THE NEW
LESBIAN STUDIES

THE NEW
LESBIAN STUDIES

Into the Twenty-First Century

Edited by Bonnie Zimmerman and Toni A. H. McNaron
Foreword by Margaret Cruikshank

The Feminist Press
at The City University of New York
New York

Published by The Feminist Press at The City University of New York
311 East 94th Street, New York, New York 10128-5684

First edition, 1996

02 01 00 99 98 97 96   6 5 4 3 2 1

Muriel Rukeyser, "To Be a Jew in the Twentieth Century," in *The Collected Poems* (New York: McGraw Hill, 1976). Reprinted by permission.
Audre Lorde, "Outlines," in *Sister Outsider: Essays & Speeches* (New York: Crossing Press, 1984). Reprinted by permission.

Library of Congress Cataloging-in-Publication Data
    The new lesbian studies : into the twenty-first century / edited by Bonnie Zimmerman and Toni A. H. McNaron, foreword by Margaret Cruikshank
       p. cm.
    Includes bibliographical references and index.
    ISBN 1-55861-135-5. — ISBN 1-55861-136-3 (pbk.) (alk. paper)
      1. Gay and lesbian studies.   2. Lesbianism—Study and teaching.   3. Women's studies.
      I. Zimmerman, Bonnie.   II. McNaron, Toni A. H.
    HQ75.15.L47 1996
    306.76'07—dc20   95-50927
                                              CIP

This publication is made possible, in part, by a grant from The Paul Rapoport Foundation. The Feminist Press would also like to thank Kay Ann Cassell, Joanne Markell, Robin Morgan, M. Jane Stanicki, and Genevieve Vaughan for their generosity.

Book design and typography by Ascienzo Design.
Printed in the United States of America on acid-free paper by Royal Book Manufacturing, Inc.

CONTENTS

PART FOUR:TRANSFORMING KNOWLEDGE

PART FIVE: WORKING WITH/IN INSTITUTIONS

ACKNOWLEDGMENTS

We wish to acknowledge our new contributors for working so smoothly with us to prepare this manuscript. We also appreciate those women with essays in the original version of Lesbian Studies who agreed to our retaining their work in our revision. In early stages of the project, Margaret Cruikshank offered us valuable advice and invaluable encouragement to bring out this expanded edition.

At The Feminist Press, Susannah Driver provided us with needed and welcome assistance as we collected essays. Florence Howe lent her support by sending us names of potential contributors. Finally, we thank Alyssa Colton for her fine copyediting.

Bonnie wishes to thank Mary Johnson, a graduate student at San Diego State University, who did preliminary bibliographic research, as well as Oliva Espín and Linda Garber for suggesting potential contributors.

Toni wishes especially to thank Bonnie for doing the major share of editorial work on first drafts of manuscripts. Her ability to shape an essay twice the necessary length into a manageable length without losing the essential fire or logic of the original is remarkable.

We end by thanking each other for being so compatible as coeditors. The labor of this project has been laced with humor and mutual affection.

FOREWORD
Margaret Cruikshank

In 1979, when I proposed the first volume of this book to The Feminist Press, the phrase "lesbian studies" boldly claimed turf within women's studies and the gay caucus of the Modern Language Association, but it was as much a consciousness-raising slogan as a description of a real phenomenon. Although in hindsight we originators of lesbian studies may look prescient and pathbreaking, I was motivated by the desire to have a good time: the lesbian sessions at NWSA were tremendous fun. It's true that I had a high-minded aim of influencing the developing disciplines of women's studies, but if lesbian studies had looked like any other kind of studies, I would not have been drawn in.

In the thirteen years since then, lesbian studies has become a "field" rather than informal groups of friends and scholars trading information and exchanging names and addresses. Now a new generation of teachers, students, and writers is extending the reach of lesbian studies. I no longer know personally most of the women doing this work. My bookshelves no longer contain all the relevant publications.

Another change is that many lesbians now hold influential academic jobs. In 1979, we were more likely to be fired from low-level jobs than welcomed for our skills and talents. Needless to say, academic lesbians today must still be extremely smart, superbly diplomatic, and not too threatening to keep their posts. One of our ongoing challenges is to figure out which eruptions of campus homophobia we will confront and which we will simply note.

As a community college English teacher, I have had the freedom to write and to publish whatever I choose. If I don't publish, I don't perish. The workload is crushing, but the chance to teach an occasional gay and lesbian studies course saves me from burn-out.

One disadvantage of being out of the academic loop is that I can't understand some of the work now being published in gay and lesbian studies. It's natural for the first people into a new territory to feel baffled by newer settlers, and inevitable that the aftercomers set off on new trails. But gay and lesbian work in obscure and needlessly difficult language reminds me of priestcraft. Some scholars seem to be writing only for each other. Their language may be an emblem of power, a sign of initiation. I want lesbian and gay books to be written in language my students can understand. Some scholars have replied defensively to this observation by claiming that complex ideas require difficult language. My retort is brief: read bell hooks, read Gloria Anzaldúa.

I worry that lesbian studies, which originally had a strong grass-roots consciousness, will get swallowed up in "gay and lesbian studies" or "queer theory." I have fought too hard for the psychic freedom to name myself a lesbian to disappear now under the queer rubric. One of the mistaken notions of queer theory is that lesbian feminism in the 1970s was all intolerance and indifference to sex! We need a history of that decade that will capture the fun, the high-spirited sense of sexual self-discovery, the euphoria of community building, and the wonder of finding our numbers large and growing larger. The laughter of the 1970s should not be forgotten.

At a time when moderate reforms like affirmative action are under attack, it is hard to predict the future of lesbian studies. At least the context today is very different from what it was when the first edition of this book was published: we are at the centers of scholarship rather than on the fringes. The original *Lesbian Studies* came to life through improvisation and mapless trekking. When the typist called to tell me she had added an article of her own on lesbian sports, because the book clearly needed to address that subject, I said, "Why not?" In the 1990s, lesbian studies is more methodical and more sure of itself. May it wear its new respectability lightly and irreverently.

INTRODUCTION
Toni A. H. McNaron and Bonnie Zimmerman

In 1982 when Margaret Cruikshank first edited Lesbian Studies, most campuses were still sufficiently hostile to lesbian and gay scholarship to make the number of courses being offered with "lesbian" in their titles quite small. Many lesbian faculty were entirely closeted or only out to faculty friends and selected students. Existing texts and resources were often obscurely located or simply inaccessible to faculty and students without the benefits of alternative bookstores or a liberal library acquisitions policy. No campus antidiscrimination policy included gay and lesbian faculty, staff, or students as a protected class. Stories still circulated about faculty being fired because they were known to be lesbian or gay, though other "reasons" were always given by their departments. This history is worth rehearsing as a context within which to consider the phenomenal rise in the sheer numbers of published books and articles; the growing call by students and faculty alike for courses and programs of study with a gay and/or lesbian focus; the inclusion of lesbians and gays not only in antidiscrimination policies but also as part of health insurance and other faculty benefits programs; and the support for both faculty research and student activities focusing on lesbian and gay subject matter and issues. This history is also important as a cautionary reminder of where we have been and where we could return if federal and state civil rights legislation is not secured or if insufficient numbers of politicians and other allies do not speak out actively in our behalf.

The very success of our social and intellectual movement is producing a virulent backlash in this last decade of the century. Cities with antigay ordinances seek to revoke them; the National Association of Scholars attacks lesbian and gay faculty on campuses across the country, accusing us of indoctrinating rather than teaching and of assigning grades on the basis of politically correct opinions rather than solid knowledge; right-wing evangelists argue that granting basic civil rights to gays and lesbians somehow constitutes special privilege; senators in Washington step up their hateful speech about "homosexuals who are destroying the very fabric of American family life" and about whom no words may be spoken in schools on pain of losing federal funding.

The moment seems perfect, then, to issue *The New Lesbian Studies,* in order to honor our past, to record our present state, and to encourage more and more lesbian faculty and students to begin or continue their exploration of lesbian history and culture. This exploration is one of the surest ways to combat false information and bigoted slander. An additional impetus for this second edition is the inescapable and important awareness of differences among lesbian scholars, differences not so apparent or articulated in 1982. As often is the case for emerging groups, early signs of lesbian studies on college and university campuses were too precious and the gains therefrom too fragile to indulge in internecine arguments. Those of us who eagerly devoured the pages of Margaret Cruikshank's volume were still primarily engaged in including lesbians as subjects rather than as objects of heterosexist and homophobic scrutiny. We were discovering primary texts and asking first-level questions about them, presenting papers at conferences in which we asked elementary critical questions and offered tentative hypotheses intended for further study and investigation. We were just beginning to feel hopeful about winning a genuine place of respect in our respective academic venues.

In the more than a decade since the publication of the first edition of *Lesbian Studies,* lesbian scholars have expanded the range and complicated the ideas of lesbian studies while questioning the very meaning of who "we" are. The list of books, anthologies, and articles available in the mid-1990s is far longer and more diverse than what existed in 1982—so much more extensive, in fact, that it is no longer possible to produce an exhaustive bibliography. The number of courses offered at universities throughout the United States and, increasingly, in other countries has grown considerably. As many of the essays included in this second edition demonstrate, the place of lesbian scholarship in disciplines such as literature, history, anthropology, and psychology seems assured, if never as solid as we would want it to be. The lesbian caucus of the National Women's Studies Association has grown to be the largest in the organization, and presentations at its meetings as well as at those of many other professional associations are numerous, strong, and exciting. The diversity of our racial, ethnic, cultural, social, and political identities grows more impressive every year. But just as we have achieved a small foothold in the academy, momentous theoretical and institutional changes have begun to reshape our understanding of the meaning and place of lesbian studies. Additionally, this country has made a shift to the political right, always a threat to the lives and work of lesbian and gay people.

Lesbian scholars of all generations are engaged in often heated debates about the future of lesbian studies. Perhaps the clearest division turns around which pathway to lesbian studies an academic lesbian will take. In 1982 virtually all of us engaged in anything resembling lesbian studies were operating from a base in women's studies or academic feminism. Today, however, many lesbian scholars align themselves with the rapidly emerging field of queer theory and with gay and lesbian studies programs. The difference is significant: lesbians coming out of a feminist base tend to use gender as a fundamental lens through which to approach any area of scholarly or human activity; lesbians coming out of a queer theory base tend to utilize sexual difference as the governing lens of analysis. Feminist lesbians are most likely to draw upon the work of Adrienne Rich and Audre Lorde; queer lesbians cite such scholars as Judith Butler and Eve Kosofsky Sedgwick. Of course, this distinction is stated rather simply here, but the broad lines of it can be seen everywhere throughout the academy. Lesbian feminists are often accused of being unreconstructedly essentialist, believing as we tend to do that lesbian identity remains a meaningful political marker. Queer theorists are just as often upbraided for failing to conduct accessible analysis of women's experiences of degradation and oppression and the collective history of this oppression. Such charges, hardened too often and too quickly in public fora, create a dangerous gulf between scholars and activists who can ill afford to be divided. These distinctions are not easily bridged and can cause serious splintering within the still frustratingly small ranks of lesbians who teach courses, conduct research, and publish in the fields of lesbian history, culture, and theory.

The most serious challenge posed by queer theory and postmodern feminism, we would argue, is to the definition and meaning of the term "lesbian." In their quest to undermine the notion of a static, unified identity or self, queer theorists question the very existence of categories, identities, and labels including that of "lesbian." As they deconstruct the binaries of male/female or heterosexual/homosexual, those of us whose academic endeavors were shaped by women's liberation, lesbian feminism, and identity politics rightly feel that the rug is being pulled out from under our feet. In the early days of women's studies programs, lesbian students and faculty were often encouraged to subsume our history, culture, and critical questions under the presumably more palatable rubric of "woman" or, on more liberal campuses, under that of "feminist." After literally years of discussion and confrontation, lesbian courses and research have become fairly standard fare in such programs. Now, with the growth of gay studies and queer theory, lesbians once again find ourselves in danger of becoming invisible. In place of the gendered terms "lesbian" or "dyke," we are invited to place ourselves under the sign of "queer"—a presumably more inclusive site for institutional struggle. As essays in this collection demonstrate, lesbian academics have very diverse responses to the invitation to "queer" ourselves.

Moreover, lesbians—and particularly lesbians who do not whole-heartedly embrace queer theory—may well be assigned a back seat not only in name but also in equal representation in critical texts, conference presentations, and course syllabi. The shift from women's studies-based lesbian studies to a queer-based lesbigay studies (to use a currently fashionable term) generates a series of provocative questions that already influence the working life of everyone in the field. For example, how does the lesbian academic justify committing her time to lesbian-exclusive rather than lesbigay research—or vice versa? Must all courses and textbooks cover lesbian and gay material? Is the theoretical underpinning of lesbian studies the promotion of lesbian history, identity, and culture(s)—or the deconstruction of heterosexuality? If it is both, how does any one scholar, course, or program determine priorities?

It is in answer to these and other questions that we—who have built our careers primarily in women's and lesbian studies—chose to accept the invitation to coedit the second edition of this groundbreaking volume. We see the value of texts that bring together lesbian, gay, bisexual, and queer scholarship. But, as the twenty-first century approaches, we continue to see the need to promote an independently defined lesbian studies. As the editors of this volume, we both strongly believe that teaching and research in lesbian studies entails asking particular questions and, more importantly, proceeding from a particular theoretical stance which will not be subsumed beneath female heterosexuality, male homosexuality, or even queer pan-sexuality.

Lesbian studies, as a women-centered field, occupies a different institutional position than gay and queer studies occupy. Lesbians working in the field are often feminist scholars specifically concerned with analyzing patriarchal social structures and institutions. This socio-political perspective can produce friction and frustration when some academic lesbians attempt to collaborate with gay colleagues. Unless gay academics have examined the privilege related to their being men in a sexist society, they will not easily comprehend some of the basic tenets likely to operate within lesbian studies. Certainly it remains the case that many gay men have not read lesbian theorists to any great extent; some are not even familiar with lesbian literature, music, or art. Contrarily, many lesbian scholars do know gay culture and theory because of the sexist cast in the formation and dissemination of knowledge. To weaken the use of "lesbian" as a significant defining term for scholarly and pedagogical investigation would seem an unnecessary loss which we do not want to see occur. And yet, as these pages will show, even among those scholars who continue to find the rubric "lesbian studies" meaningful, there is a rich and invigorating range and variety of perspectives.

In Part One of this volume, "Remembering Our Roots," we have included essays from the original *Lesbian Studies* in order to demonstrate that the present is never divorced from the past. Gaining permission from the authors we intended to reprint gave us an opportunity to speak with some of the pioneer researchers in this field, all of whom generously agreed to let us include their earlier work. These same scholars declined our request to update their content or bibliographies, preferring to let the work stand not as a present-day report or study but as a pebble whose concentric reverberations still have significance to current researchers and activists.

The range of subject matter encompassed by these early essays is worth noting: Evelyn Beck articulates the double-edged silence felt by many Jewish lesbians; Lillian Faderman begins to account for the wholesale effort by historians and biographers to efface women's relations with other women; Cherríe Moraga and Barbara Smith discuss designing a course to include Third World lesbian writing. In an essay partly funny and partly scathing, Mab Segrest presents her split existence as English professor at a southern Baptist college by day and radical lesbian feminist by night, while Paula Bennett spins a chilly tale of living and teaching from the closet. Doris Davenport names her painful invisibility both as a lesbian and an

African American trying to keep body and soul together in a conservative English department, while Marilyn Frye takes heterosexual feminists to task for their reluctance to infuse their own courses with lesbian material. Jane Gurko dares to speak of the pedagogical taboo, i.e., the presence of sexual energy in the classroom, while H. Patricia Hynes maps the treacherous course open to lesbians who choose science as their provenance.

Taken together, these nine essays challenge a huge portion of academic territory, naming many cruxes and barriers to lesbian research and teaching which remain firmly in place in our colleges and universities. We hope readers of this second edition will have their curiosities sufficiently piqued to seek out library copies of the Cruikshank volume. We encourage colleagues, especially younger ones who may not be familiar with the first edition of Lesbian Studies, to read it in its entirety, not only because it contains historically important markers of where lesbian studies was at a particular moment. Rather, these writings are important in themselves. Additionally, they are passionately conceived and often quite relevant to our present-day debates and struggles.

Following these voices from another decade, we offer thirty-one new essays by lesbian scholars and activists who represent a variety of theoretical approaches to the study of lesbianism, who come from a number of different academic generations, who demonstrate the ongoing importance of work by and about lesbians of color, who participate in lesbian studies outside the United States, and who reflect the disciplinary variety within the field. Several areas addressed in the 1982 *Lesbian Studies* have been revised and updated to include new research and new perspectives developed over the past decade. These include lesbians in the world of sport, older lesbians, and lesbian scholarship in a number of academic disciplines such as history, literature, and psychology.

Part Two, "Studying Ourselves," blends personal narratives and scholarly analyses in the effort to show that lesbian studies continues to find value in the expression and analysis of our individual and social identities. As the writers in this section demonstrate, the kind of lesbian studies an individual does is greatly affected by her (or his) social position and internalized subjectivity. This section adds to the recognized differences of age (Quam) and ethnicity (Cochran, Chan) those of disciplinary focus (Weston), personal history (McNaron), and immigrant status (Espín). Overall, we hope these pages demonstrate that although scholars no longer speak about an essential "Lesbian Self," we still place importance upon the analysis of our variously constructed lesbian selves.

Part Three, "Standing and Delivering," explores the impact of lesbian studies in the classroom. This section presents valuable information about implications of lesbian theories for pedagogy (Pellegrini and Franklin); strategies and techniques for introducing lesbian materials in diverse classroom settings such as courses on feminist psychology (Rose) and disability studies (Hillyer); and practical evaluations of women's studies and literature anthologies (Woodward, Hickok). Because of the healthy proliferation of courses treating a wide variety of issues within the broad confines of lesbian studies, we have not included specific syllabi. Instead we offer a quantitative study by Painter and Young based on a reading of many syllabi. Readers who need such pedagogical models would do well to contact any of the authors included here or to attend sessions at professional meetings which focus on lesbian materials and issues. The narratives and analyses in this section convincingly demonstrate that teaching remains the frontline for the everyday struggles to develop and promote lesbian studies.

The essays in Part Four, "Transforming Knowledge," investigate both the effects of lesbian studies on the disciplines and the concurrent impact of disciplinary approaches on lesbian studies as a field of knowledge. Although this section cannot represent every discipline in which lesbian scholars work—and we regret the absence of essays on such fields as science, health, law, art, and philosophy—we are pleased nonetheless with the expanded coverage of this edition. *The New Lesbian Studies* includes essays on anthropology (Blackwood), sociology (Schneider and Dalton), religion (Arguelles and Rivero), and film studies (Mayne), as well as on literature (Umpierre) and history (Leyva, Rupp, Ng)—two of the disciplines historically most influential in the development of lesbian studies. This section shows how traditional disciplines are being reconstructed as a result of the radical challenge of lesbian studies, and that in turn transforms not only what we know, but how we know.

Part Five, "Working with/in Institutions," looks at the ways in which lesbians and lesbian studies struggle for a place in academic institutions, in the United States and abroad. Those of us who are classroom teachers and scholars often forget the crucial work being done in other settings, such as libraries, student services, and—not surprisingly!—athletic departments. Beth Zemsky's essay provides useful information about student/faculty centers, which are slowly appearing on more and more campuses in an effort to meet more needs of lesbian (and gay) members of academic communities. Ellen Broidy demonstrates how lesbian studies is moving forthrightly into the information age. Susan Cahn provides a fascinating history of homophobia in women's athletics, while Angela Bowen argues for the importance of alliances among Black lesbians and hetero-sexual women. Moreover, while lesbian studies may have begun in the United States, in the 1990s it is a global phenomenon, as essays from the United Kingdom (Munt), Sweden (Lindeqvist), and New Zealand (Sayer) testify.

Finally, Part Six, "Theorizing Our Future," suggests a variety of ways we might think about lesbian studies as we move into the next millennium. To what extent, asks Sharon Holland, has our work moved beyond being "white lesbian studies"? How do we "queer" lesbian studies, asks Judith Halberstam, while maintaining its female specificity? Is there a way, asks Harriet Malinowitz, to reconcile the presumed opposition between poststructuralist and identity-based lesbian theory? What are the practical consequences of being a lesbian scholar in an age of queer and lesbigay studies, asks Bonnie Zimmerman? Together, these essays impel readers to clarify their own sense of the relationships between lesbian studies and the rapidly emerging fields of gay and queer studies, as well as the future of the historical interconnections between lesbian studies and women's studies programs.

Overall, *The New Lesbian Studies* interweaves a number of themes throughout its six sections including the significance of feminism within past, present, and future lesbian studies; the importance of extending the geographical boundaries within which North American lesbian scholars and activists work to include research and teaching being undertaken in countries other than our own; the vital contributions being made by lesbians of color to all future explorations by scholar-teachers in the field; and the importance of lesbian theory to many academic disciplines. Additionally, some of our authors speak about the centrality and usefulness of lesbian studies in organizing political action outside academe. Others map the theoretical landscapes being limned by lesbian researchers working in this last decade of the century and into the next.

Finally, as a guide to further study, we have included a short list of our own "favorite" books, a kind of editors' hit parade of titles published during the past ten years which we find especially germane. These resources might serve as starting points for readers interested in pursuing various aspects of lesbian studies.

In compiling and editing this anthology, we have chosen to preserve the contributors' different voices by respecting their original styles, word choices, and modes of documentation. The different styles found in this volume, as well as the different historical, theoretical, and identifying terms used, are illuminating and instructive.

Needless to say, limitations in time and space keep us from including some exciting and challenging work. But the range and diversity of content and perspective represented in this anthology accurately reflects the state of lesbian studies at the threshold of the next millennium. Lesbian scholars, teachers, and activists have made and are making an indelible mark on most fields of knowledge, and this knowledge helps us to transform our lives. As these essays demonstrate, lesbian studies in the late 1990s maintains continuity with the work of the past, while responding to new concerns and theories as they arise. Importantly, these essays also point the way toward the directions that lesbian teachers and scholars will need to follow in the future. As editors, who having been working in lesbian studies for over twenty years, we are proud and excited to help this process along.

Despite the diversity of opinions, our differences of style and perspective, all contributors to this significantly revised edition are committed to carrying lesbian studies into the next century and to mirroring as high a degree as possible of multiculturalism and diversity in theory and content. What we publish now reflects the broad outlines of an immensely varied and still expanding field of inquiry known as lesbian studies. We hope readers will find our effort challenging, materially helpful, and provocative in the best sense—a stimulus to generate and communicate what's still to be done.

PART ONE

Remembering
Our
Roots

DYKE IN ACADEME (II)

Paula Bennett

I take as my theme the first five lines of Muriel Rukeyser's "To Be a Jew in the Twentieth Century":

> To be a Jew in the twentieth century
> Is to be offered a gift. If you refuse,
> Wishing to be invisible, you choose
> Death of the spirit, the stone insanity.
> Accepting, take full life.

Before describing what it is like to be a lesbian in twentieth-century academe, I would like to explain what it was once like for me to have been a Jew—and invisible.

I grew up during the Second World War when Hitler and anti-Semitism were daily news. Like the three little black boys who play chain gang in Toni Morrison's *Sula,* I and my little Jewish friends played concentration camp. We used a laundry court, as I remember, and strung each other up from the lines. We had been raised in a neatly kept, middle-class Jewish suburb outside Boston. To my knowledge, none of us had ever been directly subjected to anti-Semitism. But Jew-hating was part of our reality, just as chain gangs were part of black reality, and like Morrison's three Dewies, we acted out our reality in our games.

When I was eleven, my parents took me out of the predominantly Jewish public school I was attending and sent me to a private girls' school in the city. I and two other Jewish children, neither of whom was in my class, had been accepted on a trial basis to see if assimilation would take in what was then a largely Episcopalian sanctuary. My parents had never been particularly observant nor had they done much to bolster my sense of pride in being Jewish. Their chief concern was the quality of my education. Problems of assimilation were beyond them. The one thing my mother said to prepare me for any anti-Semitism I might encounter, was that since Christians looked down on Jews, it was up to me to prove we were as good as anybody else by being better. It was, she said—and I'll never forget this—

"the cross I would have to carry."

Filled with fears I could not express, I chose to hide instead. As luck would have it, the first book we read that year was *Oliver Twist*. When one girl, out of bland curiosity I am sure, asked if there were any Jews in Winsor, I did not answer. I had become invisible, a closet Jew. And since I did not look Semitic or bear a "Jewish" last name, it was, unfortunately, possible for me to pass. I told only one or two close friends of my religious background and lived in almost daily terror that the rest of my classmates would find out the truth. Never very good in groups anyway, I pulled more and more into myself, isolated by my lie and by the hostile suspiciousness that it engendered in me. Eventually, the hostility and isolation—not to mention self-betrayal—took their toll, as they were bound to do, and at the end of my freshman high school year, I flunked out.

The most significant aspect of this story is that during the three years I spent at Winsor, I never once heard an anti-Semitic remark or witnessed an anti-Semitic act. Given the time period and the makeup of the school population, I am sure there was anti-Semitism, but if there was, it lived solely in what people thought, not what they said. They said nothing. Jews, as far as most Winsorites were concerned, simply didn't exist, or if they did exist, aside from an occasional query or two, their existence was not a matter worth discussing. For the rest, it was silence.

Looking back at this incident now, I am overwhelmed by how much I contributed to my own defeat. I have no way of knowing, of course, what my real reception would have been, had I "come out." But it is fairly easy to guess. Some students would have befriended me just because I was Jewish. Others, for the same reason, would have steered clear. But most, I believe, would have gotten over their initial surprise and discomfort at my difference and would have judged me for myself. I never gave them the chance. Unable to deal with or talk about my fears, I hid until hiding became too painful. Then I dropped out.

My experience at Winsor colors everything I have to say about being a lesbian in academe or anywhere else where one cannot feel free to be fully and publicly oneself. It is the experience of the closet, of a void created by fear on one side and silence on the other. It produces a form of oppression that comes not from the things people do, *but what they do not do.* At best, this experience leads to feelings of anger and alienation. At worst, it produces an attitude of apathy and indifference. For some it is a stone insanity, for others, a living hell of self-hate and self-betrayal.

I do not wish to suggest that all gay academics are miserable. A goodly number of them obviously are not. They are sound, whole individuals, well respected by their departments and profession, who have been able to fuse their public and private lives in an integrated and productive manner.

Nor would I suggest that colleges and universities are especially bad places to be if you are gay. Over the past ten years in particular, many college departments and administrations have shown themselves warmly, even enthusiastically, supportive of their gay faculty and staff. And there are now, as we know, quite a number of "happy" coming-out stories, stories which suggest that at least in particular cases many of our worst fears about coming out may prove unfounded.

The problem is that most of us do not dare to find out whether our fears are unfounded or not. Since most academic institutions maintain silence on this issue, the onus for discovering whether one will be accepted or not lies with the individual gay. For most gay academics, even the tenured, this is, apparently, too great a risk to take. Overwhelmed by fears which may or may not be justified, unable to find out simply and without risk whether their fears are justified or not, the vast majority of gay and lesbian teachers remain, however unwillingly, in the void I have described, victims of their own anxiety and a social situation which through their silence they have helped perpetuate as well as create.

Caught between silence on one side and fear on the other, the typical closeted gay academic spends his or her professional life in a state of constant duplicity, internally and externally divided by a lie that is not spoken, by an act of deception that is never acted out. Even the most mundane or natural aspects of human interaction and communication are distorted by the invisible presence of the void such duplicity creates. Talk about nights out, living arrangements, vacations, lovers, divorces is carefully censored to control how much real information is given out. Sometimes the ability to communicate on both sides becomes warped beyond recognition. Then the failure to speak becomes in itself another form of oppression. A friend of mine at Northeastern told me this story.

Joe had lived with his lover of twelve years in a house outside the city. Their relationship was well known to many of Joe's colleagues although technically speaking Joe was not "out" to his department at the time. When the relationship ended, Joe moved back into the city, sharing an apartment with a graduate student. His colleagues would then ask the graduate student how Joe was doing. They did not ask Joe directly, although it was apparent to everyone that he was going through a period of deep stress and mourning. Like Joe's colleagues, most of us are naturally reluctant to bring up private matters unless we have, in effect, been given permission to do so; but what kept Joe, who desperately wanted comfort, from giving permission was the closet, and it was the closet that prevented his colleagues in turn from showing their sincere interest and concern.[1]

There is no way to put a statistical number on this "act of oppression," because no act has occurred. No act occurs when two gay members of the same department or university can know each other for several years—as Joe and I did at Northeastern—and never share one of the single most important facts about themselves, that they are gay. No act occurs when a gay teacher, seeing a gay student at a gay bar, turns on his or her heel and walks away. The warmth, support, and human kindness lost in such cases is as intangible as it is incalculable. It cannot be measured; it can only be weighed by the heart that has felt it.

To live in the closet, in this void, is to be constantly aware of what one is *not* saying, is *not* doing, is *not* experiencing or receiving, because you are afraid to be fully, publicly yourself. In the classroom, it often means avoiding authors or themes that might cast you as a teacher or student in a questionable light. I know, for example, some lesbian teachers who will not touch Stein or Barnes because they are too obvious. I know others who will treat these writers but who will either avoid the subject of their sexual orientation or mention it only in passing. I know only a few lesbian teachers for whom teaching "out" writers is simply a matter of course, producing neither anxiety nor second thoughts. For myself, I have never been able to teach lesbian writers without feeling an enormous sense of inner division over the kind of deception such teaching involves when I myself have not come out.

Where writers themselves are not open about their sexual preference (and most are not), the closeted lesbian or gay teacher confronts an even more painful dilemma: do you say what you know or believe about Emily Dickinson, Sarah Orne Jewett, Virginia Woolf, Willa Cather, Amy Lowell, Lorraine Hansberry, May Sarton, Elizabeth Bishop, and risk the appearance of a special interest, or do you suppress the information that you have and help perpetuate the conspiracy of silence which distorts our reading of these and so many other authors? Either way, for the closeted teacher, it is a no-win situation. For the students and for scholarship, it is also a dead loss.

The consequences of the closet on research and writing are just as pernicious, affecting both the quality and the quantity of the scholarship produced. Gay and lesbian teachers are obviously suited to research on gay writers. They are sensitive to the issues. They understand the problems, having lived through them. They are more likely because of their sensitivities to recognize encoding when encoding occurs and to respect the complex validity of such hidden expression. And finally, of course, they care. But the fear of being stigmatized disables the gay or lesbian teacher in a way that straight scholars are not. At a recent meeting of the Boston Gay Academic Union, Monica McAlpine discussed her excellent article on Chaucer's "Pardoner's Tale," (*PMLA*, January, 1980). Almost the first question from the audience after the presentation was "weren't you afraid someone would take you for a lesbian?" (Ms. McAlpine is both married and straight.) The question may sound naive, but it was clearly on everyone's mind, since a ten-minute discussion followed on the perils and possibilities of research for the homosexual scholar. The tenor of the discussion was far from encouraging.

Even without the fear of stigmatization, however, gay research appears to many gay and lesbian teachers a dead end. True, it is a largely unexplored area, filled, if you look at the list of nondeclared writers, with all kinds of exciting possibilities. The fact is that like women's studies and ethnic studies, gay studies, such as they are, are an academic stepchild. They weigh less heavily toward promotion and tenure, and they are taken less seriously by scholars-at-large. Teachers committed to such areas risk being labeled and treated as second-class, that is, too "narrow" in their interest and too far outside the academic mainstream to be considered full-fledged members in good standing of their departments. The caste/class system of the universities, based on white male patriarchal models, dominates research and demands that teachers who wish to advance give most of their interest and energy to topics that carry the patriarchal imprimatur. Thus a friend of mine now bucking for tenure at a prestigious eastern university has given up a book on Amy Lowell for one on Emerson and Hawthorne instead. Her heart may be with the lesbian poet, but her head and her pocketbook tell her to stick with what she knows will be well received.

That such decisions represent the suppression of knowledge goes, I believe, without saying. Again, no one has moved deliberately to limit the freedom of speech or inquiry of the gay scholar—there is no "act of oppression" that one can name—but oppression has occurred, from within and without, and the loss to our community is one we can ill afford.

When weighed together, the various effects of the closet—on human communication, on teaching and research—have a profound effect on the gay or lesbian herself. In an article in *Concerns*, Toni McNaron describes with moving honesty what she calls the "hypocrisy and ill health" of her position before coming out to her department. It was a period when she struggled with weight, alcohol, and constant anxiety over exposure. In my own article, "Dyke in Academe," in *Concerns*, I described similar bouts I had, not with food and drink, but with self-hate and Freudian therapy, for much the same reason as Toni: it was the best way I knew to make the price of hiding or having to hide clear.

I do not want to repeat the arguments of that paper here. Suffice it to say that it is no easy matter to maintain self-esteem when, in order to preserve your job, you feel it necessary to betray yourself in a variety of major and minor ways: from not treating authors or ideas that might open you to question to not speaking out when one of your colleagues tells an offensive joke. To suffer an injustice without protest is, in my opinion, far more destructive in its consequences than the original injustice itself, since the self-betrayal silence involves eventually rots away the inner person. To betray oneself in this way for a job is certainly not a price worth paying. Yet it is a price asked constantly of lesbians and gays in our society, and having had to pay it, to any degree, makes me angrier than I can say.

Anger is not a pleasant emotion, but as I suggested in the original "Dyke in Academe" essay, it can be a preserving one. Over the years, my anger has helped me learn how to insulate myself against the worst effects of not being able to come entirely out (I am an untenured part-timer and, therefore, permanently vulnerable). I have learned not to go places where I do not feel comfortable (such as the English department offices) and not to do things that would force me to betray myself (such as write on authors I do not care for). I spend most of my free time working for those things I believe in: gay rights and lesbian literature. But this is not the kind of arrangement most academics can afford to make. Only the fringe nature of my job gives me the latitude to go so much my own way. Succinctly, since I am not asking for tenure, what I do, or do not do, does not really matter. As far as my department is concerned, I barely exist. In a curiously ironic way, the "invisibility" of the outsider remains the price I pay for my freedom.

To be an outsider, as Rukeyser suggests, can be a gift. Certainly one can achieve in alienation a degree of autonomy, a sense of choice, a clarity of vision hard to obtain in any other way. But it is a gift which to yield "full life" must be fully and completely accepted, fully and completely used. Promotion, tenure, respect, collegiality, self-esteem, human warmth, and kindness should not depend upon sexual preference any more than they should depend upon matters of race, religion, or sex. Yet because of the silence and fear that distorts our lives, they do.

We are not free, nor will we be, until this silence at last is ended and we are invisible no more.

The original "Dyke in Academe" appeared in *Concerns,* the newsletter of the Women's Caucus of the Modern Languages, spring 1980, pp. 12–24. "Dyke in Academe (II)" was presented at the panel "The Second Sex in Academia: Stress, Anger and Energy" during the Modern Language Association Convention in Houston, December 27–30, 1980. I wrote the second paper largely as a response to criticisms I received on the first version. I wish to thank in particular J. S., Carol Meyer, Jonathan Goldberg, and Joe DeRoche for their patient assistance in this drawn-out endeavor.

NOTES

1. An interesting coda to this incident occurred on the plane back from Houston when I showed this paper to one of Joe's colleagues. After lengthy discussion, I still could not convince him that Joe's fears were grounded in reality. "Everyone knows about Joe and loves him," he insisted. The fact that no one said specifically to Joe, "We know; it's okay," bore no weight with him, though it meant everything to Joe. I am not sure what one does with such well-meaning obtuseness.

BLACK LESBIANS IN ACADEMIA: VISIBLE INVISIBILITY

Doris Davenport

By way of introduction, it seems to me that i have LIVED in academia all my life: from age five to the present (age thirty-two) i have always been in school, either studying, teaching, or dropping out and in. At the present stage, i am in a PhD program (University of Southern California, English). It also seems to me that i have been a feminist all my life, and recently, a very political or politicized lesbian. i am proud of studying literature; i am equally proud of being a lesbian. But what that means is this:

i am the only Black student (that i know of) in my graduate English department. Before me, there was one other het Black woman, whom i knew slightly. In September 1979, when i first went to USC, i discovered (from a white womon student) that this Black-het had told certain people at the school that i was a feminist-dyke "going around trying to convert people." That Black sister meant to do me a lot of damage. Instead, she did me a favor. When i got to USC, i did not have to come out, so much as let a few folks know that physical seduction was the only part she had wrong. The white folks were a little confused as to how to approach me: i fit neither their stereotypes of a "Black nationalist" nor of a dyke. (i could see them thinking, about the latter, "but she doesn't 'look' like one.") It meant that i was either benignly ignored, or guardedly spoken to. i laughed and carried on.

At the same time, i got "stuck," by default, teaching the only Black literature class offered at USC. The only Black professor had quit, and with my being *Black,* i was offered the class as part of my teaching assistantship duties. i gladly accepted, since Black literature is one of my major fields. However, no one checked on my ability to teach the class. Again, stereotyped, and benignly neglected. i taught my class (well) and carried on.

Then, the following semester (January 1980), i took a class which ostensibly covered "American literature since World War II." There were no Blacks and/or wimmin on that syllabus. When i asked the professor (a middle-aged white boy) about this oversight, he said i could do a report on Leroi Jones or someone like that, or i could drop the class; that he would not alter the syllabus for me. i promptly told him no, to both alternatives, and called him on his stereotyping, and furthermore, told him that he addressed only what he could see: sex and color. i said, add to that, that i am a lesbian, so you can go ahead and insult *that* part of me too. (He was new, and apparently had not heard the "coming-out story.") He had the grace to semi-apologize privately, but our "discussion" was in front of the entire class.

Each semester in my Black literature class, i have a beginning enrollment of at least thirty-two people, mainly Black. Each semester, a few either drop the class or get mighty nasty because of my feminism and my "strict" requirements. My feminism means i point out both feminism and chauvinism in the literature and in classroom responses, especially of the males. The requirements mean that students have to do original thinking—very painful, for lots of folk. i am, to them, simply another authority figure—the enemy—and the fact that we are all Black, all students, and all in "hostile" territory does not seem to make that much sense to them. If my color means anything to them at all, it's simply that my course must be an easy A.

Almost all Black students in predominantly white schools get a grade called "automatic B" (either for Black, or because you're Black you can't do no **B**etter). Sometimes, you get "automatic A," (**A**ctually, it means the prof is guilt/racist tripping), but either way, the work you produce is not judged on its own.

It is this fragmentation, in life and academia, that i want to address. It works like this: lesbian studies (and lesbians) belong in wimmin studies. Black literature is cross-listed under ethnic studies. English departments usually fall under the general heading of esoteric studies, to most people. So what happens to a hybrid like me? i fit into all the above categories, and then some. i have never tried to camouflage the fact that i am a lesbian. In fact, some folk say i flaunt it. (i wear a ♀ necklace and ring, and have the same symbol sewn in white on my brown book bag, so it will stand out more.) Oddly enough, that is hardly ever addressed directly, even by other lesbians. For the others, the most visible and the most accessible route of attack is via my color: i get what most Black students do, with a little added shit, due to being feminist-lesbian.

The added shit means that if i say good morning, they will challenge it. Maybe it is because i am also articulate, outspoken (or, speaking period), and un-grad-school-mediocre (although i sometimes do get bored to death by the ego trips of the white boy professors). So for them, here's this live and moving target that is not only Black, but Black-and-articulate, Black and i-don't-take-no-shit, Black and lesbian feminist. All that at once is a confusing target. But they try. And i, constantly, fight back, or at least try to fight against the alienation and isolation, in anyway i can. Sometimes, i send my mind back to Paine College, especially in the spring. Frequently, i read Hurston or Toni Morrison or my own prose. Often, i get drunk and go to sleep, reminding myself that i *do* have a vision of another reality. . . .

Plus, i recently realized that i have been operating off an unconscious incentive (unconscious, but strongly and deeply ingrained). That is, the "legacy" of Black educators, a legacy of love, discipline, high standards, and commitment, which i got from attending an all-Black high school and undergraduate school. That is, the fact that all the significant teachers in my life (excluding one white womon) have been Black. On the other hand, i want to carry on or instigate a "new" tradition: that of being a Black, brilliant, lesbian, educator—open and proud.

i am in this field because i passionately love literature, although i know there is a great deal of unnecessary, humiliating absurdity involved in academia, period. Yet, i know too that i am a lesbian, feminist, poet, writer, critic, teacher, and overall goddess-given seer. Therefore, i refuse to let any of this deter me—this time. In short, i fight the fragmentation as best i can, and as often as i get wiped out i regenerate myself, but it ain't easy, and it is so alone.

i wouldn't mind if "the enemy" would stick to one issue at a time, or would fight "fair" and up front. But we all know they don't work that way. For example, last fall (October 1980),the new white chairwoman of the department informed me that the school policies prevent T.A.'s from teaching literature courses. Moreover, she doesn't think we are *prepared* (that is, we are too dumb) to teach them. So in the fall (September 1981), i will not be teaching my Black literature course, if it's up to her—in spite of the fact that i have been teaching it for the last two years. i sense, in other words, around me an aura of intense hostility-fear-awe, at almost all times. i hear people relating to an image—a projection of their diseased imaginations and other stereotypical neuroses. i find myself fighting a constant battle on at least ten levels at once, just to complete course requirements!—even while i continue to write my womon poetry and do readings. All of which is ignored in academia: i recently self-published a book of poetry and announced the Great Event in the department newsletter. To date, no one has acknowledged the book. It seems to me that the main objective is to undermine me (us) in as many ways as possible, and most of the time, i don't even think it is intentional. They can't help themselves. But none of this helps my state of mind, either. What would help me is this:

That those of us who are Black lesbians in academia would at least start a survival and support network—newsletter, once-a-month-chain letter, union, whatever, so we won't feel so alone and isolated. In other words, establish some sort of system for our mutual survival and *celebration*. A system to prevent our being individually devastated and individually negated. After all, we know that being lesbian, at this point, is not a phase we are going to "grow out of." Nor, if you are as persistent as i am, are we going to give up on what we see as our professional goals. NOR should we look for that much support from anyone else but ourselves. We have to find a way to minimize the devastating bullshit, and maximize our potential—on all levels. (It might also help if more of our sisters came out of the closet.)

i guess we are a threat to the "system" (since Black wimmin are perceived as a threat to everyone, period), but not really, and not yet. i just want to stay here, and i want my sisters to stay here, long enough to make some radical, and positive, changes. Changes in the way Black lesbians are viewed and treated in academia, and the rest of the un-real world. Changes in the way we are presented and perceived. Changes from this death-oriented world, to a more Goddess-oriented, life-loving world.

I LEAD TWO LIVES: CONFESSIONS OF A CLOSET BAPTIST

Mab Segrest

I lead a double life. By day, I'm a relatively mild-mannered English teacher at a southern Baptist college. By night—and on Tuesdays and Thursdays and weekends—I am a lesbian writer and editor, a collective member of *Feminary,* a lesbian-feminist journal for the South. My employers do not know about my other life. When they find out, I assume I will be fired, maybe prayed to death. For the past four years, my life has moved rapidly in opposite directions.

When I started teaching English at my present school five years ago, I knew I was a lesbian. I was living with Peg, my first woman lover. But I wasn't "out" politically. I had not yet discovered the lesbian culture and lesbian community that is now such an important part of my life. The first time I let myself realize I was in love with Peg, I had sat under a willow tree by the lake at the Girl Scout camp where we both worked and said aloud to myself in the New York darkness: "I am a lesbian." I had to see how it sounded; and after I'd said that, gradually, I felt I could say anything. When, three years ago, Peg left to live with a man, I knew my life had changed. I read lesbian books and journals with great excitement. I joined the all-lesbian collective of *Feminary,* then a local feminist journal, and helped turn it into a journal for southern lesbians. I started writing. I did all this while working for the Baptists, feeling myself making decisions that were somehow as frightening as they were inevitable. Early issues of *Feminary* record the process. First there is a poem by "Mabel." Then an article by "Mab." Then the whole leap: "Mab Segrest." My whole name, and not much of a chance to say, "that was the *other* Mab Segrest." I knew if I could not write my name, I couldn't write anything. I also knew: if I can't be myself and teach, I won't teach.

Since my junior year in college, over a decade ago, I have wanted to be a teacher. For a long time—before Peg and I both made the brave, reckless leap that woman makes when she loves another woman for the first time—teaching was the most important thing in my life. I have always liked school. It is fall as I write this, and

September brings back memories of new plain cotton dresses, clean notebooks, pencils sharpened to fine points, and especially a stack of new books full of things I didn't yet know. And I always—always!—loved to read. During my childhood—which, if it was full of small-town life and summers with my brother in the woods near the lake, was also full of the deep loneliness of being queer—I spent many hours with books on the front porch swing or in my father's chair by the gas heater. I have always pondered things in long conversations with myself, walking home from school, my hands slightly waving as I held forth to some invisible audience. Now in my classes I love the challenge of trying to explain a body of material clearly and in ways that catch students' interests, in spite of themselves; of looking out over a sea of consciousness, watching eyes focus and unfocus, words register or float out the back windows, every period the necessity to generate interest, every hour a hundred tiny failures and successes. Teaching is the work I love best. I can bring much of myself into it, and much of it into myself. But as a lesbian teacher in a society that hates homosexuals—especially homosexual teachers—I have learned a caution toward my students and my school that saddens me. The things my life had taught me best, I cannot teach directly. I do not believe that I am the only one who suffers.

The first time homosexuality came up in my classroom it was a shock to my system. It was in freshman composition, and I was letting a class choose debate topics. They picked gay rights, then nobody wanted to argue the gay side. Finally, three of my more vociferous students volunteered. I went home that day shaken. I dreamed that night I was in class, my back to my students, writing on the board (I always feel most vulnerable then), and students were taunting me from the desks—"lesbian! queer!" The day of the debate, I took a seat in the back row, afraid that if I stood up front IT would show, I would give myself away: develop a tic, tremble, stutter, throw up, then faint dead away. I kept quiet as my three progay students held off the Bible with the Bill of Rights, to everyone's amazement, including my own. (I certainly knew it could be done; I just hadn't expected them to do it. No one else in the class had figured any legitimate arguments were possible.) Then the antigay side rallied and hit on a winning tactic: they implied that if the opponents *really* believed their own arguments, they were pretty "funny." I called an end to the debate, and the progay side quickly explained how they didn't mean anything they had said. Then one of my female students wanted to discuss how Christians should love people even when they were sick and sinful. I said the discussion was *over* and dismissed the class. The only time I had spoken during the entire debate was in response to a male student behind me, who had reacted defensively to a mention of homosexuality in the Army with, "Yes, and where *my father* works, they castrate people like that." I turned with quiet fury—"Are you advocating it?" All in all, I survived the day, but without much self-respect.

The next year, on a theme, a freshwoman explained to me how you could tell gay people "by the bandanas they wear in their pockets and around their necks." She concluded, "I think homosexuals are a menace to society. *What do you think?*" A pregnant question, indeed. I pondered for a while, then wrote back in the margin,

"I think society is a menace to homosexuals." I resisted wearing a red bandana the day I handed back the papers.

Sometimes, friends ask me why I stay. I often ask myself. I'm still not sure. A few years ago, Anita Bryant was appointed a vice-president of the Southern Baptist Convention. A southern Baptist school is not the most comfortable place for a gay teacher to be—sitting on the buckle of the Bible Belt. I stay partly because teaching jobs are hard to come by, especially in this vicinity, where I'm working on *Feminary*. I have begun to apply for other jobs, but so far without success. But I wonder how different it would be in other places, where bigotry might be more subtle, dangers more carefully concealed. Mostly I stay because I like my students. They remind me, many of them, of myself at their age: making new and scary breaks from home and its values, at first not straying very far and needing to be told, "There's a bigger world. Go for it." Teaching them is like being a missionary, an analogy many of them would understand.

Two years ago, I came out for the first time to a student. I had resolved that if any gay student ever asked me to identify myself, I would. So when Hank came up to my desk after Christmas vacation, sporting one new earring and wanting to talk about bars in Washington, I knew it was coming.

"Where do *you* go to dance?" he asked. (At the time, there was one gay disco in the vicinity.)

"Oh," I evaded, "you probably wouldn't know it. What about you?"

"Oh, you wouldn't know it. What about you?"

"Oh, you wouldn't know it either." Then, quickly, "It's between Chapel Hill and Durham."

Me: "I think I do. It starts with a 'C'?"

Him: "Yes. *You* go there?" His eyes lit up.

Me: "Yep."

Him, politely, giving me an out: "You probably just went one time and got disgusted?"

Me: "Nope."

By this time, the class was filling with students, milling around my desk and the blackboard behind us. I suggested to Hank that we finish the conversation after class. We did—in the middle of campus on a bench, where we could see anyone coming for at least half a mile. I felt a sudden sympathy for the CIA. He asked me if he could tell his friends. I took a deep breath and said yes. But they never came to see me. I still don't know how far word has spread; every now and then I get the feeling I exchange meaningful glances with certain students. I would like for gay students to know I am there if they need me—of maybe just to know I am there—but I do not take the initiative to spread the word around. I have made the decision to be "out" in what I write and "in" where I teach, not wanting to risk a job I enjoy or financial security; but it is not a decision I always feel good about. I see the unease of most college students over sexuality—whether they express it in swaggering and hollow laughter over "queer" jokes or in timidity or in the worried looks of married students from the back row—and I know it is part of a large disease with sexuality and the definitions of "men" and "women" in society. I see how they—and most of us—have been taught to fear *all* of our feelings. And I understand all too well, when I realize I am afraid to write—to even know—what I think and feel for fear of losing my job, how money buys conformity, how subtly we are terrorized into staying in line.

The closest I ever came to saying what I wanted to was in an American literature class last year. Gay rights came up again—I think I may have even steered the discussion in that direction. And a student finally said it to me: "But what about teachers? We can't have homosexuals teaching students!" I resisted leaping up on the podium and flashing the big 'L' emblazoned on a leotard beneath my blouse. Instead I took a deep breath and began slowly. "Well, in my opinion, you don't learn sexual preference in the classroom. I mean, that's not what we are doing here. IF you had a gay or lesbian teacher, he or she would not teach you about sexual preference." I paused to catch my breath. They were all listening. "What he or she would say, *if you had a gay teacher,* is this . . ." (by now I was lightly beating on the podium) ". . . don't let them make you afraid to be who you are. To know who you are. She would tell you, don't let them get you. Don't let them make you afraid." I stopped abruptly, and in the silence turned to think of something to write on the board.

And if they ever do have a lesbian teacher, that is exactly what she will say.

SEXUAL ENERGY IN THE CLASSROOM

Jane Gurko

Sexual energy in the classroom[1]—one of those taboo subjects we all experience but rarely talk about in public, especially we who are in women's studies. It's one thing to trash male professors who exercise their *droit de seigneur,* blithely trading A's for ass without the faintest shiver of guilt over their abuse of power. But how do women teachers, in particular lesbian teachers, explain to a suspicious public the crushes, ego boosts, propositions, and temptations generated by a women's studies classroom? So we *are* in there recruiting after all, are we? (Are we?) What do we mean by "sexual energy" anyway, and what codes of ethics or behavior do we painfully fashion for ourselves as we negotiate our flimsy feminist life rafts through these dangerous patriarchal waters?

The phrase itself, "sexual energy in the classroom," suggests many possible situations: student's crush on teacher, teacher's crush on student, mutual student-teacher attraction, students' sexual interest in each other, individuals' excitement about themselves as they discover something new about their sexual identity, general excitement or interest in the subject of sexuality as it somehow relates to course content. All of these situations create problems and choices, especially for the teacher, about how to act or react: should she discuss her sexuality (whatever it is) openly? Should she encourage friendship with this student? Should she go to bed with that one?

I go back over my own experience for answers: Me, age twenty-six (pre-coming out), getting stoned one evening with a handsome male student of mine who often drives me to school from the East Bay. He tells me he has an open marriage, finds me fascinating, et cetera. I groggily but immediately button up my shirt, knowing vaguely that walking into class and facing him the next day will be impossible if I don't.

Me, age thirty, out at home but not at work, listening to a student pour out her fear of men, love of women, wondering how I can tell her that lesbianism is fine without endangering my tenure.

Me, age thirty-three, in a deep, intense friend-mentorship with one of my brightest but neediest students, suddenly confronted with the fact that my lover and I have used her cruelly (if unconsciously) as an ego boost for ourselves, leaving her always as the third wheel. (We promised intimacy, sexual and otherwise, that we couldn't or wouldn't deliver.)

Me, age thirty-five, -six, -seven, -eight, out all over the place (tenured now), listening to many attractive women confess admiration, desire, love for me, while I wonder how to refuse and affirm at the same time (the most difficult and touching question to answer: "How can I *be* you?").

My thirteen years' teaching experience, nine of them including women's studies, have brought me to a deep caution about exploiting students' intimate feelings toward me or indulging my own toward them. Yet I am conscious of wanting to be personally attractive in the classroom, not so much in looks or dress as in my energy and tone. I realize that I've worked hard at this personal attractiveness, knowing that it's a crucial part of my teaching skill. This is especially true in women's studies courses, where I can be genuine and un-gamey, a woman among women. Is this exploitation? Cheap thrills? Abuse of power? I don't think so.

Certainly I have had my share of dreams and fantasies of being the lover-hero, inner scripts which are fed by my ego-gratifying professorial position. Certainly I have been flattered and aroused by the adulation of students, especially women students. Certainly I gear up for an intense personal exchange when I enter the classroom. What then makes me a literature teacher rather than a sexual guru? Perhaps the distinction is not so absolute. Because I do think the classroom is a sexual arena, but not in the conventional, physical sense. The real sexuality of the classroom lies in the intellectual interchange itself—orgasms for the mind.

If we define sexuality as "the anticipation of orgasm" then virtually all life activity, if it is fully experienced,[2] is "sexual," since it is our psychobiological nature to build up to—climax—and unwind from whatever we do. This is true for eating, working, lovemaking, and learning of every kind. We have all experienced intense feelings of anticipation and buildup as we study a new idea or concept, then a climax or orgasm (or multiple orgasms) as the various pieces fall into place and we achieve illumination, then the denouement of seeing ramifications and applications or of having lesser understandings as we "come down" from our stint of research. Sexual energy is thus inherent in every classroom in its intellectual form. It *ought* to be there; without it, nothing is happening. As a teacher, then, I do "make love" to and with my students. If I bring my best intellectual energy to bear on the subject at hand and try to stimulate their best energy in response, am I not teaching my students to "come"?

And if intellectual excitement and climax are not only permissible but expected in the classroom, why draw an arbitrary line between that form of sexuality and the more usual, physical one? Do we not wish to heal patriarchy's vicious mind-body split, or at least not reinforce it? In an ideal society no such arbitrary distinction need be made. In an ideal learning situation there are no grades or hierarchical judgments, even though there may be one person with more experience of the subject, i.e., a "teacher." In the *most* ideal learning situation, for me, there are only two participants, and intellectual excitement can lead very naturally to sexual excitement, and the two kinds of sharing become intertwined. I have my best conversations and illuminations in bed (does everybody?).

However, the classrooms in which we teach are not ideal. They are pointedly hierarchical, the teacher is invested with the authority and obligation to grade her students on their work and is invested with many other kinds of institutional power as well: to write recommendations, to advise and consent on programs, to sign graduation forms, to Give Answers. The intellectual lovemaking process is marred by this power differential, followers of Socrates notwithstanding. Many teachers, especially feminist ones, try to lessen the pain of this difference by "free" grading schemes, student decisions on syllabi and class process, and scrupulousness in avoiding abuse of their power. But no amount of tinkering or make-believe changes the reality: teachers have power over students. I think well-intentioned feminist teachers who try to alleviate the power imbalance in the classroom by denying its presence or importance, or by pretending to give it up, do their students a disservice. Many students are misled into thinking the teacher more accessible than in truth she can be and are rightfully resentful when the teacher withdraws her personal attentions or finally "pulls rank" in some way, tarnishing the intimacy that may have developed.

It behooves us to admit and accept our institutional power and try to use it as decently as we can. As long as the classroom contract is open and understood by all ("*I* give the grades, and they will be based on thus and so"), intellectual excitement and gratification are still possible to a large degree. As a feminist teacher in a patriarchal institution, I have accepted the fact that my prostitution is an honorable one, since most women are too poor and resource-less to gain on their own all the skills and knowledge they need. Some must still come to academia for certain skills, and better they should find me there than someone less feminist or less concerned. So I will give the grades and hope for some shared learning, some mutual climaxes, despite that.

But to enter a physical sexual relationship with a person who is at the time one's student—this is not in the contract. I think it should absolutely not be done, regardless of the age, gender, or state of mind of the participants. I speak from my own experience here, and while the relationship which ensued turned out to be of long duration (eight years) and profound importance to me, it was fraught with power problems from the start; had I to do it over again, unquestionably I would wait until we were no longer in our student-teacher roles.

The problem lies in the fact that any noncoercive power imbalance tends to trigger romantic fantasies on both sides of an unequal relationship, regardless of the sexes involved. It's almost automatic in the classroom: the teacher becomes an object of hero worship, and conversely, as "hero," indulges in ego-inflating fantasies of power over her "worshipper." I believe that human sexual excitement depends largely on each lover having a fantasy of power over the other. But ideally, in my value system, lovers play out their power fantasies in a mutual and role-shifting way, avoiding any overall inequalities or dependencies. In fantasy, power-over and power-under are in fact often interchangeable, since each side by definition depends on the other. In our mutual fantasizing we are equal—and equally responsible for our dreams and expectations.

But in a classroom liaison, the teacher in *fact* has more power—it's no fantasy. The lovers cannot play with it, shift it around, manipulate it for their mutual growth.[3] There's no way the two people involved can realistically keep their student-teacher and lover-lover relationships separate, if they are going on simultaneously. The teacher will wonder, "Can I grade her classwork with as much neutrality and impersonality as I try to grade the other students? Will she accept my grades neutrally?" The student will wonder, "Is she trying to be teacher in bed? Does she accept me as her peer? Am I being graded now?" (One friend of mine facetiously remarked, "I never worry about it. I'm only attracted to A students." "Yes," I replied, "but *you* still get to fill out the report card.")

Romantic fantasies which are triggered by real power imbalances are disasters if they are acted out. Even if the attraction between student and teacher is a serious one and their relationship has potential, both must be responsible for not pushing the other into it. The teacher at the very least is morally obligated not to pursue the attraction, since she is the one less likely to be hurt by the power difference. Moreover, if she is not attracted to the student who has seriously propositioned her, I think she is obligated to (1) affirm the student's feelings; (2) tell the student that such a liaison would be inappropriate as long as they share a classroom; and (3) admit that aside from their student-teacher roles she doesn't feel ready for such a relationship at this time.

The main reason, then, to avoid physical intimacy between student and teacher is that it is virtually impossible to maintain simultaneously two differently negotiated power relations without one affecting the other. If, in some hypothetical utopia, physical sharing were as much a part of the classroom contract as intellectual sharing, then this power differential wouldn't be an obstacle, since it would be understood to exist in bed as well as at the blackboard. I doubt, however, that bed would seem so attractive if grades and student evaluations were attendant upon our individual performances there.

On the other side of the coin, a teacher-student relationship which exists outside an institution—i.e., a nonhierarchical exchange of money and services, as in a private tutoring situation—need not be bound at all by distinctions between the intellectual and the physical. If I'm paying a person to teach me a subject (anything at all, from botany to auto mechanics) and we become attracted to each other, I see no reason not to become physical as well as intellectual sharers. If, as so often happens, the original subject disappears, then it couldn't have been that important to either one of us. If we agree that money payment is no longer appropriate, that's fine too, as long as some equal exchange of skills or talents takes place.

Inside the institution, however, even an open contract about physical intimacy wouldn't make such a liaison acceptable, because there is a second reason to abstain:

numbers. Whether or not physical relations are part of the classroom contract, as long as the student-teacher ratio is more than one to one, the teacher cannot be expected to divide her energy in this way. Her ability to be an equal facilitator for *all* the students in the class will be weakened if she is giving so much intimate out-of-class energy to one or more selected few.

Everything I've said so far applies to all classrooms, regardless of subject matter, or the gender of teacher or students. Some specific distinctions between male and female (especially lesbian) teachers need to be made, however. First, lesbian teachers, particularly in women's studies courses, must go beyond the power principles I've outlined here to the simple political expediency of keeping our behavior clean. We have a responsibility to the women's studies program we serve to protect them from charges of "recruitment" and "seduction." It's painful to have to pander in any way to the prejudices of the dominant culture. But mere survival of these programs depends on such compromises, and we owe it to our students and colleagues to save personal indulgences for safer settings.

Second, the caveat about institutional power imbalance goes at least double for male teachers of female students, since even outside of their academic roles the woman is at a disadvantage.

Third is the most important difference between male and female teachers, and certainly between "regular" and women's studies classrooms. The real goal, after all, of women's studies is teaching women to take themselves seriously as women, to study and analyze their cultural history, personal experience, and position in the world; in short, teaching women to love women, both others and themselves. In such a setting, especially if the teacher is an open lesbian in an all-female group, the classroom will vibrate with sexual energy among the students themselves. Thinking, talking, working together on the subject of women's growth and freedom is, in Audre Lorde's terms, the ultimate erotic experience. No male teacher could catalyze an atmosphere quite like it. Many women students will find themselves attracted to each other in the best sense of the word. And though physical intimacy is not a necessary ingredient of this exciting ferment, it may grow out of or be added to it later.

Similarly, the students may find themselves more powerfully attracted to the lesbian teacher than to the usual male authority figure, since the lesbian teacher's energy and involvement in their mutually stimulating material is quite different. The teacher becomes a model not simply of authority, but of freedom, risk-taking (if she is open about her orientation), and (to some) radically new ideas. The lesbian teacher in turn will be more stimulated by her women's studies students than by her mixed classes, because both the material and the atmosphere free her from most of the gender-based sex games demanded in the ordinary classroom.

Both the special attractiveness of the lesbian teacher and her special sense of comfort have their pitfalls, however. On the one hand, even if she exercises her authority with scrupulous objectivity and care, misleading no one with false promises, flattery, or flirtation, the love-feeling she will inspire in some of her students may still affect the class adversely. Deprived of mothering as all women have been in patriarchy,[4] the temptation to see the lesbian authority figure as Mother is overwhelming. And in the first flush of the semester's excitement, she is the Good Mother. But as soon as it becomes clear that Mom is going to criticize, give grades, and—crucially—*not* step in and take care of one for life, inevitably anger and resentment arise. The righteous rage of life-long, centuries-long deprivation eclipses the teacher's true face, and the betrayed student sees only the Devouring Mother. Many lesbian teachers find themselves confronted midsemester by harsh and totally unexpected criticism, ranging from vituperation to full-scale mutiny. The intensity of some students' bitterness seems incomprehensible; everything had been going along so well. The experienced lesbian teacher knows how to foresee this upheaval, to recognize the storm warnings of excessive enthusiasm or personal regard early in the semester. It is not always avoidable, but at least the disruptive effects on the class can be lessened if the teacher properly understands the psychology involved and can articulate clearly her sense of what is going on both to the individual(s) and to the whole group.

On the other hand, the lesbian's special feeling of comfort in the women's studies classroom often leads her to be more personally expansive and nurturing than is wise. For myself I tend to play down specifically "maternal" behaviors or tonalities—overly solicitous inquiries about students' personal lives, bringing of food to class gatherings, too much hugging or physical touching. In other feminist settings such behavior may be genuine and appropriate, even necessary. In the classroom I think it triggers deep expectations which simply cannot be met, a kind of love which ought not to be promised. In dealing with such powerful needs, however, the teacher must always affirm even her most troublesome students' pain. We are all in this boat together, and meeting hostility with its likeness will surely sink us.

There are other particular sexual dynamics set off by a lesbian teacher in a women's studies classroom, but the Mother-trap is the most dramatic that I have encountered. I know it happens to heterosexual women teachers as well, but not, I think, with quite the same intensity. As Nancy Chodorow, Adrienne Rich, and others have pointed out, the mother-daughter relationship is profoundly lesbian (and sexual) at its core, and an openly lesbian woman will trigger those feelings at a more profound or perhaps violent level than a straight woman.[5]

In a larger sense, the dynamic created by any minority person in an authority position in a majority institution is explosive, because power in the classroom must be realigned and redefined quite drastically. Minority students suddenly have permission to feel in the "majority" or accepted role. Majority students are forced to re-examine their unconscious assumptions about being right, about owning the world, and about what kind of validation they can expect from this teacher. The teacher must make some extremely difficult choices between her responsibility to the institution which pays her and her responsibility to her own identity and honest exposure of it (and all the political perspectives and opinions which come with it) to her students. When the minority-majority axis concerns sexuality—i.e., lesbian versus heterosexual—the class is surcharged with sexual energy of all kinds from the start. If the energy remains at an intellectual level, if the teacher does not promise impossible nurturance or attention, if she affirms both her own and her students' sexual feelings without acting them out physically, and if she is open and honest about her grading responsibilities, then the class should be a fine and proper lovemaking experience—one of the only possible inside these patriarchal walls.

I am indebted in the writing of this essay to many women for suggestion of issues; but in particular to Sally Gearhart, Helene Wenzel, and Marcia Keller for dialoging with me about these ideas.

NOTES

1. Throughout this essay I refer to college-level classrooms only.

2. See Audre Lorde, "The Erotic as Power," *Chrysalis* 9 (fall 1979): 29: "the erotic is not only a question of what we do. It is a question of how acutely and fully we can feel in the doing."

3. I make a distinction here between the direct and immediate power imbalance in the teacher-student situation, and the indirect power imbalance created by class differences of two lovers. The latter power imbalance is very real and laced with inescapable problems. But I think they are resolvable, at least between the two individuals involved, since the more privileged always has the choice to share or renounce most of her privilege. This is not true for the teacher if she is to remain a teacher.

4. See Phyllis Chesler, *Women and Madness* (Garden City, NY: Doubleday, 1972), 18–19.

5. Nancy Chodorow, "Family Structure and Feminine Personality," in *Woman, Culture & Society,* edited by Michelle Z. Rosaldo and Louise Lamphere (Stanford: Stanford University Press, 1974), 53; Adrienne Rich, "Sibling Mysteries," in *The Dream of a Common Language* (New York: W.W. Norton & Co., 1978), 52; and Adrienne Rich, "Compulsory Heterosexuality and Lesbian Existence," *Signs* 5, no. 4 (summer 1980): 637.

LESBIAN LITERATURE: A THIRD WORLD FEMINIST PERSPECTIVE

Dialogue transcribed from a taped conversation, April 1981

Cherríe Moraga and Barbara Smith

"A Baseline From Which to Build a Political Understanding": The Backgrounds and Goals of the Courses

Barbara Smith: I'd taught Black women's literature, interdisciplinary courses on Black women and talked about Lesbianism as an out lesbian in my "Introduction to Women's Studies" courses, but I really wanted to do a Lesbian lit. course. Lesbian literature had never been offered by the women's studies program at the University of Massachusetts in Boston, although the program is almost ten years old. There was a gay literature course that hadn't been offered for a while. It had been cotaught by a gay man and a Lesbian, but its orientation was quite a bit different from what I had in mind.

Cherríe Moraga: Well, Lesbian literature had been taught a number of times at San Francisco State through the English department. I had also taken some other women's studies courses which focused on Lesbianism. My major motivation for wanting to teach the class was that I thought it was a perfect place to integrate a political perspective that basically centered on Lesbians of color, since my politics feel so Lesbian-identified. The other motivation came in response to taking other women's studies classes and Lesbian-related courses that were so completely white and middle-class. I wanted to teach a course that covered what I thought was missing from those classes. I thought I could bring in an integrated perspective.

B: I had no intention of teaching what I called on the first day of class "Rich White Women."

C: Indeed.

B: The Renee Viviens and Natalie Barney types. No interest whatsoever, because they do get taught, and some of them even get taught in straight literature classes.

C: The other thing is too that in gay literature classes what is usually taught are books like *Rubyfruit Jungle* and whatever stuff is as mass-market as can be. Not necessarily feminist stuff. And then, in a Lesbian course taught by a white woman, you would get racist and classist selections by default.

B: One major goal was to familiarize the women who took the course with the writing of women of color. When you teach a Lesbian literature course on white writers, there will be segments of people in the class who know the material on some level. Whereas if you're teaching the work of women of color, you're basically dealing with a blank slate, people who don't know the writers at all, who haven't heard of them. The other goal was for them to get a grasp of how the issue of racism in the women's movement connected to them. I felt that it was impossible to talk about the literature of women of color without talking about the reality of racism also.

C: One of my goals was actually to teach a course on the theory of oppression through a feminist perspective. I really wanted to talk about how Lesbians function in a positive and visionary way for a feminist future, for progressive change, social change. But at the same time, I was really clear about wanting to talk about Lesbianism as oppression and to talk about homophobia. Regardless of their color, most of the women in the class had lesbian oppression in common, which gave them some sensitivity to making connections with racial oppression and class oppression. Some of the students didn't know they were oppressed. But as in teaching a class whose students are predominantly Third World and female, there would be a source of oppression to work from.

B: There'd be a baseline from which to build a political understanding.

"People Came Around":
Our Students

B: Most of my class were white women and Lesbians. There were some white straight women and one Black straight woman, but no Lesbians of color who attended on a regular basis. I did everything possible to inform women of color about the class. I talked about this difficulty to the students from the beginning and I think at a certain point they thought I was saying that I didn't want *them* to be there, but I think that they began to understand what the significance was of having Third World women actually in attendance as we got into the subject matter. University of Massachusetts in Boston is an urban university that basically serves working-class and lower-middle-class students. The composition of the class did not reflect the racial composition of the campus. There are still, despite cutbacks, significant numbers of women of color. Not just Afro-American women, but Latinas, people from the Caribbean, Asian women, all kinds of people go there. But what began to be obvious is that the risks involved for a woman of color to take a course called "Lesbian Literature," whether she was a Lesbian or not were high, particularly if she was a Lesbian. As far as age was concerned, most of the people who took the course were in their early twenties.

C: Well, my class was also predominantly white. There were four women of color officially registered and fortunately often Third World women in the community would attend. The effect of the course? "People came around," as you would say. They had little or no exposure to the works of women of color, and they got some. In the first six weeks of the course, however, there was a great deal of tension in the room, particularly between the white women and Third World women. I experienced this tension as well. What came up was many of the white women in the room didn't know that they'd have to be dealing with racism when they came to a Lesbian lit. course.

B: Right, indeed.

C: What they told me, later, was that they had felt very intimidated by the subject matter; and that there was some unspoken resentment that this was a criterion for the course they had not anticipated. This tension didn't get resolved until enough time had passed where they indeed trusted that I wasn't just trying to make them feel bad. Instead they began to comprehend that the way I was defining "Lesbian Literature and Feminism" meant that they had to be antiracist.

B: Yep. Yep. Yep.

C: Because racism is an issue that makes white women feel so vulnerable, it early on set up a dynamic of some resistance between them and me and the women of color in the room.

B: Well, I must admit that despite what I consider to be the success of the course, I know that there were times that I felt alienated myself in the situation of virtually all-white women. I did feel like an anomaly at times. Sometimes some students weren't very sympathetic, like saying, "Isn't this hard for you to do? How can you do this? Don't you get tired of it?" I have found in all my teaching experience, I am constantly dealing with this contradiction of the powerfulness of being a teacher against the powerlessness of being Black. Most white university students have never had a Black teacher. That, in itself, is a mind trip. The teacher *is* in a position of power. I think it does a trip to white student's heads to have a Black person—a Black woman in particular—in that position over them when their general experience of Black persons in the society is in situations where Blacks are subordinate to them.

C: If not subordinate, then nonexistent.

B: Sometimes I really have the feeling in the classroom that the look in my white students' eyes is "What is she going to do next?!" Of just not knowing. . . . People have so many *negative* images of Black people. And teaching, particularly on a non-university level, has many *positive* connotations. A teacher is someone who *takes care*. In other words, their connotations of teacher are different from their connotations of Black.

C: Rightrightrightrightright.

B: Another thing is intellect. To have a Black person in a position of intellectual power over white people is UNKNOWN: You know? That's just a real mind trip on the children. (laughter) I mean how could the Black person know more than they do? AHHHHHHHHHH: (laughter) How could a Black person be teaching them anything? Just like I say in the introduction to *But Some of Us Are Brave: Black Women's Studies*[1]: "How could someone who looks like my maid or my fantasy of my maid teach me anything?

C: Right. (laughter)

B: I'm supposed to know everything. I'm white. . . . (sigh)

   C: My being a light-skinned Third World woman versus being Black meant that in my class there was less of a specifically racial or color dynamic happening. But since my being Chicana formed my politics, which determined the makeup of the course, they felt at a disadvantage because they were being graded from my perspective. I think they wondered, "How can I learn something if I wasn't born into it?" when all along we, as working-class and Third World women, have been required to learn and teach outside of our own point of reference. But the existence of Third World students in the classroom made my existence much easier. It was a positive connection. However, I did notice, Barbara, what a difference it made to the Black women in the class when you came to visit and teach a section. Here was an unmistakably visible *out* Black lesbian feminist. After your visit, in speaking to one Black woman in the class who was so moved by your appearance, I realized how rare it is to see someone like us teaching a class. I know the Latinas in the class felt that way about my teaching. The point is that I may be able to teach Black Lesbian literature well, but not like you. What I'm saying is that there's nothing like a passionate lived connection when you're teaching a subject.

   B: Indeed. And also a cultural point of reference. When I was in your class I could use language and elicit responses that were useless in my class. There was no point in talking in Black language, about Black women's writing in a class that's basically white. I might have slipped occasionally, but, like Beverly Smith's old concept, they didn't "inspire the behavior."

"The Political Significance of Being a Dyke": The Designs

   B: We had arrived at wanting to teach these courses independently, but then when we found out what each other was doing, we talked about our course outlines together and actually developed courses that were fairly similar in topics, if not in reading lists.

   C: I began the course trying to talk about the criteria on which Lesbian literature is examined. I used your definition of feminism. To paraphrase: *Feminism that is not about freeing all women, which means working-class women, women of color, physically challenged women, et cetera, is not feminism but merely female self-aggrandizement.* We took some articles like Julia Penelope Stanley and Susan Wolfe's "Toward a Feminist Aesthetic" and an article by Bertha Harris, "Notes toward Defining the Nature of Lesbian Literature" and contrasted those against Elly Bulkin's article "Racism and Writing" and your article "Toward a Black Feminist Criticism." If Lesbian feminists are doing criticism then they are responsible for doing actively anticlassist, antiracist work, using anticlassist and antiracist criteria for examining those literatures.

B: We read the same articles and I guess had similar discussions. The students in my class—and this was pretty early in the semester—were quite critical of the white women writers, like Bertha Harris, June Arnold, et cetera who did not deal with issues of race and class, and it was good to have Elly Bulkin's article as a contrast.

C: Did you discuss Lesbian feminist aesthetics much?

B: No. We hardly talked about aesthetics at all, because to me aesthetics is talking about what makes something pretty as opposed to what makes something effective. We certainly talked about that—effectiveness.

C: When we discussed aesthetics we did so in relation to color and class. This led us to then examine the white middle-class bias of what is considered good art in the first place. What we did in terms of literary criticism grew from the perspective of trying to develop some kind of integrated (that is, not male and not white) defined sense of what is good work.

B: We also did a section in the course called "Forerunners, Pre-feminist Lesbian Writing." I had an opportunity to show a slide show on Lesbian pulp fiction.[2] I wanted people to have an understanding that Lesbian literature existed pre-feminism. We had quite a debate over whether *The Black and White of It,* a recent book by Ann Allen Shockley, was feminist writing or not. I think that this was one of the first examples of how people's effort to be nonracist made it difficult for them actually to be critical of what we were discussing. In their eagerness not to be negative about a Black woman writer's work, they used different standards to approach it. In other words, because she was Black, they felt they couldn't say she wasn't explicitly feminist.

C: In my class we spent some time talking about Lesbianism outside of a feminist framework. Instead of using pre-feminist literature, however, we used some articles about specific sexual questions among Lesbians now. I felt that the majority of the women in the class came out as Lesbians through the feminist movement and had very little understanding of what it meant to be gay without the support of a woman-identified political movement. In some way, they had been sheltered from viscerally dealing with plain old queerdom. I felt that it was critical that a lot of them come to terms with that.

In contrast, I also included a section that was about Lesbian feminist visions of the future. This has been a heavy genre in Lesbian feminist writing. All the major books coming out around 1978 had a section that talked about a feminist vision in some way. Like the third section of *Gyn/Ecology,* which was supposed to be about Lesbian ecstasy. And then the last section of Susan Griffin's book *Women and Nature,* and the last section of Adrienne Rich's *Dream of a Common Language.* And also Sally Gearhart's *The Wanderground* which is a feminist fantasy. These white writers were producing a body of literature that was talking about where we should go from here. My problem was that I could never get behind any of them (with the exception of Rich, who incidentally titled her final section "Not Somewhere Else, But Here," with the emphasis on the "Here"), and I didn't understand why. So in class we used *The Wanderground* as a way to seriously examine how that vision was in some way actually exclusive. It was not an all-encompassing vision, but was directed only to a particular group of women that could indeed feel liberated by the guidelines she had set forth. One of the best parts of the class was actually when Sally Gearhart came in and we could talk with her face to face. This then brought up the issue of a Lesbian feminist writer's commitment to speaking out of her reality but at the same time with a sense of inclusiveness.

Judy Grahn's work is a perfect example of doing just that. Judy is very clear about how her class has actually affected the kind of writing she does in terms of form and content. And also affected her politics. The pivotal point of the whole class was talking about the question of ethics by focusing on "A Woman Is Talking to Death." That one long poem became the breakthrough for lots of women to really understand, not in an analytical way, or theoretical or abstract way, the political significance of being a dyke. Many white middle-class feminists write ethical poetry but you can't get underneath it. It's not concrete. Judy's stuff in a very daily way helps you see how indeed she is up against all the forms of oppression and how they all collapse in on each other.

B: We talked about how the first moral dilemma that she poses is should she help out a Black man. Isn't it interesting that the poem actually begins with race? Besides accountability, violence, accidental violence, and the white-boy stupidity that got the motorcycle rider killed in the first place, race is up front. And when was the poem written? 1973? Before most people were even thinking about racial accountability as a feminist issue.

In my class we talked about the irony of the fact that the people who were really asking practical ethical questions were perverts—the people who were talking about having enough food for people to eat, trying to end race hatred, war, what-have-you. I think that's even different from so-called revolutionary male or nonfeminist women writers who might ask those very questions but whose perspective is ruined by homophobia. So we're talking about an ethical vision one could actually live with as opposed to an ethical vision that stops short of Lesbians and gay men.

C: Along with that I think a recurring theme that comes up in Lesbian literature—which is to me the heart of why I would bother to teach the course—is some kind of personal conviction that something between women could be different than what it has been before. By focusing upon the works of Audre Lorde, Judy Grahn, and Adrienne Rich as they come together you can see this basic theme repeated. Somehow maybe it's possible that between women, racism, hunger, et cetera could be overcome.

B: As Adrienne says, "The decision to feed the world/is the real decision. No revolution/has chosen it. For that choice requires/that women shall be free."[3]

C: And along the same lines, the theme that goes through "A Woman Is Talking to Death" over and over again, is that of touching. Because she touches women she's a pervert, and yet the reality is that the true perversion or the true indecent act is when she didn't touch women.

B: Indeed, indeed.

C: Judy Grahn says, "Yes I have committed acts of indecency with women and most of them were acts of omission. I regret them bitterly."[4] And I think that there's the same kind of ethical frame of reference in Audre Lorde's work. Take a poem like "Between Ourselves," in which she writes, "I do not believe/our wants/have made all our lies/holy."[5] She refuses to use race as an excuse for imposing other forms of oppression. But it's all rooted in very concrete stuff. That's the critical difference.

B: I think the point about white working-class women being almost the only white writers who are appropriate to include in this kind of course is significant. It's not that we have a lot of white working-class writers to call upon, but the problem with white middle-class writers or upper-class women writers is that they only experience their oppression from at most two perspectives, which can limit the inclusiveness of their vision in their writing.

"Our Ideas Precede Our Means": The Materials

C: Unfortunately, things being as they are, there is very little literature by women of color, period, that's published, but particularly Lesbians of color, and so what we were both forced to do was to find it, to exchange some information ourselves and at the same time to get it from other people and copy. We had to use handouts because we don't have bound books. One of the things I wanted to say about that is that some of the strongest pieces of literature we had were on pieces of paper. One of the problems that is typically brought up about why women of color and/ or Lesbians of color aren't really discussed in women's studies courses is that there isn't any available material and part of that is true. But it takes a real invested interest and commitment to find the stuff. Because it's actually there, but it's in feminist and Third World small-press form and published randomly in periodicals.

B: It's also much easier to find, at this point, collected writings of Black Lesbian writers because of publications like *Conditions: Five,* than writing of women of color who are not Afro-American.[6] It would have been much easier to teach a course using only Black Lesbians, but it would hardly have been comprehensive. Often white women in particular think only in terms of Black and white and think if they've added a few Black women to a course they've done what's expected of them. I think what we're describing is so typical of the position of Third World Lesbian feminists which is that our ideas precede our means.

C: Exactly, exactly.

B: The hardest to find book which dealt with racial issues was actually by a white woman writer: *The Changelings* by Jo Sinclair, written in the 1950s. We had only three copies of the book to pass among thirty people. Because of that process we ended up talking about the book last as opposed to where it actually appeared on the syllabus. And that was a really great book to end on since my class was almost entirely white. Although Jo Sinclair never publicly identified herself as a Lesbian, the book was written from a Lesbian and feminist perspective, and it talks about issues of race from the perspective of a Jewish woman. In other words, it brought together many of the themes of the course because it was talking about race, but from a white woman's perspective. It was Lesbian literature in that it focused upon a friendship between a Jewish girl and a Black girl. People really got into the book seriously, and most of them felt they had never read a book like that—and of course most people will never read it because it's out of print. Some feminist publisher should seriously consider reprinting Sinclair's work.[7]

"They Taught White Men, So Why Can't They Teach Black Women?": The Third World Lesbian and Women's Studies

B: What concerns me here about this dialogue is how much of an exception is it going to be to the body of the book *Lesbian Studies* as a whole? We're going to be talking about Third World Lesbian literature, and somebody else can be talking about the marvelousness of using Mary Daly's thing as a jumping-off point.

C: Could we speak to that issue? Because we're talking to each other, we're assuming a lot of stuff as givens which are givens to us. But maybe if you could articulate exactly why we're convinced that we're probably among the few people in the country who are teaching any women's studies courses from this perspective. . . .

B: Okay. Number one, there are virtually no women of color who are out as Lesbians who are in a position to teach courses in universities. This is one of the ironies of our existence. There are Third World Lesbians, but very few have the wherewithal to be able to teach a class at a university. There are also Third World Lesbians who do teach at universities who are not out or who are not feminists. So in other words the pool of people who can teach these courses is virtually nonexistent. Very similar to how there are very few people involved in Third World women's studies from a feminist perspective, period. Like what I have found is that the people who have the politics don't have the jobs, or the credentials. The people who have the credentials and the jobs don't have the politics.

C: So you mean also white women who could be teaching stuff about Third World women . . .

B: Aren't at universities, either? Probably, probably.

C: In women's studies there aren't the Third World women. But what about the white women who are already teaching there?

B: The white women who are teaching there—they definitely don't have the perspective in the main because if they did women's studies would have a whole different look than it does. I don't think it's trashing to say that white women have been extremely limited by their whiteness and their class backgrounds, because every text, every piece of tangible evidence that you pick up indicates that. In other words it's not just an impression, it's a reality. You can document it. All you have to do is go into your women's studies section at your university and see what's being taught.

C: I think that on our various campuses, there has been at least some effort to begin. There are some white women teaching who do some Third World women's studies and are trying to do some substantial integration in the curriculum. But it's very slow.

B: Another thing is that there's little Lesbian literature taught anyway. Of all the women's studies courses taught, it might be the one taught least, because of the issues and risks involved. This brings up the issue of so-called professional security and whether you're intending on making it in the university system. I think it's also significant that the two people who taught *these* Lesbian lit. courses had *no* interest whatsoever in having careers in the university.

C: Indeed. So we didn't have as much to lose.

B: Yeah, in other words we could be Third World Lesbians, teaching Third World literature, teaching Lesbian literature. And the thing is we didn't expect a future.

C: Right.

B: Another thing I was going to say is that what really makes me angry about straight white women's studies teachers in general is like how they can never see where women of color and Lesbians would logically fit into their subject matter. Women in my classes would come back and talk about other women's studies courses they were taking simultaneously, and they would complain bitterly about the narrowness of a women's studies course that the very semester before they might have taken on face value. And I think they only had this consciousness by having been involved in my course at the same time.

C: Right, exactly.

B: But the thing is, it really makes me mad that I can look at a course outline and say, "Well, Third World women should go here, Lesbianism should go there, blah, blah, blah," and yet women's studies teachers are so totally incapable of doing this. Why?

C: I think basically the mentality of most programs is we will teach white middle-class, heterosexual women for all our courses except in the Lesbian literature course where we will teach white lesbians and in the Third World women's course where we will teach straight Third World women. And that's it. (laughter)

B: Perfect.

C: I mean then everything's covered in the curriculum.

B: Perfect, perfect.

C: So if you happen to be a Third World Lesbian, forget it. Because there's not going to be one course that you could totally relate to. Your Lesbianism gets dealt with in an all-white atmosphere and your color gets dealt with in a straight context. Then they want to know why there are no Third World women or Third World Lesbians taking women's studies.

B: Right, indeed.

C: And certainly you're not going to hear anything about Lesbianism in any other department.

B: Right, unless it's abnormal psychology.

C: And what you find in ethnic studies programs is probably not going to be very much about women.

B: Another factor is that we are active as feminists. That's another thing that would bring us to this commitment about what to do in a classroom. I don't see teaching as political work, but certainly my political consciousness affects what I think is important to teach. Which brings up the point, how translatable is this? Do we really believe white women can teach these classes? Because my feeling is, they can.

C: Oh yeah, sure.

B: It's not about them teaching it as we would teach it, but teaching it as opposed to all that alien crap that they are teaching.

C: Well, to repeat a point that has been made over and over again. If white women could teach white-boyism for so many years, why couldn't they teach Third World women's stuff? After all, they aren't white men, anymore than they are Third World women. They could particularly teach Third World women's literature because literature opens you up into the mind of another person. They taught white men, so why can't they teach Black women?

B: Hey? Well, you see, because white people are *normal.* The norm. (laughter) But in reality the reason that one thing appears easy and the other hard is that confronting the experience of women of color calls white women's lives into question in a way that the writing of white boys just doesn't. They can remain aloof. Because they're not having to examine their relative power in relationship to poor and Third World people, nor their own role as collaborators with the very people who oppress them.

C: See, I believe that the design of our Lesbian lit. courses could be applied to virtually any women's studies course.

B: Oh, of course, absolutely.

C: Hopefully, our own students have a hit now, to go into other courses and check out if the only writers being discussed are Susan Griffin, Adrienne Rich, Mary Daly, you know . . .

B: Honor Moore.

C: Honor Moore, Olga Broumas, and the only issues being examined are "transformation of language."

B: "Silences in language."

C: Yeah. "Changing silence into language." . . . It's not that for women, and particularly Lesbian, writers that this is not an important critical approach, but it's only one theme. It's only *one* way to look at our writings. It's only one mode of expressing our conflicts as Lesbian writers. Compare, for instance, how often the word "language" comes up for one writer and how often the word "seeing" or "hunger" or "touch" comes up for another. What might these two writers have in common, what is the difference between them in terms of color, class, et cetera? The point is that if you do teach a course that involves a Third World woman's perspective, a lot of the assumptions that you are making in the course are going to be turned around. I think this is terrifying to teachers because to bring in another body of information would mess up their whole system.

B: Sure. Absolutely. Without question.

C: Like, for instance, I know a woman who is nearly completing a thesis on a certain aspect of Lesbian literature. I asked her why it was she had not included the work of Third World women, she being politically a very conscious woman.

She told me that for her at this point to try to include Third World women would mean including a whole set of other issues that would alter her thesis entirely. What I began to think of then was, "Well, how valid, then, are her conclusions?" If, for instance, you're making the point that such and such is a common thread in Lesbian literature and Lesbian experience but are excluding a whole mass of people, how true are your points, ultimately?

B: Virtually not at all. You see, this is the fallacy of white knowledge.

C: Here we go. What Lesbian feminists need to be responsible for is producing a body of literature that makes people have to get up and move. Why use the word "feminist" if you're talking about a body of literature that rationalizes people's complacency? Their internal psychological dilemmas may be very interesting, but if they prevent the reader from ever having to deal with the woman down the street . . .

B: With race, class, and color . . .

C: What's happened in Lesbian literature too often is romanticizing relationships between women. We only have to look very close at home and can go off in our little enclaves and never have to be accountable to a larger struggle.

B: The criterion for women's studies courses is that they should reflect the experiences of all women.

C: AAALLLL.

B: Given the practicality, that's not always physically possible. But that's the goal. And that does not mean tokenism.

C: But if a course is designed to reflect differences and commonalities between women, then to midway introduce an issue that was overlooked—for instance, aging women or physically challenged women—should not throw the intent of the entire course off, but instead enhance its goals, whether the course be "Women and Psychology," "Women's Spirituality," what-have-you. We have to teach courses with the desire to be challenged by our students. We're all ethnocentric. There's always something more to know.

NOTES

1. Gloria T. Hull, Patricia Bell Scott, and Barbara Smith, eds., *All the Women Are White, All the Blacks Are Men, But Some of Us Are Brave: Black Women's Studies* (New York: The Feminist Press at CUNY, 1982).

2. This slide show by Maida Tilchen and others had not been distributed as of 1981. —Eds.

3. Adrienne Rich, "Hunger," in *The Dream of A Common Language* (New York: Norton, 1978), 13.

4. Judy Grahn, "A Woman Is Talking to Death," in *Collected Poems* (New York: St. Martin's Press, 1978), 125.

5. Audre Lorde, "Between Ourselves," in *The Black Unicorn* (New York: Norton, 1978), 113. "Between Ourselves" was originally published in 1976 by Eidolon Editions, Point Reyes, California.

6. At the time of this conversation, the Latina anthology *Compañeras*, edited by La Colectiva Latinoamericana, was in progress, and *This Bridge Called My Back*, edited by Cherríe Moraga and Gloria Anzaldúa (Watertown, MA: Persephone Press, 1981), had just been published. In a note, the speakers cited these two volumes and observed that "works by Lesbians of color from many racial/cultural backgrounds are becoming increasingly available in print."—Eds.

7. In 1985, The Feminist Press reissued *The Changelings*, with afterwords by Nellie McKay, Johnnetta B. Cole, and Elizabeth H. Oakes, and a biographical note by Elisabeth Sandberg. —Eds.

TEACHING ABOUT JEWISH LESBIANS IN LITERATURE: FROM "ZEITL AND RICKEL" TO "THE TREE OF BEGATS"

Evelyn Torton Beck

The patriarchy is especially good at fragmenting the loyalties of those of us who are members of more than one minority group. If we wish, in spite of the push to make us choose sides, to keep all components of our identities intact, we must be prepared to struggle, both within the minority groups to which we belong and against the dominant culture.

A consciousness of being Jewish has no doubt been with me since childhood, when, under Hitler, I experienced anti-Semitism first-hand. Thereafter, growing up in the United States (where anti-Semitism was less visible but far from dead), I was involved in a variety of Jewish activities, mostly of a cultural-political rather than a religious nature. As an adult, I integrated this continuing interest in Judaism into my professional life by offering a course in Yiddish literature in translation and by including major Yiddish writers in the world literature curriculum.

Being a conscious member of one minority group can make one more sensitive to the oppression of other groups. I had no sooner altered the curriculum to include these men when I began to notice the absence of women writers. Since it was the early 1970s, the rise of the second wave of feminism, this omission was being noticed by others as well; collectively, we began the long, slow, and exciting process of uncovering, teaching, and researching women writers. In the process, we began to notice the absence of many other minorities. Nonetheless, it was years before I was satisfied that the material in most of my classes was reasonably representative of previously excluded groups. The sole and glaring exception was the Yiddish literature class, whose texts remained solidly male. Because it was difficult to obtain translations of the few women who had written in Yiddish, I found that the only satisfying way to integrate women into the course was to shift the focus from Yiddish writers to Jewish women.

I knew from the start that I wanted the material in this course to be as integrated as in my other classes, but I was also aware that it would be a less easy process. Jewish-identified students have not always been overly eager to explore their own prejudices. Yet, for several years I had experienced oppression as a lesbian and as a result had become dedicated to making the invisible visible. Parallels came to mind. Never in all my years as a Jew had I ever dreamed of denying my people's history or my own past experience. Increasingly, as I rid myself of internalized negative prejudices about lesbians and began to see myself through my own eyes, I wanted to break through the denial that silence imposes, at least in the content of the course. So I learned to say the word lesbian out loud, without blushing or stammering or feeling as if I were leaping over a precipice; to hear it as a positive term, not only in the privacy of my home or among my lesbian friends, but out there, in the face of the patriarchy and its explicit determination to oppress and perhaps eradicate us.

This determination had the strange result of reawakening in me the memory of an older oppression. When I was in lesbian circles I often became anxious about anti-Semitism. I began to notice a new set of omissions. When lesbian and gay liberation groups spoke of needing the support of the churches, I noted that they didn't include the synagogues; when we talked of ministers, we never mentioned the rabbis. This idea wasn't new with me; there had been discussions about anti-Semitism in the movement press. In big cities Jewish lesbians had formed their own groups. I did not know what to do with this reawakened Jewish consciousness; it brought back my younger years when I had been actively involved with the Jewish struggle for survival. But now I was no longer a Zionist or even a strong supporter of Israel; nor was I an Orthodox Jew or even a believing one. I was simply a cultural Jew, a "Jewish atheist." Yet, I wanted to be visible and accepted *as a Jew* among lesbians, much as I wanted to be visible and accepted *as a lesbian* among Jews.

In the struggle to be heard, it is enormously helpful to have some visible support. While the National Women's Studies Association explicitly recommends the inclusion of lesbian/feminist material (as well as that of other minority groups) into women's studies curricula, the same kind of support is not forthcoming from the National Jewish Studies Association, which, at this time, is just beginning to recognize the contributions of Jewish women, but not yet the existence of Jewish lesbians. Where, then, does this leave the Jewish lesbian/feminist who is dedicated to being heard in Jewish as well as feminist contexts? Why insist on refining the oppressions and placing ourselves in triple jeopardy? And what happens in the classroom when we do?

With these questions still unanswered, I proceeded to plan the course on the Jewish woman, which was offered for the first time in the spring of 1978 at the large state university in which I work. We began with a history of the Yiddish language, since Yiddish is inextricably linked with women. It is a language that is both beloved and denigrated—not accidently also known as *mame loshn* ("mother tongue")—and characteristically associated with exaggerated emotion, earthiness, lack of rigor, and impurity, particularly in contrast to Hebrew, the holy tongue, associated with men's concerns—prayer and study. With this in mind, we read accounts of Jewish communities in Eastern Europe and other books that provide a historical context for the Jewish woman.[1]

The scope of the course was broad, ranging from the seventeenth century to the present, and including Europe, Canada, and the United States. Texts included works by the "fathers" of modern Yiddish literature, Mendele Mocher Sforim, Sholom Aleichem, and I.L. Peretz, as well as *Memoirs* by Gluckel of Hameln (1690; published 1932; reissued New York: Schocken, 1977) and Bela Chagall (*Burning Lights,* 1946; reissued New York: Schocken, 1963). We read fiction by Anzia Yezierska (*Bread Givers,* 1925; reissued New York: Persea 1975), Tillie Olsen (*Tell Me A Riddle,* New York: Dell, 1960), and Susan Fromberg Schaeffer (*Anya,* New York: Avon 1975); writings by Holocaust survivors, and contemporary essays and poems.

In the syllabus I also included Martha Shelley's poem, "The Tree of Begats," the first poem I had ever come across that dealt explicitly with the experience of being a Jewish lesbian.[2] As further points of reference, I included recent personal essays by other Jewish feminists including a few lesbians,[3] and with some hesitation I also assigned two short stories by the notoriously misogynistic but extremely popular contemporary writer, Isaac Bashevis Singer.[4] While these stories are no exception in Singer's oeuvre, they do deal with women's relationships to women: "Zeitl and Rickel" is an explicitly lesbian love story that ends with the death of both partners; "Yentl the Yeshiva Boy" tells the story of a young girl who poses as a man in order to be allowed to study and in this disguise ends up marrying a woman.

The majority of students who take "Yiddish Literature in Translation" are Jewish students with a strong Jewish identity, although non-Jewish students also sign up for the class. Most of the students have little feminist consciousness, and in the past close to half have been men. This semester, because of the topic and perhaps also due to the feminist questions I posed in the class flyer, about forty-five of the students were women and five were men. The format for this kind of class at our university calls for two lectures a week which are supplemented by smaller sections led by a discussion leader. It was my function to provide the lectures. I was extremely fortunate to have had the assistance of so excellent a discussion leader as Biddy Martin (an advanced graduate student in the German department at the University of Wisconsin-Madison) who had had experience in teaching introductory women's studies. Her support and sensitivity contributed greatly to the success of the class, and I am indebted to her for many of the observations in this paper.

On the very first day of class I drew parallels between anti-Semitism, racism, sexism, and the oppression of homosexuals. At this time I also introduced the idea of overlapping or multiple oppression and mentioned lesbians as part of the diversity of Jewish women. Moreover, I also pointed to the historical parallels between Hitler's persecution of the Jews and his treatment of homosexuals. Homosexuals were also exterminated in large numbers, a fact that has received little publicity. By showing that Jews are not unique in being persecuted and by placing the oppression of both Jews and homosexuals in the same concrete historical context, students began to see that oppression is never arbitrary, but is always related to power relationships and control within a society.

For most students, the idea that women have been oppressed in the society at large was not new, and they accepted it to varying degrees. But the idea that women are also oppressed within Judaism, not only by the attitudes of individual Jewish men, but by the very institutions of Judaism and the Jewish law itself, proved to be difficult for most to contemplate. It was even harder for students to believe that Jewish lesbians feel oppressed when they are not accepted into the Jewish community (unless they remain closeted of course). Most of the students had never knowingly met a lesbian, and most were so uptight about the idea that they did not even know how to express their discomfort directly. Instead, their negative attitudes came out obliquely: they objected to the "blatancy" displayed by Jewish lesbians who, like Martha Shelley and the essay writers, "made an issue" of their oppression; they failed to see the irony of their own position as Jews who were "making much of their Judaism" in a Christian world.

Yet the students liked Martha Shelley's poem a great deal and appreciated the feminist impulse behind it. They could especially understand Shelley's feelings of being cheated of full personhood as a Jewish woman: "These clean shaven rabbis merely pretend to reform/saying in English, 'Thank God for a healthy child'/and in the ancient tongue '. . . for giving us a healthy son.'" It was somewhat harder for them to empathize with Shelley as a Jewish lesbian who was insisting on her right to be who she really was, struggling to keep all parts of her identity, "I am each day less the wandering lesbian/my father dares not own." This was an oppression they had never experienced and could not understand. While most responded with absolute and unthinking anger about anti-Semitism and the Holocaust, Shelley's bitterness, particularly her refusal to bear children ("My womb, like my fist/is clenched against the world") seemed excessive. They had great difficulty seeing the ideological assumptions behind their gut feeling that some kinds of oppression produced "justified" anger, while the oppression of those they saw as "other" did not merit the same response and was therefore necessarily exaggerated and "unjustified." They were also very upset at the parallels made by one of the essay writers between Zionism (Jewish separatism) and lesbian separatism, both of which serve similar needs for autonomy. Ironically, it was the more traditional Jews who could see the parallels better than the assimilated ones (or non-Jews), even though Orthodox Judaism forbids male homosexuality and ignores lesbianism altogether.

Another way that the students' unacknowledged prejudices came to the surface was in their insistent misreading of the two Singer texts. First, they read right over Singer's explicit statement in "Yentl the Yeshiva Boy" that the two consummated their marriage. Singer is quite explicit: Yentl, disguised as a man, marries a woman who is so naïve she never notices anything unusual in their lovemaking. Moreover, he even explains that Yentl found a way to deflower the bride so that the sheets were bloody the next morning as they were supposed to be. Yet, the students were so uncomfortable with the idea of two women making love, they preferred to ignore this evidence. Second, they objected to "Zeitl and Rickel" because Singer portrayed the relationship between the two women as "perverse." It was not that they themselves approved of lesbianism. They insisted, however (against the clear evidence of the text), that Zeitl and Rickel were not *really* lesbians; the town had misinterpreted their relationship; they were, to use the old cliché, "just good friends."[5]

Friendship between two women was something they could all understand; it was something they had themselves experienced and which they valued. As a result, they worried about definitions: how could you tell for sure where friendship left off and lesbianism began? This is indeed a significant and valid question when raised in a feminist context that challenges the insistent patriarchal emphasis on lesbians as purely sexual beings. Here, however, it was clear that the students were raising these questions in order to protect themselves and their understanding of the world. They wanted badly to assume that whatever lesbianism was, it was totally different from anything they had ever known or could ever experience themselves. Because they believed it to be something essentially evil, they wanted to reassure themselves that what they had experienced had nothing to do with lesbianism. This need to protect themselves created a great distance between the students and the lesbians in the text.

Although in lecture I gave every signal I could think of (including wearing a labyris to class), I never came out on the podium. Some students picked up on the cues (particularly those who were lesbians themselves); others guessed, but some never realized that a lesbian had been lecturing to them all semester. (In private conversations I always came out if the students seemed to want to know.) I believe that this semi-out, semicloseted stance hurt the class. I believe it would have been less easy for students to distance themselves from the lesbian material if I had been explicitly out. Yet, it is hard to know how those taboo words about one's private self will affect a class. I have found it easier to be out in small classes where one can talk person to person. I am still not sure what I will do in the next large lecture class. One feels very naked standing up there alone.[6]

Singer's stories were assigned in the first few weeks of the semester, in the context of the "fathers" view of Jewish women. In the midsemester evaluations, the students' response to the lesbian material was fairly typical of heterosexuals who are confronted with lesbianism for the first time: they felt we had placed "too much emphasis" on lesbianism, although it was only one topic among at least a dozen topics we discussed. It has been my experience that any mention of lesbianism, no matter how brief, in a heterosexual environment seems to expand until it takes up all the space. Students are so unused to this most taboo topic, that once they hear about "it" all else seems to recede into the background. This is a good indication of just how important it is for us to continue to integrate lesbian material into our classrooms. Only in this way is it possible to defuse the subject and destroy the myths.

The major focus of the course had been on what it meant to be a Jewish woman, historically and in the present. Within this focus, a number of questions arose. There was a continuum ranging from "Can a woman lead her own life and still be part of institutionalized Judaism?" to "Can a woman be a lesbian and maintain a Jewish identity?" For the religious students the answers to both were negative, though there was some possibility of stretching Jewish institutions to accommodate the feminist challenge. For the religious, lesbianism didn't fit in at all. For other students the question remained: to what extent was it worth fighting to save these institutions? The cultural Jews felt it was more possible to be a Jew and a lesbian, but the heterosexual imperative in Judaism is so strong, many were not hopeful that attitudes would really change within the Jewish community. For a culture that relies on the family for its survival, the idea of lesbianism still poses a serious threat, especially since the idea of lesbian motherhood is unthinkable to most people in the Jewish community.

Nonetheless, in spite of the initial resistance, something positive did happen to the students' attitudes toward lesbianism in the course of the semester. Because the topic was integrated into the course material and not relegated to special sessions, students found it less easy to dismiss it as unimportant. And in the course of time, the idea became less strange, and they were decidedly more comfortable discussing the topic. By the end of the semester, it seemed entirely appropriate to bring in and discuss a newspaper clipping about Anita Bryant's statement that the United States needed to get rid of all Jews and homosexuals. The topic had become part of an ongoing discussion and had filtered into the students' consciousness. Those who did not speak to the issue in lecture or discussion section said that they continued to think about it outside of class. When, in one of the small discussion groups one student raised the question "Could it be that the only reason the professor brought in lesbian material is because she is a lesbian?" a number of students came to my "defense." What difference did it make why the topic was brought in? It was important that it be there, and besides, what was wrong with bringing a subject into class if it meant something personally? This was a big shift in attitude from the beginning of the semester, when almost all the students had believed that to challenge the patriarchy was to be "biased" (only the status quo was capable of objectivity); to bring in anything personal was to be unacademic; to bring in any political dimension was to be unliterary. Some students never got beyond this, and a few said they resented having their opinions shaken, but on the whole, the course was a huge success. Most said, in the final evaluations, that the course had really opened their minds; ultimately, the lesbian material was accepted as part of my commitment to teaching literature in a feminist manner, using a feminist approach.

NOTES

1. Mark Zborowski and Elizabeth Herzog, Life Is with People (New York: Schocken, 1962); Charlotte Baum, Paula Hyman, and Sonja Mickel, The Jewish Woman in America (New York: New American Library, 1977); Leslie Hazelton, The Israeli Woman (New York: Simon & Schuster, 1979). For further references see Aviva Cantor, The Bibliography on the Jewish Woman (Fresh Meadows, NY: Biblio Press, 1979). Unfortunately, none of these texts give any attention to Jewish lesbians.

2. This poem appears in the following places: Martha Shelley, *Crossing the DMZ* (Oakland, CA: Women's Press Collective, 1974), 51–52; *Ms.*, 3 July 1974, 84; Elly Bulkin and Joan Larkin, eds., *Amazon Poetry* (Brooklyn, NY: Out and Out Books, 1975), reissued as *Lesbian Poetry* (Watertown, MA: Persephone Press, 1981). I would now also include the poetry of Irena Kelpfisz, *Periods of Stress* (Brooklyn, NY: Out and Out Books, 1975).

3. These are: "The Ways We Are," *Lilith: The Jewish Women's Quarterly* 1, no. 2 (1974): 4–14; Janet Meyers, "Diaspora Takes a Queer Turn: A Jewish Lesbian Considers Her Past," *Dyke* 5 (fall 1977): 12–14. The entire issue of *Dyke* 5 is devoted to ethnic lesbians and contains some other relevant essays. A recent collection, *Chutzpah: A Jewish Liberation Anthology* (San Francisco, CA: New Glide Publications, 1977) also includes material concerning Jewish lesbians and gay men. Significantly, several of the women writing in the Jewish publications use pseudonyms in telling their stories. My anthology of writings by and about Jewish lesbians (published by Persephone) will greatly facilitate the integration of material on the subject into any curriculum. [This book, *Nice Jewish Girls: A Lesbian Anthology*, was revised, updated, and re-published in 1989 by Beacon Press. —Eds.]

4. These are: I.B. Singer, "Zeitl and Rickel," in *The Seance and Other Stories* (New York: Farrar, Straus & Giroux, 1968) and "Yentl the Yeshiva Boy," in *Short Friday and Other Stories* (New York: Fawcett, 1978). For a more detailed analysis of Singer's attitude toward women, see my article, "I.B. Singer's Misogyny," *Lilith* 6 (1979): 34–36.

5. While this was true for the majority of the students, it is important to mention that some of the students with a generally more progressive political perspective had a more positive attitude and read the texts accurately.

6. For further thoughts on being out in the classroom, see my unpublished paper, "Self-Disclosure and the Commitment to Social Change" (paper delivered at the Forum on Feminist Pedagogy, Modern Language Association, Houston, Texas, 1980).

WHO HID LESBIAN HISTORY?

Lillian Faderman

Before the rise of the lesbian-feminist movement in the early 1970s, twentieth-century women writers with great ambitions were generally intimidated into silence about the lesbian experiences in their lives. In their literature, they gave male personae the voice of their most autobiographical characters, and they were thus permitted to love other women; or they disguised their homoerotic subject matter in code which is sometimes all but unreadable, or when they wrote of love most feelingly and even laid down rules for loving well, as Margaret Anderson did, they left out gender altogether. We cannot blame them for not providing us with a clear picture of what it was like for a woman to love other women in their day. If they had they would have borne the brunt of anti-lesbian prejudice which followed society's enlightenment by late–nineteenth-century and early–twentieth-century sexologists about love between women,[1] and they knew that if they wished to be taken seriously they had to hide their arrested development and neuropathic natures. But we might expect that before the twentieth century, before love between women was counted among the diseases, women would have had little reason to disguise their emotional attachments; therefore, they should have left a record of their love of other women. And they did. However, it is impossible to discover that record by reading what most of their twentieth-century biographers have had to say about their lives.

While pre-twentieth century women would not have thought that their intensest feelings toward other women needed to be hidden, their twentieth-century biographers, who were brought up in a post–Krafft-Ebing, Havelock Ellis, Sigmund Freud world, did think that, and they often altered their subjects' papers. Other twentieth-century biographers have refused to accept that their subjects "suffered from homosexuality," and have discounted the most intense expressions of love between their subjects and other women. And where it was impossible to ignore the fact that their subjects were despondent over some love relationship, many twentieth-century biographers frantically searched for some hidden man who must have been the object of their subject's affection, even though a beloved woman was in plain view. These techniques of bowdlerization, avoidance of the obvious, and *cherchez l'homme* appear in countless pre-1970s biographies about women of whom there is reason to suspect lesbian attachments.

In our heterocentric society, the latter technique is the most frequent. What can it mean when a woman expresses great affection for another woman? It means that she is trying to get a man through that woman. What can it mean when a woman grieves for years over the marriage or death of a woman friend? It means that she is really unhappy because she had hoped to procure her friend's husband for herself, or she is unhappy because there must have been another man somewhere in the background who coincidentally jilted her at the same time—only all concrete evidence has been lost to posterity. So why did Lady Mary Montagu write to Anne Wortley in 1709 letters which reveal a romantic passion?

> My dear, dear, adieu! I am entirely yours, and wish nothing more than it may be some time or other in my power to convince you that there is nobody dearer (to me) than yourself. . . .[2]

> I cannot bear to be accused of coldness by one whom I shall love all my life. . . . You will think I forget you, who are never out of my thoughts. . . . I esteem you as I ought in esteeming you above the world.[3]

> . . . your friendship is the only happiness of my life; and whenever I lose it, I have nothing to do but to take one of my garters and search for a convenient beam.[4]

> Nobody ever was so entirely, so faithfully yours. . . . I put in your lovers, for I don't allow it possible for a man to be so sincere as I am.[5]

Lady Mary's 1920s biographer admits that Mary's letters to Anne carry "heartburnings and reproaches and apologies" which might make us, the readers, "fancy ourselves in Lesbos,"[6] but, she assures us, Lady Mary knew that Anne's brother, Edward, would read what she wrote to Anne, "and she tried to shine in these letters for him."[7] Thus, Mary was not writing of her love for Anne; she was only showing Edward how smart, noble, and sensitive she was, so that he might be interested in her.

Why did Anna Seward, the eighteenth-century poet, grieve for thirty years over the marriage of Honora Sneyd? Why in a sonnet of 1773 does she accuse Honora of killing "more than life—e'en all that makes life dear"?[8] Why in another does she beg for merciful sleep which would "charm to rest the thoughts of whence, or how/Vanish'd that priz'd Affection"?[9] Why in still another poem does she weep because the "plighted love" of the woman she called "my life's adorner"[10] has now "changed to cold disdain"?[11] Well, speculates her 1930s biographer, it was probably because Anna Seward wished to marry the recently widowed Robert Edgeworth (whom Honora ensnared) herself. After all, "She was thirty years old—better suited to him in age and experience than Honora. Was she jealous of the easy success of

[Honora]? Would she have snatched away, if she could have done so, the mature yet youthful bridegroom, so providentially released from his years of bondage?"[12]

But surely such distortions could not be made by a biographer of Mary Wollstonecraft. Even her husband, William Godwin, admitted in his memoirs of her that Mary's love for Fanny Blood had been "so fervent, as for years to have constituted the ruling passion of her mind."[13] But what was regarded as a fact of life by an eighteenth-century husband, boggles the mind of a twentieth-century scholar. For example, how was one biographer of the early 1950s to deal with the information that in 1785 Mary underwent a terrible depression and that she complained in a letter to Fanny Blood's brother, George, "My harassed mind will in time wear out my body. . . . I have lost all relish for life—and my almost broken heart is only cheered by the prospect of death. . . . I almost hate the Green [her last home with Fanny] for it seems that grave of all my comforts."?[14] The biographer states himself that at the Green Fanny's health worsened and she could no longer teach, and for that reason Mary urged her to marry a man who would take her to a warm climate where she might recover. Then he asks, quoting the above letter to George Blood, "What had happened [to cause her great depression]? Surely her father's difficulties could not have suddenly plunged her into such a despondent state; nor could loneliness for Fanny or George."[15] His explanation is that Mary must have been madly in love with the Reverend Joshua Waterhouse and had been spurned by him. The biographer admits that there is no evidence he can offer to prove his hypothesis, and even that "On the surface Waterhouse seems like the last man in the world who would have attracted Mary Wollstonecraft." But he was the only man around at the time so "apparently he did."[16] "Something drastic," the biographer points out, must have happened "to provoke such despair," and the loss of a much-loved woman friend cannot be seen as "drastic" by a hetero-centric scholar.

When there is no proof that a subject was involved in a heterosexual relationship, such biographers have been happy enough to accept circumstantial evidence rather than acknowledge the power of a same-sex attachment. Characteristically, the same Wollstonecraft scholar quotes a letter to George Blood which Mary wrote six months after Fanny's death ("My poor heart still throbs with selfish anguish. It is formed for friendship and confidence—yet how often it is wounded.") and then points out that the next sixteen lines have been obliterated by a later hand and suggests that they must have referred to her affair with Waterhouse. "Surely the censor did not go to such pains to conceal Mary's lamentations on the death of her friends," he asserts. It must have been Mary's love of a man the censor was trying to hide.[17] However, considering Godwin's complete honesty regarding Mary's affairs with Fuseli, Imlay, and himself, it is doubtful that a considerate censor would wish to spare her the embarrassment of one more youthful affair. What is more likely is that the letter was censored by someone from our century, aware of the twentieth-century stigma regarding lesbianism, who wished to spare Mary that more serious accusation.

Despite that biographer's flimsy proof of the Waterhouse affair, subsequent Wollstonecraft biographers, uncomfortable with the evidence of her attachment to

Fanny, have been happy to accept Waterhouse as fact. The myth is even propagated in a 1970s biography of Wollstonecraft by a woman. After discussing Mary's attachment to Fanny and pointedly distinguishing it from "lesbianism," she introduces Mary's "affair" with Waterhouse with the statement, "In spite of these emotions and professions [to Fanny], a certain secret disloyalty to Fanny did take place. It is rather a relief to discover it [*sic*]."[18]

The *cherchez l'homme* technique has been used most frequently by biographers of Emily Dickinson who have filled up tomes looking for the poet's elusive lover and have come up with no fewer than ten candidates, generally with the vaguest bits of "evidence." Concrete evidence that the ruling passion of Dickinson's life may well have been Sue Gilbert was eradicated from Dickinson's published letters and has become available only within the last couple of decades through Thomas Johnson's complete edition of her correspondence.[19] The earlier publications of a sizable number of Dickinson's letters was the work of her niece, Martha Dickinson Bianchi, the author of *The Life and Letters of Emily Dickinson* (1924) and *Emily Dickinson Face to Face* (1932). Bianchi, a post-Freudian, felt compelled to hide what her aunt expressed without self-consciousness. Therefore, Bianchi reproduced a February 16, 1852 (Johnson date) letter to Sue thus:

> Sometimes I shut my eyes and shut my heart towards you and try hard to forget you, but you'll never go away. Susie, forgive me, forget all that I say.[20]

What she did not produce of that letter tells a much more potent story:

> Sometimes I shut my eyes, and shut my heart towards you, and try hard to forget you because you grieve me so, but you'll never go away, Oh, you never will—say, Susie, promise me again, and I will smile faintly—and take up my little cross of sad—*sad* separation. How vain it seems to *write,* when one knows how to feel—how much more near and dear to sit beside you, talk with you, hear the tones of your voice; so hard to "deny thyself, and take up thy cross, and follow me"!—give me strength, Susie, write me of hope and love, and of hearts that *endured,* and great was their reward of "Our Father who art in Heaven." I don't know how I shall bear it, when the gentle spring comes; if she should come and see me and talk to me of you, Oh it would surely kill me! While the frost clings to the windows, and the World is stern and drear; this absence is easier; the Earth mourns too, for all her little birds; but when they all come back again, and she sings and is so merry—pray, what will become of me? Susie, forgive me, forget all that I say. . . .

Similarly, in the letter of June 11, 1852 (Johnson date) Bianchi tells us that Emily wrote to Sue:

> Susie, forgive me Darling, for every word I say, my heart is full of you, yet when I seek to say to you something not for the world, words fail me. I try to bring you

nearer, I chase the weeks away till they are quite departed—three weeks—they can't last always, for surely they must go with their little brothers and sisters to their long home in the West![21]

But by checking the complete letter in the Johnson edition we find that what Emily wrote to Sue in that letter of June 11, when Sue was about to return to Amherst from her semester-long stint as a schoolteacher, was much more in the nature of a love letter than we could have guessed from the Bianchi version:

Susie, forgive me Darling, for every word I say—my heart is full of you, none other than you in my thoughts, yet when I seek to say to you something not for the world, words fail me. If you were here—and Oh that you were, my Susie, we need not talk at all, our eyes would whisper for us, and your hand fast in mine, we would not ask for language—I try to bring you nearer, I chase the weeks away till they are quite departed, and fancy you have come, and I am on my way through the green lane to meet you, and my heart goes scampering so, that I have much ado to bring it back again, and learn it to be patient, till that dear Susie comes. Three weeks—they can't last always, for surely they must go with their little brothers and sisters to their long home in the West!

Sue Gilbert was later to marry Austin Dickinson, Emily's brother, and Martha Dickinson Bianchi was the daughter of Sue and Austin. As anxious as she was to prove that Sue played a great part in making Emily a poet and to show that they were the closest of friends, she was even more anxious to prove that Emily and Sue were *only* friends. Thus, she includes in *Face to Face* an affectionate note that Emily sent Sue on June 27, 1852 (Johnson date):

Susie, will you indeed come home next Saturday? Shall I indeed behold you, not "darkly, but face to face" or am I *fancying* so and dreaming blessed dreams from which the day will wake me? I hope for you so much and feel so eager for you—feel I cannot wait. Sometimes I must have Saturday before tomorrow comes.[22]

But what Emily really said in that note, as Johnson shows, places their relationship in quite a different light:

Susie, will you indeed come home next Saturday, and be my own again, and kiss me as you used to? Shall I indeed behold you, not "darkly, but face to face" or am I *fancying* so, and dreaming blessed dreams from which the day will wake me? I hope for you so much, and feel so eager for you, feel I *cannot* wait, feel that *now* I must have you—that the expectation once more to see your face again, makes me feel hot and feverish, and my heart beats so fast—I go to sleep at night, and the first thing I know, I am sitting there wide awake, and clasping my hands tightly, and thinking of next Saturday, and "never a bit" of you. Sometimes I must have Saturday before tomorrow comes.

Where biographers have been too scrupulous to bowdlerize they have nevertheless managed to distort lesbian history by avoiding the obvious. Sometimes this has been done to "save" the reputations of their subjects (e.g., Emma Stebbins, Alice B. Toklas, and Edith Lewis were the "companions," respectively, of Charlotte Cushman, Gertrude Stein, and Willa Cather), although illicit heterosexual affairs are seldom treated with such discretion by even the most sensitive biographers. Sometimes this has been done out of willful ignorance. For example, Amy Lowell so obviously made her "companion," Ada Russell, the subject of her most erotic love poetry that even a casual acquaintance could observe it, and Lowell herself admitted "How could so exact a portrait remain unrecognized?"[23] It did remain unrecognized by those who saw Lowell only as an overweight unmarried woman whose "sources of inspiration are literary and secondary rather than primarily the expression of emotional experience,"[24] and whose characters thus never breathe, except for those "few frustrated persons such as the childless old women in 'The Doll,'" who share Lowell's "limited personal experiences."[25]

Although many biographers of the 1970s have been much more perceptive and honest with regard to their subjects' lesbian loves (e.g., Jean Gould's *Amy: The World of Amy Lowell and the Imagist Movement* [New York: Dodd, Mead, 1975]; and Virginia Spencer Carr's *The Lonely Hunter: A Biography of Carson McCullers* [Garden City, NY: Doubleday, 1975]) we cannot assume that lesbian history will never again be hidden by scholars who live in this heterocentric world. One otherwise careful, contemporary feminist critic totally ignores Margaret Anderson's successive passionate relationships with Jane Heap, Georgette LeBlanc, and Dorothy Caruso, and explains that ambitious women of Anderson's day were forced into loveless existences. But even where lesbian relationships are admitted in biographies of the 1970s, their importance is often discounted. A recent author of an Edna St. Vincent Millay biography squeezes Millay's lesbian relationships into a chapter entitled "Millay's Childhood and Youth" and organizes each of the subsequent chapters around a male with whom Millay had some contact, all of them ostensibly her lovers. Six who had relatively short contact with her are treated together in a chapter entitled "Millay's Other Men," although the author admits in that chapter that three of "Millay's other men" were homosexual.

This essay no doubt reads like a long complaint. It is. But it is also a warning and a hope. It is as difficult for heterocentric biographers to deal with love between women in their subjects' lives as it is for ethnocentric white scholars to deal with Third World subject matter, and their products are generally not to be trusted. If we wish to know about the lives of women it is vital to get back to their diaries, letters (praying that they have not already been expurgated by some well-meaning heterosexist hand), and any original source material that is available. It is also vital to produce biographies divested of the heterocentric perspective. Women's lives need to be reinterpreted, and we need to do it ourselves.

NOTES

1. See my article, "The Morbidification of Love between Women by Nineteenth Century Sexologists," *Journal of Homosexuality* 4 (fall 1978): 73–90.

2. *The Complete Letters of Mary Wortley Montagu,* volume 1, edited by Robert Halsband (Oxford: Clarendon Press, 1965), 4.

3. Ibid., 5.

4. Ibid., 12.

5. Ibid.

6. Iris Barry, *Portrait of Lady Mary Wortley Montagu* (Indianapolis: Bobbs-Merrill, 1928), 61.

7. Ibid., 54.

8. Walter Scott, ed., *The Poetical Works of Anna Seward with Extracts from Her Literary Correspondence,* volume 3 (Edinburgh: John Ballantyne and Co., 1810), 135.

9. Ibid., vol. 3, 134.

10. Ibid., vol. 1, 76–77.

11. Ibid., vol.3, 133.

12. Margaret Ashmun, *The Singing Swan: An Account of Anna Seward and Her Acquaintances with Dr. Johnson, Boswell, and Others of Their Time* (New Haven, CT: Yale University Press, 1931), 28–29.

13. William Godwin, *Memoirs of Mary Wollstonecraft,* edited by W. Clark Durant (1798; reprinted London: Constable and Co., 1927), 18.

14. Quoted in Ralph M. Wardle, *Mary Wollstonecraft: A Critical Biography* (Lawrence: University of Kansas Press, 1951), 40–41.

15. Ibid., 41.

16. Ibid., 37.

17. Ibid., 41–42.

18. Claire Tomalin, *The Life and Death of Mary Wollstonecraft* (London: Harcourt Brace Jovanovich, 1974), 18.

19. Thomas Johnson and Theodora Ward, eds., *The Letters of Emily Dickinson* (Cambridge, MA.: Harvard University Press, 1958).

20. Martha Dickinson Bianchi, *Emily Dickinson Face to Face* (Boston: Houghton Mifflin, 1932), 184.

21. Ibid., 216.

22. Ibid., 218. I discuss these letters at greater length in "Emily Dickinson's Letters to Sue Gilbert," *Massachusetts Review* 18 (Summer 1977).

23. Letter, John Livingston Lowes, 13 February 1918, in S. Foster Damon, *Amy Lowell: A Chronicle, with Extracts from Her Correspondence* (Boston: Houghton Mifflin, 1935), 441.

24. Hervey Allen, "Amy Lowell as a Poet," *Saturday Review of Literature* 3 (5 February 1927): 558. See also Horace Gregory, *Amy Lowell: Portrait of the Poet in Her Time* (New York: Thomas Nelson and Sons, 1958), 212; and Walter Lippman, "Miss Lowell and Things," *New Republic* 6 (18 March 1916), 178–79.

25. Ibid., 568.

TOWARD A
LABORATORY OF ONE'S OWN:
LESBIANS IN SCIENCE

H. Patricia Hynes

In late spring of 1979, I submitted an entry to *Matrices*[1] announcing that four women, lesbians[2] in science, had formed a study group. We were students in geology, environmental engineering, forestry, and general science at the University of Massachusetts, Amherst. Science students are notoriously short on time for everything except labs, research reports, and unsolved problems. A unique, microscopic subset of women, lesbians in science is the only class of feminists I have known who will reject a women's studies course for yet another science course and who will pass up a once-a-year women's event to do problem number 6, one of thirty assigned that semester. The intense preoccupation with itself which science fosters is double-edged. The workload and demands on time require almost a fealty of students, and we must jealously guard our time for feminist readings, lectures, and cultural events. On the other hand, science is a context of learning in which discipline and the ability to focus and organize our work is, of necessity, quickly learned.

Eager to bring feminist passion to science, we four immediately set about to plan papers and field trips on those ideas and investigations which had originally sparked our passion for science. Our agenda spanned an exciting spectrum of subjects:

- a voyage via slides through the Yucatán in search of gynocentric myth and solar architecture in Mayan culture, and a discussion of the natural resources of this Mexican province.
- the sources, effects, and chemistry of acid rain in New England.
- a portrait of Ellen Swallow, founder of the science of ecology.
- the basics of rock-climbing, slides of rock formation, caverns, and the results

of an extensive field study of Karst geology and cavern development.
- the fundamental electronic theory of computers.
- an overview of conventional energy sources in the United States and the potential for alternative energy.
- a geological history of the Connecticut River Valley told from the vantage point of Skinner Park, overlooking the Connecticut River Valley in South Hadley.
- a walk through a forest to demonstrate the principles of woodlot management.

The diversity of ideas was deliberate: to reopen chambers of curiosity and passionate reason which are sealed off by the prohibition of science against venturing outside of one's field. If one moves on or beyond the compartmental boundary, one is suspect of being restless, intellectually immature, undisciplined, generalist, and dilettantish. One is expected to stand still and bore ever deeper, urged on by the omnipresent imperative to specialize or perish.

Ellen Swallow's ultimate failure at the Massachusetts Institute of Technology is paradigmatic of this dilemma. Swallow, the first woman to receive a degree from MIT and to teach there, distinguished herself as a water and industrial chemist, a metallurgist, a mineralogist, an expert in food and nutrition, and an engineer. In the late nineteenth century, she devised and taught the first interdisciplinary curriculum and science methods of ecology, leading students to test air, soil, water, and food. Her science of ecology, which integrated the chemistry of soil, air and water, biology, and the scientific study of the human environment, was ultimately rejected at MIT. One biographer analyzes the failure of her new science accordingly: "It was, in spite of the validity of its parts, seen as an unpedigreed, mixed breed by the specialized science aristocracy."[3] He adds that "Swallow and most of her (ecology) friends were women and too few were scientists."

The idea of a "lesbians in science" study group came to me in my second year of graduate school. I had seen myself and other women in predominantly male sciences buffeted and demeaned in the scientific milieu:

- buffeted by the cruel rites of passage that characterize initiation into a male society: intense competition, always the threat of failure and expulsion, and willful obscuring of knowledge.
- demeaned by the sexual tension our anomalous presence catalyzed, by the invisibility of our talent and stamina; and by no recourse to women in power.

It was, though, the erosion of intellectual passion that I found to be the most appalling in science. I was, and I remain, confounded by the contradiction that the more advanced our study of science, the more remote becomes the subject of our intellectual passion: nature. It is absurd that field trips in botany courses for nonscience majors and lectures in "physics for poets" (so-called pop-science) conjure up the dynamism, the variability, and the intelligence of nature, whereas fluid mechanics and advanced thermodynamics are arduous, mechanistic, and often spiritually dulling exercises in rote problem solving.

What, then, could be more appropriate for lesbians in science than to present to one another those ideas, those intellectual projects which had first fired our mental passion? With that one guide, we developed our agenda of presentations and field trips. Our meetings were thick with ideas and questions; they were always too brief. This unique collaboration created a background of pride and meaning altogether absent in science for woman-identified women.

Very simply I picture intellectual passion as a mind on fire: a fire whose metaphysical energy furiously gathers and creates ideas; a fire whose vital flames light the eyes; a fire whose heat warms the mind and expands the self. Patriarchal science has no passion. It has fractured passion into a chilling logic and pseudo-passion. Cold logic is all too familiar: it permits a nationally known toxicologist to stun his audience with larger-than-life pictures of thalidomide babies, drawing out clinical details of their deformities while bemoaning how difficult it was to do a valid statistical survey on the babies' mothers because the women were so suggestive that they could not be relied upon to know if they had taken thalidomide or not. "Furthermore," he added dryly, "women usually don't know when they get pregnant." Pseudo-passion has many guises. It is the tense excitement stirred up in students by pitting them against one another for grades, recommendations, and limited opportunities. Pseudo-passion is warmed by the prospect of inclusion in the high priesthood of science. It is the rush scientists have when doing research against time deadlines and budget constraints, in intense competition for grants, prizes, and publication. It is the bizarre fraternity and excitement men feel when they collaborate in a high-risk venture or in a climate of potential imminent tragedy. I heard one reserved chemist declare that the frenetic federal survey and cleanup operation of Love Canal in which he participated was "surprisingly exciting," one of the most exciting times in his life. In a commemorative article on the Trinity Site White Sands Missile Range, New Mexico, where the first atomic bomb was exploded, *Time* magazine quoted two men who found the site and the event it conjured up "romantic."[4]

One wonders if the unique erasure of women in science—by erasure I mean both the cover-up of what women have done and the success of the lie that women cannot do science and mathematics—is really the erasure of passion from science. Nonetheless, it has imposed a silence so great that lesbian scientists have yet to imagine a history of lesbians in science. It does not occur to ask of the lone woman honored here and there in science: Was she a feminist? Were her mentors women? Did she dedicate her work to a woman? With whom did she live? It is so remarkable that she was honored in male history at all. All a woman need do is read the life of Ellen Swallow, Rachel Carson, or Rosalind Franklin to see the silencing and erasure of women by male "colleagues" for doing brilliant, passionate, and prodigious work. Their controversies unmask that face of patriarchy in which we read the disdain for, the envy of, and the hatred of women.

My mind still reels from the impact of H. J. Mozans's work, *Woman in Science*.[5] In one sweeping history of invention by women, Mozans unwittingly discloses the take-over of creative cultural work from women by men, the destruction of female power, and the effect of that violence on the character of male science. He cites the universal myths which record the creation by women of agriculture and agricultural implements, of dwellings which warm and cool naturally, of transport and sanitary storage of water, of the mechanical arts, in brief, of all vital systems. "Tradition in all parts of the world," he writes, "is unanimous in ascribing to woman the invention, in essentially their present form, of all the arts most conducive to the preservation and well-being of the human race." With great fervor, he then describes the brilliant work of hundreds of women scientists from classical Greece to the early twentieth century. The effect is like a great chain of lights being turned on, one by one, to illuminate female genius which, with the exception of one luminary, Marie Curie,[6] has been systematically adumbrated by lies and silence.

None of us can measure or predict, I think, how it changes us to break the silence imposed by patriarchy. Presenting our ideas and projects to other women who welcome our intelligence and who know the woman-hatred in science, as in our study group, is much more than sharing ideas and gaining self-confidence. It is an act of rebellion against our own erasure. It is, too, exhilarating mental work which forges identity and meaning, identity and meaning which will never be given to a woman, no matter what degrees and prizes she achieves, by patriarchal science.

I have written this essay—as our study group proceeded—assuming that women who love science ought to study it. Why would a woman-identified woman study science when scarcely a grain of female genius is tolerated by male science, when the intention to preserve "the well-being of the human race" is only a fragile memory of the origins of science in prehistory, and when the petty passion of patriarchal science for splitting, splicing, and bombarding is so assaultive to nature? The scope of such a discussion goes beyond this short essay. I can only conclude with some open-ended remarks about women studying science.

The root of the word science is *scire,* to know, and *scientia,* knowledge. As I see it, the purpose of studying science for women is to know nature: because nature is fascinating, because we are part of nature and we depend on nature for our life, and because knowledge will guide our wise use of nature. Patriarchal science is no more what nature is about than the psychology of the female in Freud and the philosophy of female being in Jean-Paul Sartre is about women. As men assume that what they think about women is what women are, so they believe that what they theorize about nature is what nature is. I would suggest then that a woman who loves nature, who is intellectually curious and creative, would study science to identify precisely patriarchal science's definitions and construction of science. By studying and working in science, radical women can refuse to concede to men trained and degreed in science, the absolute power over nature that is assigned to and claimed by them. If, since childhood, a woman has loved the theory and inner logic of numbers, or if she wants to learn about soil, pH, bacteria, and organic matter out of some ill-defined fascination, out of a desire to grow food and flowers, or to become soil, like her own body—in dynamic chemical balance with air, water, plants, animals, and stone—then where is she to go but books, laboratories, and schools where, despite the pathology of science, she can learn some language and ideas which she can use for "the preservation and well-being of the human race" and the planet? There is another reason for studying science. Without implying that nature is female or female is nature, I see extraordinary parallels between woman-centered being and dimensions of nature. The ideas of energy, motion, and power in physics and mechanical engineering, the image of an expanding universe and moving center in astronomy, the theory of charge in chemistry, the golden mean, continuum, and infinite series in mathematics, the cycling of energy, nutrients, and water in hydrology and geology, the vital signs of ecosystems in ecology[7]—all of these intuitions of dynamism in nature have obvious, exciting parallels in feminist theory. They may clarify dimensions of oppression. They may offer new images and, ultimately, new pathways of woman-centered being.

NOTES

1. *Matrices* is a lesbian feminist research newsletter which publishes subscribers' profiles, notes, queries, calls for papers, reviews, statements, etc. For a subscription, write to Jacquelyn Zita, c/o Dept. of English, University of Minnesota, Minneapolis, MN 55455.

2. I use the word *lesbian* interchangeably with *woman-identified woman, woman-centered woman,* and *radical woman.* All of these phrases have emerged from radical-feminist thinking. They imply a separation from patriarchal thinking and male parasitism. They describe the woman determined to search out the mystery of her own history and its connections with the lives of other women. In that same spirit, the lesbian in science searches out threads of connectedness between her own existence in this world and the subject of her intellectual passion, nature.

3. Robert Clarke, *Ellen Swallow: The Woman Who Founded Ecology* (Chicago: Follett Publishing Co., 1973), 152–53. Judy Gold, a member of Lesbians in Science, has written an extremely comprehensive paper on Swallow's life and work, with a radical-feminist analysis of the reaction of male science to Swallow's precocious work.

4. *Time,* 3 November 1980, 6, 10. One man "had been looking forward to this thing for a long time. . . . The whole atomic thing during my lifetime, and this is kind of romantic." The other man had worked at Los Alamos more than thirty-five years. Speaking of the development and the testing of the atomic bomb, he said, "It's very difficult to convey the special spirit of that time and place. Working toward a common goal, people formed a strong bond and sensed they were part of something romantic—as indeed they were."

5. H. J. Mozans, *Woman in Science* (1913; reprint, Cambridge, MA: MIT Press, 1974).

6. In *Ideology in/of the Sciences,* Monique Couture-Cherki, a French physicist, exposes the method by which even such a memorable woman as Marie Curie is mediated to history as a second sex, in the following incident. Leprince-Ringuet, a distinguished French physicist, when questioned by the French media about Marie Curie, replied: "Between Pierre and Marie Curie, Pierre Curie was a creator whose very genius established new laws of physics. Marie radiated other qualities: her character, her exceptional tenacity, her precision, and her patience." Leprince-Ringuet characterized Marie Curie as a superb laboratory technician. He cast her as a model of "feminine" research skills and denied her her genius. By polarizing her and Pierre Curie's abilities, he insinuated that she, on her own, was not an exceptional scientist, but that she was, however, a most desirable life partner for an eminent male theoretician.

7. One example of drawing ideas from science for feminist analysis is the subject of a paper I wrote that was published in the *Heresies* issue on feminism and ecology, number 13. I have taken four principles of natural ecosystems and shown the parallels between the conditions of women under patriarchy and that of natural ecosystems under the stress of extreme pollution.

A LESBIAN PERSPECTIVE ON WOMEN'S STUDIES

Marilyn Frye

Looking at women's studies from my lesbian perspective and my lesbian-feminist sensibility, what I see is that women's studies is heterosexual. The predominance of heterosexual perspectives, values, commitments, thought, and vision is usually so complete and ubiquitous that it cannot be perceived, for lack of contrast. (Like the air on a calm and moderate day; the way sexism still is for many people.) Sometimes, usually because of the interruption and contrast imported by my own presence, the basically and pervasively heterosexual character of women's studies is very clear and perceptible—overwhelming and deeply disappointing. It is also, usually, unspoken and unspeakable.

Some of my colleagues in women's studies say they cannot really tell the truth or "be radical" in their teaching because it would alienate the students. I tell them not to worry about alienating people; I say that the truth is challenging, interesting, compelling, and very effective in the classroom. I also say that when one attempts just to tell the truth, the responses, whether constructive or hostile, honest or dishonest, will be the best clues to one's errors. But in my dealings with my heterosexual women's studies colleagues, I do not take my own advice: I have routinely and habitually muffled or stifled myself on the subject of lesbianism and heterosexualism, feminism and women's studies, out of some sort of concern about alienating them. Some of these women are tangibly peculiar about lesbianism and are already offended by my being uncloseted and blatant; I do not think they have noticed that I avoid discussing lesbianism and heterosexuality with them for fear their already-nervous association with women's studies would become simply untenable for them. Much more important to me is the smaller number who are my dependable political coworkers in the university, the ones in the academic world with the clearest and strongest feminist and antiracist politics, the ones with some commitment to not being homophobic and to trying to be comprehending and supportive of lesbians and lesbianism. If I estrange these women, I will lose the only footing I have, politically and personally, in my long-term work-a-day survival in academia. They are important, valuable, and respected allies. I am very careful, overcareful, when I talk about heterosexuality with them.

But the situation is asymmetrical, as it always is with minority or marginal people and majority or dominant people. What is *a topic* for them, which some can and some cannot attend to fruitfully, is a condition of life for me. I avoid "alienating" them, but they constantly and (usually) unconsciously alienate me by their mostly uncritical and apparently unalterable, to me unfathomable, commitment to heterosexuality—by which I mean deeply bound emotional and intellectual commitments to men, to reform, to integration, and to the centrality and natural necessity of heterosexual genital sex. The unwelcome weight of this heterosexualism is a salient fact of my life, and its manifestations in the politics of women's studies are becoming very clear to me and should be stated.

In my experience with women's studies it seems common and characteristic for the women instructors to assume that widespread heterosexuality and the dominance of heterosexual conceptions have always been and will always be The Way It Is for humans on this planet, in particular for women on this planet. Lesbianism is seen by most of them (but not all) as an acceptable, plausible alternative for some women and it is understood (not by all) at least at a verbal level to be clearly coherent with feminism. But they all believe that it is only realistic to understand that most women are and most women will be heterosexual, at least for the duration of any era that our practical politics can concern itself with. Women's studies programming is grounded on the assumption that the vast majority of the students are and always will be heterosexual. Hence we give them almost entirely heterosexual women's literature, the history of heterosexual women,[1] and analysis of the roles of heterosexual women in work, business, the arts, and heterosexual domestic life. It is also assumed that we should support (not just tolerate) speakers, films, workshops, classes, whole courses, which encourage women to prepare themselves to cope with life in the "dual career marriage," teach how to be married and a feminist, train them in the tricks of legislative reform so they can try to ensure that abortions will be available to them when they need them, since they obviously will not practice the only safe and sure method of contraception.[2] We presume the students are hopelessly heterosexual and cater to the interests and needs we assume heterosexual women to have, instead of assuming they are educable to other ways of living, different needs, and interests, and some non-or anti-heterosexist sensibility and politics.

Women's studies, as an institution, as I know it, actively and aggressively supports women in becoming and remaining heterosexual; it actively seeks to encourage women to believe that the personal, political, economic, and health problems associated with heterosexuality for women should be struggled with rather than avoided—that these problems are inevitable but more or less solvable (with great endurance and much work), rather than that they are unsolvable but definitely inevitable.

I am notorious in my town for my recruitment of women to lesbianism and lesbian perspectives. But what I do is minuscule. Imagine a real reversal of the heterosexualist teaching our program provides. Imagine thirty faculty members at a large university engaged routinely and seriously in the vigorous and aggressive encouragement of women to be lesbians, helping them learn skills and ideas for living as lesbians, teaching the connections between lesbianism and feminism and between heterosexism and sexism, building understanding of the agency of individual men in keeping individual women in line for the patriarchy. Imagine us openly and actively advising women not to marry, not to fuck, not to become bonded with any man. Imagine us teaching *lots* of lesbian literature, poetry, history, and art in women's studies courses, and teaching out of a politics determined by lesbian perception and sensibility. Imagine all this going on as actively and openly and enthusiastically as the program now promotes the searching out of careers and "feminist men," the development of "egalitarian marriages," and the management of heterosexual sex and the family.[3]

But the politics which women's studies purveys, even when some material by or about lesbians is included in some courses, is heterosexual politics. And according to heterosexual politics, lesbianism could never be the norm, and promoting lesbianism for women generally is somewhere between unrealistic and abusive.

The people who are primary agents in determining and promoting this politics in women's studies are the heterosexual feminists in academia. These women are (not without exception) quite good in their relations with the few lesbians they work with—supportive, tolerant, useful. But this friendly, open-minded, even appreciative attitude camouflages their continuing and firm commitment to our marginality. Their being friendly and supportive and respectful to a few lesbians (who inevitably serve as tokens) has obscured from me and from them the enduring fact that they would never take seriously any idea that lesbians and lesbianism *should not be marginal.*

I want to ask heterosexual academic feminists to do some hard analytical and reflective work. To begin, I want to say to them:

I wish you would notice that you are heterosexual.

I wish you would grow to the understanding that you choose heterosexuality.

I would like you to rise each morning and know that you are heterosexual and that you choose to be heterosexual—that you are and choose to be a member of the privileged and dominant class, one of your privileges being not to notice.

I wish you would stop and seriously consider, as a broad and long-term feminist political strategy, the conversion of women to a woman-identified and woman-directed sexuality and eroticism, as a way of breaking the grip of men on women's minds and women's bodies, of removing women from the chronic attachment to the primary situations of sexual and physical violence that is rained upon women by men, and as a way of promoting women's firm and reliable bonding against oppression.

Some heterosexual women have said in response to these sorts of sayings, "I see the connection between lesbianism and feminism, but I cannot just decide to be a lesbian. . . . I'm not sexually attracted to women: women just don't turn me on." And I want to ask, "Why not? Why don't women turn you on? Why aren't you attracted to women?" I do not mean these questions rhetorically. I am completely serious.

The suppression of lesbian feeling, sensibility, and response has been so thorough and so brutal for such a long time, that if there were not a strong and widespread inclination to lesbianism, it would have been erased from human life. There is so much pressure on women to be heterosexual, and this pressure is so pervasive and so completely denied, that I think heterosexuality cannot come naturally to many women; I think that widespread heterosexuality among women is a highly artificial product of the patriarchy. I suspect that it is not true at all that we must assume that most women are and most women will forever be heterosexual. I think that most women have to be coerced into heterosexuality. I would like heterosexual women to consider this proposition *seriously*. I want heterosexual women to do intense and serious consciousness-raising and exploration of their own personal histories and to find out how and when in their own development the separation of women from the erotic came about for them.[4] I would like heterosexual women to be as actively curious about how and why and when I became lesbian.

At this point it might seem that I am demanding of heterosexual women their respect for my choice but that I am unwilling to respect theirs. I think, though, that it is respectful of autonomy to genuinely inquire into the history and grounds of choices, and disrespectful or negligent of autonomy to let unfreedom masquerade as choice or let the declaration "It's my choice" close off rather than open up inquiry.

Millions of heterosexual women give no thought to what heterosexuality is or why they are heterosexual. Heterosexuality is understood by them to *be* sexuality, and they assume uncritically and unthinkingly that it is simply the way humans are; they do not perceive heterosexuality as *an* option. Where there are no perceived options, there can be no such thing as choice, and hence one cannot respect the choice. But well-educated, worldly, politically astute, thoughtful, analytical, feminist women do know perfectly well that there are options, and that lesbian life is an option that coheres very well with feminist politics. They do choose to be heterosexual. Respect for that choice (on my part and on their part) demands that they make that choice intelligible.

Many feminist lesbians have thought and reflected and written and worked very hard to demonstrate that our choice makes sense. We have gone forth and participated on panels and in workshops and appeared on television explaining ourselves. We have, over and over, at great personal risk and considerable cost, worked as hard as we know how to make our choice intelligible to audiences ranging from the idly curious to the skeptical to the openly hostile. Respect for heterosexuals' choice demands equally that they show, within the gentle standards of rationality recommended by womanly sensibility, that their choice can be understood as a reasonable choice. Until this has been shown I will not grant the assumption that heterosexuality can make sense for feminists, and I am not willing to continue uncritical acceptance of women's studies promoting heterosexuality for women.

Unless many heterosexual feminists start working as hard at making their choice intelligible as lesbians have worked at making ours intelligible, they should refrain from teaching and publishing and other work which openly or implicitly encourages other women in becoming or remaining committed to heterosexuality, and lesbians should refrain from supporting women's studies.

I am grateful to Sarah Lucia Hoagland for organizing the panel "Lesbian Perspectives on Women's Studies" for the 1980 National Women's Studies Association conference; what is printed here is a revision of the speech I made. My thoughts reflect discussions with my lover Carolyn Shafer, and she gave help and suggestions in the revision process.

NOTES

1. . . . or the literature and history of women *presumed* to be heterosexual. The evidence that many of the women we study were lesbians is generally overlooked—an erasure that builds an added security for the assumption of natural near-universal heterosexuality.

2. By "the only safe and sure method," I do not mean only exclusive lesbianism, but whatever would add up to total female control of reproductive sexual intercourse.

3. For a sense of magnitude of this, consider: at Michigan State the women's studies classes account for well over twelve thousand student-credit-hours each year.

4. This phrase is Adrienne Rich's. My thoughts on these things have benefitted from my correspondence with her.

PART TWO

Studying
Ourselves

FROM A LONG LINE
OF CONTRARY FOLKS
Jo Whitehorse Cochran

How do I let you, the reader, know, if you are not Native, what it is to be "of the people"? "The people": I can write this, but there may be nowhere inside you where these words have meaning, where these words reside within your experience and living. And for a Native person this is where we begin. We are tribal, communal, family beings. Even breeds like me, who live in cities, who live in lesbian families and communities, who now have no tribe, inside of me there is how I am "of the people." How I am Lakota, *Sicangu*.[1] How no matter how far away I live, how far I travel in the world, whom I love, whom I live with, what spirit I speak to, I am always a Native woman. I am imbued with a consciousness, a voice, a way of seeing that is within every cell of my being and always brings me home to the rhythms, the songs, the thoughts, the humor, the heart that is Native. That is me. I can also make that statement just as certainly about being a lesbian. Which may appear as a contradiction, but then again I come from a long line of contrary folks.

Within the women's movement in the 1980s, American Indian/Native American/ Native women began to bring our concerns forward. We spoke of "makin' it." We talked about the oppressions and violences of racism, and the survival of our children, our peoples. The suicides of our teenagers on the reservation. The sterilization of ourselves and our sisters as genocide/gynocide. The tuberculosis, diabetes, alcoholism, fetal alcohol syndrome, cancers, tumors, radiation poisoning— the illnesses the white world brought and rooted among us. The lack of health-care providers and facilities. More of our people, our children dying. The hopelessness of these lives. We articulated, as indigenous peoples in "America," how we share the economic, health-care, housing, educational, and societal status of many poorer third world nations. Our reservations in this country are often subject to some of the most difficult living conditions in the world. It was shocking to some feminists. It is our truth.

In the eighties, the ways in which we as Native women, Native lesbians, along with other straight women and lesbians of color, interacted with the white upper- and middle-class women in the women's movement changed the course of the women's movement. We began to demand that our voices be heard, in person. We began to demand our places on the boards and steering committees of feminist organizations and women's studies programs, on conference panels at political and professional meetings, in journals, and on the podiums at rallies. We further demanded our right to say it like it is for us. To give voice, face, body, and soul to our struggle in *our* communities, which looked a hell of a lot different than the "sisterhood" of the women's movement. For Native lesbians, and other women of color, the book *This Bridge Called My Back* edited by Cherríe Moraga and Gloria Anzaldúa was one of the first rallying cries.[2] It was a ground-breaking book that called up from silence the voices of women of color in the women's movement. *This Bridge* provided space for lesbians of color to come out and speak truthfully about ourselves and our communities.

During the eighties, I became involved in the women's movement through women's studies and the National Women's Studies Association. I taught Introduction to Women's Studies, and I wrote poetry and essays. Three projects helped me bring into print the voices I was longing to hear as part of the women's movement. I coedited *Gathering Ground: New Writing and Art by Northwest Women of Color; Sobreviviendo/Bearing Witness,* a special issue of *Calyx* by Latina, Chicana, and Native American women; and *Changing Our Power: An Introduction to Women's Studies.* With *Gathering Ground* and *Sobreviviendo/Bearing Witness,* I was gifted with projects, as a writer and editor, that provided a vehicle in which women of color could speak, many for the first time in print. Women of strong voice and strong vision contributed stories of heart and struggle. In the textbook *Changing Our Power,* my coeditors and I produced what we dreamed.

We searched for women writers, scholars, voices from all backgrounds, all communities, all perspectives. In the pages the publisher allotted to us, we endeavored to get to the core of what we had taught in an introductory course, and then to expand some. As an editorial threesome, we were well balanced at that time: two lesbians (now three), two moms, two white, one Native, all from different classes, one writer, one literary scholar, and one political scientist. Our journeys in life were varied, our visions of women divergent and unified. We came to find home in each other, a trust and friendship that have lasted over many years and miles.

As editor and contributor, I was challenged with writing pieces on lesbianism, Native women, child abuse and street kids, spirituality and healing. All of these topics, for students who were being introduced to women's studies, women's issues, women's lives. And further, these students, female and male, straight, lesbian, and gay, Caucasian, African, Asian, Native, Chicana, Latina, for the most part would not share my viewpoint. So my challenge was to express my ideas, my concerns, my reality in a way that they could hear. In a way that would make them think, or feel, or react in any way. In a manner that would let them know that although I write and live with my own biases, I also speak as a part of a community. And that one community I walked into was that of women and men fighting against sexual and other physical abuse of children that leads those children to run away from their homes to live on the streets. In another instance I wrote as a member of a tribe called lesbians, and in that tribe my band was the Native lesbians and mixed bloods. In another instance, I tried to expand the dialogue on women's spirituality and religions, which for me is about unity inside myself. I brought to this book, then, a personal voice from experience, and the eye of a teacher, and the perspective of a Native lesbian.

How did my perspective as a Native lesbian shape this process? *Changing Our Power* was not at first the book's title, but the title of a poem I had written, and an idea I was growing. As I worked on the book, my perspective shifted from seeing women as reclaiming our power, to seeing us as changing our power. When I looked for my mothers—the teachers, the healers, the storytellers, the warriors of my past—I came to see that we, as women, as Native women, as Native lesbians, were always powerful. Perhaps not recently, as a group voice, perhaps only as individual women, but powerful all the same. And suddenly, there was lineage there that I could look to for strength and memory. And I realized that what the mainstream white society had defined as power came from the structure of victim and oppressor. Therefore, we had to change how we claimed, used, and envisioned our power individually and as women in all of our tribes and communities. This understanding began a spiral of conversations, writing, and work among us as editors on women as victims, women as oppressors, and women as powerful and responsible for our power. Light into darkness, darkness into the light, a move to balance our true selves. And in fact, it was my search for a way to balance harmony and disharmony that sparked our transformation. For it appeared in that moment that the women's movement was predominantly concerned with difference, with victim and oppressor. My spark could not have caught fire and burned had not my coeditors, Carolyn Woodward and Donna Langston, been of like heart, mind, and creation. This was for me a great moment as a woman, and a Native lesbian working for women, although not perhaps the typical experience for other Native lesbians. This was a moment in which I knew I was visible and had a voice others would hear.

For Native lesbians in general, our stake in the women's movement and in lesbian studies has been a speaking of the reality of our basic survival in this country. A speaking of our total invisibility. We are often invisible to our peoples, invisible within the traditions of our tribes, invisible within the women's movement, invisible in the lesbian and gay rights movement, invisible in lesbian scholarship and teaching, and of course invisible in the overall society. We express the politics and voice of the outsider, always being on the furthest edge of any recognized movement. The politics, the lives, the voice that come from invisibility.

What I know as a Native person, as a Native lesbian, is an innate drive for family, tribe, and community. A place within myself where, with others like me, a rhythm of life is the vibration of home. In this way I become, I make myself visible.

Among my friends, who are of English, African, French, Cree, Irish and Potowatamee, Cherokee, Spanish, and Norwegian descent, we know each other as tribe and home. It is in part because we are lesbians; it is in part because we share a spiritual journey together that makes us of one heart. It is in part because we share the unspoken pact to be visible. What we do not share as a commonality of being Native peoples, we share in the living of a lesbian life. None of us are young anymore; we share this as we head into our forties and fifties. Most of us have been "out" for many years. I have been an "out" visible lesbian for sixteen years. I take pride as a Native lesbian that some of what younger lesbians speak of as the "old days, history, not the way it is anymore," was how I came up, how I lived. But I am too much a contrary being, a maverick, to have wanted to be born into more accepting times.

But this is still the periphery from which I've made the fabric of being a Native lesbian. This is how I have come to survive, to find my community/tribe of friends and lovers, to search for my grandmothers. First, I looked to my elders. When I came out, elders were difficult to find. Other Native lesbians were hard to find. Only one article was in print by a Native American lesbian about Native lesbians: Paula Gunn Allen's article on *koskalakas*[3] in the journal *Conditions*.[4] I looked to elders in history, my heroines, Beloved Women, leaders, healers, warriors. I found from Allen's writings that I am of the gender within Native lesbians that would be considered *koskalaka*, or by some *berdache*,[5] or in lesbian cultural terms a "butch," or, as I have come to discover, a manly-hearted woman. And as I knew from inside of me that I was born that way, it was my birthright. It is the essence of my contrary[6] nature. I am without gender as the white, Western world understands gender. I am not totally the feminine ideal woman, nor am I totally a butch ideal woman. I am both; I am the third one that has no name. I come from a world of Changers and Coyote, a world where more than two genders exist in the social consciousness. This understanding of gender goes even further back in our peoples' remembering and traditions than what is written and spoken about now. Often the gender or status assigned to "lesbians and gay men" in our tribes is not spoken of now, because it has become taboo within the tribe and the Western-white world. This is the manifestation of homophobia within both worlds. But found within the writings and research of Paula Gunn Allen and Will Roscoe[7] are the roots, the truth, of the *koskalaka* and *berdache* as members of Native society and as ceremonial and spiritual beings. I can only verify these truths from how my blood remembers as I have read these writers' works.

I came to reveal a knowing from my blood, memory from my blood, that other women, other Native lesbians such as Vickie Sears and Beth Brant, were writing and thinking about. My mother in this process, who has kept me alive, unearthed me, sung aloud to me as Native lesbian and writer, is Paula Gunn Allen. In a time when the lesbian feminist movement was fermenting and ardently breaking into the ranks of the feminist movement, there were NO faces, NO words, NO dreams, NO visions I could share in. The dreams, visions, faces, and words were predominantly those of white, middle- and upper-class academic lesbians. I know that as a Native lesbian, I share that place of no voice, no reflection in that moment in time with Asian, African, and Chicana/Latina lesbians in America. But it seemed to Native lesbians that we were even further out on the periphery, an even smaller cadre.

But as I sought the home I had come to within me as a lesbian, a lover of women as a woman, I was seeking too my direct descendants. I still seek them, as I too have become one of them for younger Native women who will come out as lesbians. I say I have become a descendant because I am now in my late thirties, I have raised a child, I am now a mother. It also means that now, as Native lesbians, we have among our ranks grandmothers who are movers and shakers, speakers and writers of the truth. This is a realization of great joy for me, to know that our lives as Native lesbians who live visibly in the world are stretching the lives of generations of Native women. Now the stories of who we are are no longer hidden, forgotten, or silent. We have remembered ourselves, which is the first and hardest step to knowing, in certainty, who we are.

This continues to be my journey as a Native lesbian, the uncovering of self. It has led me to become certain of my identity, my roots. It has led me to be a radical Native lesbian feminist during the eighties. It has led me to work in the governing of my city and county within the government and in grassroots organizations. It has led me to be a lesbian activist. It has led me to ask the greater questions of the spirit and then seek my own answers, then ask the next greater question. It has led me to claim, understand, and live as a woman of power. And this is a power that is deeply rooted in the blood and heartbeat of Native America, Native vision. It is a power that is rooted in the mother, the grandmothers, and walking in balance with all that is.

A time ago, and often, Paula Gunn Allen writes that it is important to know your mothers. Just as it is important to know your mothers, it is important to carry that knowing into your own growth into maiden, mother, grandmother. It is the Native expression of knowing where you came up from, and not forgetting, but holding this in honor and regard. The face or faces of my mothers have been obscured by time and prejudice. But we have uncovered our selves again. We are warriors and mothers, we are storytellers and healers, we are visionaries and grandmothers, we are truth-speakers. Often we are contrary beings, in the many understandings of being contrary. We live within our tribes or as outcasts amid the whites. There is no one thing that will describe or define Native lesbians. We are bringers of change in all its facets, and we are keepers of traditions. This is what I know, this is what I live, this is my truth. Ask another Native lesbian and she will reveal another story, another truth.

NOTES

1. *Sicangu* is the Brule name for ourselves in Lakota.

2. Cherríe Moraga and Gloria Anzaldúa, eds., *This Bridge Called My Back: Writings by Radical Women of Color* (1981; New York: Kitchen Table/Women of Color Press, 1983).

3. *Koskalaka* is a Lakota term meaning "double woman."

4. Paula Gunn Allen, "Beloved Women: Lesbians in American Indian Cultures," *Conditions: Seven* 3, no. 1 (spring 1981): 67–87.

5. *Berdache* is a French word for a man we might consider a cross-dresser, transgender person, but it was often applied to describe Native women who were lesbians.

6. Contrary: The idea of a contrary being is often found among Native peoples, and the Lakota especially. Contrary people often use humor, or clowning, or contrary behavior to make a point. Contrary beings are sacred beings within this understanding, like Coyote.

7. Will Roscoe, *The Zuni Man-Woman* (Albuquerque: University of New Mexico Press, 1991).

THE VIRTUAL ANTHROPOLOGIST
Kath Weston

What walks like an ethnographer, talks like an ethnographer, packs a tape recorder, jots incessant notes, publishes, travels to conferences and applies for jobs just like an ethnographer, even begs and blunders and cajoles like an ethnographer, but is not and never can be a "real" ethnographer? Welcome to the nether world of virtual anthropology, the state to which the field methodically consigns its "un-fit," a mode of inhabiting the discipline that substitutes ceaseless interrogation for all the comforts of home. How can you expect to teach based upon this sort of field work? Why didn't you study genuine families? Real women and real men? Authentic (pure, isolated, acceptable) natives? How can you have any perspective as an "insider"? Do you really call this anthropology?

The virtual anthropologist is the colleague produced as the Native Ethnographer.[1] Fixed as the one who sets out to study "her own," she attracts, disturbs, disorders. She may have acquitted herself with highest honors during her professional training. She may have spent long hours in the field, carefully researching a topic central to the intellectual history of the discipline. If she is lucky, she will carry with her a pedigree from an outstanding graduate program.(Being advantageously positioned in terms of class hierarchies helps.) If she is very smart and very, very lucky, she may eventually secure a position at a top-ranked university. (Although precisely because she has been rendered virtual she is less likely to garner such accolades.) In short, she may have gone through all the motions supposed to bring about professional legitimacy, and with it, access to those resources the profession has to offer (salary, students, coastal residence, travel, grants). Yet her work will remain suspect, subject to inspection on the grounds of authenticity rather than intellectual argument or acumen.

Too often described as a marginal figure, unfairly exiled to the periphery of the discipline, the virtual anthropologist actually moves through the professional landscape as a creature of another order. She is irredeemably Other, but not as the result of anything so blatant as an operation of exclusion based upon race, sex, class, ethnicity, nationality, or sexuality ("We don't hire/serve/need [epithet of choice] here"). Instead, "oppression" operates obliquely to incarcerate her within a hybrid category. It is as the Native Ethnographer that the virtual anthropologist finds her work judged less than legitimate, always one step removed from "the real stuff."

Curiouser and Curiouser:
The Case of Queer Ethnography

Back in graduate school, when I first decided to study lesbians and gay men in the United States, the faculty members who mentored me pronounced the project "academic suicide." I found it hard to disagree. Before I could proceed, I felt I had to reconcile myself to the possibility (probability?) that I would never get a job in "my field." (At least, I thought, I would get a book out of it: a way to present my research to a wider public.) One glance at the gloomy employment picture for ethnographers who had studied "homosexuality" reinforced this assessment. Almost none of them held appointments in anthropology, assuming they had jobs at all.

Is it simply that people were more likely to bow down before that spectral figure, homophobia, back in the early 1980s? I don't think so. Graduate students still write to me, torn between the desire to run off with their first love, queer studies, and the advice of elders to accept the more sensible arranged marriage with "another culture" that would move them securely into "mainstream" anthropology. While job prospects may have improved ever so slightly, the structural circumstances that undercut the legitimacy of queer researchers who study queer topics remain. Anthropology's colonial heritage has formed a field that disciplines its natives in a society that nativizes its queers.

The points at which I have been, and continue to be, produced as a Native Ethnographer tend to be points of evaluation. These are the sites at which the discipline fields its ethnographers: not just job interviews, but conference presentations, book reviews, particular readings of published research, and the many small interactions that mint that coin of the academic realm, national reputation (reputation as what?). Comments on such occasions range from the generic dismissal ("Fieldwork with gay people is not fieldwork") to the more refined art of the backhanded compliment ("When I saw the title for your talk, I thought it would be a really flaky topic, but you've just transformed my whole notion of kinship").

Reactions to the threat posed by the hybridity of the Native Ethnographer may be couched as expressions of concern: "Some people (not me, of course, I'm your friend) think that if we were to offer you a job here, you would become an advocate." (Don't we all advocate for something?) Then there is the repetitive deployment of that thoroughly neutral category, "fit," as in, "We love your work, but you just wouldn't fit into this department." (Ever wondered why?)

For a change of pace, inventive sorts resorted to the thinly veiled objection on methodological grounds: "Lesbians and gay men are too small a segment of society for your results to be meaningful." (As opposed to research on that multitude, the Yanomami?) "Well, there aren't many X left, but when you study the X you are studying an entire social system." (Even Marx, who aspired to a systems analysis, sought a point of entry—alienation, commodity fetishism—that offered a unique line of sight into the whole.) "But why bother with queer theory? It's just a passing fad." (Like the Sapir-Whorf hypothesis? Or game theory? How about that one-time razor's edge of anthropological analysis, structuralism?) Every bit as disconcerting as the historical and political ignorance embedded in such a litany is the utter lack of irony with which otherwise astute colleagues pose these questions.

My dance with professional death would have been humorous if it wasn't so costly. Anyone who brings the wrong color or area of competence to her work is familiar with the pressures of having to do more and better than peers to get ahead. But it is difficult to describe the unsettling experience of watching your job history recast as a cautionary tale for the benefit of graduate students still in training. Or the sense of moving through the world more ghost than legend in one's own time. Or the slow and painful realization that the portable inquisition is likely to follow you even if you someday manage to secure a "good" position. Not that the vagaries of the job market made it easy for many applicants to land the job of their dreams. Still, in my case, there was the telltale specificity of the grounds for incredulity and dismissal: Explain why you call this anthropology.

Mistakenly concluding that my subjection to reality checks in an interrogative key was the consequence of conducting research on a stigmatized topic, mentors devised tactics to mitigate the effects of a risky focus of study. Arranged in chronological order, their advice went something like this: As long as you do theory, everything will be okay. Write your way out. Just finish your dissertation. Just get your degree. Once you sign a book contract, things will start to change. Just wait until the book is in press. Wait until the book comes out in print. Wait until people have time to read the book. Maybe that second book manuscript will turn the tide. Perhaps if you broadened your geographic area a bit (say, from lesbians and gay men in the United States to "Western civilization")?

What these routinized strategies for establishing professional credentials failed to take into account are the processes that can render an anthropologist virtual. For that peculiar anthropological subject/object, the Native Ethnographer, career strategies that rely solely on meritocracy or a move to the disciplinary center necessarily prove inadequate. To the degree that queerness is read not only through your research but through your body, hybridity becomes impossible to ignore.

Going Ethnographer

If one is not born an anthropologist, neither is one born a native. Natives are produced as the object of study that ethnographers make for themselves (Appadurai 1988, Fabian 1983). Coming of age "there" rather than "here" is generally enough to qualify you for this anthropological makeover. Expatriates, of course, need not apply: suitable candidates must be able to lay claim to the ethnicities and nationalities assigned to their place of origin. In Europe and the United States (anthropology's "here"), attribution of native status becomes a bit more complicated.

Assignees tend to occupy a sociohistorical location that makes them suitable for exoticization. Darker skin and deviance are always a plus.

With their self-absorption, sexual obsession, love of pageantry, celebration of the body, and party-going nature (please!), queers could have been sent over from central casting to play the savages within. Stereotypes all, but stereotypes that are remarkably continuous with the construction of the primitive in the annals of anthropology. Much as accusations of idleness placed European beggars in a structurally analogous position to those certifiable savages, the "Hottentots" (Coetzee 1985), so the facile reduction of fieldwork among lesbians and gay men to "an extended vacation" evokes the frivolous, childlike behavior in which barbarians everywhere wallow.

Of course, lesbians and gay men do not offer the "best" natives for study. In representation, if not in action, they appear too modern, too urban, too here and now, too wealthy, too white. Below the perceptual horizon are queers with rural origins, immigrant status, empty pocketbooks, racial identities at variance with the Anglo. Ironically, the gay movement's problematic tendency to draw analogies between sexual and racial identity—as though all gays were white and people of color could not be gay—has encouraged even white queers who study queers to be taken as "insider" ethnographers in a way that heterosexual white middle-class anthropologists studying their "own" communities are not.

Unlike "primitive" or "savage," the term native has made something of a comeback in recent years. This particular return of the repressed has occurred after a pluralist fashion that takes little notice of the power relations that produce different types of nativity. (I'm a native, you're a native, we're natives, too.) But each nativizing move can only be understood in its specificity with respect to race, ethnicity, sexuality, religion,or residence.

As the century turns the corner, queers are constructed not just as natives tethered to the symbols of residence or birth, but as natives-cum-savages. Like primitives, who got such a bad rep after ethnologists decided they had not evolved to the point of practicing monogamous marriage, queers have been saddled with a sexuality that is popularly believed to evade the strictures of social control. For lesbians and gay men of color, these representations become overdetermined, given the racist legacy that primitivizes and hypersexualizes everyone but the Anglo.

As postmodern-day savages, queers have only a few, mostly unsavory, choices: they can be lazy or restless, noble, self-indulgent, or cruel. The articulate presence of these domestic but not domesticated natives is doubly disturbing because it disrupts the homogeneity of "home," that imagined space of sameness and security that shadows "the field."[2] To the degree that the queer who studies queers has been nativized, she joins a long line of African-American, American Indian, South Asian Indian, Mexican, and Brazilian anthropologists trained in "American" universities. Like it or not, she is bound to incite professional insecurities about a changing world in which natives not only read the ethnographies that purport to explain them, but also threaten to show up in a graduate program near you.[3]

So it is not surprising that the aspiring anthropologist who is known to be "that way" finds herself reduced to her sexuality with the presumption that queer nativity is a prior attribute brought with her into higher education. Forget for a moment the complexities of history and circumstance that undercut the utopian vision of a perfect native. Ignore the possibility that our anthropologist may not understand her sexuality in terms of identity categories and identity politics. Table every theory you know that tells you identities do not produce transparent, shared experiences waiting to be expressed. Set aside the differences of race and religion and class and nationality that guarantee she will never be the consummate "insider" familiar with every nuance of a bounded community. Never mind that her own discipline is implicated in constructing the (queer) native as an internally homogeneous category. When she embarks upon a career in anthropology, she is likely to be seen as native first, ethnographer second.

If you want to understand the conflicts, suspicion, and general volatility of social relations that surround the lucky incumbent of the Native Ethnographer position, an understanding of hybridity becomes indispensable.[4] Hybridity is a compound (Native Ethnographer), rather than the sum of an additive relationship that mixes two intact terms (*native + ethnographer*). Think back to that mystical moment in chemistry class when the instructor explained the difference between mixtures and compounds. A mixture is something like a teaspoon of salt stirred together with a spoonful of pepper. Given lots of time, good eyes, and a slightly maniacal bent, a person can sort a mixture back into its original components, placing the pepper, grain by grain, in one pile, and the salt in another. A compound is another matter altogether. Compounds also combine disparate elements, but they join those elements through a chemical reaction that transforms the whole into something that does not resemble either of its constituent parts. Water is a compound of oxygen and hydrogen. Put the two together in certain proportions under particular conditions, and you will find a liquid where you might expect a gas. Trying to divide water into its elements mechanically, molecule by molecule, drop by drop, would be a fool's errand. Assuming that you understand the properties of water because you once inhaled "pure" oxygen could lead to early death by drowning.

A person cannot understand what it means to be positioned as a Native Ethnographer by reading an essay or two on representations of savagery and then brushing up on the latest in interview techniques. Attempting to grasp each term in isolation is as fruitless as trying to spot the elements of hydrogen and oxygen in your morning cup of coffee. If you come up with anything at all, it is likely to be your own reflection.

If there is anything that creates the Native Ethnographer as a particular sort of hybrid, it is the act of studying a "people" defined as one's own. Or more accurately, it is the performance of this research activity in the context of the same set of social relations that produces inanities like the characterization of "insider" fieldwork as one long party. (I don't know what kind of parties you go to, but spin the bottle looks pretty good next to 350 days of field notes.) All of this is a social product. Studying "one's own" is no more a matter of natural affinity than nativity is the consequence of birth. Veterans who study warfare are not nativized in the same way as queers who study sexuality, and their work is much less likely to be read off their bodies.

Colleagues who misrecognize hybridity as an additive relationship search in vain for the advocate hiding behind the professional mask, the savage in ethnographer's clothing. Meanwhile, the anthropologist who finds herself mired in nativity in the eyes of colleagues can attempt to extricate herself by "going ethnographer": emphasizing observation over participation, or insisting on the legitimacy of her research ("I did fieldwork, too, you know").

Although these offensive and defensive moves may seem opposed in the high-stakes game of authentication, they share an insistence on the importance—indeed, the possibility—of separating the ethnographer from the native. But the two terms cannot be neatly distinguished once the discipline has brought them into a relationship of hybridity. As a compound state, hybridity represents something more complex than an "intersection" of separate axes of identity. The operations that transform the whole into something qualitatively different than the sum of its parts make it impossible to tease out the various ways in which research area and nativity combine to provide a basis for discrimination.

Was it studying the United States or the way you stood with your hands in your pockets (too butch) that led the interviewer to pose that hostile question about "real fieldwork"? Funny, another guy asked the same thing when the job specified a geographic focus on the United States, so maybe it's not area after all. But if it wasn't area and it wasn't the hands in the pockets (still not sure about that one), maybe it was because you couldn't put to rest those lingering fears that, if appointed, you would become a crusader for "your people." Geez, what if it was all three?

When Native Ethnographers attempt to prove themselves real in the face of the inevitable interrogation, they face the old duck dilemma: however convincingly they may walk and talk, quack and squawk, as they perform the time-honored rituals of professional legitimation, they will look *like* an ethnographer before they will be taken as (a real) one. As hybrids, they are continuously produced in the cyberspace of the virtual.

In the course of professionalization, Native Ethnographers emerge from graduate programs that promise to transform the benighted Them (natives) into the all-knowing Us (anthropologists). On the job market they labor under the suspicion that greets shape-shifters, those unpredictable creatures who threaten to show up as Us today, Them tomorrow. The very presence in the discipline of queers who study queers could complicate this dichotomy between Us and Them in useful ways. But in the absence of the thoroughgoing reevaluation of the anthropological project that an understanding of hybridity entails, the irresolvable question that faces the virtual anthropologist remains: How will *these* ethnographers make their Other?

This chapter is an abridged version of a section of a longer essay forthcoming in Jim Ferguson and Akhil Gupta, eds., *Anthropology and "the Field"* (University of California Press). My thanks to Deb Amory, Jared Braiterman, Susan Cahn, Kristin Koptiuch, Thaïs Morgan, Geeta Patel, and participants in the Anthropology and the Field Conference organized by Jim Ferguson and Akhil Gupta (Stanford University and the University of Santa Cruz, 1994) for the irreverent comments and lively conversation that helped make this paper what it is today.

NOTES

1. "Native" is a problematic term that keeps people in their place by essentializing their characters, bounding their communities, and otherwise subjecting them to the disciplinary legacies of racism that emerged from colonial rule (Bhabha 1984, Narayan 1993). In this essay, I capitalize Native Ethnographer to underscore the category's status as representation rather than birthmark.

2. For a critique of "home" as a locus of safety and familiarity, see Martin and Mohanty (1986) and M.B. Pratt (1991). On the discomfort and ambivalence associated with the racialized and sexualized colonial stereotype that produces the native, see Bhabha (1984, 1986).

3. Cf. Ashcroft et al. (1989). For authors who write explicitly, though not always contentedly, from the position of "native anthropologist" or "insider ethnographer," see Abu-Lughod (1991), Jones (1970), Limón (1991), Narayan (1993), and Sarris (1991).

4. For theoretical treatments of the concept of hybridity, see Lugones (1994) and Patel (1994). For examples of the concept's incorporation into discussions of multiculturalism, see Lowe (1991) and West (1993).

BIBLIOGRAPHY

Abu-Lughod, Lila. 1991. Writing against culture. In *Recapturing anthropology*, edited by Richard Fox. Santa Fe, NM: School of American Research Press.

Appadurai, Arjun. 1988. Putting hierarchy in its place. *Cultural Anthropology* 3, no. 1:36–49.

Ashcroft, Bill, Gareth Griffiths, and Helen Tiffin. 1989. *The empire writes back: Theory and practice in post-colonial literatures.* New York: Routledge.

Bhabha, Homi K. 1986. The other question: Difference, discrimination, and the discourse of colonialism. In *Literature, politics, and theory,* edited by Francis Barker et al. New York: Methuen.

———. 1984. Of mimicry and man: The ambivalence of colonial discourse. *October* 28:125–33.

Coetzee, John M. 1985. Anthropology and the Hottentots. *Semiotica* 54, nos. 1/2:87–95.

Fabian, Johannes. 1983. Time and the other: How anthropology makes its object. New York: Columbia University Press.

Jones, Delmos J. 1970. Toward a native anthropology. *Human Organization* 29:251–59.

Limón, José. 1991. Representation, ethnicity, and the precursory ethnography: Notes of a native anthropologist. In *Recapturing anthropology.*

Lowe, Lisa. 1991. Heterogeneity, hybridity, multiplicity: Marking Asian American differences. *Diaspora* 1, no. 1: 24–44.

Lugones, Maria. 1994. Purity, impurity, and separation. *Signs* 19, no. 2:458–79.

Martin, Biddy and Chandra Talpade Mohanty. 1986 Feminist politics: What's home got to do with it? In *Feminist studies/critical studies,* edited by Teresa de Lauretis. Bloomington: Indiana University Press.

Narayan, Kirin. 1993. How native is the "native" anthropologist? *American Anthropologist* 95, no. 3: 671–86.

Patel, Geeta. 1994. Home, homo, hybrid: Queerness in India. Unpublished ms.

Pratt, Minnie Bruce. 1991. Identity: Skin blood heart. In *Rebellion: Essays, 1980–1991.* Ithaca N.Y.: Firebrand Books.

Sarris, Greg. 1991. What I'm talking about when I'm talking about my baskets: Conversations with Mabel McKay. In *De/colonizing the subject: The politics of gender in women's autobiography,* edited by Sidonie Smith and Julia Watson. Minneapolis: University of Minnesota Press.

West, Cornel. 1993. *Race matters.* Boston: Beacon Press.

THAT WAS THEN AND THIS IS NOW

Toni A. H. McNaron

In 1964, when I began work at the University of Minnesota, there were no publicly defined lesbian or gay faculty. Perhaps on a few campuses in California or New York City, such academics could declare their sexual orientation, but in an overwhelming majority of cases, we were silent, reluctant to risk credibility and jobs by announcing our gayness or lesbianism. This self-monitoring, based on homophobic displays such as those exhibited by Senator Joseph McCarthy's House Un-American Activities Committee and routine police raids of gay bars, allowed universities and colleges to keep their heads in the sand. Administrators could avoid even thinking about the needs or concerns of lesbian and gay faculty since none of us ever voiced any.

When I arrived at the University of Minnesota, there were two unmarried women and one unmarried man in the English department. While one of those women seemed asexual, the other lived with another woman in a secluded river house an hour and a half from the university. The man was elegant in all regards, had three or four close friends in other departments who, like him, were "single," and traveled to England or Europe once a year for a more relaxed and open life.

Efforts to make friends with the tenured woman living on the river were singularly daunting. Since neither of us was capable of publicly acknowledging our lesbianism, our social moves were opaque at best. Rather than reaching out to me, she seemed threatened by my presence. Much later I would come to understand that this woman worried that I might somehow encroach on the ground she had won for herself. She was accepted by the departmental patriarchs because she cast herself as "one of the boys," drinking more old-fashioneds than they during extended lunch hours at downtown hotels, cursing at least as vividly, and winning often at weekly poker marathons.

Though I felt genuine kindness and understanding coming my way from the elegant man, his carefully imposed silence about his own life, together with our combined terror of being "found out" by colleagues, left us with powerful lacunae conversationally and emotionally. Aside from these tortuous encounters, I was convinced for years that there were no other lesbians or gay men at the University of Minnesota. Two decades later, Audre Lorde's discussion in her luminescent *Cancer Journals* of the waste that attends upon women's use of prosthetics to disguise radical mastectomies would resonate profoundly with me. Like them, no lesbian or gay faculty could "find" one another because we too were in hiding, making heroic attempts to pass for heterosexual and usually being thought of as pathetically asexual.

In my early years, socializing within my mostly male department was confusion enough. If I stayed with my colleagues, their own conversations became so stiff as to make all of us distinctly uncomfortable. For many of them, making small talk with a female colleague seemed too large a challenge. If I retired to the kitchen with my colleagues' wives, conversation again ground to a halt. Those women's lives in the mid-sixties often revolved around children or their homes—subjects that certainly interested me. But in front of me such topics seemed to become boring in the speakers' eyes, so we were left with little to talk about except what we had just eaten or were about to eat.

Because my partner and I were entirely closeted, I never took her to such social events. Because I denied my private life, I prevented anyone from asking about me as a human being. I remember with a wince any number of painful conversations between me and an older colleague or his wife. These people extended themselves in a vague way, hoping, I'm sure, to help me feel more a part of the academic scene. We were usually at the annual fall cocktail party; everyone paired except me (the other lesbian skipped these functions, declaring herself allergic to large groups). Conversations usually went something like this:

"Well, Toni, and how are you finding Minneapolis/your students/the winter/ our art galleries/the symphony/your neighborhood?"

"Oh, just fine, thank you," I would say, gulping my drink or sandwich in a frantic gesture to buy some time while I thought about what I could say next to the person trying so hard to set me at my ease.

"Are you making friends, meeting people, or are you lonely for someone special back in Madison?" The tone behind the last phrase was always hopeful, encouraging, reminiscent of my mother's queries each holiday visit during college as she became increasingly uneasy with my failure to present some nice young man for her to meet.

Utter panic. My "someone special" was at home studying the MMPI, Rorschach blots, or theories of personality development. So how was I to answer so innocuous a question? "No, I'm not meeting people—it takes all my spare time to manage my secret life, thank you."

During my first decade at Minnesota, my closet deepened as did my dependence on alcohol. I believe it is the rare person who can sustain a central secret about themselves without resorting to some numbing agent. Rather than enumerate the waste from that period, I want to leap into the present.

Thirty years after my arrival on campus, I am in the midst of a sabbatical devoted to writing an ethnographic and narrative study of lesbian and gay faculty from across the United States who have been in the academy for at least fifteen years— a project for which I have been awarded a salary augmentation, enabling me to complete it within a year. Professionally, I am asked to contribute to many lesbian scholarly publications; I teach lesbian literature or culture when I'm not offering Shakespeare, Milton, or Woolf courses; and I serve on editorial boards for several feminist and lesbian journals and presses.

How did I get from there to here? The three most important factors in my metamorphosis are the flowering of women's studies in academe, sobering up, and coming out at work. Within women's studies I finally found an intellectual and emotional "home," a place that valued strong women with new ideas and questions. I remain committed to feminist academic pursuits because I admire, love, and enjoy working with and for women.

My personal health and productivity depend as well, however, on factors outside myself. For instance, in 1973, the American Psychological Association removed homosexuality from its catalogue of diseases, reducing it to a potential neurosis rather than an inevitable psychosis. Since 1980, student activists have been asking for greater inclusion of lesbian and gay material in relevant courses, for space and support services for gay/lesbian/bisexual concerns, and for coherent clusters of courses, if not full-fledged programs focusing on gay and lesbian studies. Scholars inside and outside the academy are generating, with dizzying speed, new knowledge based on gay and lesbian research. The concomitant presentation of such research at conferences held by virtually every professional academic discipline fosters a growing context within which younger faculty members may feel freer to teach courses and conduct scholarship focusing on lesbian and gay issues. The legal recognition of sexual orientation as a potential target for bias and harassment, together with the recent upsurge in hate speech on campuses nationwide, are forcing many top-level administrators to come to grips with the virulence with which homophobic attitudes can be held and expressed even in such supposedly accepting environments as their own.

These factors converge to the consternation of those who object to a more tolerant attitude toward lesbians and gays. But the changes they prompt are consistent with academic rhetoric that promises an open exchange of ideas as one of the centerpieces of scholarly discourse.

For some time now, theorists have argued that invisibility is one of the mainstays in preserving prejudice and injustice. I can keep my prejudices in tact as long as I think I don't know anyone who fits some category I find offensive. If I learn that someone with whom I work, someone more or less like me, is a member of this offensive group, I have several options. I can automatically and unthinkingly reject a person who moments before I admired, liked, and associated with easily. I can extend my definition of acceptability to include this representative of the offending group as an "exception." Or I can begin to question culturally received constructs that depend upon groups of people being marginalized, stigmatized, and discriminated against.

Recently I was asked to participate in a panel at a training session for University of Minnesota staff. In the question period, I was asked what heterosexual coworkers can do to make my working environment friendlier. Here are my responses:

- Ask me about what my partner and I did over the weekend, for a major holiday, or on our vacation.
- Once I've told you my partner's name, file it away the same way you do the names of coworkers' spouses so you are able to refer to her specifically rather than having continually to resort to some distancing and mildly insulting generic, i.e. "And how is your partner?"
- Think of me, my partner, and our cherished animals as a family that enjoys the same activities and feels the same stresses as your own, compounded by our not being legally defined as a family.
- Speak out when you hear anti-lesbian or antigay jokes. Let the teller know that you do not find them funny, that you have friends, relatives, and coworkers who are gay or lesbian, and you don't like to hear unfair and denigrating remarks about them.
- If you're an affectionate person, extend your usual physical and verbal contacts to me when the occasion warrants.

When I consider the new generation of lesbian and gay faculty, teaching, publishing, writing dissertations, and organizing conference sessions, I feel a rush of excitement. But I also feel a little like Thomas Gray, the late eighteenth-century English poet, who wrote about his feelings as he stood on a rise overlooking students at his old school, Eton. From his vantage point, their flamboyant play was shadowed by knowledge gained from bitter experience. I want to warn my colleagues that our gains are dangerously fragile, that history can repeat itself unless we all work very hard to prevent it.

For their part, these wonderfully assertive individuals sometimes look at old-timers like me with a mixture of indulgent sufferance and sentimental trivializing, sure within themselves that the world has indeed changed permanently. If they could read some of the three hundred questionnaires I have collected for my sabbatical project, they would understand graphically that progress in gay and lesbian studies has come in distinct pockets and that the extraordinary window of opportunity within research and publication that I currently celebrate could be closed by the same people who have opened it.

I begin my fourth decade at the university full of hope and gratitude to all who labor to remember that I and my lesbian and gay colleagues do indeed exist. We teach hard and well, we conduct lively and important research, we serve on the panoply of committees that help make the university function. We are eager to be included in all academic networks, including the alumni association. And, most importantly, we want to do all these things as visible lesbians and gays who are valued not in spite of our sexual identities but in part at least because of them. This is my wish for the future here at Minnesota. With the active support of heterosexual allies, it will materialize. Without that support, too many of us will feel it necessary to remain in closets that shut out the light of human companionship and shrink the spirits confined within them.

This essay, solicited in early 1995, was initially rejected by the executive editor of *Minnesota*, the alumni magazine of the University of Minnesota. I protested this homophobic attempt at censorship to the university's president, who counseled that I meet with the editor. Accompanied by Beth Zemsky, the director of our L/G/B/T office, I agreed to such a meeting. The editor reversed her decision when her state advisory board voted unanimously that the contents of my article were exactly the kind of thing they wanted to see in their magazine. The essay was originally published in *Minnesota* (May–June 1995): 46–48.

THE IMMIGRANT EXPERIENCE IN LESBIAN STUDIES

Oliva M. Espín

A large proportion of the world's immigrants and refugees are women.[1] The United Nations estimates that 80 percent of all refugees in the world are women and their children (U.S. Committee for Refugees 1990). The current estimate is that the foreign-born population in the United States is about twenty million (Rogler 1994). Demographic studies have demonstrated that the composition of the gay and lesbian population in North America is very much like that of the entire North American population (Tremble, Schneider & Appathurai 1989). As it is true for all other groups of women, one can assume that lesbians are present in significant numbers among immigrants. The usual difficulties in obtaining adequate statistics on gay and lesbian populations also prevail concerning this population of immigrants and refugees.

Although the experiences of women in international migration have begun to draw attention from researchers, policy makers, and service providers (e.g. Cole, Espín & Rothblum 1992; Gabaccia 1992), the lesbian experience is mostly absent from these studies. In fact, little is known about the experiences of both heterosexual and lesbian immigrant women in such "private" realms as sexuality, sexual orientation, and identity. Yet, as we know, sexuality and related issues are not private, which explains why so many cultures and countries try to control and legislate them. Indeed, as one historian observes, "Sexual behavior (perhaps more than religion) is the most highly symbolic activity in any society. To penetrate the symbolic system implicit in any society's sexual behavior is therefore to come closest to the heart of its uniqueness" (Trumbach 1977, 24).

We know that the sexual and gender role behavior of women serves a larger social function beyond the personal in all societies. It is used by enemies and friends alike as "proof" of the moral "rectitude" or decay of social groups or nations. In most societies, women's sexual behavior and their conformity to traditional gender roles signify her family's value system. Thus, in many societies, a lesbian daughter as well as a heterosexual daughter who does not conform to traditional morality can be seen as "proof" of the lax morals of a family. This is why struggles surrounding acculturation in immigrant and refugee families center frequently on daughters' sexual behavior and women's sex roles in general. For parents and young women alike, acculturation and sexuality are closely connected; in many immigrant communities, to be "Americanized" is almost synonymous with being sexually promiscuous (Espín 1984, 1987b).

Moreover, the self-appointed "guardians of morality and tradition" that are ever-present among immigrant "communities" are deeply concerned with women's roles and sexual behavior. Considering that immigrant communities are more often than not besieged with rejection, racism, and scorn, those self-appointed "guardians" have always found fertile ground from which to control women's sexuality in the name of preserving "tradition." While young men are allowed and encouraged to develop new identities in the new country, girls and women are expected to continue living as if they were still in the old country. They are more often than not forced to embody cultural continuity amid cultural dislocation. Groups that are transforming their way of life through a vast and deep process of acculturation focus on preserving "tradition" almost exclusively through the gender roles of women. Women's roles become the "bastions" of traditions. The "proper" behavior of women is used to signify the difference between those who belong to the community of immigrants and those who do not (Yuval-Davis 1992, 285). Needless to say, lesbians present unique challenges to immigrant communities while, at the same time, the expectations of their communities create enormous pressures on lesbians who belong to immigrant families, particularly for those who come out while in adolescence. The authors of a study of Canadian youth note that "The rift that occurs between parent and child over sexual orientation is set in the context of an existing conflict, as the child pulls away from the Old World culture to espouse the North American way of life" (Tremble, Schneider & Appathurai 1989, 255).

Even as an adult, to be a lesbian in the midst of an immigrant community involves not only a choice about one's own life but also a choice that affects the community's perception of itself and of her family. Coming out may jeopardize not only family ties, but also the possibility of serving the community in which the talents of all members are important assets. Because many lesbian immigrants are single and self-supporting and take advantage of the opportunities for employment and education in the United States, they are frequently involved in services and advocacy in their communities. At the same time, they may also feel tensions about serving their community, fearful of discovery and rejection by that same community (Espín 1987a, 1990).

Immigration, even when willingly chosen and eagerly sought, produces a variety of experiences with significant consequences for the individual. No matter how glad the immigrant may be to be in a new country, the process often results in the loss of people with shared experiences; strain and fatigue from the effort to adapt and cope with cognitive overload; feelings of rejection from the new society, which may lead to alienation; confusion in terms of role expectations, values, and identity;

"culture shock"; and a sense of uprootedness and impotence; and an inability to function competently in the new culture.

When immigrants cross borders, they also cross emotional and behavioral boundaries. Becoming a member of a new society stretches the boundaries of what is possible in several ways. One's life changes, and one's identity may as well. In the new culture, new social expectations lead to transformations in identity. The identities expected and permitted in the home culture may no longer be expected or permitted in the host society. Most immigrants eagerly or reluctantly crossing geographical borders may not expect to cross the emotional and behavioral boundaries as well.

For lesbians, the crossing of borders and the subsequent crossing of boundaries take specific forms. Migration—and the acculturation process that follows—open up different possibilities for them (Espín 1984, 1987a, 1987b, 1990). Frequently, newly-encountered sex-role patterns combined with greater access to paid employment for women creates possibilities to live a new lifestyle that may have been previously unavailable. One case in point is an openly lesbian life. For example, some women become employed outside the home for the first time in their lives after the migration. Many of them encounter new opportunities for education. All of them are confronted with new alternative meanings of womanhood provided by the host society. The crossing of borders through migration may provide for many women the space and "permission" to transform their sexuality and sex roles. For lesbians, an additional border/boundary crossing takes place that relates to the coming out process. Coming out may have occurred in the home country. It may have occurred after the migration, as part of the acculturation process. Or, in some cases, it may have been the motivating force behind the migration. Many lesbians experienced discrimination because of their sexuality before the migration.

Although lesbianism is not only about sex, it is, obviously, closely connected with sexual behavior and identity. Sexuality is a universal component of human experience, yet how it is embodied and expressed is not. Sexuality is culturally variable, not an immutable, biological force. Even what is considered to be sexual or not in one cultural context is often strikingly different for people in different cultural environments. These cultural constructs inextricably inform the expression of all lesbian sexuality and demand learning "how to be a lesbian" in the host country regardless of previous experiences in the home country. Cultural traditions, colonial and other forms of social oppression, national identity, and the vicissitudes of the historical process inform the development and perception of female sexuality and the creation of patterns of behavior among lesbians. Worldwide, definitions of what constitutes appropriate sexual behavior are strongly influenced by male sexual pleasure. Even for lesbians, these definitions carry a strong weight—if not altogether a conscious one. These definitions are justified in the name of prevalent values in a given society: nationalism, religion, morality, health, science, and so forth. Worldwide, women are enculturated and socialized to embody their sexual desire or lack thereof through their particular culture's ideals of virtue. A social group's expectations are inscribed in women's individual desire and expressed through their sexuality. That is not to say that gay men's sexuality is not subjected to conscious and unconscious controls by society. However, the expectation of conformity to society's sexual norms exercises pressures on all women's sexuality, regardless of sexual orientation.

All pressures on immigrant women's sexuality, however, do not come from inside their own culture. The host society also imposes its own burdens and desires through prejudices and racism. Lesbians who have come out in their country of birth may have developed patterns of behaving and relating that may not fit the prevalent accepted codes of behavior among lesbians in the new country. Even though racism may be expressed subtly, the immigrant woman finds herself between the racism of the dominant society and the sexist and heterosexist expectations of her own community. The racism of the dominant society makes the retrenchment into "tradition" appear to be justifiable, while the rigidities of tradition appear to justify the racist/ prejudicial treatment of the dominant society. Moreover, the effects of racism and sexism are not only felt as pressure from "the outside," but also become internalized, as are all forms of oppression.

Immigrant women who are lesbian develop their identity against the backdrop of these contradictions. Thus we need to increase our knowledge and understanding of how the contradictions and interplays of sexuality/gender and racism in both the home and host cultures are experienced and made sense of by lesbian immigrants.

My own research seeks to increase knowledge and understanding of sexuality- and gender-related issues among immigrant and refugee women (Espín 1994). Specifically, it explores the main issues and consequences entailed in crossing both geographical and psychological borders and boundaries and analyzes how sexuality and identity in lesbian women are affected by the migration. Both the importance of geography and place and the role of a second language are crucial in understanding the experience of immigrant lesbians.

Immigrants are preoccupied with geography—that is, with the effect of the *place* in which events in the life course occur. This phenomenon has two components. One is the engrossment with the vicissitudes of the actual country of origin that gives that place a sense of being almost *not* real in spite of its constant psychological presence in the life of the immigrant. The other is a fixation on "what could have been" that translates into ruminations about life's crossroads. "The migration experience creates an emergent phenomenology of incessant reference group comparisons and trade-offs between the benefits of the host society and the losses incurred in departing from the society of origin" (Rogler 1994, 704). Reflections about life's possibilities had the immigrant continued to live in the country of birth or immigrated to another country, or had the immigration taken place at this or that stage of life, as well as other what-ifs are frequently present.

For immigrant lesbians this preoccupation is tied to the process of coming out, to the development of a lesbian identity as well as the development of one's sexual orientation. Some lesbians are preoccupied with the relationship between childhood events and having become a lesbian. To this, the immigrant lesbian adds thoughts, concerns, and general "what could have been" ideas concerning her lesbianism, concentrated in a basic question: Would I have become a lesbian if I had not emigrated? The Cuban-American lesbian writer Achy Obejas illustrates these concerns in a recent story, when she ponders,

> What if we'd stayed? What if we'd never left Cuba? . . . What if we'd never left[?]
> . . . I wonder, if we'd stayed then who, if anyone . . . would have been my blonde
> lovers, or any kind of lovers at all. . . . I try to imagine who I would have been if
> Fidel had never come into Havana sitting triumphantly on top of that tank, but
> I can't. I can only think of variations of who I am, not who I might have been
> (Obejas 1994, 124–25).

This preoccupation is of course connected with the process of acculturation that all immigrants experience in their adaptation to their new country and all lesbians and gay men undergo in the process of coming out. The immigrant lesbian acculturates as an immigrant and sometimes as a lesbian at the same time. Even when she was a lesbian before the migration, she needs to learn to be a lesbian in her new cultural context. If she comes to the United States from a background other than European, she also has to acculturate as a so-called minority person.

I am specifically interested in discerning lesbians' comfort with descriptive terms about lesbianism in their first language. The preferential use of one language over another is deeply related to identity, but also to other factors not yet studied. (See, for example, Espín 1984, 1987b, 1992, 1994). For lesbians, the integration of the two languages when addressing sexuality may be a step towards integrating both cultural backgrounds. Conversely, the exclusive preference of one language over another may be an effort at compartmentalizing the contradictions inherent in being a lesbian and an immigrant. Through formal and informal interviews I have explored how variations in speakers' comfort (or discomfort) when addressing sexuality in the mother tongue or in English have emerged (see, for example, Espín 1994, 1995). Even among immigrants who are fluent in English, the first language often remains the language of emotions (Espín 1987b, 1992). Thus, speaking in a second language may distance the immigrant woman from important parts of herself. Conversely, a second language may provide a vehicle to express the inexpressible in the first language (either because the first language does not have the vocabulary, or because the person censors herself from saying certain taboo things in the first language) (Espín 1984, 1987b, 1994). I contend that the language in which messages about sexuality are conveyed and encoded influences the language chosen to express sexual thoughts, feelings, and ideas and reveals important clues to one's identity process.

Two apparently contradictory patterns concerning language emerge for the lesbian immigrants I interviewed. It is apparent that some of them can express themselves better in their first language. However, although it is easier to use their first language's vocabulary in terms of vocabulary, they apparently feel that it is easier to talk about sexuality and related topics in English. Perhaps feelings of shame prevent them from addressing these topics in the same depth when using their first language.

Other immigrant lesbians I interviewed, on the other hand, seem unable to have conversations about sexuality in their first language because they actually do not know the vocabulary needed to talk about sexuality in their native language. These women usually migrated at an earlier age than the first group, frequently before or during early adolescence. They developed their knowledge of sex, and obviously, came out while immersed in English. Some of the women who manifest this second pattern explain that they cannot conceive of "making love in their first language" while those in the former scenario feel unable to "make love in English."

Is the immigrant lesbian's preference for English when discussing sexuality motivated by characteristics of English as a language, or is it that a second language offers a vehicle to express thoughts and feelings that cannot be expressed in the first language? Or does the new cultural context, in which English is spoken, allow more expression of the woman's feelings? Acquired in English, these experiences and expressions may become inextricably associated with the language (as happens with professional terminology acquired in a second language). In any case, many immigrant lesbians resort to English when describing their sexuality.

For a number of different reasons, it is apparent that the field of lesbian studies is enriched by understanding the lesbian experience in international perspective, particularly in reference to immigrant lesbians in North America. In addition, the transitions experienced during the migratory process may provide additional insights in the process of coming out for all lesbians. They are a metaphor for the crossing of borders and boundaries that all lesbians confront when refusing to continue living in "old ways." The immigrant's acculturation into a new society is "first and foremost a process of disassembling and reassembling social networks" (Rogler 1994). Similarly, the process of coming out involves a disassembling and reassembling of one's life and social networks. The immigrant's ruminations about "what could have been" are paralleled by lesbians' concerns about past events seen in a new light. In other words, an examination of continuities and discontinuities induced by the migration also sheds light on the continuities and discontinuities induced by the coming out process. Students of lesbian studies will benefit from seeing their experiences reflected and reproduced in different cultural contexts, and in the migratory process itself. Learning how other social groups negotiate lesbian identity and the coming out process cannot but expand an understanding of the alternatives available to all lesbians.

NOTES

1. The legal distinctions between immigrants and refugees are usually colored by the political persuasion of governments. That is not to say that there are no distinctions in the experiences of danger, trauma, or control over decision-making concerning the migration between these two populations. In my work, I consider refugees those individuals whose internal experience is that they have been either "pushed out" from their countries or lucky enough to escape a dangerous situation, regardless of what the actual political situation may have been from the perspective of observers. Immigrants are usually

perceived as having migrated willingly, although in some cases that is also open for interpretation. In this paper I usually use the terms "immigrant" or "migrant" to describe both immigrants and refugees because the lesbian experiences I am discussing tend to apply to women from both populations.

WORKS CITED

Cole, E., O. M. Espín, and E. Rothblum, eds. 1992. *Shattered societies, shattered lives: Refugee women and their mental health.* New York: Haworth Press.

Espín, O. M. 1984. Cultural and historical influences on sexuality in Hispanic/Latin women. In *Pleasure and danger: Exploring female sexuality,* edited by C. Vance. London: Routledge and Keagan Paul. (2nd. ed., London: Pandora, 1994).

———. 1987a. Issues of identity in the psychology of Latina lesbians. In *Lesbian psychologies: Explorations and challenges,* edited by Boston Lesbian Psychologies Collective. Urbana: University of Illinois Press.

———. 1987b. Psychological impact of migration on Latinas: Implications for psychotherapeutic practice. *Psychology of Women Quarterly* 11, no. 4:489–503.

———. 1990. Ethnic and cultural issues in the "coming out" process among Latina lesbians. Paper presented at the 98th Annual Convention of the American Psychological Association, August, Boston, MA.

———. 1992. Roots uprooted: The psychological impact of historical/political dislocation. In *Shattered societies and shattered lives.*

———. 1994. Crossing borders and boundaries: Life narratives of immigrant lesbians. Paper presented at the 102nd Annual Convention of the American Psychological Association, August, Los Angeles, CA (Presidential Address, Division 44 of the APA, Society for the Psychological Study of Lesbian and Gay Issues).

———. 1995. 'Race', racism, and sexuality in the life narratives of immigrant women. *Feminism and Psychology* 5, no. 2:287–302.

Gabaccia, D., ed. 1992. *Seeking common ground: Multidisciplinary studies of immigrant women in the United States.* Westport, CT: Praeger.

Obejas, A. 1994. *We came all the way from Cuba so you could dress like this?* Pittsburgh, PA: Cleis Press.

Rogler, L. H. 1994. International migrations: A framework for directing research. *American Psychologist* 49, no. 8:701–8.

Tremble, B., M. Schneider, and C. Appathurai. 1989. Growing up gay or lesbian in multicultural context. In *Gay and lesbian youth,* edited by G. Herdt. New York: Harrington Park Press.

Trumbach, R. 1977. London's sodomites. *Journal of Social History* 11. Cited in Necef, M.U., 1994. The language of intimacy. In *Middle East studies in Denmark,* edited by L.E. Andersen. (Odense, Denmark: Odense University Press, 1994).

U.S. Committee for Refugees. 1990. *World refugee survey: 1989 in review.* Washington, DC: American Council for Nationalities.

Yuval-Davis, N. 1992. Fundamentalism, multiculturalism and women in Britain. In *Race, culture and difference,* edited by J. Donald and A. Rattansi. London: Sage.

OLD LESBIANS: RESEARCH AND RESOURCES

Jean K. Quam

Who are old lesbians? For researchers who have tried to answer that question there are several dilemmas. In much of the earliest research, men and women were lumped together, because it was presumed that being gay or lesbian made them more similar than gender made them different. In addition, studies were mainly based on purposive samples of relatively small size carried out in New York or California on middle-class, white professionals. Lipman (1986) concluded that "Research on homosexuals in all its forms tends to lack methodological rigor" (53).

Many of the early studies also defined "old" in different ways. Because of the difficulty of finding samples, the subjects were "old" at age forty. From gerontological research, it is widely accepted that there are at least two groups of old adults—the young-old who are active and fairly well-off financially and physically; and the old-old who are frail and feel the full impact of reduced income and diminishing health. We know more about the younger group, but almost nothing is known about the older group. Many lesbians over age sixty grew up in an era in which sexual orientation was a private matter. They feared being seen as immoral or illegal and ostracized if their private lives were made public.

It is estimated that 3.5 million lesbians and gay men are over the age of sixty (Ryan and Bogard 1994). Women increasingly outnumber men as they age, and they are the fastest growing segment of the population over the age of eighty-five. In gerontological literature, only a handful of studies since the mid-1970s have focused on either old lesbians included in research on old gay men (Quam and Whitford 1992, Berger 1984, Minnegerode and Adelman 1978) or on old lesbians alone. The first study of old lesbians was Chris Almvig's (1977) which surveyed seventy-four white, professional lesbians aged fifty to seventy about their attitudes toward aging and lesbian identity. This was followed by Raphael and Robinson (1980), who interviewed twenty lesbians aged fifty to seventy-three and found high self-esteem and strong friendship ties. Kehoe (1989) studied fifty white lesbians aged sixty-five to eighty-five who were coping well with aging. Marcy Adelman (1986) also interviewed lesbians in this age group for her book *Longtime Passing: Lives of Older Lesbians*. Most recently, in the field of nursing, Deevey (1990) used Almvig's questionnaire with seventy-eight lesbians aged fifty to eighty-two to add evidence to positive feelings about aging among old lesbians. The most recent literature has explored the health-care needs of old lesbians (Gentry 1992, Hitchcock and Wilson 1992, Deevey 1990) and the risks of disclosure of one's sexual orientation to professional health-care providers (Hitchcock and Wilson 1992, Lucas 1992).

Some feminist writers now refer to "old" lesbians rather than "older" lesbians, suggesting a greater acceptance of the aging process. Baba Copper (1988) illustrates this point best:

> I am an old woman. I am sixty-six. Part of the reason I self-identify as old is a need to escape the prissy category of older woman. This label claims descriptive power over women from eighteen to eighty . . . calling myself an old woman is radical . . . like other words that feminists are reclaiming by proud usage, I would take to myself the word everyone seems to fear (48–49).

Many of the issues of aging that concern old lesbians also afflict old heterosexual women—loneliness, poor health, and insufficient income (Quam and Whitford 1992). However, Ryan and Bogard (1994) point out that old lesbians have lifelong income disadvantages such as lack of spousal or survivor benefits, lack of tax benefits or inheritance rights, and work histories in marginalized lower-income jobs. Reduced income in old age leads to an inability to afford good quality health care.

Perhaps more is being understood as old lesbians write and speak about themselves. Some are angry about being ignored by the women's movement, which tends to focus on younger women's issues, and about being overlooked by the gay and lesbian movement, which is also frequently ageist. Barbara Macdonald's writings have been the most widely quoted as she has magnificently described her feelings as an old lesbian (Macdonald and Rich 1983). She cites painful examples of being excluded at gatherings of lesbians of all ages, such as at a Take Back the Night march. She wonders aloud where all the old lesbians have gone as she confronts her aging body and her relationship with a younger lover.

Elsa Gidlow, a lesbian poet, is interviewed in a film and book, both titled *Word Is Out* (Adair and Adair 1978). She has also written about her life (Gidlow 1984) as has Monika Kehoe (1984), who also wrote one of the most widely recognized research reports on old lesbians, *Lesbians over Sixty Speak for Themselves* (1989). The lives of Del Martin and Phyllis Lyon, founders of Daughter of Bilitis (the first international lesbian organization), who have been a couple for over forty years, are presented in *Positively Gay* (Martin and Lyon 1979). To these must be added the writings of Audre Lorde, particularly *The Cancer Journals* (1980) and her collection of essays, *A Burst of Light* (1988). In both works, Lorde writes as a middle-aged and, later, an old lesbian who is living with cancer. Much of the poetry of Adrienne Rich illustrates the passion of an old lesbian writing about her life and her relationships.

One of the most intriguing old lesbian writers was May Sarton. In a 1979 interview, Sarton identified herself as bisexual, worrying that her work had not been fully accepted by the public because she was seen as a lesbian (Ingersoll 1991). Sarton saw her novel *Mrs. Stevens Hears the Mermaids Singing* (1965) as her coming-out novel because it was so autobiographical. In her later work, Sarton portrayed issues about the lives of old lesbians. In both *A Durable Fire* (1972) and *Journal of a Solitude* (1973), she writes about a love affair with a woman at age fifty-eight. *Recovering* (1980) focuses on her breast cancer and her changing relationships with women. In *The Education of Harriet Hatfield* (1990), her first novel to explicitly portray a lesbian as the leading character, Harriet painfully and successfully reconstructs her life after the death of a long-time partner.

A new text in which several old lesbians have written essays about their lives is *Lambda Gray: A Practical, Emotional and Spiritual Guide for Gays and Lesbians Who Are Growing Older* (Farrell 1993). Jeanne Adelman, at age seventy-three, remembers deciding at age sixty to live the rest of her life as a lesbian. Vashte Doublex, a sixty-seven-year-old artist, poet, writer, and editor of *We are VISIBLE,* a newsletter for "ageful" women, is interviewed, as are Sharon Raphael and Mina Robinson Meyer, cofounders of the National Association of Lesbian and Gay Gerontology (NALGG). In this book, Marcia Freedman, a fifty-six-year-old lesbian, writes of confronting her own aging, her mother's death, and her lesbian relationships.

Another recent text, *Gay Midlife and Maturity,* (which was originally a special issue of the *Journal of Homosexuality*), has a collection of articles that includes a few on old lesbians (Lee 1991). Marcy Adelman writes about interviews conducted with twenty-five old lesbians in the San Francisco area and makes some conclusions about developmental issues for both gay men and lesbians as they age. Other articles include Beth Dorrell's description of a support network for an eighty-four-year-old terminally ill lesbian; Richard Friend's theory of successful aging for older lesbians and gay men; and Margaret Cruikshank's survey of lesbian and gay aging studies. Cruikshank offers an excellent summary of gerontological research on old lesbians.

In Lillian Faderman's historical study, *Odd Girls and Twilight Lovers: A History of Lesbian Life in Twentieth-Century America* (1991), old women are generally absent until the 1980s. She pinpoints the 1987 West Coast Conference and Celebration by and for Old Lesbians as "the birth of the angry old woman" (289). She also credits Barbara Macdonald and Baba Copper with leading the way, telling young lesbians that they are not their mothers, grandmothers, or role models, and exhorting gerontologists not to make old lesbians the focus of their research.

Several recent films have included old lesbians. The Canadian *Company of Strangers* follows seven old women who become lost on a bus trip. The group includes Mary Meigs, a seventy-one-year-old lesbian writer. *Word Is Out,* an award-winning documentary, features Pat Bond in addition to Elsa Gidlow, while *Acting*

Our Age showcases Shevy Healy, an old lesbian from San Francisco. *Silent Pioneers* presents a black grandmother who has come out to her children and grandchildren and a closeted lesbian who wants to know more about the lesbian community after the death of her lover of fifty-eight years. *West Coast Crones* focuses on interviews with nine old lesbians from a variety of classes, races, and professions.

Recently there has been a trend for both old gay men and old lesbians to develop and participate in social service groups and organizations specifically designed to meet their unique needs. Perhaps the best known is Senior Action in a Gay Environment (SAGE), which was established in 1978 and now has affiliates in several states and in Canada. Another group, Gay and Lesbian Outreach (GLOE), is based in San Francisco and provides information and referral about social and health services, advocacy, counseling, legal advice, and social activities (Hubbard et al. 1992, Goldberg 1986). Organizations that are specifically focused on old lesbians include the Old Lesbian Organizing Committee (OLOC), several chapters of Slightly Older Lesbians (SOL), and West Coast Crones (NALGG 1993). Smaller groups come and go as energy and interest allow.

Two professional organizations that have been created specifically to collect and disseminate information available about lesbians as they age are National Association of Lesbian and Gay Gerontology (NALGG) founded in 1978 and the Lesbian and Gay Aging Interests Network (LGAIN) of the American Association on Aging (ASA), founded in 1993. NALGG developed an archive on materials now located in the San Francisco State University Gerontological Library and produces an outstanding bibliography on lesbian and gay aging that is regularly updated.

Currently, research is developing on the health-care needs of old lesbians and how they cope with their aging. Several new anthologies on aging have expanded our understanding, as has new research in the field of gay and lesbian studies. Controversy persists as to who should do research, and under what conditions old lesbians should be studied. But the fact remains that the number of old lesbians is increasing and more information from research, biographical work, fiction, and film can provide a more accurate picture.

WORKS CITED

Adair, N. and C. Adair. 1978. *Word is out.* San Francisco: New Glide Publications.

Adelman, M., ed. 1986. *Long time passing: Lives of older lesbians.* Boston: Alyson Publications.

Almvig, C. 1982. The invisible minority: Aging and lesbianism. Syracuse, NY: Utica College of Syracuse University.

Berger, R. M. 1984. Realities of gay and lesbian aging. *Social Work* 29, no. 1:57–62.

Copper, B. 1988. *Over the hill: Reflections on ageism between women.* Freedom, CA: The Crossing Press.

Deevey, S. 1990. Older lesbian women: An invisible minority. *Journal of Gerontological Nursing* 16, no. 5:35–39.

Faderman, L. 1991. *Odd girls and twilight lovers: A history of lesbian life in twentieth-century America.* New York: Penguin Books.

Farrell, L. F., ed. 1993. *Lambda gray: A practical, emotional, and spiritual guide for gays and lesbians who are growing older.* North Hollywood, CA: Newcastle Publishing.

Gentry, S. E. 1992. Caring for lesbians in a homophobic society. *Health Care for Women International* 13, no. 2:173–80.

Gidlow, E. 1984. Casting a net: Excerpts from an autobiography. In *New lesbian writing,* edited by Margaret Cruikshank. San Francisco: Grey Fox Press.

Goldberg, S. 1986. GLOE: A model social service program for older lesbians. In *Longtime passing.*

Hitchcock, J. M. and H. S. Wilson. 1992. Personal risking: Lesbian self-disclosure of sexual orientation to professional health care providers. *Nursing Research* 41, no. 3:178–83.

Hubbard, W. S., K. R. Allen, and J. A. Mancini. 1992 The GLOE Program: Social services and support for older gay men and lesbians. *Generations* 16, no. 3:37–42.

Ingersoll, E. G., ed. 1991. *Conversations with May Sarton.* (Jackson, MS: University Press of Jackson).

Kehoe, M. 1989. *Lesbians over sixty speak for themselves.* New York: The Haworth Press.

Kehoe, M. 1984. The making of a deviant. In *New lesbian writing.*

Lee, J. A. 1991. *Gay midlife and maturity.* New York: Harrington Park Press.

Lipman A. 1986. Homosexual relationships. *Generations* 10, no. 4 (summer):51–54.

Lorde, A. 1980. *The cancer journals.* Argyle, NY: Spinsters Ink.

———. 1988. *A burst of light: Essays by Audre Lorde.* Ithaca, NY: Firebrand Books.

Lucas, V. A. 1992. An investigation of the health care preferences of the lesbian population. *Health Care for Women International* 13, no. 2:221–28.

Macdonald, B. and C. Rich. 1984. *Look me in the eye: Old women, aging and ageism.* San Francisco: Spinsters Ink.

Martin, D. and P. Lyon. 1979. The older lesbian. In *Positively gay,* edited by B. Berzon and R. Leighton. Los Angeles: Mediamix Associates.

Minnigerode, F. A., and M. R. Adelman. 1978. Elderly homosexual women and men: Report on a pilot study. *The Family Coordinator* 27, no. 4:451–56.

National Association for Lesbian and Gay Gerontology. 1993 *Lesbian and gay aging resource guide.* San Francisco: NALGG.

Quam, J. K. and G. S. Whitford. 1992. Adaptation and age-related expectations of older gay and lesbian adults. *The Gerontologist* 32, no. 3:367–74.

Raphael, S. M. and M. K. Robinson. 1980. The older lesbian: Love relationships and friendship patterns. *Alternative Lifestyles* 3, no. 2:207–29.

Ryan, C. and R. Bogard. 1994. *What every lesbian and gay American needs to know about health care reform.* Washington D.C.: Human Rights Fund Campaign.

Sarton, M. 1965. *Mrs. Stevens hears the mermaids singing.* New York: W. W. Norton.

———. 1972. *A durable fire.* New York: W. W. Norton.

———. 1973. *Journal of a solitude.* New York: W. W. Norton.

———. 1980. *Recovering: A journal.* New York: W. W. Norton.

———. 1990. *The education of Harriet Hatfield.* New York: W. W. Norton.

DON'T ASK, DON'T TELL, DON'T KNOW: SEXUAL IDENTITY AND EXPRESSION AMONG EAST ASIAN-AMERICAN LESBIANS

Connie S. Chan

Although identity is a fluid concept in psychological and sociological theory, we tend to speak of identities in fixed terms. In particular, those aspects of identity associated with observable physical characteristics, such as race or gender, are perceived as unchanging ascribed identities. Examples include identifications such as Chinese woman, or Korean-American woman, or even broader terms such as woman of color that group together individuals who are not of the hegemonic "white" race in the United States. We base these constructions of identity upon physical appearance and an individual's declaration of identity. However, even these seemingly clear distinctions are not definitive. For example, I, a woman of Asian racial background, may declare myself a woman of color because I see myself as belonging to a group of ethnic/racial minorities. However, my biological sister could insist that she is not a woman of color because she does not feel an affiliation with our group goals, even though she is a person of Chinese ancestry. Does her non-affiliation take her out of the group of people of color? Or does she remain in regardless of her own self-identification because of her obvious physical characteristics? Generally, in the context of identities based upon racial and physical characteristics, ascribed identities will, rightly or wrongly, continue to be attributed to individuals by others. It is left up to the individual herself to assert her identity and demonstrate to others that she is or is *not* what she might appear to be upon first notice.

The issue of *sexual* identity is more ambiguous still, whether taken as a concept by itself or in context with cultural, racial, ethnic, or gendered identities. With sexual identity, even more than with other aspects of identity, it is generally those individuals who would be considered "sexual minorities," such as lesbians, gay men, and bisexuals, who define and declare their sexual identities. Unless there is a specific focus upon sexual orientation, few in the "majority" would identify themselves as heterosexual. Given the assumption that heterosexuality is the norm, it is a political statement to acknowledge a sexual identity. Even if it is one identity among several, and one is not prioritizing it over racial, ethnic, gendered, or professional identities, individuals who declare a sexual identity may become identified primarily in those terms. Perhaps it is because of this "primacy effect" of transgressive sexual identity that lesbians of color may be reluctant to take on a label of a sexual identity. When they do, it can overshadow their racial/ethnic identity, which affords a sense of social belonging and group cohesion.

In research on Latina lesbians, East Asian-American lesbians, and gay men, Oliva Espín (1987) and Connie Chan (1989) found that most respondents preferred to be validated for both their ethnic and sexual identities. Instead, their experience was that they were perceived as being primarily lesbian/gay once their sexual identities were known, negating their ethnic/racial identities as Latina or Asian-American, or even their gendered identities as women.

Cultural background may also significantly determine how individuals include sexuality in their sense of identity. Non-Western cultures such as in East Asia may not have a concept of sexual identity similar to that we know. Our models of sexual identity development and the paradigms of identity for the individual self may not be applicable for individuals who have non-Western cultural backgrounds. While it is impossible to generalize about the characteristics of "people of color" as an inclusive group, or to group non-Western cultures together, some of the issues of sexual identity addressed here in relation to East Asian Americans are applicable to other ethnic minority groups.

Since sexuality is contextual, what it means to have a sexual identity is related to the meaning given to sexuality for females in a given culture. Thus the range of sexual behaviors which are considered acceptable, the forms of expression, the concept of sexual identity, who may express which forms of sexuality, as well as what are perceived to be deviations from these norms, are all cultural factors which must be considered in understanding the formation of sexual identity.

As a social movement, defining and declaring one's homosexual identity has been likened to "discovering a map to explore a new country" (D'Emilio 1983). Choosing an "out-of-the-norm" sexual identity, such as that of a lesbian or a gay man, individuals declare a separateness and individuality in sexuality that also identifies them as a members of a self-defined sexual minority group. These declarations of identity are both individual and internal in a psychological sense, and also external and group-based in a political and social sense, and have been crucial in the making of the gay/lesbian movement as well as the Civil Rights movement.

Much as people of color defined themselves in terms of their race in the 1960s and 1970s, homosexual men and lesbian women, by identifying and declaring a sexual minority status, chose to define themselves in this category as a means of empowerment and group cohesion. To achieve this empowerment, both sexual minorities and racial minorities chose to accentuate aspects of themselves which heretofore were viewed as negative and stigmatized (race or sexuality), and to express pride, not shame, at minority status.

It has been widely accepted in psychology that individuals who accept a previously stigmatized identity generally pass through several stages of development en route to embracing their new identities. Vivienne Cass's model of homosexual and lesbian identity formation (1979) has been frequently cited as describing the process through which an individual develops an integrated identity. Cass posits that an individual begins with a self-awareness that some of his/her feelings and behaviors can be defined as homosexual/lesbian, creating conflict about a sexual (and perhaps social) identity that had previously been defined as heterosexual. From this basic premise of self-awareness, an individual goes through six stages through which s/he accepts, has pride in, and, finally, integrates a lesbian/gay identity with other aspects of self.

This model, while generally perceived as being universally applicable, does not exist within a vacuum, and it presupposes that favorable social conditions which make possible the affiliation and identification described are present. In stages four and five, individuals seeking identity acceptance have increased contact with other homosexuals and immerse themselves in homosexual culture and community. A lesbian/gay presence in urban areas in some countries allows this to occur far more readily than in places where no homosexual culture exists.

Moreover, sexual identification is not merely a naming of how one perceives one's own sexuality or sexual expression, but it is also a political identification. There are individuals who do not consider themselves lesbian or gay who engage in sexual activity with same-sex partners; there are also individuals who consider themselves lesbian or gay who do not have sexual contact with same-sex partners. What was once known as a homosexual identity has developed into a lesbian/ gay identity, which, in addition to being a strategy for group formation and cohesion, is seen as a way to address discrimination and a form of resistance against conformity and restriction. Trends in queer theory and culture take this resistance one step further with the refusal to fit into fixed categories of heterosexual, homosexual, or bisexual.

The significance of the naming is crucial, however, to the construction of a sexual identity. If, as Foucault states, without the name, there is only the "half-life of an amorphous sense of self," is this the situation, now, at the end of the twentieth century, where East Asian-American lesbians and gay men find themselves? In their East Asian cultures of origin, East Asian Americans do not have the category of lesbian, gay man, or bisexual as identities by which to define themselves. There is not only a lack of labels but also a fundamental difference in the construction of sexuality, sexual expression, and sexual identity, as well as of identity itself, from those we know in the West.

A crucial distinction between traditional East Asian culture and Western culture is the idea that sexuality and sexual expression is a private matter. Any direct and open discussion of sexuality is unusual in East Asian cultures, as sexuality is considered to be a very sensitive subject. Even among one's closest friends, a discussion of sexuality is considered to be awkward and highly embarrassing at best, and at worst, strictly taboo (Tsui 1985). This extreme discomfort with open and direct discussion of sexuality is sometimes misread and misconstrued by Westerners as *asexuality* or as an extreme repression of sexual interest on the part of East Asian Americans. Both perceptions, though common, are incorrect. However, what is presented publicly is very different from what is tolerated and expressed in private with sexual intimates.

The distinction between a private and public self is an important concept in East Asian cultures. The public self is that which conforms to gendered and familial role expectations and seeks to avoid actions which would bring shame not only upon oneself but also upon one's family. Within the Asian part of an East Asian American's culture, there is little support for an *individual* public identity of any kind beyond the familial. As a psychological concept of self-definition, an individual's identity, forged against a backdrop of social forces, may be perceived as being universal, but is in fact a Western concept. In East Asian cultures such as Chinese, Japanese, and Thai, the concept of individual identity, whether by self-definition or ascribed, may not exist. Instead there is only a group identification and an identity as a family member.

Much as there is no identity outside of the family's, there is no concept of a sexual identity or of external sexual expression beyond the familial expectation of procreation. Sexuality would be rarely expressed in the context of one's public self, only within the private self. Especially for women, the private self is never seen by anyone other than an individual's most intimate family and friends. (In some cases, she may choose never to reveal a private self to anyone.) The dichotomous nature of the public and private self is far more distinct than in Western culture, where there is more fluidity between the two. The relevance of this public/private split within East Asian culture is that there is not only very little public expression of sexuality, but the private expressions of sexuality may take on different forms for East Asian Americans. Erotic behavior, for example, may be expressed only privately and in indirect ways that may be misperceived as nonerotic in nature by Westerners unaccustomed to subtle nuances such as a change in the register used by two women having a conversation: the brush of a hand against another person, language patterns reflecting affection and non-discernable to the casual observer; and quick glances, perhaps holding the gaze just a second longer than might be expected. With private sexual expression, what one sees is not necessarily what is being conveyed, unless one is familiar with the cultural nuances.

Popular and erotic images of East Asians contribute to the myth of asexuality or passivity in sexual expression, particularly for East Asian females. For East Asian-American women, the historical visual sexual images in film have been of two basic types: "(1) the Lotus Blossom Baby (i.e. china doll, geisha girl, shy Polynesian beauty) and (2) the Dragon Lady (prostitute, devious madam). . . . Asian women in film are, for the most part, passive figures who exist to serve men" (Tajima in Fung 1991). Since Asian women are supposedly passive and compliant, both sexually and in relation to men, they have been "fetishized in dominant representation" (Tajima in Fung 1991), in stereotypes that certainly limit the range of sexuality depicted. Moreover, in the absence of a body of lesbian pornography, whether in film or magazines, images of East Asian lesbians are rarer still in widely-distributed markets. Even Chinese-American novelists such as Maxine Hong Kingston, Amy Tan, and Gish Jen, while exploring bicultural issues, do not give strong representation of Asian-American women as sexual beings of *any* orientation.

Two notable exceptions are the short documentary *Women of Gold,* which profiles Asian-American lesbian athletes at the 1990 Gay Games, and poetry, essays and stories written by Asian-American lesbian writers Kitty Tsui, Willyce Kim, and Merle Woo. In a poem, Kitty Tsui describes her attempts to integrate both aspects of her total identity—her lesbian self with her Chinese-American self—while at a dinner banquet with her extended family. There is slightly more inclusion of Asian-American lesbians and gay men in lesbian/gay literature, but without accessible representations of Asian lesbian women that are erotic and politically viable, media images provide little support for a lesbian or bisexual identity among Asian Americans that is not similar to Western cultural identity.

Thus it appears that the paradigms of sexual identity formation and sexuality to which we in the West are accustomed must be adapted if we are to understand the "Asian" cultural influence upon sexual expression in East Asian-American lesbians. Only if sexuality can be expressed without disrupting the integrity of an individual's prescribed role within the family can it be tolerated. With only a sketchy identity as a person distinct from the identity as a member of a family, having a sexual identity or identifying an "alternative lifestyle" may be literally inconceivable except to those who are much more Western-acculturated. A common perception results: that proportionately fewer "out" lesbian, gay, and bisexual people are Asian Americans. If that perception is numerically accurate, it can be explained by cultural prohibitions against public expression of sexual orientation.

Asian Americans who identify openly as lesbian are likely to be more acculturated and to have been more influenced by U.S. or Western culture. A study of lesbian/gay East Asian Americans supports this theory, indicating that East Asian-American lesbians and gay men, while preferring to be recognized for both (sexual and ethnic) aspects of their identity, if forced to choose between affiliations, identified more closely as lesbian/gay, as well as American (Chan 1989). This study's sample of self-identified East Asian-American lesbians and gay men was already skewed towards a more assimilated and Westernized population, since it included those who considered themselves to be lesbian or gay. Even so, some of the results indicate that East Asian-American lesbians and gay men respond to pressures from both their East Asian and American communities. Respondents were more likely to come out to non-Asians than to other Asians (reflecting the pressure to maintain privacy within the Asian culture), and many had not disclosed their sexual identity to their parents, even though they had been out an average of 6.2 years. Responding to American expectations, some did report wanting to belong and feel part of a gay and lesbian community, and even sought dates with white lesbians/gay men to feel more comfortable with the hegemonic "lesbian/gay scene."

In conclusion, sexual identity is not an essential, fixed given for any individual, nor is it developed within a vacuum. Lesbian and gay identities have evolved over a two-hundred-year span in the West, heavily influenced by social and political conditions such as the initial sexual categorization by sexologists, the formation of male homosexual identity, the construction of the "New Woman" stereotype in the early twentieth century, and the politicization of lesbian, gay, bisexual, and queer identities during the past two decades.

But these modern homosexual identities are still Western constructs. There are no comparable sexual identities in East Asian culture. Even if a Chinese woman in Beijing were to have a lesbian identity (and well she might), she would have to define herself through Western cultural concepts. For an East Asian American who is defining a sexual identity, she also must adapt Western models of sexuality and sexual expression to meet her own needs. At the same time, such lesbians would have to respond to East Asian cultural influences, which entail different family responsibilities, degrees of privacy, and forms of sexual expression which are considered to be acceptable for females. Balancing the Western pressure to come out and be openly lesbian against the East Asian cultural demand for privacy requires juggling contradicting forces. While some women may never openly admit or act on their homosexuality, others will embrace the Western model enthusiastically; still others will be openly lesbian only in safe (generally non-Asian) environments.

However, East Asian cultural restrictions on the open expression of sexuality may actually create less of a dichotomy between heterosexual and homosexual behavior. Instead, given the importance of a private expression of sexuality, one could theorize the existence of fluidity within a sexual behavioral continuum. The cultural prohibition against defining or declaring sexual orientation/identity may ironically result in a broader range of acceptable behaviors, even as public identities are more rigidly defined.

Lesbian studies and women's studies have tended to focus on the evolution of people whose primary political and "ethnic" identification is as lesbian or gay, and who have been able to organize a multidimensional way of life on the basis of their sexuality. But we need to focus upon other forms of sexuality—other ways in which lesbian and homosexual relations have been organized, understood, named, and left deliberately unnamed (Chauncey 1989). We need to be careful not to view the evolution of a homosexual or lesbian identity only through a Western lens, expecting perhaps that non-Western cultures, with modernization, will eventually achieve greater openness about such behavior. Cultural differences in the construction of identity and in the expression of sexuality have to be taken into account. We are just beginning to know which questions to ask.

WORKS CITED

Cass, V. C. 1979. Homosexual identity formation: A theoretical model. *Journal of Homosexuality* 4:219–35.

Chan, C. S. 1989. Issues of identity development among Asian-American lesbians and gay men. *Journal of Counseling and Development* 68:16–20.

Chauncey, G. 1989. Christian brotherhood or sexual perversion? Homosexual identities and the construction of sexual boundaries in the World War I era. In *Hidden from history: Reclaiming the gay and lesbian past.* Edited by M. Duberman, M. Vicinus, and G. Chauncey. New York: Meridian.

Cochran, S., V. Mays, and L. Leung. 1991. Sexual practices of heterosexual Asian-American young adults: Implications for risk of HIV infection. *Archives of Sexual Behaviors* 20:381–91.

D'Emilio, J. 1983. *Sexual politics, sexual communities: The making of a homosexual minority in the United States, 1940–76.* Chicago and London: University of Chicago Press.

Espín, O. 1987. Issues of identity in the psychology of Latina lesbians. In *Lesbian Psychologies.* Edited by Boston Lesbians Psychologies Collective. Urbana: University of Illinois Press.

Fung, R. 1991. Looking for my penis: The eroticized Asian in gay video porn. In *How do I look? Queer film and video,* edited by Bad Object Choices. Seattle: Bay Press.

Tsui, A. 1985. Psychotherapeutic considerations in sexual counseling for Asian immigrants. *Psychotherapy* 22:357–62.

Tsui, K. 1983. *The words of a woman who breathes fire.* San Francisco: Spinsters Ink.

PART THREE

*Standing
and Delivering:
In the
Classroom*

LESBIAN STUDIES SYLLABI, 1982–1994

Dorothy Painter and Willa Young

Asked to write an essay on the state of lesbian studies as reflected in academic syllabi, the most obvious starting point is the first source we knew of for models for such work: *Lesbian Studies* edited by Margaret Cruikshank. There, the words of Madeline Davis provide a context for where we have been and how far we have come:

> Since the early 1970s, numerous courses on lesbianism, lesbian literature, lesbian history, and other topics relating to lesbian life have been taught in colleges and universities across the country, sometimes under the auspices of women's studies programs. More often, a daring soul from English or psychology has braved the shock and outrage of administrators and has fought to offer a course in a more traditional department. Although these courses have differed significantly, the women who have conceived, researched, and taught them have shared similar experiences. We have had few models either for syllabus development or for teaching methods, and we have faced the special problems related to teaching and learning about our own lives in the context of an academic environment (93).

The other commonly shared experience of teachers of lesbian studies was that one was almost always working alone, at least within one's own university. Organizations such as the National Women's Studies Association (NWSA) and the Modern Language Association (MLA) had caucuses through which members might meet and share suggestions and offer support to one another; however, on a day to day basis, there was often only one person doing lesbian studies on campus. The nine syllabi which are reproduced in the Appendix of *Lesbian Studies* represent not only where we as teachers of lesbian studies have been; they also created the pedagogical framework upon which many of us have built.

Although the full text of those syllabi may be found in *Lesbian Studies,* the naming of these early teachers of lesbian studies who shared their syllabi and who often taught in academic isolation seems appropriate: Barbara Smith, Cherríe Moraga, Joy Fisher, Julia Penelope, Joan Nestle, Evelyn Beck, Madeline Davis, Melanie Kaye, and Ann Schroeder and Niki Rockwell (217–35).

Our current project of surveying lesbian studies courses began in 1989 for a presentation at the annual conference of the National Women's Studies Association. We wrote to every women's studies program listed with NWSA and asked them either to send us copies of syllabi for all lesbian (or lesbian and gay) studies courses which had ever been taught at their institution or else to forward our letter to the appropriate individual, if the course(s) had been taught or were being taught in a different academic unit. We received syllabi or detailed information about twenty-one different courses. For the second stage of our survey, we acquired all of the syllabi sent to the Lesbian Caucus of NWSA in 1994 at the request of the past caucus coordinator, Annette Van Dyke. Only one of the twenty-three syllabi received from the 1994 request was for a course taught before 1989. Hence, we collected two groups of syllabi: those dated 1983 to 1989 and those dated 1989 to 1994.

The following types of information for both sets of syllabi may be found in the following tables:

Table I .... Characteristics
Table II .... Subject Areas
Table III .... Level
Table IV .... Evaluation
Table V .... Topics

In addition, the authors and texts appearing most often will be listed for both sets of syllabi. After presenting the information for the two sets of syllabi, we will discuss trends in lesbian studies as reflected by the syllabi and suggest future directions.

Until the 1990s, all courses were either lesbian only or lesbian and gay. The one syllabus we received in the later group which is clearly a queer theory course is included; however, its content and theoretical grounding are significantly different from the lesbian studies course, except for one week which is devoted to the theoretical perspective of lesbian feminism.

Although many lesbian studies courses from both of our samples include relevant information on the history of gay men as it relates to lesbians and the lesbian movement, courses were only viewed as lesbian and gay if the content of the course (and usually the title) reflected the combining of these two communities as a significant assumption, focus, or emphasis of the course. Hence, a course entitled "Gay and Lesbian History" which combines the history of gay men and lesbian women across time periods is lesbian and gay; however, a course on "Lesbian Lives" which includes a unit on a historical period combining lesbian and gay history to show the formation of the first separate lesbian organizations is a lesbian-only course.

Table I
CHARACTERISTICS

	1983–1989	1989–1994
Lesbian only	16	19
Lesbian and gay	5	2
Lesbian, gay and bisexual	0	1
Queer	0	1
Both contemporary and historical	15	15
Contemporary only	5	
		3
Historical only	1	4

The syllabi from 1972 to 1981 centered primarily around lesbian literature and culture. The courses which followed in the 1980s began to broaden the perspective.

Table II
SUBJECT AREAS

	1983–1989	1989–1994
Interdisciplinary	11	13
Literature	5	1
Socal science	2	2
History	1	4
Literature and theory	1	0
Film	1	1
Psychology	0	1
Intersession	4	2
(or short summer session)		

Although a large number of syllabi in both groups are clustered around the sophomore and junior class level, a couple of major shifts can be seen from the early to the latter group. First, the level of the course is much easier to discern, often because it is stated, from the 1989–1994 syllabi than from the earlier group. Second, none of the syllabi in the 1983–1989 group contain any mention of prerequisites. Regardless of the difficulty of the readings, the courses appear to be open to any student with an interest in the topic. Conversely, the 1989–1994 syllabi all contain prerequisites except for one course which is clearly introductory in nature. Although the prerequisite is often only an introductory course in English or women's studies, some level of knowledge is required.

Table III
COURSE LEVEL

	1983–1989	1989–1994
Introductory	3	1
Sophomore or junior level	9	16
Advanced undergrad and graduate	0	3
Graduate level only	0	1
Label not given	9	2
No prerequisites	21	1

Methods of evaluation have expanded over the years to include the use of more varied activities for student assessment. All courses used more than one type of evaluation with the most popular being attendance and participation and written papers. Attendance and participation are important components of many classes; however, the lesbian studies course syllabi both emphasized their importance and also often included other in-class activities such as leading class discussions, contributing class discussion questions, giving presentations, or participating in class debates. Although these activities may look different on the surface, they underscore the assumed importance of active student input into the educational process. Another form of active student participation is the response paper. Response papers did not appear on any of the pre-1989 syllabi but are a significant form of activity in over a third of the post-1989 lesbian studies courses. Requiring students to keep a journal remained a frequently used evaluation tool across both samples.

Table IV
METHODS OF EVALUATION

	1983–1989	1989–1994
Attendance and participation	14	14
Research or analytical papers	14	11
Response papers	0	8
Exams	10	7
Journals	9	5
Class presentation	5	6
Research project	4	6
Group presentation	2	4
Book report	4	3
Group project	1	3
Grade contract	4	0
Lead class discussion	1	3
Written questions over readings	1	2
Non-written project	1	1
Discussion out of class (required)	0	2
Clippings notebook	0	2

Table IV, *continued*

	1983–1989	1989–1994
Attend Lesbian events	0	1
Attend and view films	0	1
Autobiographical paper	0	1
Annotated bibliography	0	1
Self-evaluation	0	1
Meet with instructor	0	1
Project chosen by class	0	1
Structured debate	0	1
Content analysis (gay and lesbian press)	0	1
Literature review	0	1

During the time periods covered in both sets of syllabi, a grounding in history was deemed important; thus, the most frequently occurring topic was the study of historical lesbian communities. Many other topics appear commonly on both the earlier and later syllabi, but there was a shift worthy of note. For instance, although racism, class bias, and anti-Semitism appeared often as topics on the earlier syllabi, they were eclipsed in the later syllabi by a new topic: difference. Racism was sometimes included in the topic name, such as "racism and difference"; but overall, the focus shifted from prejudice and oppression to recognitions of variations among groups. Sexuality, identity, and theory became more frequent topics in the later syllabi, while social movements, homophobia, and literature received less attention. Interestingly, in the more recent syllabi, motherhood and families were combined as a topic whereas in the earlier syllabi they had been separated. While lesbian culture was a popular topic in both sets of syllabi, a topic that emerged in the 1989–1994 syllabi was lesbian communities. Legal issues was also a new topic that surfaced in the later syllabi. Among the topics listed on numerous earlier syllabi that did not appear at all in the later group were health and gay men. Topics that occurred across the time period with roughly the same frequency included coming out, lesbianism and feminism, and politics.

Tabel V
TOPICS

	1983–1989	1989–1994
Human communities	17	20
Racism/difference	15	11
Sexuality	9	15
Social movements	14	14
Identity	9	15
Homophobia/heterosexism	13	6
Literature	12	7
Theory	5	12
Coming out	10	7

Tabel V, *continued*	1983–1989	1989–1994
Motherhood/families	9/6	11
Relationships	9	10
Culture	9	10
Lesbian communities	0	8
Lesbianism and feminism	7	6
Classism (as separate topic)	7	0
Politics	6	5
Anti-Semitism (as separate topic)	7	0
Legal Issues	0	5
Gay men	5	0
Health	5	0

Across all the syllabi, from 1983 to 1994, students in lesbian studies courses were most likely to be exposed to lesbian scholarship and writing via a required reading packet of articles selected and assembled by the instructor, which was then purchased by students at a copy service. Eleven of the older syllabi and sixteen of the newer ones used reading packets. The text most often required in the 1983–1989 syllabi was *The Well of Loneliness* (six times), but *Zami: A New Spelling of My Name* and *Rubyfruit Jungle* were also both used four times. Otherwise, there were no patterns of text selection found in the early syllabi. The most used text (seven times) in the 1989–1994 collection of syllabi was *Hidden From History. Zami: A New Spelling of My Name, Rubyfruit Jungle, A Restricted Country, The Well of Loneliness,* and *Odd Girls and Twilight Lovers* were each used four times in the later syllabi. As in the earlier syllabi, there were no other visible trends in text selection.

Since most of the required readings were not books, we reviewed the use of other assigned readings and found that there were indeed trends in authors whose works were included regularly. For instance, although few syllabi used books by Audre Lorde, and none used a book by Adrienne Rich, their works were utilized in nearly all courses. The most popular authors in the early set of syllabi were Audre Lorde, Virginia Woolf, Adrienne Rich, Margaret Cruikshank, Cherríe Moraga, Ellie Bulkin, Marilyn Frye, and Evelyn Beck. Although some of those authors' works sustained their popularity into the more recent syllabi, there were significant changes. The later syllabi most often cited articles or book excerpts by Audre Lorde, Barbara Smith, Adrienne Rich, Joan Nestle, Jewelle Gomez, Marilyn Frye, Lillian Faderman, Gloria Anzaldúa, Judy Grahn and the Radicalesbians. Clearly, some content areas and the works of several authors are becoming institutionalized components in lesbian studies courses, but this standardization is not apparent in the lists of required texts in syllabi. Patterns of regular use, however, are evident via examination of the listings of other assigned readings. Overall, we conclude that the best syllabi exhibit the interweaving of writings on differences and a variety of lesbian studies topics. They ground students in a historical context and provide interdisciplinary, culturally-sensitive exposure to theoretical frameworks and contemporary lesbian issues, and they end the term by asking students to continue deliberation on the future of lesbian cultures, lesbian communities, and lesbian studies.

Just as many syllabi indicate that some lesbian studies courses end with discussions envisioning the future, we too close our discussion in that manner. We hope the growth of lesbian studies continues in both disciplinary and interdisciplinary courses. Given that there currently is unprecedented intellectual interest in lesbian topics and research, we anticipate additional compelling scholarly publications becoming available for the continued growth of lesbian studies courses. These new works will not displace, but will stand beside, the readings that are fast becoming the classics of lesbian studies. Finally, we expect that scholarship based on study grounded in lesbian realities will enrich the possibilities for continued commitment to furthering feminist scholarship and intellectual growth within a distinctly lesbian context.

WORK CITED

Cruikshank, Margaret, ed. 1982. *Lesbian Studies: Present and Future*. New York: The Feminist Press.

INTEGRATING LESBIAN STUDIES INTO THE FEMINIST PSYCHOLOGY CLASSROOM

Suzanna Rose

I continue to be amazed at how difficult it is to integrate a lesbian studies perspective fully into my feminist psychology courses, even after teaching them for twenty years. And even as an out lesbian with a research specialization in lesbian sexuality and relationships, I find it a daunting task. This is not to suggest that I have avoided trying, because I am pleased with most of my efforts. However, an event occurs at least once a semester to remind me that I have not come far enough in exorcising my own "isms" to think that I understand what a "true" lesbian-centered approach would be.

Most recently, this realization was brought home to me by having a young, outspoken African-American lesbian feminist student, Tonya, sit directly in front of me each day as I taught Psychology of Women. Tonya and I had been in an antiracism group together for the past year and I had encouraged her to take my course when she entered the university, thinking she would find a home for her feminism in women's studies. I did not anticipate the stress I was to feel later as I viewed my lectures through her eager—and sometimes cynical—eyes. What does a psychology of women course have to say of relevance to an out twenty-four-year-old, working-class, African-American lesbian? Her interests definitely were not represented in the standard text. It would be up to me, a forty-four-year-old, privileged, white woman professor, to provide that relevance. It was a responsibility that I only partially fulfilled. However, facing her unspoken expectation on a daily basis made me aware of a level of inclusiveness I had yet to attain in covering lesbian, race, and class issues in my teaching. I began to think more consciously about what litmus tests I use to evaluate my teaching from a lesbian studies' standpoint. In this essay, I will apply two criteria, *inclusiveness* and *tolerance*, to evaluate how effectively I integrate lesbian studies into my courses. Then I will discuss some issues concerning how personal development affects one's ability to meet these criteria.

Inclusiveness refers to the extent to which lesbians are included in the curriculum. A minimal inclusiveness criterion would require that at least one lecture deal with lesbianism; a more stringent one would demand that material on lesbians be integrated throughout the course. I conscientiously apply both criteria to all the feminist psychology courses I teach, including undergraduate ones on the psychology of women, female sexuality, and homosexuality, as well as graduate courses on human sexuality and women and mental health. I allow at least one week of class time in every course for exclusive attention to lesbian issues, as well as regularly bring up the applicability of other topics to lesbians.

Deciding *what* content to include requires more strenuous intellectual effort. The courses I teach fall within the areas of psychology of women or lesbian and gay psychology. Each poses a different problem in terms of enhancing lesbian visibility. The subdiscipline of psychology of women is defined by an implicit heterosexism that marginalizes lesbians. The major textbooks convey an unquestioning acceptance of women's emotional, intellectual, and sexual commit-ment to men. Thus, topics such as theories of personality, achievement, work, nonverbal behavior, biology, health, sexuality, therapy, and violence are framed in terms of heterosexual relations. Solutions to social or economic problems implicitly assume women's continued heterosexuality. Men are to be reformed, but not avoided. Lesbianism most often is represented as an "alternative lifestyle" or "sexual variation" rather than as a challenge to heterosexuality. Typically, origins of sexual orientation and the mental health consequences of being lesbian are explored, usually to illustrate that lesbians are not really deviant. The wide diversity among lesbians in terms of race, social class, age, and ability is rarely mentioned.

Lesbians receive more attention within lesbian and gay psychology than within psychology of women, but generally less than gay men. Due to a gender bias in the research base that defines what questions are asked and who is studied, topics such as origins of sexual orientation, lesbians and gays in the military, discrimination in employment, homophobia, and HIV/AIDS more often are slanted toward gay men. Furthermore, a feminist perspective is often lacking in much lesbian/gay/queer writing. Lesbians' and gay men's common oppression frequently is explored without mention of patriarchy or institutionalized sexism; the different gender status of lesbians and gay men is virtually ignored. Consequently, lesbians' experiences as women are made invisible. For example, research and activism on homophobic violence focus on criminal assaults aimed at gay men (Jenness and Broad 1994), while other violence experienced by lesbians—including rape (unless it is specifically perpetrated against a woman because she is a lesbian), loss of child custody due to being a lesbian, or racist violence against lesbians of color—is not included in this definition.

Meeting the inclusiveness criterion requires that lesbian-feminist issues be addressed systematically in both types of courses. Two significant elements are now available: First, the burgeoning body of knowledge on lesbians in the form of specialized journals such as *Psychology of Women Quarterly, Women and Therapy, Feminism and Psychology,* and *Journal of Homosexuality.* Articles on heterosexist bias in psychological research, diagnosis, and therapy, and in research on lesbians and gays in the military also have appeared recently in mainstream journals such as *American Psychologist* (e.g., Herek 1993, Morin and Rothblum 1991). Book publishing on lesbian issues in psychology is flourishing as well (e.g., Garnets and Kimmel 1993, Greene and Herek 1994, Rothblum and Brehony 1994). Contemporary topics include lesbians of color, relationships and sexuality, pregnancy, child custody and adoption, and health and aging, as well as mental health. A second positive influence on lesbian visibility is the progressive stance concerning sexual orientation taken by the profession of psychology. Recommended changes in language have been the most significant. For example, the use of the phrase "lesbians and gay men" has been recommended as the appropriate replacement for the terms "homosexual" or "gay" in the latest edition of the widely used *Publication Manual* of the American Psychological Association (1994, 51). The rationale given for the guideline is that "homosexual" or "gay" might be interpreted as including only men. Since 1975, the APA has also been an advocate in the wider society against the stigma of mental illness associated with homosexuality and for lesbian and gay civil rights (Garnets et al. 1991, 971). The APA has submitted *amicus curiae* briefs supporting lesbian and gay rights in five landmark cases before the courts (Bersoff and Ogden 1991). The APA also requires that doctoral programs seeking accreditation have a nondiscrimination policy that includes sexual orientation. The APA's actions have legitimized lesbianism as a valid area of inquiry within psychology and eased the way for bringing up lesbian issues in the classroom.

Clearly, it should now be possible to meet the inclusiveness criterion in coursework. The material and perspectives described above are available to make integration of lesbian issues throughout courses possible. Furthermore, it is relatively easy to evaluate the inclusiveness criterion by determining how much course content pertains to lesbians. However, one possible consequence of thorough integration is that students will be threatened by hearing "so much" about lesbians. Lesbian faculty report that a too rapid or too extensive (to heterosexual students) focus on lesbians may result in a loss of credibility for teachers whose opinions might be seen as "biased."

Tolerance is the second criterion I use to evaluate whether courses include a lesbian studies' perspective. An increase in the amount of tolerance students express toward lesbianism over a semester as assessed by anonymous feedback from students concerning their likes and dislikes at several points during the semester frequently is used to determine whether the tolerance criterion has been met. Increasing students' tolerance demands that teachers attend to the process of learning. Three techniques I use to promote tolerance are familiarization, developing empathy, and shifting paradigms.

Familiarization increases tolerance by reducing the shock effect associated with the mention of lesbians. The topic of lesbianism is made so commonplace that it loses its novelty. One easy strategy to increase familiarity is to use specific language. I am careful to specify that a lecture will cover heterosexual dating or heterosexual and lesbian domestic violence instead of labeling those lectures "Dating" or "Domestic Violence." Another familiarization technique is to ask students regularly to apply concepts to populations with different sexual orientations (or races). For example, most women's studies and psychology courses begin with a discussion of stereotypes. Cultural stereotypes of women include traits like nurturance, gentleness, or not being dominant or aggressive. Having students generate stereotypic traits for white lesbians or African-American heterosexual women quickly serves to illustrate that cultural stereotypes of women are based on notions about heterosexual white women. Thus, the technique reveals the unstated biases concerning sexual orientation and race. A similar point can be made in a lesbian and gay studies course by generating traits of "homosexuals" and then asking students how applicable each trait is to the stereotype of a "lesbian," thereby illuminating the former's implicit male bias.

Familiarization exercises with a more explicit focus on sexuality are useful in countering the deep anxiety associated with it in our culture. This anxiety extends to textbook authors, faculty, and students alike. For instance, I recently was shocked to realize, mid-semester, that the syllabus for Psychology of Homosexuality (which I was teaching for the first time) did not include anything about lesbians' or gay men's sexual practices, nor did any of the four texts I had assigned! I immediately revised the syllabus to include two lectures on the topic. Then it occurred to me that a discussion of tribadism and oral sex with sixty students was going to require more introduction. I decided to modify and use a vocabulary brainstorming technique that had been very effective previously in human sexuality classes. In small groups, students generated as many synonyms (scientific, slang, or personal) as they were able for terms such as "intercourse," "masturbation," "oral sex," and "anal sex." Then different groups were asked to read their lists. The exercise resulted in a lot of nervous laughter but increased students' comfort when asking questions.

Developing empathy, my second technique for enhancing tolerance, is actualized by exposing students to guest speakers and through written assignments. Any teacher who has ever invited a lesbian panel, particularly a racially diverse one, to class is well aware of its potential for positive impact. Written assignments can be used to reinforce empathic responses elicited by speakers. One assignment with which I have had a great deal of success requires students to write a short paper based on an interview with someone who differs from themselves on two of the following dimensions: sexual orientation, gender, race, age (minimum fifteen-year difference), or social class. Students individually or in small groups generate a list of interview questions that I review, and later report on their experiences to the group. Another assignment that works well is to ask students to write a three-to-five-page essay about what it would be like (or was like) to come out to one's family. A third exercise to build empathy about the oppressiveness of the closet requires that students display a visible interest in lesbianism/homosexuality in one or more settings, including going to a bookstore and asking where the books on lesbians are or carrying an obviously lesbian book openly in public places. Having heterosexual students hide their sexuality from their friends, family, and employer for a week and write about the experience also is an excellent consciousness-raising technique.

The empathy exercises described above are largely aimed at making heterosexual students aware of issues lesbians (or gay men) face, but can be modified to increase empathy among lesbian and gay students for diverse groups in their own community. For instance, lesbian students may be asked to select a lesbian of a different race or social class as an interview participant, to write an account about what it would be like for a lesbian of a different race to come out in the racial community that the student knows, or to ask in bookstores about what materials are available for lesbians of color or about racism in the lesbian/gay community.

The third aspect of the tolerance criterion, *shifting paradigms,* encourages students to see heterosexuality from a lesbian viewpoint or to find other ways to challenge heterosexism. Students tend to be less defensive toward and less threatened by a paradigm shift if it occurs after sufficient familiarization and empathy experiences. Asking students to participate in a "heterosexuality panel" is one of the best paradigm-shift methods I have used. Four or five students are asked to volunteer to represent the heterosexual population on a panel. A list of questions commonly asked of lesbian and gay panels, reversed to target heterosexuality (e.g., "When did you first realize you were heterosexual?") or ones more challenging of heterosexuality, (e.g., "Why are so many heterosexual men child molesters?") are then distributed to the rest of the students, who are encouraged to ask them of panelists. The heterosexual panel is extremely effective if it immediately follows a lesbian panel, which can be done if a class period of two to three hours is available. Student responses to the combined empathy-paradigm-shift exercise have been overwhelmingly positive. Most notably, the implicit superiority of heterosexuality that is conveyed by the need to have a lesbian panel is revealed once the roles are reversed.

A paradigm shift also can be promoted in sexuality courses by having small groups discuss how sexual orientation and gender affect definitions of the term "have sex." Participants are asked to generate a list of all sexual behaviors that are likely to "count" as "having sex" for each of four groups: heterosexual women, heterosexual men, lesbians, and gay men. The exercise illustrates that definitions of having sex for men usually involve male orgasm (their own or a male partner's) regardless of sexual orientation, but that female orgasm is used less often by women as the main criterion. Having sex is most likely to be defined by heterosexual women as vaginal intercourse with male orgasm. What lesbians are likely to count is least obvious. The exercise shows that sex researchers' conclusions that lesbians "have sex" less often than heterosexuals and gay men (e.g., Blumstein and Schwartz 1978) could be due to differences in definitions among the groups, as well as male-centered cultural definitions of sexuality.

Guided fantasies are another way to achieve a paradigm shift. Reading (or having students write) a fantasy about a world in which heterosexuality is outlawed highlights the moral justifications and institutional forces used by the dominant culture to oppress the nondominant group. Religious pronouncements and cultural values supporting the superiority of same-sex relationships help make this point (e.g., "heterosexuals are responsible for the population explosion, therefore their sexuality must be controlled or prohibited"). An exercise that may be used on its own or as a complement to the guided fantasy above is to have students brainstorm about what *advantages* might be associated with lesbian (or same-sex) relationships (i.e., no oppressive gender roles, understanding the body of someone of the same sex, resulting in better sex, et cetera).

Success at meeting the tolerance criterion is more difficult to evaluate than for inclusiveness. The only way I can really tell whether students have become more tolerant toward lesbians is to read student evaluations. I know from surveys I have taken early in the semester that about 40 to 55 percent of students in my classes agree with the statement "I disapprove of homosexuality as a lifestyle for others." By the end of the semester, only about 10 percent of students make negative comments about lesbians specifically. More common are remarks such as "[hearing about lesbianism] opened me up to a deeper understanding and acceptance" or "made me aware of my own prejudices."

The last issue that I want to discuss is how much one's own personal development affects one's ability to meet the inclusiveness and tolerance criteria. The example of my response to Tonya, the young African-American lesbian mentioned earlier, characterizes the dilemma colleagues and I often face when trying to balance two cultures—the heterosexual academic world and the lesbian one—in the classroom. I have noticed that being able to cope with the pressure of biculturalism or to tip the balance toward using a lesbian frame of reference is directly related to the strength of three components of my personal development as a lesbian-feminist faculty: internalized homophobia, vision, and self-nurturance.

Internalized homophobia among lesbian faculty is frequently discussed in terms of how it affects coming out in the classroom and the comfort level with bringing up lesbianism (e.g., Zimmerman 1994). Distancing oneself from very open, outspoken, or obvious (e.g., "butch") lesbians is another form of internalized homophobia I have seen many lesbian faculty express. Vision and self-nurturance are the components of my personal development that positively influence what I can accomplish from a lesbian studies' standpoint. Vision refers to my own ability to shift paradigms, to see the world in a lesbian-centered way. My and colleagues' normal strategies for enhancing vision include reading widely, actively participating in the lesbian community, and consciously reflecting on how heterosexism and sexism affect us. Self-nurturance pertains to assessing and meeting the emotional and physical needs that accompany the challenging of oppression.

These three components are deeply intertwined. My vision has been profoundly and positively affected by my competence at self-nurturance, which also enables me to contend with my internalized homophobia more effectively. For example, I have become more aware of how my effectiveness at coming out is as much about me as about "them"; my fears and reactions are as important to its success as are students'. How confident, apologetic, curt, or defensive I am determines, in large part, how they will react. Thus, I focus more on appreciating the strain it puts on me to tell from twelve to two hundred students at a time that I am a lesbian. I also quit motivating myself through criticism (e.g., "Tenured faculty *should* come out") and began praising and rewarding myself. Now I set aside several hours the day before my coming-out class for a long walk or other exercise during which I may or may not contemplate what I will say. After coming out, I take the rest of the day off. This small amount of self-nurturance has paid off. I am much more relaxed and creative about what to say.

In conclusion, like many other lesbian faculty, I now have the academic tools and the teaching experience necessary to meet the criteria of inclusiveness and tolerance that are relevant to lesbian studies. What appears to be needed to make us more effective and perhaps to move us to a new level of understanding is to look more deeply inside, to use ourselves as a guide for where we need to go next. By the phrase "using ourselves," I mean doing more than simply identifying how we have internalized the "isms." I am referring to shifting some focus to our fears and needs and using them as a springboard for teaching. I do not have many examples to offer of how this will work, because I have only started to get serious about this type of analysis. However, it is reasonable that, after several decades of lesbian-feminist scholarship and activism, we might want to turn in this promising direction.

WORKS CITED

American Psychological Association. 1994. *Publication manual*. 4th ed. Washington, DC: APA.
Bersoff, D. N. and D. W. Ogden. 1991. APA amicus curiae briefs: Furthering lesbian and gay male civil rights. *American Psychologist* 46:950–56.
Blumstein, P. and P. Schwartz. 1983. *American couples*. New York: Morrow.
Garnets, L. et al. 1991. Issues in psychotherapy with lesbians and gay men: A survey of psychologists. *American Psychologist* 46:964–72.
Garnets, L. and D. C. Kimmel. 1993. *Psychological perspectives on lesbian and gay male experiences*. New York:Columbia University Press.
Greene, B. and G. M. Herek, eds. 1994. *Psychological perspectives on lesbian and gay issues: Vol. 1. Lesbian and gay psychology: Theory, research, and clinical applications*. Thousand Oaks, CA: Sage.
Herek, G. M. 1993. Sexual orientation and military service. *American Psychologist* 48:538–49.
Jenness, V. and K. Broad. 1994. Antiviolence activism and the (in)visibility of gender in the gay/lesbian and women's movements. *Gender and Society* 8:402–23.
Morin, S. F. and E. D. Rothblum. 1991. Removing the stigma: Fifteen years of progress. *American Psychologist* 46:947–49.
Rothblum, E. D. and K. A. Brehony. 1994. *Boston marriages: Romantic but asexual relationships among contemporary lesbians*. Amherst, MA: University of Massachusetts Press.
Zimmerman, B. Lesbian studies in an inclusive curriculum. *Transformations* 5:18–27.

TEACHING FEMINIST LESBIAN DISABILITY STUDIES

Barbara Hillyer

When I designed my course on women and disability, I chose the only texts which specifically addressed women's experience of disability (as distinct from men's or a disembodied generic person's). It wasn't until a student reacted to these texts with homophobic defensiveness that it occurred to me that I was also teaching a lesbian studies course.

It hadn't occurred to me that I was *not* doing so; I just hadn't thought about it at all. I take this curious unconsciousness on my part to be a reflection of my own well-integrated stage of coming out and, at the same time, a reflection of the state of the arts in feminist disability studies, where lesbian experience is either central to the discussion or conscientiously included. What is curious about this situation is that until recently, disability studies scarcely recognized the experience of women as a separate category and feminist studies ignored disability.

What changed, beginning in the late 1980s, was that a few feminist theorists (notably Julia Penelope 1990 and Sarah Lucia Hoagland 1988) began including disability experience in their illustrations of lesbian linguistic and ethical dilemmas. About the same time, three key volumes in feminist disability studies were published: Michelle Fine and Adrienne Asch's *Women with Disabilities* (1988), Jenny Morris's *Pride against Prejudice* (1991) and my *Feminism and Disability* (1993). One foundation for these was an anthology of disability stories, *With the Power of Each Breath,* edited by Susan Browne, Debra Connors, and Nanci Stern (1985). These personal experience narratives were strongly influenced by the tradition of lesbian coming-out stories and many were written by lesbians. *With Wings* (1987), edited by Marsha Saxton and Florence Howe, contains similar personal experience narratives along with fiction and poetry, integrating lesbian experience with many other kinds of disability stories. Connie Panzarino's *The Me in the Mirror,* published in 1994, uses autobiography for a powerfully political end.

With the Power of Each Breath was especially important to my students because it personalized disability issues for them. When a homophobic response to these stories surfaced, most students were able to argue that the writers' lesbian perspective was incidental to what they were saying about disability. "A heterosexual woman would talk about her husband as Maureen Brady does about her lover," they argued. What I added was that lesbian coming-out stories were a well-established genre by the mid-eighties, that lesbians are used to thinking and writing about their lives in this way and would find it natural to respond to Browne, Connors, and Stern's call for papers. Equally important, however, is the fact that lesbians are much more likely than most heterosexual women to have attended thoughtfully to our own embodiment and to think of ourselves as integrally at one with our bodies. Such self-consciousness is also uniquely available to women with disabilities (Hillyer 1993, chapter 9). Lesbians with disabilities have a written tradition within which to conceptualize such an integral self-body connection.

Thus, remarkably, I found myself responding to a student's homophobic response by asserting the intellectual superiority of a lesbian perspective for conceptualizing women's disability narratives.

Connie Panzarino's autobiography, *The Me in the Mirror,* shows how her lesbian and feminist activism grew out of her disability activism and reflects on how these movements interact. Because it is a personal experience narrative, it engages students in much the same way as the stories in *With the Power of Each Breath,* and does so with more political analysis of even the most apparently personal experiences.

In my own book of feminist theory about disability, I include a chapter (Hillyer 1993, chapter 8) on disability passing in which I compare it to lesbian passing, citing the advantages and disadvantages of passing and suggesting strategies for maintaining one's integrity while passing and while coming out. Here again, the existence of an extensive literature, both scholarly and personal, about passing and the coming-out process makes lesbian studies the most appropriate context in which to examine the complexities of living a deliberately duplicitous life and the hazards of not doing so.

In addition to the basic minority status that makes passing seem desirable, I cite certain other traits that make the two groups comparable: being socialized by persons who do not share the stigma; being treated like members of the more privileged group; having learned to conform to the privileged group's standards of behavior and appearance; having available civil rights movements of rather short duration; being minorities within other civil rights movements; and being women whose sexuality is at issue when their minority status is known. All of these items are open for discussions in the classroom, as are the passing situations which the chapter describes in more depth.

Except for that one chapter, my book does not explicitly come out as a lesbian book, though I cite many lesbian authors and use the word "lesbian" freely. This is, after all, a feminist theoretical work of the early nineties, and by this time most feminist writers know that difference, including lesbian difference, must be addressed in our work. Thus, Jenny Morris's theoretical feminist disability book, *Pride against Prejudice,* includes lesbian experiences and provides the teacher/

student/reader with an opportunity to observe heterosexual self-consciousness.

Morris identifies herself as heterosexual, but she includes one lesbian in the group of eight women whose stories help to form the center of her book, and she identifies other disabled lesbians who have commented on the manuscript or written about disability. She does not label any of her other sources "heterosexual" though she does mention their husbands and children. Generally she uses the terms "partner" and "lover" rather than "husband" or "boyfriend." This usage and the fact that she is self-consciously heterosexual are in themselves evidence of the impact of lesbian studies on feminist theory.

Simply to say, "I am a heterosexual woman" or "from a heterosexual perspective," suggests the possibility of other options. Not to do so is to collaborate with the culturally pervasive heterosexist assumption. Similarly, when I point out that Morris names "racism, sexism, or heterosexism" but explores only racism (170–75), or mentions "gays and lesbians" but doesn't incorporate them into an example or discussion, it becomes clear that naming and inclusion are not the same. When students encounter this analysis in the classroom, their own unconscious heterosexism is challenged and, if they are lesbians, their existence is acknowledged, in some cases for the first time in a classroom.

By this time in the semester's work, Fine and Asch's collection of scholarly articles, *Women with Disabilities,* seems unremarkable in its conscientious inclusion of at least some feminist analysis in each essay and its infrequent references to sexual orientation. It does provide an opportunity to discuss how scholarly language flattens the diversity of disability expression and makes necessary the very editorial skills that Fine and Asch exercise to keep a feminist perspective central in the collection. The editorial insistence on including a feminist perspective is one important strength of the anthology. The editors have been much less able to encourage even an acknowledgment of lesbian existence. Only one writer, Marilyn Rousso, names the heterosexual bias of her research, stating that "by no means is it intended to devalue other forms of sexual expression." The others ignore lesbian experience, perhaps because they are so focused on gender socialization to be feminine and appealing to men or else on the assumption of the asexuality of women with disabilities. Nowhere is it suggested that acculturation to be less feminine might help a woman consider the possibility that sexual orientation away from men might be possible. The most glaring omission of lesbian possibility in the volume is Barbara Simon's essay on never-married women. She states that one reason these women do so well is that they have many friends, usually including one special, close friend with whom the woman has daily contact, but she never mentions that some of these friends may be lesbians, nor does she mention that her research categories excluded the possibility of finding out that some "subjects" might be lesbians.

In contrast, Asch and Fine are scrupulous about including "sexual orientation" in their lists of complexities of discrimination; they also speak of "heterosexual women," of "intimate relationships with men (and women)," and of "heterosexual and lesbian partners". In the context of a statement about the low marriage rate for women with disabilities, they point out that although Browne, Connors, and Stern include many lesbian contributors, none mentions an ongoing intimate relationship. In their epilogue, they include in a list of topics not yet addressed the experience of disabled women in relationships with women or men as partners. These are indicators of willingness to include lesbians, but in fact the book does not do so. Perhaps one reason for the omission is the tone of objectivity in the language, which doesn't merely cover up the absence of lesbians in the research design, but also renders inappropriate any discussion of desire in favor of a more abstract attention to gender, femininity, marriage, and reproduction.

Finally, in teaching my course, I use some films which provide occasions for discussions of lesbian issues. *Lifetime Commitment: A Portrait of Karen Thompson* graphically presents disability as a lesbian issue, showing how being closeted, being lesbian, being "gay," being in a committed relationship, having no legal protection, and being the object of heterosexist discrimination interact with being disabled. *Passion Fish,* which I use to support an extended discussion about the relationships between women with disabilities and women care givers, is about the development of an intense, primary relationship between two apparently heterosexual women of different races, classes, and (dis)abilities. Without directly focusing on the question of whether they are lesbians (presumably not), the film certainly opens the matter of the "lesbian continuum," as both women's "recoveries" (from spinal cord injury, alcoholism, upper-class southern small-town socialization and northern urban ghetto socialization) brings them to acceptance of each other's primacy in their lives.

Although the texts I used in this course enabled me to do lesbian education with these students, I don't think there are sufficient materials to support a "Lesbians and Disability" course. This would be a moot point in my university and, I suspect, in most. Enrollments are low in more general courses about disability and we have no core in lesbian or gay studies. *With the Power of Each Breath* could easily be used to support a unit on disability in a course on lesbian experience, though I would urge the teacher of such a course to be familiar with the theoretical issues raised in *Pride against Prejudice* and *Feminism and Disability.* Most other disability literature, like the contributors to *Women with Disabilities,* either ignores lesbians or mentions them only in lists of oppressed people. At present, the best strategy for incorporating lesbian experience in teaching about disability is to use it in such examples as Karen Thompson or Connie Panzarino. Raising consciousness by naming lesbians and heterosexuals and by taking care with language should be as routine as naming ability status and avoiding ableist assumptions.

What do I make of the realization that lesbian studies is so integral to this apparently nonlesbian course? First, feminist disability studies is such a new phenomenon that there are very few available resources for the classroom. Those few, however, are solidly feminist and come from a lesbian-influenced feminist tradition. Thus, in my course at least, the textbooks enabled the students and me to use a lesbian studies perspective. Second, women's experience of disability forces an awareness of embodiment which calls into question key aspects of our cultural ideology (for example, of beauty and of productivity), which powerfully influence lesbians along with everyone else. Third, lesbian personal experience narratives have been the model for the coming-out narratives of women with disabilities. Third, similarities between lesbian passing and disability passing permit discussion of the ethical problems and societal causes of deliberate dissimulation. Fourth, problems in relationships between women with disabilities and their paid or intimate care givers provide insight about lesbian relationships and about the lesbian continuum. Fifth, some lesbians have disabilities and some women with disabilities are lesbians; discrimination against either group impacts the other.

What I learned as a teacher from the lesbian dimension of my Women and Disability course is that I am no longer able to choose not to teach lesbian studies. Feminist materials make it essential as do my own experience and the way in which lesbian and queer studies have problematized women's experience of embodiment.

WORKS CITED

Browne, Susan, Debra Connors, and Nanci Stern, eds. 1985. *With the power of each breath: A disabled women's anthology.* San Francisco: Cleis.

Fine, Michelle and Adrienne Asch, eds. 1989. *Women with disabilities.* Philadelphia: Temple University Press.

Hillyer, Barbara. 1993. *Feminism and disability.* Norman: University of Oklahoma Press, 1993.

Hoagland, Sarah. 1988. *Lesbian ethics: Toward new value.* Palo Alto, CA: Institute of Lesbian Studies.

Morris, Jenny. 1991. *Pride against prejudice: Transforming attitudes to disability.* Philadelphia: New Society Publishers.

Panzarino, Connie. 1994. *The me in the mirror.* Seattle: Seal Press.

Penelope, Julia. 1990. *Speaking freely: Unlearning the lies of the fathers' tongues.* New York: Pergamon.

Saxton, Marsha and Florence Howe, eds. 1987. *With wings: An anthology of literature by and about women with disabilities.* New York: The Feminist Press at CUNY.

QUEER COLLABORATIONS: FEMINIST PEDAGOGY

Ann Pellegrini and Paul B. Franklin

Some leading questions:

- What does it mean for a self-identified "gay man" and a self-identified "lesbian," both of whom not so incidentally identify themselves as feminists, to collaborate in and out of the classroom?
- In order to present a unified front, whatever that is, must one term drop out, and which one would it be?
- Is the privileged political/pedagogical nexus through which such a "coupling" takes place necessarily a "queer" one?
- How is such a queer coupling, if that, indeed, is what it is, viewed or understood by others, such as students or colleagues?

Part of what motivates our asking these critical questions is our personal experiences as graduate students at Harvard. Between 1992 and 1994, we cowrote and copresented a paper, cochaired another academic panel, and cotaught a women's studies seminar. Among the issues these experiences focused for us is the value of feminism for "homosexual insiders." It seems to us, and we will try and make this claim clearer below, that the abject status of feminism among queers on college campuses today may derive in part from generational differences. Of course, these differences are mediated by the changing historical, social, political, economic, and epidemiological scene of homosexuality. In order to situate our analysis we want to begin by rehearsing some of our own telling encounters.

At the Second National Graduate Student Conference on Lesbian, Bisexual, and Gay Studies, in the spring of 1992, we jointly presented a paper entitled "A Different Story: When We Queers Cum Together." This was a paper we wrote collaboratively over an intense three-day writing binge. Following our presentation, in both the formal question-and-answer period and later in informal conversations, the question we were asked most often was how did we write it. What were the mechanics of our creative process? Did we each work privately and then meet to compare notes and assemble the dialogue on display here?

It seems to us that for many of our interlocutors the question of formal mechanics—"how did you write it?"—was actually a question of interpretation: as if knowing how we wrote it would provide the hermeneutic key to what we wrote, to the substance of our arguments. We were also challenged by some audience members as to whether or not our dialogue was in fact "dialogical." For some, our paper seemed too much of one voice: Ann's. For others, it seemed too much of one affect: camp. (In other words, Paul's.) Yet doesn't this pattern of identification-authoritative voice versus affective tone, lesbian-feminist seriousness versus camp frivolity—rather unqueerly replicate the binary regimes of hetero/homo, male/female, masculine/feminine that feminist and queer theories are dedicated to subverting?

If our performance caused gender trouble it surely was not the kind of trouble we had hoped to get ourselves into. Who is to say that "lesbianism" formally, essentially, or by definition excludes camp? Why must the effete gay man, who also, not insignificantly, happens to take feminism as his theoretical and political point of departure, lose his voice—even when that voice warbles in a higher register?

These concerns seemed to raise, without ever explicitly stating, the question or "problem" of collaboration. Innocently, "collaboration" might name work done in common. Less innocently perhaps, there looms the specter of war-time treachery. As Wayne Koestenbaum writes: "Double writers bear the stain of [collaboration's] political meaning: the sense lingers that they, like collaborators in Vichy France, have compromised themselves, have formed new and unhealthy allegiances, and have betrayed trusts."[1]

This crisis of collaboration—"which side are you on?"—also appeared when we cotaught "Voices of Liberation: From Women's Lib to Gay Lib, 1965–1975," at Harvard in the spring of 1994. In fact, it was our political and pedagogical commitment, in planning and teaching this course, *not* to take sides. Rather, as we outlined in our course description, we proposed to explore the historical and political confluences of the American women's and (lesbian and) gay movements through what was arguably the most critical decade in each of their developments. We emphasized the contribution of the women's movement and its radical politics to revolutionary changes in gay identity immediately before and after Stonewall. We set particular stress upon identifying points of tension between and within these two movements, especially in relation to the different priorities placed upon gender oppression, sexual identity, and sexuality, race, and class.

The relation of lesbianism to feminism on the one side and to gay liberation on the other is especially fertile ground for elucidating the contradictions of revolutionary feminism and gay liberation. One of the ways we attempted to frame and localize these various tensions was through privileging "the" lesbian. The very practice of this course was intended to demonstrate, by way of our example, that a gay man and a lesbian could effectively work together and mutually embrace their—

which is to say: our—shared histories through feminism.

What interests us here are the reactions and responses of some of the students who enrolled in the seminar to the challenges our "joint appearance" and shared praxis seemed to represent. They missed much of the political point of our collaboration because they took collaboration among "queer people" for granted. All the students in the class—queer, straight, and bisexual—came to political consciousness in the shadow of AIDS. The forms of radical protest with which they were most familiar, growing up as they did in the Reagan/Bush era, were the "zap" actions of ACT UP and Queer Nation. That lesbians and gay men might work together and make common cause was, to our students, business as usual. Of course, not only does this assumption idealize the always tenuous alliances between lesbians and gay men, but it also occludes fragmentations of race and class. Similarly yet more generally speaking, many queers of Generation X seem to presume that bisexuality and bisexuals now fit seamlessly into both feminist and gay *and* lesbian liberation movements and, what's more, where bisexuals did not fit, that this was due to the biphobia of lesbians and gay men. For both of us, however, when we were undergraduates, the inclusion of bisexuals and bisexual issues into our respective campus lesbian and gay organizations was hotly debated and divisive.[2]

As these examples indicate, our starting points and those of our students were vastly different. And this was despite the fact that there were "only" eight years between ourselves and the undergraduates. But, as we had to caution ourselves not to forget, eight years is two full collegiate generations (and two presidential terms). As we understood it, the point of our collaboration was to pause and consider what is being left behind in the self-promotions of gay and lesbian studies. That is, which "selves" are being promoted? What is the force of the "and"?[3] Has feminism, particularly that version of feminism glossed under radical and/or radical-lesbian feminism, become the new "old maid"?[4] As a lesbian ("lesbian") and a gay man who came out and of age in and through feminism, we have been startled and alarmed by the critical lack of feminist identification and politics among not only gay and bisexual male students, but even among lesbian, bisexual, and heterosexual female students. In a "postfeminist" age, we saw this course as an opportunity both to remind students of the living debt we all owe radical feminism and to resurrect something of the challenge and complexity of identity politics. Certainly, where our own personal, theoretical, and political commitments were concerned, we actually "inverted" the expected alignments of identity politics.

Our individual investments in identity politics are not identical, but are inflected by our different embodied histories (differences which are in no way reducible to anatomical "sex") and are also mediated by different kinds and uses of theory. Paul's more-than-strategic attachment to identity politics stems from his belief and indeed insistence that only identity politics can incorporate him; only identity politics can maintain the corporeality of his body, a corporeality which is too often put into jeopardy and, therefore, under erasure. For her part, Ann worries about the ways in which, as Judith Butler argues, "identity categories tend to be instruments of regulatory regimes," recolonizing the very people and "identities" in whose name they might seem to speak and whose possibility of speech they might seem to condition.[5] Certainly, a particular and historically specific relation to lesbian-feminist identity politics conditioned Ann's coming out as a "lesbian" and conditioned also her intelligibility as a "lesbian subject." Yet, if today Ann can only cite (and site) "the lesbian" and herself "as lesbian" in and through quotation marks, this equivocal (self-)description marks neither the failure of politics nor the loss of nerve, but instead remarks the always phantasmatic psychical and political wish for self-identity, self-knowing, and self-certainty that coming out as anything at once promises and defers. The quotation marks around "lesbian" also signal the powerful reflexes of the closet as one passes from one region of unknowing to another.[6] No longer the question or the anxiety "do they know about me?" but "what do they know when they know about me?" and, even, "what do I know when I know myself as lesbian?" Within the classroom context, coming out or being out might seem simultaneously to invite and to foreclose new kinds of identifications between those who would teach and those who would be taught.[7] Nor, as we shall argue more clearly below, are these two positions mutually exclusive.

From discussions, inside and outside the classroom, with two students in particular—one out lesbian and one out gay man—it became evident that it was Paul who was seen to represent gay (male?) liberation, while Ann was a type for women's liberation. Neither of us would disclaim these identifications. But, is that all there is to "it" or to "us"? Moreover, doesn't this way of placing us recapitulate the gender divisions we were trying to make complex in this historically-focused course? Perhaps we did not carry out our pedagogical goals as effectively as we had hoped or planned. But it is also possible that our re-situation as "typical" gay man and "typical" lesbian woman testifies to the powerful reflex of binary thinking even among the most converted. We do not exclude ourselves from this criticism.

Less typical perhaps was our position within the larger institutional structure of Harvard University. We were not faculty pure and simple, but graduate students. We took the initiative in proposing this course to the chair of women's studies and to other women's studies faculty. Permission to teach this course depended on the chair's willingness and ability to plead our case before the administration. Harvard does not allow graduate students to teach their own courses, and, therefore, it was only through the full support of the women's studies department that we received special dispensation to do so. We were appointed as "special instructors," but were paid as teaching assistants.

In many ways, it was precisely our liminal position as graduate students that enabled us to teach this course, the very first gay and lesbian history seminar ever offered at Harvard. And it was also our generational position vis-à-vis the tenured faculty who "authorized" our course which allowed us to imagine it in the first place. For we are among the first generation of graduate students who were out as undergraduates, out as graduate students, and who will be or already are out as faculty members—a "privilege" not generally available to those who came before. The content and meaning of being out have changed and will continue to change at each of these stages.

However, our ambiguous standing—almost faculty—also created some complex pedagogical issues inside the classroom. If the students who enrolled in our seminar presumed a certain familiarity and camaraderie with us, this was less presumptuous than it might first have appeared. In addition to extensive teaching, both of us had been resident advisors in Harvard's undergraduate housing system for four years. In this capacity, each of us had lived among literally hundreds of undergraduates, advising them on issues of sexual harassment, race, and sexual diversity—not to mention our own academic disciplines. Interestingly, each of us was initially hired to serve more "narrow" communities. Ann was specifically hired to advocate for women and promote a feminist voice in her residential house, while Paul was explicitly hired as his house's "in-house faggot." Each of us was asked, in her/his own way, to compensate for the perceived shortcomings in house life.

Because we were two of the few out and politically active queer residential advisors, we were repeatedly called upon by undergraduates, administrators, and colleagues (queer and straight) to speak for "our people." We dare say this is an experience not unfamiliar to out faculty as well—whether those faculty be out as queer or out, say, as Black or Latina. The upshot of this over-signification, due itself to an under-representation, was that we were supposed to speak as one. Yet, when we did speak as one, this required another set of explanations and self-justifications.

We are not begrudging the roles we were asked to play, roles we willingly took up: those of role models. What we are questioning is whether this performance ultimately is a "good" thing for students or for us. The question is: What do we give up in the name of safety? Certainly, the presence of queer faculty and students in the same classroom may create a safety zone on both sides. However, it may also create the illusion of identification where it might be more accurate to speak of projection. Here we are alluding to the complicated, and sometimes messy, dynamics of transference and countertransference. As teachers and role models, we are potent sites of identification for our students as they are, in different ways, for us. Here it is worthwhile to acknowledge our own investments in and identifications with our students. For our students were, for us, also points of (mis)identification. At this writing, one year since teaching "Voices of Liberation," it now seems to us that our assumption (narcissistic wish?) that the issues that had framed and informed both the campus politics of our undergraduate days and our own coming-out narratives would be the *same* issues framing our students' narratives was, fundamentally, a *misrecognition of our students as ourselves*. In this sense, then, our identifications with our students were impossibly nostalgic. That is, we saw in them the students we never really were. "Never really were" not merely for the "obvious" reason that lesbian and gay studies was not on the curricular menu of the undergraduate institutions we had attended, but, more centrally, "never really were" because the very impossibility of identification is what makes *any* identification work.[8] When, where, and how do we actively interrupt these transferences and countertransferences? Can queer pedagogy only "speak" itself as therapy?

To the extent that queer pedagogy has been, in some ways, conditioned by therapeutic techniques, this should come as no surprise. The "perverse" logic of homosexuality's historical medicalization and pathologization[9] demands no less than the talking cure. A similar claim might be made with respect to the queer classroom's kissing cousin, the women's studies classroom. Indeed, the consciousness-raising techniques practiced in the latter space, which were taken over from Freudian analysis (and which Freud himself expropriated from Bertha Pappenheim, a.k.a. Anna O.), are the historical foundations for queer pedagogies. This nexus—Freud, feminism, homosexual identities, progressive pedagogies—brings us full circle. Queer collaborationists, indeed!

Questions concerning the process and product of queer and queerly feminist pedagogy are politically vital to the ongoing project of liberation inside and outside the classroom. We argue—or have tried to argue—as much in this paper. At minimum, our process of writing has enacted (for us, at any rate) an ideal of collaboration, namely, struggling word by word to hear each other, even and especially in our differences. Our "coupling" embodies the productive and provocative tensions of collaborating across differences, real and imagined. Asking on what and on whose terms lesbians, gay men, bisexuals, and feminists of all persuasions can and do speak to one another provides a necessary starting point and material context for the actualization of a fuller pedagogical method.

For us, the process of teaching and writing collaboratively and performatively conjures, even if it can never fully instantiate, that dream of a future perfect—that modality which, as Alice Jardine says, "implies neither that we are helpless before some inevitable destiny nor that we can somehow, given enough time and thought, engineer an ultimately perfect future."[10] And, after all, the classroom is where the future begins.

We would like to thank Barbara Johnson, Marjorie Garber, and Alice Jardine for enabling the two of us to teach collaboratively. We acknowledge as well our many students who have challenged us, in ways we are just coming to realize, to continually rethink what it means to be out in the classroom.

NOTES

1. Wayne Koestenbaum, *Double Talk: The Erotics of Male Literary Collaboration* (New York: Routledge, 1989), 8.

2. Perhaps the controversy over bisexuality and bisexuals was to our generation what current debates regarding transgender are today. Of course, to say that bisexuality is today less embattled an issue than it was a decade ago is *not* also to say that it is no longer being fought over and about. For a discussion of the political and cultural history of bisexuals and bisexuality see Marjorie Garber, *Vice Versa: Bisexuality and the Eroticism of Everyday Life* (New York: Simon & Schuster, 1995).

3. Similar questions have been raised with respect to the place of men in feminism and feminist theory. See the controversial anthology *Men in Feminism,* edited by Alice Jardine and Paul Smith (New York: Methuen, 1987) and *Engendering Men: The Question of Male Feminist Criticism,* edited by Joseph A. Boone and Michael Cadden (New York: Routledge, 1990).

4. Here we are side-stepping questions (and ongoing controversies) of definition—what is radical feminism? how is it to be distinguished (if it is) from cultural feminism and reform feminism?—and periodization. For two representative yet opposing analyses of these questions see Alice Echols, *Daring*

to Be Bad: Radical Feminism in America, 1967–1975 (Minneapolis: University of Minnesota Press, 1989) and Verta Taylor and Leila J. Rupp, "Women's Culture and Lesbian Feminist Activism: A Reconsideration of Cultural Feminism," *Signs* 19, no. 1 (autumn 1993):32–61.

5. Judith Butler, "Imitation and Gender Insubordination," in *The Lesbian and Gay Studies Reader,* edited by Henry Abelove, Michèle Aina Barale, and David M. Halperin (New York: Routledge, 1992), 308.

6. Ibid, 309.

7. See Ann Pellegrini, "Classics and Closets: When Teachers Come Out in the Classroom," *Women's Review of Books* 9, no. 5 (February 1994): 11–12.

8. For an important examination of what is at stake—psychically, pedagogically, and politically—in identification, see Diana Fuss, *Identification Papers* (New York: Routledge, 1995). See also Ann Pellegrini, *Performance Anxieties: Staging Psychoanalysis, Staging Race* (New York: Routledge, 1996).

9. By "medicalization and pathologization" we mean to refer to the ways in which "the homosexual" and "the lesbian" were subjected to and, in no small fashion, subjectivated by the "expert" knowledge of medico-scientific practitioners. A "foundational" discourse in the production of the modern homosexual is psychoanalysis and its precursor, sexology. To say this is not to deny that there were and still are circulating other explanatory systems in and through which "the homosexual" and "the lesbian" have been conceptualized, regulated, and "experienced" (such as legal and moral-theological frameworks). For a helpful discussion of the medicalization of homosexuality and lesbianism (which we wish to resist eliding in our discussion), see George Chauncey, Jr., "From Sexual Inversion to Homosexuality: The Changing Medical Conception of Female Deviance," in *Passion and Power: Sexuality in History,* edited by Kathy Peiss and Christina Simmons (Philadelphia: Temple University Press, 1989).

10. Alice Jardine, "Introduction to Julia Kristeva's 'Women's Time,'" *Signs* 7, no. 1 (autumn 1981):5.

LESBIAN IMAGES IN SELECTED WOMEN'S LITERATURE ANTHOLOGIES, 1980–1994

Kathleen Hickok

When I analyzed women's literature anthologies in 1981 for the first edition of *Lesbian Studies,* I found that while lesbian authors were widely included, their sexual orientation was frequently suppressed or misrepresented. Homophobic editorial statements were common, and lesbian content, when present, was generally covert. An alert reader could construct a lesbian reading of various poems, plays, and stories, but I thought a heterosexual reader in 1981 would be unlikely to do so. Of thirty-five anthologies of women's literature then in print, I found eight that I could recommend. Lillian Faderman's *Surpassing the Love of Men* was just out, and the collection *Lesbian Poetry,* edited by Joan Larkin and Elly Bulkin, was available from Persephone Press. But otherwise, the images of lesbians in women's literature anthologies were blurry, negative, and/or stereotypical.

Revisiting the issue in 1994 for this edition, I have found lesbian content much improved in the new anthologies, in both quantity and quality. Lesbian or bisexual authors are more likely to be identified as such. The number of anthologies including lesbian literature constitutes a greater proportion of the available texts. And the representation of lesbianism is generally more positive, distinctive, and realistic than before. Specialized anthologies abound, organized by genre, time period, theme, and/or identity (race, color, class, sexual orientation, religion, age, ability, etc.). I discovered fifty current anthologies in which lesbian content appears, and twenty-five more that are entirely lesbian literature.

For this bibliography, I defined "literature" to include poetry, fiction, plays, personal essays, and autobiographical writings. After looking at more than two hundred books, I decided to limit my scope to anthologies in which most or all of the literature is from the nineteenth or twentieth centuries, where significant lesbian content can reasonably be expected. I omitted thematic collections (which are plentiful) unless the theme was very broad, and I eliminated most collections that included male writers. I also omitted texts in which lesbian content is entirely absent; my goal is not to indict books that exclude lesbian literature but to identify and describe those that include it. All books listed are currently available in the United States and were published in the U.S. or Canada between 1980 and 1994. All prices given are approximate and subject to change.

The best available general literature anthologies are *The Norton Anthology of Literature by Women: The Tradition in English,* edited by Sandra M. Gilbert and Susan Gubar (New York: Norton, 1985; paper $34.95), and *Images of Women in Literature,* fifth edition, edited by Mary Anne Ferguson (Boston: Houghton Mifflin, 1991; paper $35.00), although there is still room for improvement in both. A new edition of the *Norton Anthology* is planned; however, Mary Anne Ferguson has died, and the future of *Images of Women in Literature* is in doubt.

Limitations of space made it impossible to include all seventy-five items I found, so I have focused on two categories. Part One lists anthologies that focus on women of color, or on class, age, religion, or disability. Where appropriate, I have noted the lesbian authors and/or content. Part Two lists lesbian anthologies followed by brief descriptive comments. I hope this bibliography will be a useful resource for teachers of women's studies and women's literature who wish to diversify their courses.

To conclude, women's literature anthologists of the past fifteen years have been focusing on our differences as women. However, in the number and variety of lesbian collections, we have achieved a kind of lesbian pluralism. Let's hope that the advent of "queer studies" doesn't obscure the visibility of our developing lesbian literary tradition.

I. Women's Literature Anthologies by/about Women of Color or about Class, Religion, Aging, or Disability

Black Sister: Poetry by Black American Women, 1746–1980, edited by Erlene Stetson. Bloomington, IN: Indiana University Press, 1981. Paper $10.95. Authors include Angelina Weld Grimké, Alice Dunbar-Nelson, Pauli Murray, Mae V. Cowdery, June Jordan, Audre Lorde, and Pat Parker.

Black Women's Blues: A Literary Anthology 1934–1988, edited by Rita Dandridge. New York: MacMillan, 1992. Cloth $40.00. This prose anthology contains letters, plays, stories, autobiographical narratives, novel excerpts, and political essays. "I Am Your Sister: Black Women Organizing across Sexualities" by Audre Lorde is the only piece directly pertaining to lesbians, and it is, significantly, the book's last selection, as the final sentence in *Black Women's Blues* is, "I am a Black Lesbian, and I *am* your sister."

Calling Home: Working-Class Women's Writings, edited by Janet Zandy. New Brunswick, NJ: Rutgers University Press, 1990. Paper $12.95. Includes short selections by Beth Brant, Barbara Smith, Audre Lorde, Dorothy Allison, Judy Grahn, Cherríe Moraga, and others.

The Colour of Resistance: A Contemporary Collection of Writings by Aboriginal Women, edited by Connie Fife. Toronto, Canada: Sister Vision Black Women and Women of Color Press, 1993. Paper $17.95. A diverse collection of poetry and fiction by indigenous American and Canadian women "exploring the diversity of culture and sexuality."

Cuentos: Stories by Latinas, edited by Alma Gomez, Cherríe Moraga, and Mariana Romo-Carmona. New York: Kitchen Table/Women of Color Press, 1983. Paper $9.95. Authors identified in the biographies as lesbian include Gloria Anzaldúa, Cherríe Moraga, Aurora Levins Morales, Aleida Rodriguez, and Luz Maria Umpierre.

Double Stitch: Black Women Write about Mothers and Daughters, edited by Patricia Bell-Scott, Beverly Guy-Sheftall et al. Boston: Beacon Press, 1991. Paper $12.00. Authors include June Jordan, S. Diane Bogus, Gloria Joseph, Gloria T. Hull, and Audre Lorde. Joseph's essay "Black Mothers and Daughters: Traditional and New Perspectives" includes a section called "Black Lesbian Mothers."

A Gathering of Spirit: A Collection by North American Indian Women, edited by Beth Brant (Degonwadonti). Ithaca, NY: Firebrand Books, 1988. Paper $10.95. About 20 percent of the contributors to this volume are identified as lesbians, including the editor; lesbian sensibilities are respected throughout.

Home Girls: A Black Feminist Anthology, edited by Barbara Smith. New York: Kitchen Table/Women of Color Press, 1983. Paper $13.95. More than half the contributors to this collection are lesbian, as is the editor. One entire section of the text is titled "Black Lesbians—Who Will Fight for Our Lives But Us?"

Infinite Divisions: An Anthology of Chicana Literature, edited by Tey Diana Rebolledo and Eliana S. Rivero. Tucson: University of Arizona Press, 1993. Paper $19.95. Although the editors expressly acknowledge in their introduction a growing lesbian presence in Chicana literature, the short poems "Ever Since" by Veronica Cunningham, "Whole" by Ana Castillo, and "Making Tortillas" by Alicia Gaspar de Alba were the only lesbian selections I could find.

Life Notes: Personal Writings by Contemporary Black Women, edited by Patricia Bell Scott. New York: Norton, 1994. Cloth $25.00 Lesbian writers include Shamara Shantu Riley, Barbara Smith, Audre Lorde, Sapphire, and a pseudonymous author who calls herself Yin Quilter.

Making Face, Making Soul: Creative and Critical Perspectives by Feminists of Color, edited by Gloria Anzaldúa. San Francisco: Aunt Lute, 1990. Paper $15.95. Lesbians represented include Barbara Smith, Janice Gould, Beth Brant, Gloria Anzaldúa, Chrystos, Michelle Cliff, and Pat Parker.

Making Waves: An Anthology of Writings by and about Asian American Women, edited by Asian Women United of California. Boston: Beacon Press, 1989. Paper $18.95. Authors include Kitty Tsui, Chea Villanueva, and several others whose biographies indicate they are lesbians. In an essay entitled "Asian American Lesbians: An Emerging Voice in the Asian American Community," Pamela H. writes, "The burgeoning Asian American lesbian movement is just beginning to gain notice from more well-established movements. . . . there are hundreds of other Asian lesbians beginning to collect their voices, and they want to be heard."

Moon Marked and Touched by Sun: Plays by African-American Women, edited by Sydne Mahone. New York: Theatre Communications Group, 1994. Paper $15.95. The editor includes homophobia with racism and sexism as cultural oppressions that exclude black women playwrights from mainstream American theater. *Cage Rhythm,* by Kia Corthron, is the only play in the book to include lesbian content.

Nine Plays by Black Women, edited by Margaret B. Wilkerson. New York: New American Library (Mentor), 1986. Paper $5.99. The editor mentions the lesbian content of *No* and *A Season to Unravel* by Alexis De Veaux and *Long Time Since Yesterday* by P. J. Gibson; however, these two playwrights are represented by different plays in the anthology.

Shadowed Dreams: Women's Poetry of the Harlem Renaissance, edited by Maureen Honey. New Brunswick, NJ: Rutgers University Press, 1989. Paper $12.95. The editor acknowledges June Jordan and Cheryl Clarke and credits Gloria T. Hull for re-covering the lesbian writing of Alice Dunbar-Nelson and Angelina Weld Grimké. The book contains woman-identified and homoerotic poems by these two and several others: Mae V. Cowdery, Marjorie Marshall, and Gladys May Casely Hayford.

Shattering the Myth: Plays by Hispanic Women, edited by Linda Feyder. Houston, TX: Arte Publico, 1992. Paper $13.00. Cherríe Moraga's play *Shadow of a Man* is the only relevant selection in this collection of six plays, and it is somewhat oblique.

Sisterfire: Black Womanist Fiction and Poetry, edited by Charlotte Watson Sherman. New York: Harper Perennial, 1994. Paper $12.00. Includes Jewelle Gomez, Deb Parks-Satterfield, Sapphire, and several other identifiably lesbian contributors. A section on sisterfriends begins and ends with lesbian selections; a section on sex contains three or four more.

The Things That Divide Us, edited by Faith Conlon, Rachel da Silva, and Barbara Wilson. Seattle: Seal Press, 1985. Paper $10.95. "This is an anthology of fiction by women that addresses both the positive aspects of diversity among women and the destructive effects of misunderstanding and separation." Relevant authors include Becky Birtha, Valerie Miner, Sarah Schulman, and others.

This Bridge Called My Back: Writings by Radical Women of Color, edited by Cherríe Moraga and Gloria Anzaldúa. Watertown, MA: Persephone Press, 1981. Reissued by Kitchen Table/Women of Color Press, 1984. Paper $9.95. A highly influential mixed-genre, multi-ethnic feminist text with the goal of breaking silences, breaking barriers between women, and, as Toni Cade Bambara writes in the book's foreword, making revolution "irresistible." The book contains poems, stories, personal narratives, speeches, essays, and letters.

The Tribe of Dina: A Jewish Women's Anthology, edited by Melanie Kaye/Kantrowitz and Irena Klepfisz. *Sinister Wisdom* 29/30. Boston: Beacon Press, 1986. Paper $14.95. Both editors being lesbian, this collection honors a lesbian sensibility throughout. Julie Greenberg, Sarah Schulman, Elana Dykewomon, Joan E. Biren (JEB), and several other lesbians are included.

The Unforgetting Heart: An Anthology of Short Stories by African-American Women (1859–1993), edited by Asha Kanwar. San Francisco: Aunt Lute Press, 1993. Paper $9.95. These stories are arranged chronologically to track cultural change; they illustrate "oppressions on the basis of sex, race, class, caste, and sexual preference" —and African-American women's resistance to them. Of the five stories from the 1980s, two are relevant: "Johnnieruth" by Becky Birtha and "The Life You Live (May Not Be Your Own)" by J. California Cooper.

When I Am an Old Woman I Shall Wear Purple: An Anthology of Short Stories and Poetry, edited by Sandra Martz. Watsonville, CA: Pâpier Maché Press, 1987. Paper $10.00. Jess Wells's touching story, "Two Willow Chairs," begins, "This is a lesbian portrait." Other contributors include Terri Jewell and Karen Brodine, but their pieces about memory loss, aging, and women's worth are not specifically lesbian in content.

With the Power of Each Breath: A Disabled Women's Anthology, edited by Susan Browne, Debra Connors, and Nanci Stern. San Francisco: Cleis Press, 1985. Paper $10.95. About 10 percent of the contributors to this book are identifiably lesbian, including Maureen Brady's "The Field Is Full of Daisies and I'm Afraid to Pass."

With Wings: An Anthology of Literature by and about Women with Disabilities, edited by Marsha Saxton and Florence Howe. New York: Feminist Press, 1987. Paper $14.95. The goals of this joint project of The Feminist Press and the Boston Self-Help Center include providing "a literary forum for the exploration of the experiences of disabled women, white or members of minority groups, heterosexual or lesbian, and of different social classes." Authors self-identified as lesbian include Rebecca Gordon, Adrienne Lee Lauby, Adrienne Rich, and Barbara Ruth.

The Woman That I Am: The Literature and Culture of Contemporary Women of Color, edited by D. Soyini Madison. New York: St. Martin's Press, 1994. Paper $29.95. About a dozen of the one hundred writers from four different ethnicities are identified in the biographical notes as lesbian. Selections in which lesbianism is foregrounded come from Chrystos, Pat Parker, Paula Gunn Allen, and Barbara Smith. Only one lesbian selection appears in a section on growing from girlhood to womanhood (Merle Woo's "Letter to Ma"), and, surprisingly, no explicitly lesbian selections appear in the section on love and sexuality.

II: Lesbian Literature Anthologies

Chicana Lesbians: The Girls Our Mothers Warned Us About, edited by Carla Trujillo. Berkeley, CA: Third Woman Press. Paper $12.95. A multi-genre anthology of selections by twenty-five Chicana lesbians, including Cherríe Moraga, Monica Palacios, Gloria Anzaldúa, Martha Barrera, and Ana Castillo.

Chloe Plus Olivia: An Anthology of Lesbian and Bisexual Literature from the Seventeenth Century to the Present, edited by Lillian Faderman. New York: Viking Press, 1994. Paper $21.95. An eight-hundred-page anthology compiled by the lesbian historian who wrote *Surpassing the Love of Men: Romantic Friendship and Love between Women from the Renaissance to the Present* (1981) and *Odd Girls and Twilight Lovers: A History of Lesbian Life in Twentieth-Century America* (1991). The book is intended as the first literary anthology "that collects the work of a variety of 'lesbian' writers of the past and present and offers it in a historical and theoretical framework."

Dykescapes: Short Fiction by Lesbians, edited by Tina Portillo. Boston: Alyson, 1991. Paper $8.95. Seventeen storytellers, including Lee Lynch and Pamela Gray, "explore such diverse themes as racism, death, lesbian parenting, prison relationships, and interracial love and sex. . . . role-playing, fat-positivity, and intergenerational affairs."

In a Different Light: An Anthology of Lesbian Writers, edited by Carolyn Weathers and Jenny Wrenn. La Mesa, CA: Clothespin Fever Press, 1989. Paper $9.95. A collection of work by authors who read in the Lesbian Writers Series at the Los Angeles bookstore A Different Light between 1984 and 1988. Includes S. Diane Bogus, Jess Wells, Judith McDaniel, and one poem each by Judy Grahn and Paula Gunn Allen.

Inventing Ourselves: Lesbian Life Stories, edited by Hall Carpenter Archives Lesbian Oral History Group. New York: Routledge, 1989. Paper $12.95. Oral histories of fifteen "ordinary" British lesbians. The Hall Carpenter Archives were formed in 1982 and closed in 1989.

Lesbian Culture, An Anthology: The Lives, Work, Ideas, Art and Visions of Lesbians Past and Present, edited by Julia Penelope and Susan Wolfe. Freedom, CA: Crossing Press, 1993. Paper $21.95. This book documents and preserves artifacts of lesbian culture in the twentieth century, mostly since the 1960s. The editors' goal in defining and affirming lesbian culture is not to fix or contain it but to encourage its growth.

Lesbian Love Stories, edited by Irene Zahava. Freedom, CA: Crossing Press. Vol. 1, 1989; paper $10.95. Vol. 2, 1991; paper $9.95. The characters in these stories "are of different ages, colors, sizes, and backgrounds." The collection includes tales of betrayal, loneliness and fear; accounts of pain and loss, of fights and breakups."

Lesbian Plays, Vol. 1, edited by Jill Davis. Portsmouth, NH: Heinemann, 1988. Paper $13.95. Vol. 2, edited by Debby Klein. Heinemann, 1989. Paper $14.95. Volume One includes work by Jill Posener, Libby Mason, Jackie Kay, and Jill W. Fleming. Authors in Volume Two are Catherine Kilcoyne, Sandra Freeman, Sue Frumin, and Cheryl Moch.

New Lesbian Writing: An Anthology, edited by Margaret Cruikshank. San Francisco: Gray Fox, 1994. Paper $7.95. Classic prose and poetry anthology from the editor of *The Lesbian Path* (1980) and the first edition of *Lesbian Studies* (1982). Contains fourteen pages of author photographs.

Nice Jewish Girls: A Lesbian Anthology, edited by Evelyn Torton Beck, new and updated edition. Boston: Beacon Press, 1989. Paper $15.00. "The first plank in building bridges of safety between Jewish lesbians and non-Jews in the lesbian community," according to the editor, this revised anthology continues to be timely and informative.

Our Lives: Lesbian Personal Writings, edited by Frances Rooney. Toronto, Canada: Second Story Press, 1991. Paper $14.95. Women's themes from a lesbian perspective: love, friends, family, children, religion, work, et cetera, as recorded in private journals, diaries, letters, poems, and stories. U.S. authors include Tee Corinne, Jean Mountaingrove, Sapphire, and zana.

Out of the Class Closet: Lesbians Speak, edited by Julia Penelope. Freedom, CA: Crossing Press, 1994. Paper $14.95. Lesbians from diverse classes, races, and ethnic backgrounds tell their stories and articulate theories of class difference among women. Includes imaginative literature as well as social essays.

The Penguin Book of Lesbian Short Stories, edited by Margaret Reynolds. New York: Viking Press, 1994. Cloth $27.50. Contains thirty-two twentieth-century stories with lesbian content, written by both lesbian and nonlesbian authors. Lesbian contributors include Dorothy Allison, Jewelle Gomez, Renee Vivien, Colette, Jeanette Winterson, and others.

Piece of My Heart: A Lesbians of Colour Anthology, edited by Makeda Silvera. Toronto, Canada: Sister Vision Black Women and Women of Color Press, 1991. Paper $16.95. A multi-genre anthology dedicated to Audre Lorde. Authors are mostly but not exclusively Canadian.

Torch to the Heart: Anthology of Lesbian Art and Drama, edited by Sue McConnell-Celi. Red Bank, NJ: Lavender Crystal Press, 1994. Paper $18.95. A unique collection of nine plays by lesbian writers plus lesbian artwork. Some of the plays have been produced in New York at the New York City Lesbian and Gay Center or the WOW Cafe; others are new. The one full-length play, *Sins of the Mothers,* is by Pamela Simones.

Two Friends, and Other Nineteenth-Century Lesbian Stories by American Women Writers, edited by Susan Koppelman. New York: Meridian, 1994. Paper $10.95. Includes selections by Rose Terry Cooke, Elizabeth Stuart Phelps, Constance Fenimore Woolson, Octave Thanet (Alice French), Mary E. Wilkins Freeman, Kate Chopin, Alice Brown, and Sarah Orne Jewett.

The Very Inside: An Anthology of Writing by Asian and Pacific Islander Lesbian and Bisexual Women, edited by Sharon Lim-Hing. Toronto: Sister Vision Black Women and Women of Color Press, 1994. Paper $16.95. A 450-page book containing more than fifty contributions by women originating from different parts of the Asian and Pacific diaspora, including Korea, China, Vietnam, Japan, the Philippines, and elsewhere. The editor is a third-generation Jamaican-born Chinese lesbian living in the United States.

Women on Women: An Anthology of Lesbian Short Fiction, edited by Joan Nestle and Naomi Holoch. New York: NAL/Dutton. Vol. 1, 1990; paper $11.00. Vol. 2, 1993; paper $12.00. Volume One contains stories and novel excerpts mostly from writers well known in the lesbian community in the United States: e.g., June Arnold, Bertha Harris, Jewelle Gomez, Judith McDaniel, Valerie Miner, Leslea Newman, Lee Lynch, and Dorothy Allison. Volume Two contains more recent writers; it is grimmer in tone, reflecting perhaps, the political climate of 1992–93.

Virtually all quoted passages, except for very recent titles, come from the books themselves. Quotations in the annotations for very recent books were taken from *Lambda Rising News, The Lesbian Review of Books, The Women's Review of Books,* or publishers' announcements. A useful reference work is *Contemporary Lesbian Writers of the U.S.: A Bio-Bibliographical Critical Sourcebook,* edited by Sandra Pollack and Denise Knight. Westport, CT: Greenwood Press, 1993. Cloth $99.50.

LESBIANISM IN INTRODUCTORY WOMEN'S STUDIES TEXTBOOKS: TOWARD A RECOGNITION OF DIFFERENCE?

Carolyn Woodward

¿Como poder decir lo que yo siento?
How to articulate these multiple voices always in dialogue?
— Maria Luisa "Papusa" Molina[1]

Every introductory textbook in women's studies speaks from a position of women's marginality in a sexist society. But women are marginalized differently by variables such as class, race and ethnicity, age, dis/ability, religion, sexual orientation, and linguistic practice, and not every women's studies introductory textbook speaks from a clear understanding of multiple identities. Here in the United States in the late twentieth century, we are living through a paradigm shift in human understanding, in which Enlightenment ideas of the rule of the same have been challenged by the facts of diversity. How do we learn to acknowledge differences— the multiplicities in each person, the multiplicities among groups of people? How do we hear our multiple voices "always in dialogue"? In the introductory women's studies classroom, people meet out of a desire to investigate such topics as oppression, stereotyping, gender roles, and social action. Recognition of differences can make the classroom a site of struggle toward community.

Since the late 1960s, lesbianism has been a major force in feminist theory and praxis. But in 1982 Bonnie Zimmerman noted that "[h]eterosexism is alive and well" in introductory women's studies texts, in the pages of which "there are feminists and then there are lesbians; there are women and then there are lesbians."[2] Today, no introductory women's studies text entirely excludes material on lesbianism, and several include more than token coverage. Few of these books, however, represent lesbianism as a center in feminism, and fewer still represent differences among women with the sort of inclusivity that creates movement among centers and margins and allows space for the confrontations out of which we can begin to shape healthy communities.

In 1981, *This Bridge Called My Back: Writings by Radical Women of Color,* edited by Cherríe Moraga and Gloria Anzaldúa, burst onto the scene of feminist activity in the United States. Section headings read like a primer of the theory and praxis that oppression cannot be hierarchized but must be understood in its intersections of sexism, racism, classism, and homophobia: The challenge that *This Bridge* presents is emphasized by its revolutionary expression of varied and sometimes mixed genres—in essays, certainly, and also in poetry, fiction, and letters. Today, nearly fifteen years after its first publication, *Bridge* continues to anger and inspire its readers. This is testimony to its brilliance. However, that *Bridge* continues to be "new" may be testimony, as well, to a studied ignorance among women who write textbooks and plan curricula for women's studies programs. Where are the texts that build on the startling ideas and ways of theorizing that *Bridge* presents?

Although every introductory women's studies textbook published in recent years testifies to the power of *Bridge's* call for an honoring of difference, most of these texts marginalize the topic of difference itself, or attempt to present diversity but lack a clear theoretical base. Only four books attempt to meet the challenge of community based in difference: *All American Women: Lines That Divide, Ties That Bind,* edited by Johnnetta B. Cole (1986); *Changing Our Power: An Introduction to Women Studies,* edited by Jo Whitehorse Cochran, Donna Langston, and Carolyn Woodward (third edition forthcoming in 1995); *Feminist Frontiers III,* edited by Laurel Richardson and Verta Taylor (1993); and *Making Face, Making Soul/Haciendo Caras: Creative and Critical Perspectives of Women of Color,* edited by Gloria Anzaldúa (1990).

Each of these four books aims to present material on lesbianism, homophobia, and contributions of lesbians to feminist thinking in the context of their interrelatedness with such topics as gender, class, race and ethnicity, dis/ability, age, and linguistic practice. In the introductory chapter to *All American Women,* Johnnetta B. Cole writes that "U.S. women" are both "bound by our similarities" and "divided by our differences,"[3] and she quotes Audre Lorde's challenge that we learn to use "'human differences as a spring board for creative change within our lives'" (Cole 28). Discussions of lesbianism are integrated into this chapter: in Cole's note that "privilege can and does coexist with oppression" (6), in a consideration of various sorts of discrimination in the labor force, in an assertion that "family" needs to be redefined, and in a review of the women's movement of the 1970s and early 1980s. However, Cole's book—published in 1986 and not yet revised—is disappointing in that the only section to address lesbian concerns with more than marginal consideration is on sexuality and reproduction.

Changing Our Power intends to introduce women's studies as "a theoretical and academic arm of the feminist movement—the movement that struggles to free women from structured and systematic oppression, and that therefore analyzes and resists oppressions of race, class, body type, pattern of loving, and age, as well as those of gender."[4] As this statement suggests, the text insists that women's studies not lose its ties to activism. Further, specificities of difference are addressed both in separate chapters and as part of the material in more general discussions. Lesbianism is centrally addressed in at least one piece of writing in each unit, and the topics of lesbianism, homophobia, and/or contributions of lesbians are integrated into discussions in each introductory chapter and in at least eighteen other chapters.

While *Changing Our Power* is intended for the beginning women's studies student and includes perspectives from philosophy, history, the social sciences, and the arts, *Feminist Frontiers III* is written from a sociological perspective and would work well in a variety of upper-division women's studies courses. In their introduction, Laurel Richardson and Verta Taylor write that feminist scholars "look at *both* commonalities and differences [and] understand systems of oppression as interlinking: race, class, ethnicity, sexual orientation, and other systems of domination inflect how one experiences gender oppression."[5] The topics of lesbianism, homophobia, and/or lesbian contributions are addressed both in separate selections and frequently as integrated material in more general discussions.

Making Face, Making Soul/Haciendo Caras works well as a central text for women's studies courses on both the introductory and more advanced levels. In her introduction, Gloria Anzaldúa announces no less a goal than "changing culture and all its oppressive interlocking machinations"; she intends her collection "to make accessible to others our struggle with all our identities, our linkage-making strategies and our healing of broken limbs."[6] In *Haciendo Caras,* margins of difference from the dominant culture connect and in their multiple dialogues make a center in which community becomes possible. Lesbians are an integral part of this central consideration of difference and community. Although lesbianism is sometimes treated as a separate topic—as in Paula Gunn Allen's "Some Like Indians Endure"—more commonly it is assumed as one of the positions from which a writer may speak. And lesbianism is important in the selections that address the question of how to build community out of the meetings of difference, as in Anzaldúa's "*La conciencia de la mestiza*: Towards a New Consciousness."

In both *Haciendo Caras* and *Changing Our Power,* lesbianism is represented in some of its own multiplicities.[7] Also, both *Changing Our Power* and *Haciendo Caras* insist that theory and action must not be separated, and in this way each of these texts can work to strengthen ties between women's studies programs and feminist activism in the communities beyond academe. Language in both of these texts is deliberately free of "academic" constructions (such as the use of specialized vocabulary or the passive voice), and sometimes is downright gritty. And, evidencing the example of *Bridge,* each of these two texts presents theory in varied and sometimes mixed genres and includes work by previously unpublished writers alongside material by recognized theorists. Thus, these two texts challenge the dominance of "high theory" and its perpetuation of other kinds of dominance, including the dominance of heterosexism. As Anzaldúa says in *Haciendo Caras,* "In our *mestizaje* theories we create new categories for those of us left out or pushed out of the existing ones" (xxvi).

These texts present the revolutionary idea that community must form not in spite of but because of and be enabled by differences. In the context of this idea, lesbianism and all other "marginal" identities are themselves centers of theory and action. In seven other texts available for the introductory women's studies course, however, this theoretical underpinning is lacking, which weakens their representation of lesbianism. Two books—*Women's Studies: Thinking Women* (1993) and *Modern Feminisms: Political, Literary, Cultural* (1992)—take as their centering focus a commitment to the concept of cultural pluralism and/or the recognition of diversity in feminist thought. However, because these texts lack a commitment to making difference itself the center of social change, "pluralism" and "diversity" remain vague, and lesbian concerns do not seem clearly connected to other issues. In their preface to *Women's Studies,* Jodi Wetzel, Margo Linn Espenlaub, Monys A. Hagen, Annette Bennington McElhiney, and Carmen Braun Williams state that they seek "to encourage pluralism and the appreciation of the unique differences in each of us."[8] Significant treatment of lesbian issues occurs in the section on women's relationships and in the unit on the future of feminism. Readings by Audre Lorde and Julia Penelope are included in the section on the shaping of gender, and Beth Schneider's 1984 analysis of lesbians' workplace participation is one of the readings in the unit on economics. But lesbian perspectives are not specified in the sections on women and politics, women and the law, women and spirituality, or women in the arts.

Modern Feminisms provides a rich collection of excerpts from British and North American feminist documents and theories from the early twentieth century to the present. In her preface, Maggie Humm states her aim "to encapsulate the diversity of feminist views—about race, sexuality, language and creativity, politics and class. . . ."[9] Lesbian perspectives are represented in nearly all of the text's seventeen sections, with works by Virginia Woolf, the Combahee River Collective, Gloria Anzaldúa, Mary Daly, Charlotte Bunch, Adrienne Rich, Luce Irigaray, Audre Lorde, Carroll Smith-Rosenberg, Teresa de Lauretis, and Barbara Smith. Because Humm's text surveys several theoretical arguments and academic disciplines, it can be effectively combined with *Changing Our Power* and/or *Haciendo Caras* in an introductory course in feminist theory. However, it must be noted that the section titled "Lesbian Feminism" represents only that thinking that can be categorized as classic "radical feminism." And in its explication of developments in feminist thought, the text lacks a focus other than the "ambiguity" that Humm believes must accompany the recognition of diversity (403).

In their introduction to the third edition of *Feminist Frameworks: Alternative Theoretical Accounts of the Relations between Women and Men* (1993), which surveys various philosophies of feminism, Alison M. Jaggar and Paula S. Rothenberg write that because "many feminists are no longer willing to apply the term 'feminist' to any perspective not thoroughly multicultural and inclusive in its starting point,"[10] their text features sections on multicultural feminism and global feminism. However, theoretical consideration of homophobia and/or of sexualities, or of specifically lesbian philosophies, are found only in the sections on radical feminism and on multicultural feminism. And it is only in the sections on family and on sexuality that social issues of concern to lesbians are significantly addressed.

Four other texts respond to the impetus toward recognition of difference with gestures that do little more than add and stir. In the fifth edition of *Women: A Feminist Perspective* (1994), Jo Freeman acknowledges diversity with the creation of Part VII: Feminism and Diversity. But diversity permeates our society; the concept needs to permeate curricula, not be set aside in a separate section. In *Women,* attention to lesbian issues is limited to Rose Weitz's cross-cultural analysis of sanctions faced by lesbians, Lisa Ransdell's consideration of twentieth-century lesbian feminism in the United States, and brief mentions in a few other essays. And in Freeman's historical overview of the U.S. women's movement, lesbian politics are represented by her claim that a gay-straight split that "consumed most of the time and energy" of small grassroots feminist groups during the late 1960s and early 1970s occurred "because a vocal group [that] articulated lesbianism as the essential feminist idea" eventually dominated the groups, the result being a diminished political impact on the larger society.[11]

Freeman's generalizations do not accurately represent what was happening in the country as a whole. In a 1993 article in *Signs,* Verta A. Taylor and Leila Rupp discuss some of the complexities of lesbianism/feminism in groups in Columbus, Ohio, between 1970 and 1990.[12] And during the late 1960s and early 1970s I lived in Seattle, Washington, where in no sense were the energies of grassroots organizations sapped by a gay-straight split. For example, a diverse group of women were served by the grassroots programs at the University Young Women's Christian Association: Abortion Referral Service, Rape Relief, Aradia Women's Clinic, Mechanica (jobs for women in the skilled trades), the Women's Divorce Cooperative, and the Lesbian Resource Center. Indeed, for a time there was a women's art gallery and poetry space at the YWCA—and it featured such memorable pieces as the "Mount Rainier Diaphragm" sculpture and the accompanying "Ode to a Diaphragm." One small group predominated by lesbians did emerge in Seattle during this time—Leftist Lezzies, which worked on such issues as Indian fishing rights, the rights of Filipino cannery workers, the establishment of legal precedent in cases of women defending themselves against abuse (the Yvonne Wanrow case), the protection of gay and lesbian civil rights in employment and housing, and the election to Congress of Mike Lowry, who today is serving as the governor of Washington State.[13] In trivializing the work of small groups and presenting lesbian politics in terms of an ostensible dominance that prevented constructive action, Freeman's analysis is both false and damaging.

Questions of difference and diversity are treated as problems that must be addressed, but are not conceptualized as sources of positive energy, in Sheila Ruth's *Issues in Feminism: An Introduction to Women's Studies* (second edition, 1990).

In this text, the difference of lesbianism is not integral to feminism: Ruth makes brief mention of lesbians, lesbianism, or heterosexism in the introductions to only three of her nine chapters, and lesbian identity is a central consideration in only two of the text's many individual articles.[14] There is nothing on lesbianism either in a chapter on the origins of female subordination or in a chapter on societal institutions and discrimination, and none of the individual pieces in the chapter on feminist activism treat either the theory and praxis of lesbianism or the work of lesbians.

In the preface to the third edition of *Women in American Society: An Introduction to Women's Studies* (1994), Virginia Sapiro says that she treats "the diversity of women" in an "integrated" rather than "segregated" manner. Certainly, questions of difference need to be integrated, but differences must, as well, be highlighted for separate considerations—otherwise, it is all too common, for example, for white, middle-class, young heterosexual women to dominate. In this text, lesbians are considered primarily as victims of oppression, for example as mothers who lose our children in custody cases. We appear as targets of demeaning labels (but not as women who claim and give power to some of these terms, such as "dyke"). Our concerns are not integrated into sections on the family or on health care. And it is only in the section on sexual orientation and sexual practices that we are considered as contributors to feminist theory and praxis. All this is especially frustrating, given that Sapiro has added to her third edition a unit of commonality and difference in which she states her commitment to a "complex" model of understanding the social bases of oppression, in which one takes care to identify "the circumstances under which the role of gender is especially contingent on other specific aspects of social existence."[15] Her text as a whole does not demonstrate her commitment to this model.

In 1983, the Hunter College Women's Studies Collective published *Women's Realities, Women's Choices*. A great deal of dialogue about difference and community has occurred in the last decade-plus, and although the book is still in print, its consideration of these issues is outdated. The only section to significantly treat issues of concern to lesbians is the chapter "Choosing Alternatives." The difference of lesbianism is given token attention in sections on the family, religion, and politics; there is nothing on lesbian theory or praxis in either the section on feminist theory or the section on political action in the 1980s.

In this discussion, I have noted (1) texts that encourage movement among centers and margins, (2) texts that focus on a loosely defined cultural pluralism, and (3) texts that demonstrate only token recognition of difference. Just what, then, do we in women's studies mean when we say "feminism"? In the definition that has guided my consideration of women's studies curricula, feminism links theory and activism and is always recharging the positive energy for community that is produced when we meet as allies who acknowledge our differences. In women's studies classrooms, I have participated in border-crossing dialogues that have led to the formation of community, and in those dialogues I have witnessed teaching from persons marked by differences from the Eurocentric, patriarchal, and heterosexist ideals of Enlightenment humanism. Because of this, I have come to believe that difference itself can engender radical theory and action, and that in our differently marked alliances we can generate sufficient love and power to eradicate the ideology of domination that permeates our society. In Barbara Smith's words, "Anything less than this is not feminism, but merely female self-aggrandizement."[16] Those of us who write, teach, and plan curricula in women's studies will do well to attend to these hopes for building community from our differences.

NOTES

1. Maria Luisa "Papusa" Molina, "Fragmentations: Meditations on Separatism," *Signs* 19, no. 2 (winter 1994): 452.

2. Bonnie Zimmerman, "One Out of Thirty: Lesbianism in Women's Studies Textbooks," in *Lesbian Studies: Present and Future*, ed. Margaret Cruikshank (New York: The Feminist Press, 1982), 130.

3. Johnnetta B. Cole, ed., *All American Women: Lines That Divide, Ties That Bind* (New York: The Free Press, 1986), 1.

4. Jo Whitehorse Cochran, Donna Langston, and Carolyn Woodward, eds., *Changing Our Power: An Introduction to Women Studies*, 2nd ed. (Dubuque, IA: Kendall-Hunt, 1991), xvii.

5. Laurel Richardson and Verta Taylor, eds., *Feminist Frontiers III* (New York: McGraw-Hill, 1993), 1, 2.

6. Gloria Anzaldúa, "Haciendo caras, una entrada," in *Making Face, Making Soul/Haciendo Caras: Creative and Critical Perspectives by Women of Color* (San Francisco: Aunt Lute, 1990), xvi.

7. See, for example, in *Haciendo Caras*, Audre Lorde's "I Am Your Sister: Black Women Organizing Across Sexualities"(321–25), which critiques homophobia among black women, and Jewelle Gomez's "I Lost It at the Movies" (203–6), a hilarious and celebratory narrative about "lesbian money" and acceptance of sexual difference among three generations of women; and *Changing Our Power* for Jo Whitehorse Cochran's poem about lesbian battering, "I Am Laughing" (297–99), and Cochran, Langston, and Woodward's affirmation in their general introduction that "we are creating together as women— friends and lovers—a change, a changing in our power" (xix).

8. Jodi Wetzel, Margo Linn Espenlaub, Monys A. Hagen, Annette Bennington McElhiney, and Carmen Braun Williams, eds., *Women's Studies: Thinking Women* (Dubuque, IA: Kendall-Hunt, 1993), xviii.

9. Maggie Humm, ed., *Modern Feminisms: Political, Literary, Cultural* (New York: Columbia University Press, 1992), xi.

10. Alison M. Jaggar and Paula S. Rothenberg, *Feminist Frameworks: Alternative Theoretical Accounts of the Relations between Women and Men*, 3rd ed. (New York: McGraw-Hill, 1993), xiii.

11. Jo Freeman, "From Suffrage to Women's Liberation: Feminism in Twentieth-Century America," in *Women: A Feminist Perspective*, 4th ed. (Mountain View, CA: Mayfield Publishing, 1989), 517.

12. See Verta A. Taylor and Leila Rupp, "Women's Culture and Lesbian Feminist Activism: A Reconsideration of Cultural Feminism," in *Signs* 19, no.1 (autumn 1993): 32–61.

13. During the early 1970s, I directed the Abortion Referral Service at the University YWCA in Seattle. I thank Karen Rudolph for information about the Seattle group Leftist Lezzies (personal conversation, August 1994).

14. These are Elsa Gidlow's "The Spiritual Significance of the Self-Identified Woman" and E.M. Ettorre's "A New Look at Lesbianism." Additionally, lesbianism figures into an excerpt from Audre Lorde's *The Cancer Journals*.

15. Virginia Sapiro, *Women in American Society: An Introduction to Women's Studies*, 3rd. ed. (Mountain View, CA: Mayfield, 1994), 102.

16. Barbara Smith, "Racism and Women's Studies," in *Changing Our Power*, 11. The essay originally appeared in *All the Women Are White, All the Men Are Black, But Some of Us Are Brave: Black Women's Studies*, edited by Gloria T. Hull, Patricia Bell Scott, and Barbara Smith (New York: The Feminist Press at CUNY, 1982). Other pioneering work toward a feminism that demands a paradigm shift

in human understanding may be found in Gloria Anzaldúa's "La prieta" in *This Bridge Called My Back: Writings by Radical Women of Color,* edited by Cherríe Moraga and Gloria Anzaldúa, 2nd ed. (Latham, NY: Kitchen Table/Women of Color Press, 1983), 198–290; Audre Lorde's "The Master's Tools Will Never Dismantle the Master's House," in *Sister Outsider: Essays and Speeches by Audre Lorde* (Trumansburg, NY: The Crossing Press, 1984), 110–13; and bell hooks's *Ain't I a Woman: Black Women and Feminism* (Boston: South End Press, 1981).

PART FOUR

Transforming Knowledge

BREAKING THE SILENCE: PUTTING LATINA LESBIAN HISTORY AT THE CENTER

Yolanda Chávez Leyva

1994. Marty sits on a mustard-colored flower-patterned recliner in her living room. "What was it like for lesbians when you were young? Did anyone ever talk about it?" I ask her, hoping for a story.

She shakes her head, "No," and repeats the phrase that has become so common to me, "Everybody knew but no one talked about it." She has lived her entire life in a small, now mid-sized, Southwestern city where everyone in town knew everyone else. I've seen photographs—young women with short haircuts, jeans rolled up to the ankle, white socks and loafers, all smiles. "Norma García," she begins, "was always in love with Dora. Every time there was a picnic, she'd have me a sing a song for Dora." Then Marty begins singing, "Nunca . . ." "Norma's eyes always teared up when I started singing."

"What happened to the woman she was in love with?" I ask. "I don't know, she got married. They say she married a gay man. That's what they say." Her voice drifts a bit. "It was harder back then than now."[1]

It is a forty-year-old story told casually one evening in a darkened living room, in part a story of unrequited love, universal in its pathos, yet also much more. It is also a story of silences. Latina lesbians have survived both because of that silence and the protection it has provided, and despite the many limits and compromises it has imposed. Silence has been for us a paradox—both protecting us and harming us. In recent years, Latina lesbians have undertaken to break that silence, their voices singing in intricate harmonies and disharmonies with every word spoken, with every poem written, with every story told. To remember our history is to draw together the pieces from many continents and from myriad experiences, from those of the fifth-generation Chicana to those of the *recién llegada*, the most recent immigrant. To speak our history is to learn the words that we were called and that we called each other—*marimachas, jotas, tortilleras, manflores, patas, amigas íntimas, cachaperas, primas,* girlfriends, lovers.

It must begin with an understanding that Latina lesbian history, or more accurately, *histories,* since we are a diverse people, must be looked at on their own terms rather than as simply an extension, or sidebar, to the evolution of white lesbian identity. The trajectory of Latina lesbian histories challenges the models, the chronology, the very language set forth by scholars of white lesbian and gay history. Regional differences, disparate economic opportunities, intersections of racism and sexism, immigrant status, nativity, ethnic affiliation, varying degrees of assimilation, and, finally, cultural and religious values, often distinct from those of the dominant society, create a unique context for Latina lesbian history. It is within this multiple context, then, that we can begin to explore the evolution of Latina lesbian sexuality, community, and political identity.

Despite the emergence over the last two and a half decades of an important body of work documenting the historical evolution of both a modern lesbian identity as well as the emergence of lesbian communities in the United States, in most histories Latina lesbians remain barely visible, appearing only when we become visible to the white lesbian community. In spite of assurances of cultural sensitivity, scholars present gay and lesbian people of color in marginal roles. We are labeled "subcultures," on the "periphery" of the lesbian community, "constituencies within the gay population."[2] Our history is viewed from afar, through the eyes of others. Latina lesbian history, like the histories of other peoples of color, requires new and creative methodologies—a truer telling of these histories calls for a conscientious effort at what Ann Ducille labels "centering the periphery."[3]

Language becomes an integral tool, and challenge, in any effort to center the periphery. As Ducille points out, there is "a pressing need to revise the language by which people of color are written in our scholarship" (127). The cultural values and assumptions associated with such words as "heterosexual," "homosexual," "lesbian," or "gay" make their use problematic. As Madeline Davis and Elizabeth Kennedy disclose in their path-breaking study of the lesbian community in Buffalo, New York, their narrators "rarely used the word lesbian," preferring to use "butch and femme" or "butch and her girlfriend." With this acknowledgment, Davis and Kennedy go on to define lesbians as "all women in the twentieth century who pursued sexual relationships with other women."[4] The question of who can or should be classified historically as a lesbian and whether sexual contact is a requisite is an ongoing debate within lesbian studies. When applied across cultures, the question becomes even more clouded. Across cultures, even the meaning of words as seemingly obvious as "manhood" or "womanhood" cannot be assumed.

Latinas in the United States, to varying degrees, have been socialized into a system that amalgamates white U.S. values and culture with that of Latin America. This assimilation into white American culture has proceeded at different rates, and with different consequences, dependent upon the historical context. How that amalgamation has played out in women's sexual identification is not entirely clear, particularly since the public sexual identities available to women, have been historically quite limited. As Donna Guy suggests in her recent article on Latin American gender history, however, women have been able to "maintain various sexual identities disguised within the conformity of roles of daughters, wives, and widows."[5] The task of the historian, then, is to uncover the layers of mystery and mystification which obscure the spectrum of women's true sexual identities.

1972. We're sitting together at the kitchen table. She's sixty years old and she likes to tell stories. "I was just seventeen years old in 1929 and I would go dancing with my husband's sister. She was a wonderful dancer. When we first met I didn't know how to dance at all. She said, 'Don't worry. I'll teach you.' So every Sunday afternoon we'd go to the tardeada and we'd dance. I fell in love with her. I was really in love with her, not my husband. I could hardly wait until Sunday afternoons just to dance with her." She laughs, her eyes twinkle. For a minute she's a seventeen-year-old with beautiful legs and full red lips in the arms of another woman.

Where do we fit into the stories of such women? In another time would she have spent her life with a woman? What opportunities were available to her to center her life around women? And where does this story fit into lesbian history? It also raises some important questions regarding the acceptability of "being in love" with another woman. The narrator of this story did not consider herself a lesbian nor did she consider her emotional and erotic feelings towards her sister-in-law as abnormal. Did she consider herself "heterosexual" however? Although scholars often refer to heterosexuality as if its definition were universal, it, like homosexuality, is socially constructed. While we are beginning to understand more clearly the expanded options available to heterosexual men within the Latin American social and cultural system, we know very little about what heterosexuality means today, or what it has meant historically to women. If we hear the voices of women at all, often all that we know is what women *said* they felt. It is much more difficult to uncover what the bonds between women truly meant to those women.

What opportunities have been available, historically, for Latina women to develop such bonds? As Oliva Espín points out, Latino culture encourages women to depend heavily on each other rather than on men.[6] In addition, sex-segregated activities, from social activities to church functions, provide opportunities for women to form deep, often intense, relationships with each other. In fact, the Catholic Church, so often cited for the ways in which it has limited women's opportunities, may also have created some spaces for women. Without discounting the ways in which religious conventions limited women's ability to be themselves, it is as important to understand the ways in which women maneuvered within such institutions. Since the colonial period, for example, the option to live in all-women religious communities provided an escape from societal restrictions for some women. It is telling that Sor Juana Inés de la Cruz, a Mexican nun who was the most famous writer and thinker of her century, has become an idol for many contemporary Latina lesbians.

1992. At a lesbian house party I meet two women, fairly recent immigrants to the United States. They've migrated here from Mexico because they want to work, and because they want to live more freely as lesbians, although they won't use that word. They are very active in their parish, working in women's groups that organize bazaars and religious processions. "We go to confession every Saturday," María confides. "And every Saturday, I tell the priest, I love Elisa. The priest says it's good. God wants us to love each other. Then I tell him we have sex. He gets mad and lectures me and tells me to do penance. Then during the week I make love to Elisa. It starts all over again. So the next Saturday, I'm back in the confessional, telling the priest that I love Elisa."

It would be extremely misleading, however, to assume that the Catholic Church was or is the only religious avenue open to women in Latin America. African, as well as Native American, religions have survived, and even flourished, in Latin America despite ongoing attacks by the Catholic Church. Women have found different options available to them within these systems wherein they can express their sexual identities. The work of Cuban writer and folklorist Lydia Cabrera, for example, provides evidence of a strong lesbian presence within Santería from the nineteenth century to the present.[7]

The formation of a sexual identity is a complex, ongoing process that involves both the individual and the community. An individual's sexual identity is but one component which determines a person's place within her community. In turn, sexual identity helps to shape a person's definition of community. A recent survey conducted at a national Lesbiana Latina conference asked women to answer who they thought of when they heard the word "community": "Latinas, lesbians, homosexuals . . . because they all aptly describe me." "Familia, extended through neighborhoods." "I think of the women that give me support and I think of the Latino community as a whole." "Gays and lesbians." "I see it in layers. Closest to me are other Chicanas with similar experience, then other Chicanos, then other Latinos and lesbians."[8] What these answers reveal are definitions which incorporate very personalized relationships (family, neighborhoods) with sexual identity (gay, lesbian, homosexual), ethnic identity (Chicanas/Chicanos) and as a broader political identity (Latinos).

Remaining within the family and community are vital survival strategies for Latinas struggling to cope with what has often been a hostile, violent, racist outside environment.[9] In addition, fewer economic opportunities have lessened the avenues available to many Latinas to leave their families. Finally, although the pressure on daughters to remain at home until marriage has eased in recent years, it continues to be an important consideration when investigating the ways in which Latinas, particularly lesbians, have negotiated their lives. When scholars of lesbian history posit that one prerequisite for the formation of a lesbian identity is the opportunity to leave the family unit, they ignore the possibility that such an identity can be negotiated with the family unit. Latina lesbian history challenges a number of other aspects of the Anglo-lesbian paradigm of the emergence of modern lesbian identity: urbanization, which allows individuals to lead relatively anonymous lives; economic opportunities, which allow women to become self-supporting; a public culture that allows lesbians to find each other; and finally, the eroticization of individuals by intellectuals who view sexuality as central to a person's identity.[10] These factors take on different meanings and nuances, not yet fully understood, when we look at Latina lesbian experiences in the United States.

The importance of community, like family, both shapes and is shaped by the interplay of sexual identity, ethnicity, and gender. Community is yet another paradox that has created spaces for Latina lesbians while at the same time acting as an agent of control. The desire and need to remain within the community, however individually defined, raises a number of important issues. What compromises have Latina lesbians made in order to remain within their communities? In what ways have Latina lesbians created forms of resistance to that silence? And how has silence allowed lesbians to maintain a place within their communities? Why was it possible, in the first place, to continue "not talking about it"? At what moment did lesbianism become such a threat that it was constructed as a threat to the whole race? Was it when the silence was broken? What happened within families and within communities when that unspoken contract—silence in return for some type of acceptance—was severed?

One response is that ethnic identity has become a form of sexual control. The construction of lesbianism "as a sickness we get from American women and American culture" works to control women's sexual behavior by threatening to take away their ethnic identity, by implicating them as not *true* Latinas.[11] This is a serious threat to many women. This construction strives to take lesbianism away as a possible option for women with strong ethnic identities. Well into contemporary times, women seeking to expand their options continue to face accusations of being too Americanized, *vendidas* (sell-outs) or *agabachadas* (a derogatory term for Anglicized). For example, in the early 1970s, women and men engaged in often heated debates regarding the implications of the nascent Chicana feminist movement, which called for an analysis of women as an oppressed group and which sought to find solutions to the needs and issues of Chicanas.[12] According to sociologist Alma García, Chicana feminist lesbians experienced even harsher attacks by cultural nationalists who saw women solely as wives and mothers.[13] The connections between lesbianism and feminism and the use of ethnic identity to control women deserve fuller investigation.

1974. Small, one-story yellow and white houses encircle a bare dirt courtyard. Tiny square cement porches are surrounded by plants and flowers, which despite the deadening heat, flourish in old coffee cans painted red and blue and purple. I see four or five children running across the yard, an old woman sitting on a chair staring at the traffic, and a middle-aged woman hanging laundry on a sagging clothes line. All around, the desert heat sits heavy. That's where La Sylvia lives—I've heard about her from the neighborhood kids even before I started seeing her at the gay bar. They hang out at her house; she listens to them, gives them advice when they ask. She has a steady girlfriend. I see them most weekends at the bar with Sylvia's best friend, Charlie. La Sylvia and Charlie are always together. Charlie could almost pass for a man—her lean body in men's clothing, usually jeans, western shirts, and boots. Only the hint of breasts reveal her to be a woman. They drink their beers, heads leaning towards each other, telling stories, taking long drags on cigarettes. Sometimes Charlie tells us about all her old girlfriends and La Sylvia just smiles. I'm eighteen years old, dealing with my own emerging identity, and always in awe of these two butch women. Twenty years later I can look back and see how their very look was a form of resistance—without words, they declared their identity in that neighborhood where everyone "just knew" but never really talked about it.

The emergence of a Latina/o lesbian and gay movement in the last twenty-five years has heightened the debate surrounding ethnicity and sexuality. In recent years, for example, the Radical Right, often with the cooperation of conservative segments of communities of color, has endeavored to place gays and lesbians in opposition to people of color. These efforts have attempted to erase the place of Latina/o lesbians and gay men within our own communities. In response, activists have declared their unwillingness to deny any one part of their ethnic, gender, and sexual identities. This conscious effort to embrace all the separate parts of identity is a hallmark of gay and lesbian political organizing within communities of color.

The history of political organizing incorporating ethnicity and sexuality begins with the inception of the gay rights movement itself. According to John D'Emilio, people of color began organizing separately within a year of the Stonewall Riot.[14] In the decade following the 1969 riot, Latina lesbians and Latino gay men organized across the United States. El Comité de Orgullo Homosexual Latino-americano (New York City), Comunidad de Orgullo Gay (Puerto Rico), Greater Liberated Chicanos (Los Angeles), and the Gay Latino Alliance (San Francisco) emerged in the early 1970s. By the 1980s, Latinas Lesbianas Unidas (Los Angeles), Ellas (Texas), and Las Buenas Amigas (New York City) gave voice to Latina lesbians. In 1987, a group of activists formed LLEGO, the National Latina and Latino Lesbian and Gay Organization.[15]

The genesis of a Latina/o lesbian and gay movement raises important analytical questions. There has been little analysis of the relationship between the civil rights movement within communities of color and organizations of gays and lesbians of color. D'Emilio has suggested that the "rhetoric and politics of such groups as the Black Panthers and the Young Lords" may have inspired, or at least provided a backdrop, for the actions of young gay men of color who participated in the Stonewall Riot (240–41). Hence, we might question Lillian Faderman's conclusion crediting white "radicals" with "foster[ing] awareness in minority lesbians, who now began to see themselves as a group with lesbian and feminist political interests" (Faderman 1988, 285). This artificial separation of one part of a political identity from another does a disservice to the true history of lesbians and gay men of color. It reflects the distorted vision of Latina lesbians and other lesbians of color which comes across in so many studies of U.S. lesbians. Rather than the true picture, what we see is a mirror image, a reversal of what is really there. Furthermore, if the gay rights movement in this country owes its inspiration to the civil rights movement, how much more can gay people of color themselves claim a connection? How did an understanding of what it meant to be a person of color in the United States influence individuals' understanding of what it meant to be lesbian or gay?

Latina lesbian history puts Latina lesbians at the center. It is a history that challenges scholars to look at the story from a new angle—from the inside looking out rather than from the outside looking in. It calls for new language, new explanations, new ways to understand the evolution of Latina lesbian sexuality, community, and political identity. It is a call "to come to terms with our past in order to develop a better future where we can all grow together."[16]

NOTES

1. The names in these stories are pseudonyms.

2. Lillian Faderman, *Odd Girls and Twilight Lovers: A History of Lesbian Life in Twentieth-Century America* (New York: Penguin Books, 1991), 285; John D'Emilio and Estelle Freedman, *Intimate Matters: A History of Sexuality in America* (New York: Harper and Row, 1988), 324.

3. Ann Ducille, "'Othered' Matters: Reconceptualizing Dominance and Difference in the History of Sexuality in America," *Journal of the History of Sexuality* 1, no. 1 (1990): 107.

4. Madeline Davis and Elizabeth Kennedy, *Boots of Leather, Slippers of Gold: The History of a Lesbian Community* (New York: Routledge, 1993), 6.

5. Donna Guy, "Future Directions in Latin American Gender History," *The Americas* 52, no. 1 (July 1994): 9.

6. Oliva Espín, "Cultural and Historical Influences on Sexuality in Hispanic/Latin Women: Implications for Psychotherapy," in *Pleasure and Danger: Exploring Female Sexuality,* edited by Carole S. Vance (Boston: Routledge & Kegan Paul, 1984), 155.

7. Lydia Cabrera, *El Monte; Igbo-Finda; Ewe Orisha. Vititi Nfinda.* (Miami, FL: Ediciones Universal, 1975), 58–59.

8. Lesbiana Latina survey, conducted by Yolanda Leyva at *Adelante con nuestra visón:* First National Latina Lesbian Leadership and Self-Empowerment Conference, Tucson, AZ, 16–18 September 1994.

9. Ana Castillo, "La Macha: Toward a Beautiful Whole Self," in *Chicana Lesbians,* edited by Carla Trujillo (Berkeley, CA: Third Woman Press, 1991), 38.

10. See, for example, Faderman, *Odd Girls and Twilight Lovers,* and Davis and Kennedy, *Boots of Leather, Slippers of Gold.*

11. Oliva Espín, "Issues of Identity in the Psychology of Latina Lesbians," in *Lesbian Psychologies: Explorations and Challenges,* edited by Boston Lesbian Psychologies Collective (Urbana, IL: University of Illinois Press: 1987), 40.

12. See, for example, Sonia A. López, "The Role of the Chicana within the Student Movement," in *Essays on La Mujer,* edited by Rosaura Sánchez (Los Angeles: University of California, Chicano Studies Center Publications, 1977); Alfredo Mirandé and Evangelina Enríquez, *La Chicana: The Mexican American Woman* (Chicago: University of Chicago Press, 1979).

13. Alma M. García, "The Development of Chicana Feminist Discourse, 1970–1980" in *Unequal Sisters: A Multi-Cultural Reader in U.S. Women's History,* edited by Ellen Carol DuBois and Vicki L. Ruiz (New York: Routledge, 1990).

14. John D'Emilio, *Making Trouble: Essays on Gay History, Politics and the University* (New York: Routledge, 1992), 261.

15. Dennis Medina, "Gay and Lesbian Latinos/as: A History of Organizing," *Nuestra Herencia,* (Washington, DC: LLEGO, 1994.) See also Gonzalo Aburto, "Abriendo caminos, nuestra contribución" in the same issue.

16. Liz, "My Name Is Liz (Oral History)," in *Compañeras: Latina Lesbians,* edited by Juanita Ramos (New York: Routledge, 1987), 80.

FINDING THE LESBIANS IN LESBIAN HISTORY: REFLECTIONS ON FEMALE SAME-SEX SEXUALITY IN THE WESTERN WORLD

Leila Rupp

The central question facing students of lesbian history is: Where are the lesbians? This is not just a question of sources, despite the fact that one often feels a bit like Gretel, desperately searching for the bread-crumb trail leading out of the woods. So many of the sources for lesbian history have been destroyed, both by women fearful of leaving a trace and by hostile outsiders determined to wipe out any evidence of the existence of women who loved and had sex with other women. Blanche Wiesen Cook reports that Lorena Hickok—who remembered "the feeling of that soft spot just north-east of the corner of your mouth against my lips" in one of her surviving missives—and Esther Lape fed to the fire letters they had exchanged with Eleanor Roosevelt after the First Lady's death.[1] And in sixteenth-century Geneva, a jurist recommended leaving out the customary description of the crime for women sentenced to death for same-sex sexual relations lest other women, equally weak-willed and lascivious, be tempted to follow their example.[2] But the trail has not entirely vanished. The problem is less one of sources than of definition: who, among the women whose stories we can find, can be called a "lesbian"?

The question comes up at all because, until the late nineteenth century, the concept and identity of "lesbian" in the modern sense did not exist. Of course, women had long loved and engaged in sexual relationships with other women, and the existence of such behaviors was no secret, despite attempts to keep it quiet. But loving a woman did not place one in a category based on sexual object choice—that is, the sex of one's partner was not all-determining—until Western culture devised a classification scheme that differentiated people known as "heterosexuals" from those considered "homosexuals." If we confine "lesbians" to those who have claimed the label and identity, if only to themselves, our history is very short.

Historians interested in female same-sex sexuality, along with lesbian activists, have taken different approaches to the question of who counts and who does not. Adrienne Rich's concepts of "lesbian existence" and the "lesbian continuum," which include woman-identified women who resisted compulsory heterosexuality in a variety of ways, have proven influential.[3] However, the "sex radical" position in the "sex wars" of the 1980s has called attention to the denial of sexuality implicit in such a definition.[4] In her classic article, Blanche Wiesen Cook claimed as lesbians all "women who love women, who choose women to nurture and support and to create a living environment in which to work creatively and independently. . . ."[5] But do we then forget about sex? Is it not important?

These are questions with which lesbian historians must grapple. The historical evidence that we have, at this point in time, tends to reveal three different phenomena connected to "lesbian history" or, put more precisely, the history of female same-sex love and sexuality: romantic love between women, transgendered behavior, and sexual acts. In almost all cases, we are left still unsure what the evidence really means in light of our modern conception of lesbian life and lesbian identity.[6]

A few examples illustrate the problem. We now know a great deal about "romantic friendships" and "Boston marriages" between eighteenth- and nineteenth-century middle- and upper-class women in the industrialized Western world.[7] Although scholars are beginning to question just how acceptable they were, passionate attachments between women, often lasting through marriages, were at the very least relatively common and openly discussed without disapproval. Thus Molly Hallock Foote wrote to her friend Helena in the early 1870s: "I wanted so to put my arms round my girl of all the girls in the world and tell her . . . I love her as wives do love their husbands, as *friends* who have taken each other for life. . . ."

And when Helena decided to marry, Molly wrote to proclaim her love and passion and also addressed her fiancé: "Do you know sir, that until you came along I believe that she loved me almost as girls love their lovers. *I know I loved her so.* Don't you wonder that I can stand the sight of you."[8] Although this last suggests that, for Molly at least, marriage did interfere with her romantic friendship, the fact remains that Molly and Helena's love was not something to be hidden from the men in their lives.

To take another example, African-American poet Angelina Weld Grimké, the grandniece of abolitionists Sarah and Angelina Grimké, formed a romantic friendship with her school friend Mamie Burrill. In 1896, Burrill wrote to Grimké: "Could I just come to meet thee once more, in the old sweet way, just coming at your calling, and like an angel bending o'er you breathe into your ear, 'I love you.'" Angelina, later that year, expressed her own longing: "Oh Mamie[,] if you only knew how my heart beats when I think of you and it yearns and pants to gaze, if only for one second upon your lovely face."[9] But Grimké, perhaps because of the increasing suspicion towards women's relationships that accompanied the creation of the deviant category of the lesbian and her own experience of a broken heart, came to obscure her desires in her published poetry. Yet in unpublished lyrics and published verses addressed to a gender-unspecified lover, Grimké poured out the pain of an unidentified lost love.

Women's expressions of love for one another, during a period in which such declarations did not immediately point to a sexual relationship, leave us uncertain about the actual nature of such ties. Did women, conceptualized by the mainstream society as lacking in sexual desire, love and kiss and caress and sleep with each other but not "have sex?" Does it matter?

We also have evidence of women who crossed the gender line by taking on the clothing, work, and social roles of men and marrying women. Catharine Linck, in eighteenth-century Germany, disguised herself as a man to serve in the army. After her stint in the military, she took on a man's job and married a woman, making a dildo and testicles from leather and pigs' bladders in order, as the court in a similar case put it, to "counterfeit the office of a husband." She was discovered when her wife, after an argument, confessed to her mother that Catharine was a woman. Like other women in early modern Europe who claimed both the occupational and sexual privileges of men, she was executed for her crimes.[10]

On the other side of the Atlantic and more than 150 years later, a French-born San Francisco woman by the name of Jeanne Bonnet took to wearing men's clothes. Arrested frequently for her penchant for male dress, Bonnet refused to pay a penny of her fines and instead went to jail, proclaiming her intention never to change her ways. In 1875, she organized a gang of ex-prostitutes who swore off men, arousing the ire of their pimps. Waiting for a gang member who was probably her lover, she was shot to death in 1876.[11]

By the turn of the century in the United States and Europe, as Bonnet's story begins to suggest, cross-dressing women, in the past always isolated from one another, began to come together in urban areas. Within the sexual underworld of big cities, women who dressed as men but did not try to pass as one came to be known as "dikes," from the term for a man all dressed up or "diked out" for a night on the town. Both urban working-class women and wealthy women in bohemian circles affected male dress for a variety of reasons, giving rise to the association made by such sexologists as Havelock Ellis between same-sex sexuality and gender "inversion."[12] At the height of the Harlem Renaissance, the African-American cultural flowering of the 1920s, bisexual and lesbian performers such as Ma Rainey and Gladys Bentley sang of "bulldaggers," connecting a preference for male attire and female company, as in Rainey's "Prove It on Me Blues": "Went out last night with a crowd of my friends, /They must've been women, 'cause I don't like no men./It's true I wear a collar and a tie. . . ."[13]

If transgressions of the gender line outraged mainstream Euroamerican society and found tolerance in the heady days of the Harlem Renaissance, some Native American cultures, primarily in western North America, included a cross-gender role, at least before the late nineteenth century. Women known as *hwame* (Mohave), *kwiraxame* (Maricopa), *tw!nnaek* (Klamath), *koskalaka* (Lakota), or *warrhameh*

(Cocopa) took on the mannerisms, clothing, and work typical of men, and they also married women. Although the cross-gender role had complex spiritual meanings, it is significant that the sex and gender systems of these cultures, prior to the impact of Euroamerican imperialism, made a place for such individuals. Although the cross-gender female became a social male, her sexual behavior with her wife was not considered heterosexual but rather rated its own terminology.[14]

Although in many of the cases of women who crossed the gender line we also have evidence of sexual activity, we are left with many puzzling questions. Did the early modern European and U.S. women who defied their societies and risked death or imprisonment to take on the roles of men do so in order to pursue relationships with women? Or were their motives primarily social and economic, but passing as a man required sexual interaction with women? Does it matter? What about their wives? Should the *hwame* and *koskalaka,* who took on a cross-gendered lifestyle in a spiritual context, be considered lesbians?

Finally, we come to examples of sexual acts between women. As already suggested by the case of Catharine Linck, our evidence generally comes from court records, notoriously difficult documents to analyze. For one thing, women accused of sexual acts had every reason to deny having committed them, and women caught with other women had cause to portray themselves as innocent victims. In the case of Benedetta Carlini, a seventeenth-century Italian abbess, and Bartolomea Crivelli, a younger and less powerful sister in the convent, Crivelli testified to the investigating Church authorities that Carlini had forced her into "the most immodest acts." According to their report, ". . . Benedetta would grab her by the arm and throw her by force on the bed. Embracing her, she would put her under herself and kissing her as if she were a man, she would speak words of love to her. And she would stir on top of her so much that both of them corrupted themselves."[15]

As in the case of Catharine Linck, we have evidence of a sexual act, but what does it mean? Another court case, this one from the early nineteenth century, raises some of the same questions but also makes a link between sexual behavior and romantic friendship. In the case made famous by Lillian Hellman's play, *The Children's Hour,* two Scottish schoolteachers confronted an accusation by one of their students that they came to each others' beds, lay one on top of the other, kissed, and shook the beds. The student, Jane Cumming, born of a liaison between an Indian woman and an aristocratic Scottish man serving the Empire in the East, reported that Jane Pirie said one night, "You are in the wrong place," and her friend, Marianne Woods, replied, "I know" and asserted that she was doing it "For fun." Another night, she said, Pirie whispered, "Oh, do it, darling." And Cumming described, through her tears, the noise that she heard as similar to "putting one's finger into the neck of a wet bottle."[16] Such testimony forced the judges in this case to make an impossible choice between believing that respectable romantic friends might engage in such behavior or that decent schoolgirls could make up such tales. As one judge put it, "Are we to say that every woman who has formed an intimate friendship and has slept in the same bed with another is guilty? Where is the innocent woman in Scotland?"[17] Only Jane Cumming's Indian heritage helped to resolve the dilemma. Surely, many of the judges decided, she had learned of such behavior in India and used her knowledge to get out of a school she found too strict.

If not evidence of actual sexual behavior, this case at least brings to our attention a conception of lesbian sexuality. The question for the court was whether Pirie and Woods kissed, caressed, and fondled "more than could have resulted from ordinary female friendship," suggesting a line into sexuality that could be crossed.[18] That such relations did exist in the guise of romantic friendship is confirmed in the remarkable nineteenth-century diary of Englishwoman Anne Lister, an upper-class, independent, mannish woman who described her numerous sexual affairs with women, some of them married. In 1819, she detailed an encounter with the love of her life, Marianne, who married for economic and social status but continued her affair with Lister, eventually passing on a venereal disease contracted from her husband through his own extramarital exploits: "From the kiss she gave me it seemed as if she loved me as fondly as ever. By & by, we seemed to drop asleep but, by & by, I perceived she would like another kiss & she whispered, 'Come again a bit, Freddy.' . . . But soon, I got up a second time, again took off, went to her a second time &, in spite of all, she really gave me pleasure, & I told her no one had ever given me kisses like hers."[19]

Fed up with waiting for Marianne's all-too-healthy husband to die, Lister went off to Paris in 1824, where she almost immediately began to court a widow, Mrs. Barlow, staying at the same pension. One night, Mrs. Barlow came to her room and climbed into bed with her: " . . . I was contented that my naked left thigh should rest upon her naked left thigh and thus she let me grubble her over her petticoats. All the while I was pressing her between my thighs. . . . Now and then I held my hand still and felt her pulsation, let her rise towards my hand two or three times and gradually open her thighs, and felt . . . that she was excited."[20]

Such explicit descriptions of sexuality, recounted in a woman's own words outside the walls of a courtroom, are a historical treasure. Most of the evidence we have of women's sexuality, like the cases of Benedetta Carlini and Woods and Pirie, is far more ambiguous. Lister was a woman who, before the invention of the term "homosexuality" in 1869 and before the emergence of the first lesbian cultures around the turn of the century, not only loved and desired women but saw this as her defining characteristic. She knew the term "Saffic," considered her attraction to women natural, and proclaimed proudly that "I love, & only love, the fairer sex & thus beloved by them in turn, my heart revolts from any other love than theirs."[21]

Her experiences bring together the previously disparate worlds of romantic friends, transgendered women, and same-sex lovers. The standard story of lesbian history in the Western world tells of class-divided experiences, with peasant and working-class women such as Catharine Linck and Jeanne Bonnet serving as forerunners of the butches and femmes of the 1950s, and middle- and upper-class women such as Molly Foote and Angelina Weld Grimké foreshadowing the lesbian feminists of the 1970s. Anne Lister's story makes clear that this is far too simple a depiction. We have assumed that, because women did not have access to public space in the same ways that men who cruised the parks and public latrines and taverns of eighteenth-century European cities did, same-sex communities could not form until the turn of the nineteenth century. But perhaps the first "lesbian communities" can be found in the drawing rooms of respectable society as well as in the ranks of prostitutes and other women within the sexual underworld of big cities.

There is no simple way to find the lesbians in lesbian history, just as there is no agreed-upon definition of a lesbian in late twentieth-century U.S. society. That the test of romantic love, or rejection of traditional femininity, or genital sexual relations with another woman, or even identity is not sufficient to "find the lesbians" has become clear through an understanding of cultural differences within the contemporary lesbian world.[22] We must continue to search for the bread crumbs that have not been gobbled up and, valuing each one for what it can tell us, find our way out of the dangerous forest of ignorance about women's same-sex love and sexuality in the past.

NOTES

1. Blanche Wiesen Cook, *Eleanor Roosevelt: Volume One, 1884–1933* (New York: Viking, 1992), 479, 15.

2. Judith Brown, "Lesbian Sexuality in Medieval and Early Modern Europe," in *Hidden from History: Reclaiming the Gay and Lesbian Past,* edited by Martin B. Duberman, Martha Vicinus, and George Chauncey, Jr. (New York: New American Library, 1989), 75.

3. Adrienne Rich, "Compulsory Heterosexuality and Lesbian Existence," *Signs* 5 (1980): 631–60.

4. The struggle over sexual expressiveness and regulation between, on one side, feminists who emphasized the dangers of sexuality and the need to fight pornography as a form of violence against women and, on the other side, those who stressed its pleasures, became a national issue after the 1982 "Scholar and the Feminist IX" conference at Barnard College. See Carol S. Vance, *Pleasure and Danger: Exploring Female Sexuality* (Boston: Routledge & Kegan Paul, 1984), 441–53, and Lynne Segal and Mary McIntosh, *Sex Exposed: Sexuality and the Pornography Debate* (New Brunswick, NJ: Rutgers University Press, 1993).

5. Blanche Wiesen Cook, "Female Support Networks and Political Activism: Lillian Wald, Crystal Eastman and Emma Goldman," *Chrysalis* 3 (1977): 43–61.

6. Martha Vicinus, "'They Wonder to Which Sex I Belong': The Historical Roots of Modern Lesbian Identity," *Feminist Studies* 18 (1992): 467–98, also considers these questions.

7. See Carroll Smith-Rosenberg, "The Female World of Love and Ritual: Relations between Women in Nineteenth-Century America," *Signs* 1 (1975): 1–29; Lillian Faderman, *Surpassing the Love of Men: Romantic Friendship and Love between Women from the Renaissance to the Present* (New York: William Morrow, 1981) and *Scotch Verdict* (New York: Quill, 1983); Lisa Moore, "'Something More Tender Still than Friendship': Romantic Friendship in Early Nineteenth-Century England," *Feminist Studies* 18 (1992): 499–520.

8. Quoted in Smith-Rosenberg, 7–8.

9. Quoted in Gloria T. Hull, *Color, Sex, and Poetry: Three Women Writers of the Harlem Renaissance* (Bloomington: Indiana University Press, 1987), 139.

10. See Faderman, *Surpassing the Love of Men,* 51–52.

11. The San Francisco Lesbian and Gay History Project, "'She Even Chewed Tobacco': A Pictorial Narrative of Passing Women in America," in *Hidden From History.*

12. George Chauncey, Jr., "From Sexual Inversion to Homosexuality: Medicine and the Changing Conceptualization of Female Deviance," *Salmagundi* 58–59 (fall 1982–winter 1983): 114–46.

13. Quoted in Sandra R. Lieb, *Mother of the Blues: A Study of Ma Rainey* (Amherst: University of Massachusetts Press, 1981), 124. See also Eric Garber, "A Spectacle in Color: The Lesbian and Gay Subculture of Jazz Age Harlem," in *Hidden from History,* 318–31.

14. See Evelyn Blackwood, "Sexuality and Gender in Certain Native American Tribes: The Case of Cross-Gender Females," *Signs* 10 (1984): 27–42; and Paula Gunn Allen, *The Sacred Hoop* (Boston: Beacon Press, 1986).

15. Quoted in Judith Brown, *Immodest Acts: The Life of a Lesbian Nun in Renaissance Italy* (New York: Oxford University Press, 1986), 117–18.

16. Faderman, *Scotch Verdict,* 147.

17. Ibid., 281.

18. Ibid., 82.

19. Anne Lister, *I Know My Own Heart: The Diaries of Anne Lister* (1791–1840), edited by Helena Whitbread (London: Virago, 1988), 104.

20. Anne Lister, *No Priest But Love: The Journals of Anne Lister from 1824–1826,* edited by Helena Whitbread (New York: New York University Press, 1992), 65.

21. Lister, *I Know My Own Heart,* 145.

22. See, for example, Makeda Silvera, "Man Royals and Sodomites: Some Thoughts on the Invisibility of Afro-Caribbean Lesbians," *Feminist Studies* 18 (1992): 521–32, and Carla Trujillo, *Chicana Lesbians: The Girls Our Mothers Warned Us About* (Berkeley, CA: Third Woman Press, 1991).

LOOKING FOR LESBIANS
IN CHINESE HISTORY
Vivien Ng

Several summers ago, I picked up a copy of Paula Martinac's *Out of Time*[1] and read it from cover to cover in one sitting. In this delightful lesbian ghost story (of sorts), strange things happen to Susan Van Dine, a perennial graduate student, after she "lifts" an old photo album from an antique store in New York City. I was especially taken by the way Susan was able to reconstruct gradually the lives of the four women whose photographs made up the album. At the time, I had just started my research on early Chinese feminists, a daunting task that involves lifting the layers of neglect and distortion that had shrouded their lives for so long. I could not help but fantasize, "If only 'my' women would communicate with me the way Harriet and Lucy did with Susan!"

"My" women founded *New Chinese Women Magazine,* a Chinese-language monthly that was published from 1906 to 1907 in Tokyo, Japan. The founding editor, Yan Bin, was enrolled at Waseda University Medical College, one of the most prestigious institutions in Japan. Chinese students began studying in Japan in ever-increasing numbers in 1900 after the disastrous Boxer Rebellion, which ended with the sacking of Beijing by the combined forces of eight imperialist powers. After this humiliation, even the conservative Manchu government conceded the need to educate the young minds of China Western-style. Japan was favored by many Chinese students for a number of reasons, among them the more-or-less hands-off policy adopted by the Japanese government toward anti-Manchu political activities of the Chinese residing there. In 1900, the number had burgeoned to almost ten thousand. *New Chinese Women Magazine* estimated that in 1907, at least one hundred Chinese women were enrolled in various schools in Tokyo.

Unlike Yan Bin, who opted for medical education, the majority of Chinese women were enrolled at the Aoyama Girls' Practical School, which was founded by Shimoda Utako, an ardent proponent of women's education who once had an audience with Queen Victoria. Regardless of their differing life goals, there was a strong sense of community and sisterhood. As early as 1903, they formed the all-female Mutual Love Society, with about twenty charter members. Their stated mission was ambitious: "To rescue the two hundred million Chinese women, to restore their basic and fundamental rights, to enable them to possess the idea of nationhood, so that they may ultimately perform their duty as women citizens." In 1904, in response to Russia's occupation of Manchuria, members of the Mutual Love Society organized the "Resist Russia Volunteer Brigade." Thus, very quickly, the Mutual Love Society expanded its embrace of women's rights to include anti-imperialist struggle.

The militantly nationalistic orientation of the Mutual Love Society was probably shaped by one of its members, the dashing Qiu Jin, who self-identified as a swordswoman, and who wore men's clothes as a political statement. Much has been written about Qiu Jin's anti-Manchu revolutionary work in Japan and China, as well as her subsequent arrest and execution by the Manchu government in 1907. In recent years, there has been a burgeoning interest in China as well as in Taiwan, and in Qiu Jin's life and work. Hong Kong television even aired a mini-series based loosely on her life. Even so, there are gaps in our knowledge about this dynamic woman's life.

As a lesbian historian, I am eager to identify and write about lesbians in modern Chinese history. Ever since I published "Homosexuality and the State in Late Imperial China,"[2] which deals mainly with male homosexuality in seventeenth- and eighteenth-century China, I have been on a single-minded mission to write about Chinese lesbians. I became even more determined after I met a graduate student from China who was pursuing a PhD degree in Chinese history at New York University. She confessed to me that after having been assigned Adrienne Rich's essay on compulsory heterosexuality in a Chinese history seminar, she complained to another student from Asia about the relevance of their reading assignment. She declared at the time: "There are no lesbians in China!"

My search for lesbians in Chinese history has thus led me to my project on early Chinese feminists, on "my" women. One promising area of investigation is the nature of the friendships that bonded so many of the early Chinese feminists together. One noteworthy example is Qiu Jin's relationship with Wu Zheying, who was a poet, renowned calligrapher, and reformer in her own right. The two met in 1903 shortly after Qiu Jin's arrival in Beijing with her husband and quickly became inseparable. Both lamented the fact that they had met too late and their time together was too short (Qiu Jin was already seriously contemplating leaving China for Japan). The following year, on the seventh day of the Chinese New Year, Qiu Jin and Wu Zheying exchanged a formal pledge of eternal friendship, an occasion that Qiu Jin marked with a poem called "Orchid Verse." The next day, Qiu Jin appeared before Wu Zheying in a man's suit and presented her with a pair of shoes and skirt, explaining to her dear friend that, "These items were part of my trousseau. Now that I have decided to wear men's clothes, I have no need for them. Please keep them in remembrance of me after we part." In 1907, after Qiu Jin was executed, Wu Zheying, at great risk to herself, collected Qiu Jin's remains so she could give her friend a proper burial.

Were Qiu Jin and Wu Zheying lovers? June Chan, a Chinese-American lesbian activist in New York City, includes pictures of Qiu Jin in her famous slide show on Asian lesbians. However, historians of China (Americans as well as Chinese) prefer not to address the issue because they find even the suggestion of lesbianism too intimidating. Many are also wary of being accused of imposing Western constructs on China. In other words, they succumb to the belief that lesbianism is a Western cultural invention, and that to label a Chinese woman "lesbian" is tantamount to forcing on her a Western identity. In my opinion, their "caution" stems from homophobia and not from theoretical considerations similar to those articulated by Gloria Anzaldúa in "To(o) Queer the Writer—*Loca, escritora y chicana.*"[3]

What do I think? Have I found the necessary "proof"? Take, for example, the formal pledge of friendship. Can I call it a "commitment ceremony"? What about "Orchid Verse"? Can I make a connection with the marriage resisters in China? Anthropologist Marjorie Topley has referred to the phenomenon of marriage resistance as a movement.[4] Topley and Andrea Sankar estimate that marriage resistance arose in three districts in the Pearl River Delta from approximately 1865 on through 1935;[5] however, I have come across a reference to it in the 1853 edition of *Shunde County Gazetteer*: "Girls in the county form very close relationships with one another and like to make vows of sisterhood with others of the same village. They don't want to marry, and if forced to marry, they stay in their own families, where they enjoy few restrictions. They don't want to return to the husband's family, and some, if forced to return, commit suicide by drowning or hanging."[6] In the 1904 publication *Nüren jing* (Canon for women), the section on filial piety includes a denunciation of marriage resistance (the compiler's commentary is indicated here by the use of brackets):

> Recently, there has developed a custom [this custom is deplorable] that is passed on from woman to woman. [Imitating and learning every step; forming Golden Orchid bonded sisterhood.] These women practice celibacy, vowing never to marry. [Blasphemous!] They refer to the husband's family as "cocoons." [Father-in-law, mother-in-law, husband, children, etc. bind their bodies and deprive them of their freedom. The analogy "cocoon" signifies suffocating bondage until death.][7]

What was the nature of the relationship between women in the sworn sisterhoods (Golden Orchid Society)? We have evidence—written records and interviews conducted by anthropologists—that sexual relationships sometimes developed. So, my question is: when Qiu Jin wrote her "Orchid Verse," was she aware of the Golden Orchid sworn sisterhood of marriage resisters? More importantly, did she choose "orchid" for her title to describe a particular kind of friendship with Wu Zheying? This is impossible to answer. I know that in 1908, in the Paris-based Chinese magazine *New Century*, a short piece about the marriage resistance movement/custom was published, indicating a degree of interest in the subject by radical intellectuals at the time. But it may be impossible to prove that Qiu Jin had personal knowledge about the Golden Orchid sworn sisterhood.

Did Yan Bin, founding editor of *New Chinese Women Magazine,* know Qiu Jin? I think so, even though I cannot prove it. Yan Bin arrived in Tokyo in the spring of 1905, while Qiu Jin was still actively involved in various fundraising efforts to enable her female compatriots to gain economic independence from their families. I suspect that Yan Bin was there when Qiu Jin convened an emergency meeting of Chinese female students in Tokyo in early fall 1905 to pressure her friend Chen Xiefen to resist her father's arrangement to have her marry a wealthy Cantonese merchant as his concubine. At that meeting, when Chen protested that she could not violate her father's wishes, Qiu Jin answered her sharply: "A man who forces his daughter to become a concubine violates life itself. Moreover, this matter affects the reputation of all of us here. You have got to cancel your engagement!" Such strong language was received with great enthusiasm and, in the midst of an eruption of thunderous applause, Chen quietly withdrew from the meeting.[8] (Chen later did indeed break her engagement.) What a defining moment in the history of Chinese feminism! Qiu Jin herself had divorced her husband and given up custody of her children before she left China for Japan. Does this make her a "marriage resister"?

Qiu Jin returned to China in 1906 to take a more direct part in the revolutionary movement to overthrow the Manchu dynasty. Later that same year, a number of Chinese women, under the vigorous leadership of Yan Bin, founded in Tokyo the *New Chinese Women Magazine.* This radical publication saw only six issues—it was shut down by the Japanese government when the entire sixth issue was confiscated because one of its articles supported the use of political assassinations. But during its short life, the magazine was able to sustain a large circulation (estimated at ten thousand copies per issue and circulated throughout East Asia and even Southeast Asia), thus proving its timeliness and popularity.[9]

The cosmopolitan orientation of the founding editors and the keen interest they had in the feminist movement in the United States and Europe are clearly evident in the pages of the magazine. Each issue contained news about developments concerning women in other countries, and at least one prominent Euro-American woman was featured in every issue. These biographical profiles reveal much about the types of women the editors wanted their Chinese readers to emulate: Margaret Fuller (presented as a journalist), George Eliot (novelist), Mary Lyon (college president), Florence Nightingale (nurse), Lucretia Mott (abolitionist), Mary Livermore (public speaker), and Joan of Arc (national savior).

My imagination runs rampant with possible scenarios. Did Yan Bin and her coeditors pick Margaret Fuller only because she was a journalist and therefore a role model for them? Were there other, unstated reasons? Had they read the *Memoirs of Margaret Fuller Ossoli,* published in 1852, two years after Fuller's death? Did they know that Fuller was involved in a passionate relationship with Anna Barker? There are many questions but too few answers.

Yan Bin was clearly the driving forced behind this successful magazine. Her signature was everywhere. I often wonder how this remarkable woman managed to find the time to be a medical student, editor, essayist, polemicist, playwright, and feminist agitator all at once. I am privileged to catch glimpses of her public persona through her writings, but what was she really like? What happened to her after the magazine was shut down? Did she finish her medical training? Did she manage to track down and reunite with her "dearest and most intimate" friend, Lo Ying, about whom she had written a moving biographical sketch? I have come across only a brief reference to the fact that Yan Bin did return to China (date unknown) and became the headmistress of a girls' school in Shanxi province (another possible lesbian scenario?). Very little else is known. What about the other writers for the magazine? Alas, I need supernatural help, of the kind Susan Van Dine received in *Out of Time,* to reconstruct as fully as possible the lives of this first generation of Chinese feminists, some of whom may well have been lesbians.

My conviction that there were/are lesbians in China is based on the essentialist belief in the universal experience of "homosexuality." At the same time, I understand (as other lesbian historians do) that sexuality is socially constructed; thus I know that it is impossible for me to find/locate exact precursors of my own experience. Perhaps what I am trying to do is not to establish beyond a reasonable doubt whether Qiu Jin "slept" with Wu Zheying or whether Yan Bin did so with Lo Ying, but to reclaim the rich emotional lives of these remarkable women.

NOTES

1. Paula Martinac, *Out of Time* (Seattle: Seal Press, 1990).

2. Vivien Ng, "Homosexuality and the State in Late Imperial China," in *Hidden From History: Reclaiming the Gay and Lesbian Past,* edited by Martin Duberman, Martha Vicinus, and George Chauncey, Jr. (New York: New American Library, 1989), 76–89.

3. Gloria Anzaldúa, "To(o) Queer the Writer—*Loca, escritora y chicana*," in *Inversions: Writings by Dykes, Queers and Lesbians,* edited by Betsy Warland (Vancouver, B.C.: Press Gang Publishers, 1991), 249–63.

4. Marjorie Topley, "Marriage Resistance in Rural Kwangtung," in *Women in Chinese Society,* edited by Margery Wolf and Roxane Witke (Stanford, CA: Stanford University Press, 1975), 67–88.

5. Andrea Sankar, "The Evolution of the Sisterhood in Traditional Chinese Society: From Village Girls' Houses to Chai T'angs in Hong Kong" (University of Michigan PhD dissertation, 1979).

6. Quoted in Janice Stockard, *Daughters of the Canton Delta: Marriage Patterns and Economic Strategies in South China, 1860–1930* (Stanford, CA: Stanford University Press, 1986), 160.

7. *Nüren jing* (1971 Taibei reprint ed.), *jüan* 1: 21b.

8. Guo Yanli, *Qiu Jin Nianpu* (Chronological biography of Qiu Jin), (Jinan: Jilu Press, 1983), 77; footnote 48.

9. Li Yuning, "Zhongguo xinnüjie zazhi ti chuang kan zhi nei han" (The founding of *New Chinese Women Magazine* and its contents), in *Zhongguo funü shi lun wen ji* (Essays on history of women in China), edited by Li Yuning & Zhang Yufa (Taibei: Commercial Press, 1981), 179–241, especially 241, footnote 71.

SCREENING LESBIANS
Judith Mayne

At the beginning of *Vampires and Violets,* the first book devoted entirely to an analysis of lesbians and film, Andrea Weiss observes that her study follows from a contradiction. "The relationship of lesbians to the cinema has always been complex," notes Weiss, ". . . it resembles a love-hate affair which involves anticipation, seduction, pleasure, disappointment, rage, and betrayal" (4). If lesbians have a long history of a love for the movies—despite the failure of the movies to reciprocate—then it comes as no surprise that much of the work in lesbian film studies focuses on examining this apparent paradox. Just as this paradox underlies the concept of lesbian spectatorship, so too does the notion of lesbian spectatorship itself inflect the various components of lesbian film studies: film history, theory, reception, and artistic representation. This does not mean that lesbians respond in one particular way to the cinema, or that there is a universal "lesbian viewer," but rather that in significant ways, lesbian culture, lesbian communities, and lesbian identities have been shaped by the ways in which films are watched, imagined, and understood. Given that the experience of watching films involves sitting in a darkened theater and engaging in fantasies that may well be forbidden outside the movie theater (or outside the home theater of the video-lit living room), it makes sense that spectatorship would hold a particularly central role in the changing definitions of lesbianism.

Spectatorship has been one of the most important concerns of contemporary film studies, yet it has also been defined in very contradictory ways, sometimes referring to how real people respond consciously to films, sometimes to how the institutions of the cinema project an ideal spectator. The tension between "real people" and "projections" not only is not easily resolved, but also is indicative of the contradictory qualities of film viewing, including the love-hate relationship of lesbians and the movies. Theorizing spectatorship involves examining both what spectators bring to the cinema and what the cinema imposes on spectators, and most important, the various spaces between the two (see Mayne 1993). While for some, the love-hate relationship of lesbians and film might be a dilemma to be resolved or a conundrum to be avoided, I'd like to suggest that lesbian spectatorship offers a unique perspective to current work on lesbian representation and lesbian theory, precisely because spectatorship involves such an engagement with contradiction. Although there may be risks involved in speculation on lesbian spectatorship, from false universals to a complete disregard for history, current examples and analyses of the dynamics of lesbian spectatorship suggest complex models that account for the varieties of lesbian experience as well as the specifics of history.

The reception of *Fried Green Tomatoes* (1991), for instance, suggests that lesbian viewing involves much more than a simple identification with (or rejection of) cinematic images. *Fried Green Tomatoes* is one of many recent films (from *Basic Instinct* to *Bad Girls*) that simultaneously opens up and closes down lesbian possibilities. *Fried Green Tomatoes* appropriates the codes and conventions of Hollywood romance to visualize the relationship between Ruth and Idgie, from longing gazes exchanged meaningfully to the contrasting styles of butch and femme, not to mention scenes so loaded with lesbian symbolism (the beehive in particular) they seem to burst. In my circle of lesbian friends, *Fried Green Tomatoes* was extremely popular, but the popularity of the film was definitely of a love-hate variety. The decision of GLAAD (the Gay and Lesbian Alliance Against Defamation) to award the film a prize for best lesbian content may have been a strategic decision to try to foreground not only the invisible visibility of lesbians on screen, but also lesbians in the audience (Pryor 1992). But many lesbians were as surprised by the award as those legions of heterosexual viewers supposedly unaware that they had even been exposed to lesbian content. Perhaps the GLAAD award brought attention to the paradox of lesbian visibility (i.e., there and not there at the same time), but most lesbians I know do not confuse the experience of watching *Fried Green Tomatoes* with identifying the film as "lesbian." In other words, lesbian spectatorship does not mean that a film must *be* a lesbian film in order to be read from a lesbian perspective.

Lesbian spectatorship vis-à-vis *Fried Green Tomatoes* is not confined to "finding the lesbians" in the film or insisting that the only way the film makes sense is in lesbian terms, even though those strategies are a part of lesbian film culture. Rather, lesbian spectatorship is concerned with that space between visibility and invisibility. There is something liminal about the experience of watching *Fried Green Tomatoes*, knowing that what is totally obvious to you will be invisible to others. This flirtation with lesbianism is matched, in a very peculiar way, by the film's insistence upon a racist narrative, in the sense that the film presents a supposedly enlightened antiracist character in a decidedly racist way. bell hooks identifies correctly the racist dynamic central to the film, but her opposition between the "progressive" quality of the film for white lesbians (versus its backlash racist narrative) is off the mark: "In *Fried Green Tomatoes*, we may be transgressing a boundary about how lesbianism is pictured, but the images of black people in that film fit every sort of stereotype. . . . The film was simply a modern plantation story with a white-lesbian twist" (Jones 1992). No lesbians I know—including white lesbians—are ready to claim the film as "progressive," and in any case, if lesbian spectatorship is to be a useful concept, it cannot be reduced to a checklist of what films are "progressive" and what films aren't. Far from being progressive on one front and reactionary on another, this film marginalizes lesbianism and African Americans in similar ways, particularly by recycling old plots (the "plantation" film, the "female friendship" film [Holmlund 1994, Vickers 1994]).

Fried Green Tomatoes and the subsequent discussion, analysis, criticism, vilification, and adoration by lesbians foreground the paradox of lesbian spectatorship—our simultaneous visibility and invisibility, as well as our ability to love and hate the cinema at the same time. For lesbian spectatorship is not just what happens when lesbians watch the film, but also and especially what happens once we leave the movie theater.

This paradox of lesbian spectatorship does not only occur vis-à-vis mainstream Hollywood films. Consider Julie Dash's film *Daughters of the Dust*, an independent feature that has been shown at festivals and museums, on PBS, and is currently available on video. Dash's film weaves a complex visual portrait of an African-American community, with particular attention to women's relationships to each other, including a lesbian relationship between Yellow Mary and Trula. Dash's representation of the relationship is subtle, but the cues are fairly unmistakable— at least to those ready to see them. For many African-American lesbians, *Daughters of the Dust* is a powerfully affirming film, and while I believe that many white lesbians share in that vision, there is also something challenging about the film for lesbians, since it does not adopt strategies of either disavowal or clear-cut identification; the lesbian relationship is simply one of many relationships among black women, and the screen time it is allotted is minimal. In interviews, however, Julie Dash has made clear that she did indeed intend to portray a lesbian relationship, without necessarily "naming" it as such (hooks and Dash 1992, 67).

When I attended a screening of *Daughters of the Dust* with three white lesbian friends, the paradoxes of lesbian spectatorship came into sharp relief. During the film, we all exchanged knowing nudges during the scenes with Trula and Yellow Mary. But during the discussion that followed the film, we were thrust into a very different kind of viewing space. Questions quickly focused on the peripheral role of Trula, and members of the audience, white and black, questioned her role and her identity, and a range of possibilities were offered in what appeared to be a massive defense reaction—call her anything, but don't call her a lesbian. Viewing *Daughters of the Dust* included the pleasure of watching a beautiful portrait of an African-American women's community, as well as the discomfort of hearing a denial of lesbian content in the discussion that followed; here too, lesbian spectatorship occupied the paradox of simultaneous visibility and invisibility.

The title of my essay is meant to be ambiguous in just this sense, for lesbian spectatorship involves the exploration of how lesbians have been both represented on the screen and rendered invisible, or "screened out." It is tempting to say that up until just a decade or so ago, lesbians were "screened out" of the cinema, and that it is only recently that complex and vital representations of lesbians have taken shape, largely in the works of independent directors. I am writing this essay at a time when the visibility of lesbian film and video seems to be at an all-time high. The fact that, for example, Rose Troche's *Go Fish* was picked up for major distribution by the Samuel Goldwyn Company, or that Weismann and Fernie's *Forbidden Love* is available on the Showtime premium cable network, suggests something a bit more profound than lesbian chic. In addition to extremely visible success stories such as these, many more lesbian artists are producing exciting, challenging works which are being screened at festivals, in classrooms, and in museums. From Cheryl Dunye's witty experimental videos (*She Don't Fade, The Passion and the Potluck*), which depict truly diverse lesbian communities, to Midi Onodera's films (*Ten Cents a Dance, The Displaced View*), which examine the intersections that comprise lesbian identities, lesbian film and video is at an all-time high rate of productivity.

It is tempting to argue that there is a clear and absolute dividing line between the past, when lesbians were uniformly "screened out," and the present, when lesbians are finally being "screened" in full and complex ways. But the separation is false to the extent that much of the exciting new lesbian work in film and video is devoted to revising, reappropriating, and revisioning images and narratives that supposedly belong to the not-so-enlightened past. In other words, lesbian spectatorship itself is a crucial dimension of contemporary lesbian work in film and video. Many lesbian artists have made lesbian spectatorship a central dynamic of their work, not just because they address lesbian viewers, but also because they examine the ways in which lesbians have been imagined and imaged in the past, and how those images change when redefined and reappropriated by contemporary lesbian subjects. The strategies for such revisions are diverse. They include the citation of classic films with lesbian subtexts, often repeating scenes over and over or placing particularly juicy scenes side by side. For example, in *Meeting of Two Queens,* Cecilia Barriga takes classic scenes from the films of Greta Garbo and Marlene Dietrich and re-edits them to create a narrative of lesbian desire—of the two stars for each other, and of lesbian viewers for the two stars. *Dry Kisses Only,* a video by Kaucylla Brook and Jane Cottis, is a kind of primer on lesbian spectatorship in this sense. Scenes from classical Hollywood films are re-read, focusing on the relationships between women that really do seem quite homoerotic, particularly when the requisite heterosexual romances are removed.

But there is a more problematic side to this re-reading of classical Hollywood films, for there is a long history in Hollywood of extremely racist characterizations of African-American women to facilitate or to mediate the relationships among white women. Clips of interactions between Bette Davis and Mary Astor in *The Great Lie* are included in *Dry Kisses Only,* and the pleasure of this foregrounding is undeniable. But in *The Great Lie,* Hattie McDaniel plays the role of confidante and servant to Bette Davis, and in many ways functions as yet another invisible presence, one that is not ameliorated by citing the film in a lesbian re-reading. Put another way, the rediscovery of lesbian possibilities engages all that is possible as well as all that is problematic in classical Hollywood cinema. Cheryl Dunye's work-in-progress takes another perspective on re-reading the classical Hollywood cinema, one that highlights the intersections of race and sexuality; she imagines a love affair between characters based on Hattie McDaniel and lesbian Hollywood director Dorothy Arzner (Rich 1994, see also Rich 1993).

Other recent work examines the ways in which lesbian communities create lesbian spectatorship. *L Is for the Way You Look,* a video by Jean Carlemusto, begins with the videomaker's voice-over narration: "I can trace an entire history of my life from age five on as a series of crushes on movie stars, television personalities, and rock goddesses. . . . These crushes were my way of figuring out who I was and what I wanted to be like." The video portrays a variety of these crushes, and in particular looks at how a Dolly Parton sighting becomes an elaborate exercise in lesbian spectatorship. Su Friedrich's film *Damned If You Don't* cites the film *Black Narcissus* and then proceeds both to deconstruct and reconstruct that classic film's preoccupation with desire among women as portrayed in a convent. All of these works offer theoretical perspectives on lesbian spectatorship, so it becomes obvious that contemporary lesbian film and video offer much inspiration for lesbian film studies. Particularly in terms of lesbian film history, the following questions arise: What does it mean to look at film history through the perspective of lesbian spectatorship? Is lesbian film history a series of absences, of erasures, of de-lesbianization? Or is it a series of triumphant, if very disparate, moments where, through sheer will or accident, some kind of lesbian visibility does make it to the screen? Or is it both, often at the same time? Consider, for example, the 1933 film *Queen Christina,* which fits easily and handily into both forms of history. On the one hand, the film does indeed de-lesbianize the life of Queen Christina. Yet, at the same time, the film offers distinct lesbian pleasures—Garbo herself, of course, not to mention one of the classic (if brief) scenes for lesbians, where Christina kisses Ebba, her lady in waiting, on the lips. If the lesbian moments of the film are brief and fleeting, then it would appear that de-lesbianization wins out. However, the romantic figure of Don Antonio, played by John Gilbert, brings a comic edge to the heterosexual plot. Gilbert overplays the role, and often appears to be parodying the very role of romantic hero he is supposed to embody. In other words, the de-lesbianizing of the legend of Queen Christina is not entirely successful. Given the presence of Garbo and the facts surrounding Queen Christina's life, this film foregrounds issues of lesbian desire and de-lesbianization. But is *Queen Christina* the exception in Hollywood, or does it magnify issues that are present in many, perhaps all, classical Hollywood films? In other words, lesbian film history might well reveal the extent to which lesbian desire and lesbian representation have been managed and negotiated rather than simply obliterated in Hollywood.

Lesbian film studies are defined, theoretically, at a curious intersection between feminist film theory and so-called queer theory. Feminist film theory has been associated with psychoanalysis generally and takes an approach to the cinema that examines how sexual difference is produced and managed. While the genesis of queer theory is complex, much of the work in queer film theory appears to be a response, explicit or not, to feminist film theory. Queer film theory insists upon the wide range of responses to the cinema that are not reducible to the paradigm of sexual difference. However, just as many lesbian commentators on feminist film theory have noted the extent to which "sexual difference" really means heterosexuality, so have lesbian commentators on queer theory noted how often "queer" really means "gay male." Teresa de Lauretis's work has been crucial in this context, for she has reclaimed psychoanalysis for an understanding of lesbian desire and representation, while critiquing both feminist theory and queer theory (1994). De Lauretis's work supports an approach to theory that is specific and attentive to the complex and limited factors that surround the evolution of particular concepts (see Bad Object Choices 1991, 137).

In that spirit of specificity, and following the example of those lesbian film and video makers who revise and re-read images from the past, I would like to conclude with some reflections on an article entitled "The Sapphic Cinema," which appeared in 1960 in *The Ladder*, the journal of the Daughters of Bilitis. Author LauraJean Ermayne notes that "in sober point of fact," few films can qualify as "little more than lesbianoid—only semi-sapphic in content—for *The Well of Loneliness* and the real butchnik pix in bilitiscope and sapphonic sound are still among the 'shapes' of things to come" (5). Ermayne then goes on to list eleven films, a "pitiful little list of films with at least a tinge of interest for the Uranian" (5). Many of the films listed are virtually unseeable today, and only two of them—*The Children's Hour* and *Maedchen in Uniform*—continue to appear on lists of lesbians in the movies.

But despite the inaccessibility of many of the films on Ermayne's list, the "sapphic cinema" described foregrounds lesbians' relationship to the movies as a peculiar love-hate relationship—we bemoan the absence of interesting, exciting, tantalizing images, yet we take enormous pleasure in making lists, teasing out the implications of what is there, cataloguing possibilities. I am struck, in reading the piece in *The Ladder*, by how important the cinema has been to a sense of lesbian visibility and lesbian representation.

The "sapphic cinema," as defined in this piece, is only secondarily a function of the films themselves; rather, it is in the act of cataloguing, of pastiche and recombination, and in the simultaneous work of "decoding" (a secondary character in one film is described as "obviously a lesbian"), that lesbian spectatorship is defined. The preponderance of European "art film" titles suggests the white, middle-class aspirations for which *The Ladder* has been criticized (notice that no B movies of the 1950s appear here, no women-in-prison films). This preference for European films reflects a desire to see not just lesbianism on screen, but particular configurations of lesbianism that conformed to ideologies of class and race, i.e., that offered the "legitimacy" of "high art."

Ermayne is drawn to the European art film; contemporary "lists" of lesbian films seem to gravitate towards classic Hollywood films (especially those featuring Dietrich and Garbo) and independent films by lesbian directors. If Ermayne's list suggests a desire for a particular aesthetic of lesbianism, current lists suggest a desire to find that erased presence in mainstream culture, while simultaneously inventing new languages of visibility.

Understanding lesbian spectatorship is the process of both compilation (where have lesbians appeared?) and self-reflexivity (how is "lesbian" being defined? How is a character "obviously lesbian"?). In Ermayne's piece, lesbian viewers are given the authority to read a film as lesbian, regardless of explicit lesbian content—a reading that, although based on the observations of "real people," is also steeped in theoretical considerations like those named above. In other words, then, lesbian spectatorship is given particular force and meaning, and while this might seem obvious to a contemporary lesbian audience, it is crucial to appreciate the extent to which this affirmation of lesbian spectatorship is not only a part of the history of lesbian film studies, but also a definition of its very possibility.

FILMS AND VIDEOS: SOURCES FOR RENTAL & PURCHASE
Barriga, Cecilia. 1991. *Meeting of two queens.* Women Make Movies.
Brooke, Kaucyila and Jane Cottis. 1990. *Dry kisses only.* Women Make Movies.
Carlomusto, Jean. 1991. *L is for the way you look.* Women Make Movies.
Dash, Julie. 1990. *Daughters of the dust.* Kino International.
Dunye, Cheryl. 1991. *She don't fade.* Video Data Bank.
———. 1993. *The passion and the potluck.* Video Data Bank.
Fernie, Lynne, and Aerlyn Weismann. 1993. *Forbidden love.* Women Make Movies.
Friedrich, Su. 1987. *Damned if you don't.* Women Make Movies.
Onodera, Midi. 1986. *Ten cents a dance.* Women Make Movies.
———. 1988. *The displaced view.* Women Make Movies.
Troche, Rose. 1994. *Go fish.* Samuel Goldwyn. Women Make Movies.

WORKS CITED
Bad Object Choices, eds. 1991. *How do I look? Queer film and video.* Seattle: Bay Press.
de Lauretis, Teresa. 1994. *The practice of love: Lesbian sexuality and perverse desire.* Bloomington: Indiana University Press.
Ermayne, LauraJean. 1960. The sapphic cinema, *The Ladder* 47, (April):5–9.
Holmlund, Christine. 1993. Cruisin' for a bruisin': Hollywood's deadly lesbian dolls. *Cinema Journal* 34, no. 1:31–52.
hooks, bell and Julie Dash. 1992. Dialogue between bell hooks and Julie Dash. In *Daughters of the Dust: The making of an African-American woman's film,* by Julie Dash with Toni Cade Bambara and bell hooks. New York: The Free Press.
Jones, Lisa. 1992. Rebel without a pause (interview with bell hooks). *Village Voice Literary Supplement,* October, 30.
Mayne, Judith. 1993. *Cinema and spectatorship.* London and New York: Routledge.
Pryor, Kelli. 1992. Women in love: Hollywood has it both ways with *Fried Green Tomatoes. Entertainment Weekly,* 28 February, 6–7.
Rich, B. Ruby. 1993. When difference is (more than) skin deep. In *Queer Looks,* edited by Martha Gever, John Greyson and Pratibha Parmar, 318–39. New York and London: Routledge.
———. 1994/1995. A is for Arzner. *Out,* December/January, 108–11.
Vickers, Lu. 1994. Excuse me, did we see the same movie? *Fried Green Tomatoes. Jump Cut,* no. 39 (June):25–30.
Weiss, Andrea. 1992. *Vampires and violets: Lesbians in the cinema.* London: Jonathan Cape.

LESBIAN TANTALIZING IN CARMEN LUGO FILIPPI'S "MILAGROS, CALLE MERCURIO"

Luzma Umpierre

For Lourdes Torres and Ann Russo

As a reader of Puerto Rican literature, I have yet to find a narrative text written by a woman that deals with the subject of lesbianism openly. I have often thought of reasons for this absence, and the main one I have come up with is that the writer fears the consequences of identifying herself and of being identified as a lesbian in Puerto Rican society.

As readers, we tend to look for works that validate our experiences and the perceptions we have of life that open new windows for our imagination and intellect. In the absence of narrative texts that portray lesbian characters, situations, issues, and concerns in the literature of Puerto Rico, and not being prone to assume an "existential" posture about it, i.e., "alone without lesbian texts in the world of Puerto Rican letters," I have set myself to reading narratives from the island, especially those written after 1970. I read from what I call a homocritical perspective, bringing out of the critical closet the perceptions I have as a lesbian reader and the way in which I approach texts.

This search for texts that narrate close relationships between women has not been totally fruitless; it has turned up a few close relationships among women. Some of Rosario Ferre's short stories, for example, probably would win a first prize in my lesbian-look-alike-short-story contest, for a number of her stories portray close positive relationships between women.

But my reading as a lesbian has also produced a feeling of being tantalized into an almost voyeuristic posture by texts that portray close relationships between women. The fact that these stories don't portray these relationships as lesbian, and that writers of these stories are unwilling to admit to using lesbian themes, leaves me asking: Am I a female voyeur reading these texts as if through a keyhole, or do these texts really contain material that tantalizes me as a lesbian reading them into a homocritical view?

In one of the best articles I have read on lesbian readers, "Ourself behind Ourself: A Theory for Lesbian Readers," Jean Kennard proposes a method which she labels as "polar reading" for "lesbian readers and others whose experience is not frequently reflected in literature." "Polar reading," she adds, "permits the participation of any reader in any text. . . . It does not, however, involve the reader in denying herself. The reader redefines herself in opposition to the text; if that self-definition includes lesbianism, this becomes apparent in any commentary she may make on her reading."[1] As interesting as Kennard's proposal is, it focuses in the realm of the reader and does not discuss the other pole: certain texts which are tantalizing for a lesbian, reading. To clarify my terminology, the term "lesbian readers" is used in this article following Kennard's concept of it; a "lesbian, reading" is my term and refers to a lesbian reading a text and looking for clues that indicate a lesbian relationship. If the "lesbian, reading" is a critic, this may lead her to a "homocritical" posture; again, this is my term, which means to arrive at a homosexual interpretation of a given work.

In an article on contemporary narratives written by women in Puerto Rico after 1970, Magali García Ramis mentions that what joins the works of this group of writers is the use of irony to criticize how women, in order to lead a tranquil life in Puerto Rican society, have had to adhere to archaic, unfair, unjustifiable social, political, and cultural situations.[2] While reading her article, I was struck by the few lines that she devotes to Carmen Lugo Filippi's short story, "Milagros, calle Mercurio." García Ramis says that the main character, Milagros, apparently liberates herself from her mother and religion by becoming a prostitute and that this liberation is then bound to make her more of a slave.

I'll admit to reading these lines nervously for I had, two years before in 1985, taught that same short story to my undergraduates in a Caribbean literature course from a very different perspective. I had focused then on the obsession of the narrator, Marina, with Milagros, a teenager. From my point of view, Marina was the main character and I had read the story's ending as the fulfillment of one of Marina's fantasies with Milagros—the symbolic cutting of her hair. Granted, I had had a male Puerto Rican student in class angrily contest my reading, but several women students helped enhance my interpretation by admitting that they too had had an "interesting" experience dealing with Marina as a narrator.

García Ramis's article made me ask if I had read myself into the story, if I had done a "polar reading" as Kennard suggests, or did the story have encoded in it a lesbian motif that could have tantalized me into that homocritical reading? I went back to read the story, now suspicious of both García Ramis's and my readings.

One of the first things that attracted me to the story was the first-person narration and the fact that Marina, the narrator, was a dropout from the university after studying comparative literature for three years. The fact that she was now a hairdresser, narrating this story as if telling it to a client, had brought me close to the text. My hairdresser in

Puerto Rico is always telling me stories about herself and others while doing my hair. But while these things attracted me to the text, something in Marina herself drove me out—her *ínfulas de grandeza* (her self-aggrandizement). Marina admitted also to wanting to deflate the ego of any woman who stood before her. This "come on/push back" tension in the reading continued until the appearance of Milagros. Marina had made such a case for her disdain of women whom she labeled as *"perfectos monigotes con ínfulas de grandes damas"*[3] (perfect clowns who feel they are great dames), that the appearance of a woman of whom she says: *"La recuerdo tan vivamente"*(I remember her vividly, 205) pulled me back into the story. In this new homocritical reading, it was obvious to me again that Marina was the main character, thus disqualifying García Ramis's positioning of Milagros. But the fact still remained in my mind that García Ramis omitted Marina and had seen Milagros's embarkment into prostitution as the ending of the story.

A critic of Puerto Rican literature and a writer herself, García Ramis focused on Milagros's change from an apparently good, obedient, and religiously observant young woman, loyal to her mother and the Pentecostal Church, to a stripper in a local bar for dirty old men. This particular reading of Milagros's change follows a traditional dichotomy within the island's literary criticism and its people's views on/of women, that of virgin/whore, which is so preponderant that texts seem to be reduced to this one opposition. Unlike García Ramis, I was not living on the island at that time. I was at a distance; I could allow myself to accept the tantalizings of Lugo Filippi's text. I could listen to Marina's story. A few examples of Marina's discourse and narrative technique will help me illustrate the story I heard from Marina.

In her description of Milagros and her first reaction to her, Marina admits that *"Contemplarla suscitaba en mí un extraño fenómeno de correspondencias"* (Looking at her brought up in me the strange phenomenon of mutuality, 206). Given that Marina has confessed an attraction for Milagros, another voice now appears in the text, one that talks to Marina as *"tú"* (you) while describing the fantasies that Marina has of Milagros's hair. This voice, which I describe as the voice of fantasy, becomes the narrator for several pages, describing imaginary conversations with Milagros and the actual pursuit of Milagros by Marina. This voice that made Marina's fantasies come out of the closet was crucial for me as a reader, for it glued me to the text. But I was a lesbian, reading. What if I had been García Ramis or an island woman critic who was straight? Some of my women students had partially responded to this question. They had seen these passages as a sign of "illness" in Marina, a flaw, something sick, statements which I had contested as heterosexist. But my students who felt this way had no doubt that Marina was the main character—they too were hundreds of miles away from the island.

Going back to the text, after these pages of second-voice revealing (lesbian, reading) or disturbing (heterosexist, reading), narration, the narrative voice returns to the first person. It is no surprise then that Marina's closeted voice, the "I" who interacts in front of others, makes negative statements about women of the kind we saw at the beginning of the story. She calls Milagros *"madonita"* and asks: *"¿Sería una retrasada mental con aires de modelo sanjuanera?"* (Could she be mentally retarded with the airs of a model? 209). The "come on/push back" feeling came over me again. Marina and her story were playing games. When the story line dealing with Marina's fantasies had become revealing to me as a lesbian, reading, but perhaps disturbing to a straight person reading the story, as we would say in Puerto Rico: "regained *compostura*" (composure)—societal *compostura*. Thus, Marina had to go back to downplaying women—she had to push them back.

But *compostura* is short-lived because a gossip makes her appearance with news of the fact that Milagros has been living a double life: "*aleluya*" (virgin) by day "*guayanilla*" (whore) by night. Milagros has been seen in a bar in Guayanilla working as a stripper. The second-person "fantasy" voice comes in once again to displace Marina's "I." Marina is about to visualize Milagros's striptease and be aroused by it. This is taboo. Marina is a woman character in Puerto Rican literature. How can she be allowed to eroticize Milagros in such detail?

Thus, another interesting element comes into play. Marina takes on a male persona in her fantasy—that of Rada, the police officer called to the scene of the striptease. At that point a true *caja china* (Chinese box) occurs before our eyes: the second voice narrates what Marina imagines seeing through Rada's eyes. Given the high sexual charge, a double closet door has appeared to make it "safe." Within Puerto Rican society, Rada is allowed to enjoy and be aroused by the sight of Milagros's erotic dance; Marina is not. Nonetheless, the scene remains sexually charged. This playful trick by the text is crucial, in regard to García Ramis's "safe" reading of Milagros as turning to prostitution. After all, Rada is the one who allegedly sees Milagros, and the bar is a men's bar. In my homocritical reading, Milagros strips for Marina but in order to bring that about, the text has established a safe distance via the second voice narrating Marina's fantasies of what Rada saw. The story's "come on/push back" tension has now acquired a greater complexity.

It is obvious to me as a lesbian, reading, that Marina is aroused by Milagros from the moment she meets her. But given the taboos of Puerto Rican literature and society, the core of the story has to be layered with sugar coating to make it palatable, and it also has to open a "proper" way out. The text, I think, plays straight attraction games with me as a lesbian, reading. It invites me to come in and take it, read its story, Marina's story and then pushes back with the interjection of the second voice and the further distancing using Rada's/Marina's vision.

After the striptease, the second narrative voice observes that Marina cannot sleep because she is thinking of Milagros's actions. This description is a sign that Marina has allowed herself to be aroused by Milagros sexually, and I link this to a passage earlier in the story in which Marina imagines having Milagros in her life as an intelligent woman companion. Both facts are narrated in the second voice, conveniently—a lesbian, reading, could perceive Marina fantasizing a lesbian lifestyle; a nonlesbian, reading, could perceive this other voice as a voice of admonishment.

The story plays overtly to critics/readers who reduce stories written by Puerto Rican women after 1970 to the virgin/whore dichotomy. Covertly, however, the text tries to make of the lesbian, reading, a female voyeur. *Her* reading perhaps is only a product of her homocritical mind. As we would say in Puerto Rico, the writer of the text has covered all the bases of her baseball game.

The ending of the story is equally convenient. Milagros arrives at the beauty salon and says, *"Maquíllame en shocking red, Marina, y córtame como te dé la gana"* (Make me up in shocking red, Marina, and cut my hair as you wish, 216). I, as a lesbian, reading, thought immediately of Marina's fantasy world coming true, becoming real: Milagros is asking her to do whatever she pleases. Given the sexual attraction I have read, this would be, as we would say in vulgar or earthy Puerto Rican slang, her chance to *"meter mano,"* to get involved. However, if I have conveniently paid attention to the second voice as admonishment, if I have not wanted to see Marina looking behind Rada and have only seen a man being aroused by a woman, if I have taken Marina's inability to sleep because of the recurrent images of the striptease as signs of Marina's fear of becoming a "loose" woman like Milagros, I could say that Marina faces a temptation: she is being asked to help Milagros become more of a prostitute by acquiring the image, "the look," of one. The second-voice narrator ends the story with the words: *"Un temblequeo . . . comienza a apoderarse de tus rodillas . . . Marina ¿qué responderás?"* (A shaking . . . takes over your knees . . . Marina, how will you respond? 217). The question is not only addressed to Marina but to the reader: what kind of a reading have you had? How far has your imagination's *"mercurio"* (mercury) gone up or down?

García Ramis maintains that Puerto Rican women have had to adhere to archaic, unfair, unjustifiable social, political and cultural situations in order to lead a tranquil life on the island. I would add that women writers of narrative fiction in Puerto Rico have had to deal with self-repression when it comes to openly writing short stories with/on lesbian characters and themes. Therefore, they leave their texts open-ended, in multiple layers of encoding, and with characters who wear multiple masks. And their texts are tantalizers to a lesbian, reading. If the homocritical reader bites the hook, the text can always conveniently close its closet door and leave the critic outside feeling like a voyeur and the characters inside, trapped as strippers or sickly obsessive women. I invite women writers of Puerto Rican fiction to open the doors of their minds and loosen their pens to allow their characters to leave the closet in a dignified way. Only then will my reading as a lesbian not be seen as polar or my homocriticism as extremist in the history of criticism in my home country. We could generate an inclusive theory of text production and reading that allows us to express and include all of ourselves freely.

NOTES

1. Jean E. Kennard, "Ourself behind Ourself: A Theory for Lesbian Readers," in *Gender and Reading: Essays on Readers, Texts and Contexts,* edited by Elizabeth A. Flynn and Patricinio P. Schweikart (Baltimore: Johns Hopkins University Press, 1986), 77.

2. Magali García Ramis, "Para que un día Luz María pueda comprar los zapatos que le dé la gana," *Caribán* 5–6 (1985): 6, 30–31.

3. Carmen Lugo Filippi, "Milagros, calle Mercurio," in *Apalabramiento,* edited by Efraín Barradas (New Hampshire: Ediciones del Norte, 1983), 204. All subsequent quotes will be indicated by page number in the text.

QUEER EVERYDAY LIFE: SOME RELIGIOUS AND SPIRITUAL DYNAMICS

Lourdes Arguelles and Anne M. Rivero

On a recent occasion we attended a Roman Catholic service for a gay male friend who had died of complications of AIDS. The service had been planned by the born-again Christian parents of our friend. Unlike in most services, in which the purported virtues of the dead are extolled and the failings conveniently overlooked, the priest used this occasion to condemn the lifestyle of the departed while pleading for mercy for his soul. We left the service, as did most of our gay and lesbian friends, extremely angry.

Several weeks after the first service had taken place, another memorial service was held by the lover and some friends of the departed. Though we did not attend, we were told that during the service a gay-identified Roman Catholic priest delivered a celebratory farewell to our deceased friend and used the biblical story of David and his loving partner Jonathan to legitimize same-sex love in the eyes of God and society and to comfort the grieving partner. Among the attenders of both services were members of the deceased's support group, whose spiritual practice derived from the channelled text *A Course in Miracles* (Foundation for Inner Peace, 1975). Also in attendance were gay men and lesbians whose spiritual practices and institutional allegiances included Wicca, Buddhism, Santería, eco-feminist/green spirituality, and gay and lesbian caucuses in various Judeo–Christian denominations. Some of those present considered their spiritual home to be traditional twelve-step programs. Present also were those for whom conventional religion was a thing of the past tied to a life of heterosexism and other oppressions they had purposefully left behind. Among these queers were men and women who saw in homoeroticism itself a spiritual practice capable of yielding a culture and an ethic. This approach to queer spirituality has been discussed at length by David Halperin in his seminal work on Foucault (1995).

This story is by no means unique. In it we see the range and variety of religious and spiritual beliefs and practices found in most urban queer communities. This exponential growth of the spiritual marketplace and frequent blurring of boundaries of the many contributing trends and forces speaks not only of the religious inclinations and spiritual longings of gay men and lesbians but also to the underlying anxiety pervasive in postmodern society amidst both traditional religious intolerance and a new wave of fundamentalist religious revival.

Unfortunately, the extensive, intensive, and often problematic nature of gay and lesbian religious faith and spirituality is more often than not absent from academe. With a few notable exceptions, religious studies departments continue to marginalize this area of scholarly endeavor while one or two women's studies courses will cover in survey fashion the rich feminist and lesbian contributions to religious studies. In queer, gay, and lesbian studies' offerings, the situation is aptly summarized by a student: "Unless it is about the threat of the religious right, the topic is for independent study only." In many of these courses, the add-on lecture on religion and spirituality in everyday life is more the norm than the exception. Further, few social-science oriented researchers investigating queer everyday life focus on its religious and spiritual dimensions. Even within the humanities broadly defined, offerings in queer studies seldom incorporate religion and spirituality as areas of legitimate inquiry and study. Yet more often than not, in the margins of our own queer scholarly establishment and the centers of our own everyday lives, religious and spiritual explorations, affirmations, debates and struggles continue to flourish.

Queers and the Bible

The pervasiveness of religion-based influence in the everyday life of queers, coupled with the continued role of the Bible as a source of parental/patriarchal authority, has made the exploration and establishment of positive links between biblical writings and same-sex eroticism extraordinarily important for many of us. In the late fifties and early sixties, a series of social-psychological studies lent credence to the possibility that a person's homophobic symbolic attitudes based upon religious ideology could be changed to more gay-affirmative attitudes through exposure to newer and more appropriate interpretations of biblical sources (Herek 1984). Not surprisingly, we find that queer religious scholars and spiritual practitioners, as well as queer activists in the frontlines of struggle against the religious right, are engaged in the task of re-reading and re-interpreting those passages that have been traditionally used in Judeo-Christian traditions to condemn same-sex love and that have become "texts of terror" for gays and lesbians (Wilson 1995). Though often disagreeing on methods, these scholars, practitioners, and activists underscore the irrelevant nature of prohibitions in the context of advanced industrial societies. They have noted, often wittily, that contemporary Christians and Jews disregard the majority of the other prohibitions listed in these sources. Influenced by Latin American liberation theology, as well as feminist and other radical theologies, gay-identified theologians began to ask questions such as,

"Why were particular regulatory passages in Leviticus written?" "Why the severity of punishments and the bullying language that frames these proscriptions?" Simultaneously, scholars began to analyze traditional interpretations of some of the most damning biblical stories, particularly that of Sodom, leading to the now popular queer notion that the sin of Sodom is not homosexuality but rather the dual sins of gang rape and lack of hospitality (McNeill 1976; Boswell 1980, 1994; Spong 1992).

As queer scholarly and not-so-scholarly revisions of seemingly condemning passages progressed, so did simultaneous reclaiming of stories with positive portrayals of same-gender intimacy and sexual love, such as the stories of David and Jonathan and of Naomi and Ruth (Horner 1978). Gradually these stories began to serve as scriptural examples validating same-sex love in contemporary gay and lesbian ceremonies and rites of passage such as marriage rituals, blessing ceremonies, and funeral or memorial services.

Some of our scholars, uncomfortable with these reclamations of biblical "ancestors," have repeatedly cautioned against the view of a monolithic, independent form of homoerotic expression traversing time and culture in the context of a benign queer-accepting Bible (Arguelles and Rivero, *Queer Spiritualities*). Additionally, some of the more progressive gay and lesbian clergy and religious scholars routinely caution against unqualified acceptance of religious ceremonies and traditions which are anchored in patriarchal customs and world views (Jacobson 1994).

Queers and Islamic Traditions

Queer efforts to understand the connections and conflicts between religion and homosexuality and to search for some degree of integration in individual lives are also in progress in the world of Islam, the other major world faith that looks to the patriarch Abraham as its spiritual father. Since Islamic religious attitudes and practices vary greatly in different historical periods and with geographical region, queer scholars must take care not to generalize about sexual beliefs.

Unlike the sexually restrictive Judeo-Christian tradition, Islamic tradition considers hetero-sex to be a healthy and natural urge of every human being. Because of human imperfection, however, sexuality in the earthly realm needs regulation primarily through the institution of heterosexual marriage. Celibacy and adultery, either heterosexual or homosexual, are seen as serious threats to the social order and to God's expression on earth. Homosexual and lesbian behavior are also considered forms of adultery, but are seen specifically as a revolt against God, violating the order of the world. As a result, examples do exist of extreme punishment in specific geographic regions, especially in particular historical periods—such as the "Ayatollah revolution" in contemporary Iran—in which a particular Islamic nation-state has perceived itself as threatened from the outside.

Not surprisingly, women and men who engage in same-sex love, or who desire to do so, historically have sought to migrate from repressive Islamic societies in search of a more open and tolerant space in which to express their sexualities as well as their spiritualities. In organized groups and as individuals, they have sought to reclaim from their religious and cultural traditions such gay and lesbian "ancestors" and ritual practices as can be found (see, for example, Chittick 1983). Simultaneously, non-Islamic gay scholars such as Andrew Harvey (1994) have helped to revive popular awareness of Sufi homoerotic mystical traditions and practices.

Queers and Hindu and Buddhist Traditions

Stepping away from the traditions and influences of the Abrahamic religions with their multiple proscriptions against homosexual behavior, one encounters ancient faiths and systems of belief—Hinduism and Buddhism—which depict instances of same-sex love straightforwardly and positively. In the enormous corpus of scriptures and sacred texts of Hinduism, for example, queers have found only a few mildly negative references to homosexual behavior. In fact, in the oldest surviving Hindu scriptures, the Vedas, homosexual behavior is routinely ignored. In addition, Hindu mythology includes instances of thinly veiled homoeroticism, including numerous gods who change sex in order to engage in intercourse with someone of their previous sex, and others who are pictured as half male and half female. In tantrism—a Hindu and sometimes Buddhist practice purportedly leading to enlightenment—the male, and recently female, practitioner is at times encouraged to develop opposite sex traits, sometimes through participation in carefully prescribed homoerotic/homosexual symbolic or ritual acts.

In the various branches of Buddhism, passages condemning homosexual behavior also seem scarce. Wherever homosexual behavior is prohibited, it is because all expressions of sexuality are seen as impediments to spiritual progress. Unlike the Abrahamic traditions, Buddhism does not necessarily consider marriage and procreation a reflection of divine will and its core teachings tend to promote gender equity rather than male dominance (Gross 1993).

Turning from same-sex carnal relations to homoerotic emotion and attachment, one finds that in the Jataka, or tales of the lives of the Buddha, same-sex love is extolled while marriage and heterosexual relations are systematically disparaged (Zwilling 1992). This comes as no surprise in a tradition that favors monasticism over lay life as a route to enlightenment. The Buddha-to-be is often depicted in the company of a devoted male companion who assists him in his quest for spiritual development. Although homosexual behavior has been known to exist among Buddhist male monastics, very little information exists on Buddhist nuns. However, the Vinaya and other texts do address the matter of sexually nonconformist women, which suggests that same-sex love may have been detected among nuns during the period in which these texts were compiled (Zwilling 1992). Further, the poetry of Buddhist nuns of the sixth century B.C.E., "special friendships" between women have been consistently noted (Murcott 1991). These texts, known as Therigatha, await critical queer readings.

One might expect that contemporary societies in such countries as India, China,

Japan, Tibet, and Thailand, whose cultural frameworks are permeated by Hindu and Buddhist spiritual traditions, would be more affirming, or at least accepting, of same-sex eroticism than those societies influenced by Abrahamic traditions. This does not seem to be the case, however, and, with the exception of Thailand, most of these societies hold same-sex love to be a punishable offense. Many scholars blame colonial experience for the lack of congruence between current negative social attitudes and older spiritual attitudes and practices.

Currently, these postcolonial Eastern societies are being influenced by U.S. and other Western gay and lesbian movements, as well as by mass tourism, increased urbanization, formal Western-style education, and evolving women's movements. Such processes of globalization contribute to the visibility and viability of gay and lesbian peoples. These newer identities and relationships are beginning to coexist—albeit under very difficult circumstances—with more covert indigenous traditions of same-sex love (Arguelles 1990).

Ironically, the re-examination and reclamation of portions of Eastern wisdom traditions pertinent to gays and lesbians are largely taking place in the advanced industrial West as lesbian/gay exiles from Asian societies, together with queer Western students of Eastern thought, have renewed traditional practices. In the nineties it can be said—to paraphrase what the poet Gary Snyder once said about women—that the single most revolutionary aspect of the practice of Eastern traditions in the West is that many open gays and lesbians participate at all levels—and this despite the fact that heterosexism is alive and well among some Buddhist students, practitioners, and institutions.

Queers and American Indian Traditions

If one were to devise a continuum of acceptance and validation of same-sex eroticism in spiritual contexts, one could probably locate the Abrahamic traditions at the most negative end, the various Eastern traditions strung along the middle, and original forms of American Indian traditions at the most positive end. Before European conquest and colonization, a great number of American Indian societies assigned powerful spiritual and social roles to individuals who were gender-mixed in activities, behaviors, and attire, and who engaged in same-sex eroticism (Williams 1986; Callender and Kochems 1986). Commonly referred to as *berdache* or two-spirited people, such individuals, from a Western perspective, might be considered gender-blended or gender-confused. From within their own cultural frameworks, however, they were often understood to represent a third or fourth distinct gender. With the systematic obliteration of American Indian cultures and cosmologies and the colonial imposition of Judeo-Christian beliefs, the prominent role of the two-spirited being and its supporting mythologies declined or retreated, but did not disappear altogether. In the conclusion to his biographical work on the Zuni two-spirited We'wha, Will Roscoe (1991) writes:

> The American Indians are using their knowledge of the berdache role to give

meaning and purpose to their lives today. . . . The viability of the berdache symbol is further attested by the diverse individuals who are drawn to it, not only Indians and not only gay men and lesbians . . . where as a role model or as an archetype of wholeness, the multidimensional image of the berdache reminds us that our debates about sex and gender involve ethical choices relative to our own time and place; choices rather than the application of presumed natural or social laws. . . ."

Gay, Lesbian, and Queer Religions and Spiritualities

Western lesbians and gay men have struggled to appropriate and transform religious and spiritual traditions of the past and present and of the East and West. In many cases efforts have been made within the existing frameworks of established churches and religious organizations. In some of these institutions gay clergy have been accepted and holy unions of gay or lesbian couples are now routinely performed. In less accepting or in openly condemning churches or denominations gay and lesbian caucuses serve the dual purposes of support and advocacy.

In addition, efforts to find a spiritual home have produced autonomous institutional forms such as the Universal Fellowship of Metropolitan Community Churches (MCC), the leading gay church in the United States with satellites in Europe, Africa, and Latin America. MCC increasingly has made an effort to accommodate religious traditions other than Christianity, diverse gay populations, and progressive nongays within its midst.

Other autonomous forms of gay and lesbian spiritualities have emerged outside the framework of any institutional base, and are, from the viewpoint of any of the mainstream religious structures, extremely unconventional. One of these, the Radical Fairies movement, attracts gay men interested in exploring and developing an alternative gay-centered spiritual tradition. Lesbians in North America, England, and continental Europe have likewise formed loose, nonmainstream networks for spiritual work. In the late sixties and early seventies several lesbian witches' covens emerged in the United States (Adler 1986; Budapest 1986; Lozano and Foltz 1989). More recently, increasing numbers of lesbians from diverse ethno-racial and class backgrounds have been joining the neopagan movement of earth-centered spiritualities, which often personify the life force as a feminine spiritual energy or goddess. Women who identify not only as lesbian, but as queer, are appropriating ancient shamanic rituals involving gender fluidity, often generating questions of racism and cultural imperialism (Gaard 1993).

Along with many other segments of Western societies, queers of various ethnicities, races, and economic backgrounds have entered the "New Age" spiritual marketplace in search of spiritualities and practices that fit their personal values, experiences, and needs. Many seek hope and affirmation in dealing with the realities and anxieties of breast cancer, HIV/AIDS, and other chronic or terminal illnesses, as well as with the aftermath of child abuse, battering, rejection from their families, and exclusion from their churches of origin. Organizations and groups stemming from the *Course in Miracles* (Foundation for Inner Peace, 1975) have become spiritual homes for many gay men and lesbians. Some New Age approaches, as yet too young to be called traditions, draw upon various Eastern and Western metaphysics along with "channeled" material and guidance. Recovery meetings, based on the twelve steps of Alcoholics Anonymous, and sometimes combined with New Age spirituality, have become a recognized part of lesbian spiritual culture, as well as targets of criticism.

In gay and lesbian communities of color still other forms of spiritual reclamations balance ethno-racial with gay, lesbian, or queer identities. In these communities there has been a strong pull toward the discovery of and return to root spiritualities lost through colonization, social integration, acculturation, and/or transnational migration. The reclamation of the ceremonial status of lesbian and/or gender-blended people, including the *berdache* tradition, now has a positive significance for gay/lesbian/queer American Indians (Gunn Allen 1986; Gould 1990; Brant 1993; Roscoe 1993). They see the blending of these traditions with new ways as a means to revitalize indigenous cultures on the verge of extinction. Ceremonial gayness and lesbianism become a means of salvation. Reactions from nongay segments of the Native American populations have varied from acceptance to derision. Moreover, some non-American Indian gays and lesbians have found in this ceremonial tradition a mythical, psychological, and social empowerment unavailable in most other spiritual traditions—a highly controversial development among native communities, as well as among American Indian queers (Gaard 1993).

Latinos and blacks of Caribbean origins in the U.S. East Coast area have renewed interest in homoerotic identities and components within Santería, an Afro-Cuban tradition. Though such aspects of Santería have always been an integral part of the lives of Cuban homosexuals (Arguelles and Rich 1984), these influences are becoming more salient in lesbian communities of color (Villasenor 1994). Some younger Afro-Caribbean spiritual healers are returning to fundamental Yoruban traditions, resurrecting forgotten or neglected *orishas* (Yoruban spirit beings) such as Inle, who can be construed as a transgendered spirit. Still other queer Latinos/as and blacks have found themselves "called" by the school surrounding the Yoruba-Lucumi priestess Luisah Teish (1985).

Another reclaiming of tradition can be seen among U.S. queer Latinos/as of Mexican ancestry. In these communities hybrid indigenous-Hispanic rituals and ceremonies which deal with healing or death have been rediscovered and modified for use in coping with the pain and loss inherent in transnational migration and in everyday life as an immigrant or refugee. The reclamation of root spiritualities and the development of neoshamanic mythologies and practices among these and other lesbians of color in the United States cast a different light on the processes of ethnic identity development, resistance to cultural exclusion, and crisis management (Arguelles and Rivero 1995).

The return to root spiritualities and to more fundamental beliefs undergirding certain spiritual practices is paradoxical in the context of parallel movements toward religious fundamentalism which have risen in the late twentieth century all over the world. These fundamentalist movements seem to emerge when people see their identity at risk and seek to fortify it by a selective retrieval of rigid doctrines, beliefs, and practices from a sacred past. Queer retrieval of root spiritualities and its return to precolonial and seemingly nonhomophobic traditions can be seen as one line of defense among many against movements such as Islamic fundamentalism and the new Christian right, which are currently seeking to threaten very directly gay and lesbian existence and freedoms. Though different in dogma, these religious fundamentalisms may be seen as a reaction against selected processes inherent in both modern and postmodern social and economic realities.

Conclusion

The current evolution of lesbian, gay, and queer life globally has included a struggle to understand more clearly and interpret appropriately traditional religious scripture so as to neutralize the prejudices that have arisen from it. It has also included attempts by queers to insert themselves individually and collectively into mainstream religious institutions.

Many queers have found the results of such efforts inadequate to meet their spiritual needs and have turned away from Judeo-Christian mainstream religious practices and institutions to create alternative spiritualities and religious institutions and in some cases to reclaim their root spiritualities or seek a spiritual home in the religious practices of non-Western peoples and American Indian communities. This latter trend has given rise to very serious questions of racism and cultural imperialism. In fact, American Indians have argued that some of these practices which involve extracting spiritual rituals from native communities are genocidal in nature (Smith 1991).

At the same time, the flame of religious fundamentalism has erupted into a powerful backlash against any small progress toward increased acceptance, compassion, and inclusion of queers in major religious traditions, in society, and in public worship. The explorations, affirmations, debates, and struggles around these and related issues will undoubtedly continue in the years to come. The end of the story cannot yet be written. But it is increasingly urgent that scholars in lesbian, gay, and queer studies creatively integrate into their investigative and pedagogical work the exciting and problematic religious and spiritual dimensions of queer everyday life. Nothing less will do.

WORKS CITED

Adler, Margot. 1986. *Drawing down the moon.* 2nd. ed. Boston: Beacon Press.

Arguelles, Lourdes and Anne Rivero. *Queer spiritualities.* Unpublished manuscript.

————. Forthcoming. Working with gay/homosexual Latinos with HIV disease: Spiritual emergencies and culturally-based psycho-therapeutic treatments. In *Culture and difference: Critical perspectives on the bicultural experience in the United States,* edited by Antonia Darder. New York: Bergin and Garvey.

Arguelles, Lourdes. 1990. Same-sex eroticism and spirituality: Conversations with some women in India. Paper presented at the First Lesbian, Gay, and Bisexual Studies Conference, Harvard University, Cambridge, MA.

Arguelles, Lourdes and B. Ruby Rich. 1989. Homosexuality, homophobia, and revolution: Notes toward an understanding of the Cuban lesbian and gay male experience. In *Hidden from history: Reclaiming the gay and lesbian past,* edited by Martin L. Duberma et al. New York: New American Library.

Boswell, John. 1980. *Christianity, social tolerance, and homosexuality.* Chicago: University of Chicago Press.

———. 1994. *Same-sex unions in pre-modern Europe.* New York: Villard Books.

Boudhdiba, Abdelwahab. 1985. *Sexuality in Islam.* Translated by A. Sheridan. London: Routledge and Kegan Paul.

Brant, Beth. 1993. Giveaway: Native American lesbian writers. *Signs* 18, no. 4:944–47.

Budapest, Zsuzsanna. 1986. *The holy book of women's mysteries,* vol. 1. 2nd ed. Oakland, CA: Susan B. Anthony Coven, No. 1.

Callender, Charles and Lee Kochems. 1986. Men and not-men: Male gender-mixing statuses and homosexuality. In *The many faces of homosexuality: Anthropological approaches to homosexual behavior,* edited by Evelyn Blackwood. New York: Harrington Park Press.

Chittick, William C. 1983. *The Sufi path of love: The spiritual teachings of Rumi.* Albany, NY: SUNY Press.

Devi, Shakuntala. 1977. *The world of homosexuals.* New Delhi: Vikas Publishing House.

Foundation for Inner Peace. 1975. *A course in miracles.* Tiburon, CA: Foundation for Inner Peace.

Gaard, Greta. 1993. Ecofeminism and Native American cultures: Pushing the limits of cultural imperialism? In *Ecofeminism: Women, animals, and nature,* edited by Greta Gaard. Philadelphia: Temple University Press.

Gould, Janice. 1990. *Beneath my heart.* Ithaca, NY: Firebrand.

Gross, Rita M. 1975. *Buddhism after patriarchy: A feminist history, analysis, and reconstruction of Buddhism.* Albany: State University of New York Press.

Gunn-Allen, Paula. 1986. *The sacred hoop.* Boston: Beacon Press.

Halperin, David M. 1995. *Saint-Foucault: Towards a gay hagiography.* New York: Oxford University Press.

Harvey, Andrew. 1994. *The way of passion: A celebration of Rumi.* Berkeley, CA: Frog, Ltd.

Herek, Gregory. 1984. Beyond homophobia: A social psychological perspective on attitudes towards lesbians and gay men. *Journal of Homosexuality* 10:1–21.

Horner, Tom. 1978. *Jonathan loved David: Homosexuality in biblical times.* Philadelphia: Westminister.

McNeill, John J. 1976. *The Church and the homosexual.* Kansas City, KS: Sheed, Andrews, and McMeel.

Jacobson, Rabbi Devorah. 1994. Personal communications, June.

Lozano, Wendy G. and Tanice G. Foltz. 1989. Into the darkness: An ethnographic study of witchcraft and death. Paper presented at the annual meeting of the Association for the Sociology of Religion, San Francisco, August.

Murcott, S. 1991. *The first Buddhist women: Translations and commentary on the Therigatha.* Berkeley, CA: Parallax Press.

O'Flaherty, Wendy Doniger. 1980. *Women, androgynes, and other beasts.* Chicago: University of Chicago Press.

Roscoe, Will. 1991. *The Zuni man-woman.* Albuquerque: University of New Mexico Press.

Smith, Andy. 1991. For all those who were Indians in a former life. *Ms.,* November–December, 44–45.

Spong, John Shelby. 1992. *Rescuing the Bible from fundamentalism.* San Francisco: Harper San Francisco.

Teish, Luisah. 1985. *Jambalaya.* New York: Harper and Row.

Villasenor, Antonia. 1994. Personal communications, July.

Williams, Walter. 1986. *The spirit and the flesh: Sexual diversity in American Indian culture.* Boston: Beacon Press.

Wilson, Nancy. 1995. *Our tribe: Queer folks, God, Jesus, and the Bible.* San Francisco: Harper San Francisco.

Zwilling, Leonard. 1992. Homosexuality as seen in Indian Buddhist texts. In *Buddhism, sexuality, and gender,* edited by Jose Ignacio Cabezon. Albany: State University of New York Press.

THINKING SOCIOLOGICALLY ABOUT LESBIANS

Beth E. Schneider and Susan Dalton

Lesbians have not been the subjects of study for very many sociologists. Most lesbian and feminist scholars in the last ten years have devoted themselves to work on women more generally. But a solid core of researchers in the last decade has made substantial contributions to understanding the social psychology and social organization of lesbian lives in the United States.

We have selected some of the work of that small group of scholars and organized it around four themes: social movement activities and organizations; legal inequalities and employment problems; creation and celebration of families; and identity, difference, and politics. Most writing by this group of women refers to and/or draws from a few key texts written by lesbian scholars in other fields, especially Gayle Rubin and Adrienne Rich. To garner insight into the ways race/class/gender and sexuality simultaneously affect lesbian lives, sociologists, teachers, and researchers often turn to the humanities and the collected and individual works of such writers and poets as Gloria Anzaldúa, Cherríe Moraga, Barbara Smith, and Audre Lorde. At present, there seems to be no research by sociologists in the United States that is focused exclusively on lesbians of color.

Nevertheless, the few social scientists who have taken on the challenge of studying lesbians sociologically have made exciting contributions to the larger field of sociological inquiry and are important players in our understanding of the everyday social and cultural lives of contemporary lesbians. Sociologists writing in the subfield of social movements challenge other scholars to theorize more deeply about the relationships between gender, sexuality, and lesbian/gay/bisexual political analyses and protest movements. Their own efforts can be seen in the pieces we discuss that focus on the lesbian community in the 1950s, the women's movements of the 1970s and 1980s, AIDS organizations, and lesbian and gay antiviolence projects.

In sociological studies of the legal and economic systems, Gould and Schneider offer insightful examinations of the complicated ways that sexism and heterosexism operate within and upon lesbian lives. Gould (1984) presents a timely sociological analysis of child custody cases that begins the process of untangling the effects of sexism and heterosexism on their outcomes. Schneider's analysis of work settings done in the early 1980s still offers the only sociologically-grounded study of the innovative ways lesbians use female-dominated workplaces to build supportive, egalitarian, and often loving relationships (Schneider 1984). Moving beyond the use of the lesbian family as merely a site from which to critique the heterosexual nuclear family, the work of Weston and Lewin, each in its own way, increases our understanding of lesbian mothers and how they come to negotiate gender, sexuality, and parenting. Weston (1991), in a book that grapples with questions of the construction of kinship in lesbian and gay communities, demonstrates the ways in which lesbian mothers use kinship ties as a primary avenue through which parents make bold claims asserting their right to be recognized as family. Lewin (1993) details the paths many lesbian mothers follow to renegotiate their "radical" lesbian identity in light of their new, more traditional mother identity.

And finally, it is within the area of identity, difference, and politics that lesbian sociologists are beginning to engage queer theory. Here, sociologists are most thoroughly documenting and theorizing about the exciting shift away from a monolithic lesbian identity toward much more complex, vibrant, multifaceted individual and collective identities.

Social Movement Activities and Organizations

Some sociologists contribute to the social historical investigation of lesbian participation in the development of lesbian and gay social movements, often paying special attention to the ways gender is made visible or invisible in social movement activities organized around sexuality. Two examples were published in 1994 in a special issue on sexuality of the journal *Gender & Society*. Kristen Esterberg, in "From Accommodation to Liberation: A Movement Analysis of Lesbians in the Homophile Movement," applies a theory about ethnic groups—competition theory— to a reexamination of the organization Daughters of Bilitis. In documenting the changes in political strategies of lesbians from DOB's inception in 1956 to its demise in the early 1970s, Esterberg demonstrates how an increasingly gendered analysis of "female homosexuality" challenges some of the underpinnings of an ethnic group analysis of lesbian and gay identities. She concludes that DOB and its magazine, *The Ladder*, could not compete successfully with a variety of new women's groups of the early women's liberation movement for resources and active membership. Esterberg's work resonates with that of Rose Weitz (1984), who, ten years earlier, applied deviance theory as a framework by which to trace the political development of the San Francisco lesbian community from 1956 to 1972. Weitz analyzed the contents of *The Ladder* and identified three distinct political phases through which contributors moved: from an apolitical period encouraging integration and conformity, to a period in the 1960s of writings focused on confrontation and rejection of the negative aspects of the homosexual identity, to a final change during which many San Francisco lesbians became radical and began calling for the open celebration of the lesbian lifestyle. Weitz observed that this move proved to be so far removed from the original intent of Daughters of Bilitis that *The Ladder* broke with the organization and its more conservative ideologies, leading soon to the demise of each. Based on interviews with lesbians from communities in the east and midwest, Verta Taylor and Nancy Whittier (1992) document the processes involved in the formation of a politically identified community of lesbian feminists at both local and national levels primarily in the 1970s and 1980s. These women generated a collective identity built on the creation of a woman's culture that accentuates differences between men and women and fosters the development of a shared consciousness, encouraging women to engage in a wide range of social and political actions that challenge the dominant system of heterosexuality. In laying out this process, Taylor and Whittier look at the meaning to lesbian feminists of events such as music festivals and institutions such as women's bookstores.

A variety of different kinds of activities have been examined for the more recent years. In their paper "Antiviolence Activism and the (In)Visibility of Gender," Valerie Jenness and Kendal Broad (1994) analyze public documents of thirty-two lesbian and gay antiviolence projects to describe the nature of their activities, the ways in which the work has incorporated the feminist analysis of sexual terrorism, and the feminist critique of the violence-against-women movement. In a critique of the work of these organizations—which argues that "gay and lesbian activism has been explicitly preoccupied by homophobia, only implicitly concerned with institutionalized heterosexism, and not at all concerned with patriarchy"—they add a critical voice to ongoing debates about the relationship of sexuality to gender. The authors explain how a lack of attention to gender leads to a misunderstanding of violence against gay *men* and *lesbian* women, and, very specifically, renders invisible violence directed at lesbians of color. In a related paper, Jenness (1995) extends the empirical analysis of this activism, showing how the problem of violence against lesbians and gay men is made an issue by local and national organizations through the documentation of incidents, creation of crisis-oriented programs, educational campaigns, and street patrols.

Lesbians have been deeply and uniquely involved in community activities and social movements dealing with AIDS. Nancy Stoller and Beth Schneider each offer different approaches in understanding these efforts. Reviewing a history of the variety of political responses that have emerged among lesbians involved in both the feminist and the lesbian/gay movements from the late 1960s to the 1980s, Stoller (1995) suggests that lesbians' participation in activities around AIDS and the extent to which it is a priority is structured by one of four political perspectives: (1) "women/lesbians make a distinctive contribution"; (2) "equal rights for women/ lesbians within the AIDS world"; (3) "lesbians and gay men must form coalitions"; and (4) "lesbians need separatism." Stoller explores the particular AIDS politics engaged in by lesbians that are consistent with attachment to each of these approaches and examines generational differences in lesbians' AIDS activities. Schneider (1992) writes about lesbians' involvement with AIDS work through an examination of five social domains: friendship networks, employment, sexual relationships, women's health, and politics. She argues that lesbian involvement was greatest when lesbians had important social/political bonds with gay men, when they were employed in health professions, when they were in the process of changing lovers or sexual partners, and when they recognized the ways in which local and national politics about which they cared deeply were being affected by AIDS.

Paula Rust has undertaken extensive research on lesbians' perceptions of bisexuality and on bisexual women and their relationships to the lesbian/gay movement. In her various published articles and a book that brings together her analyses, Rust (1995) argues that the existence of bisexual women is experienced as a threat to lesbian identity, community, and politics. That bisexuality is perceived as a threat is an indicator of problems and complexities in lesbian ideology, most particularly in its acceptance of a dualistic view of sexuality. Her survey and interview data from more than four hundred women address some of the issues directly related to her argument, such as how lesbians explain and depoliticize bisexuality; how bisexual and lesbian women explain the nature of bisexuality; and how the notions of bisexuality put forward by both lesbians and bisexual women undermine the radical potential of bisexuality to transform sexual politics.

Legal Inequalities and Employment Problems

Surprisingly little sociological work in this period focuses directly on systems of oppression. Exceptions include Meredith Gould, who examines the law, and Beth Schneider, who looks at employment. Gould (1984) examines how lesbianism is interpreted by jurists to challenge dominant perceptions of femininity and the organization of female sexual roles. She argues that "lesbianism challenges the structures and institutions of gender" and that "lesbian shocks precisely because it undermines every dominant sociocultural stereotype of women" (150). Gould concludes that while lesbians, like heterosexual women, must face a sexist legal system, as lesbians they also face a heterosexist legal system that further discriminates against them. This is most obvious in child custody cases: "Sexist law intuitively confers custody on the female parent while heterosexist law sees conferring custody on a lesbian as morally impossible" (155).

Based on quantitative analysis of answers to questionnaire items by 237 lesbians, Schneider (1986) documents the coming-out experiences of lesbians in employment, as well as with workplace affairs and sexual harassment. Schneider found that the workplace offers an important context for the beginning of sexual relationships for lesbians . Because most lesbians are employed in female-dominated settings, lesbians have greater opportunity to meet partners at work and have more equitable workplace relationships (that is, with coworkers) than do heterosexual women. Female-dominated work settings operate in other complex ways for lesbians. When lesbians are closeted, they are subject to much the same sort of sexual harassment as other women (1993); on the other hand, those settings facilitate sociability and coming out at work (1986).

Creation and Celebration of Families

Despite hostility and discrimination toward lesbian relationships and lesbian families, research on families done during this period, primarily by urban anthropologists, conveys a highly positive portrait of lesbian experiences. Kath Weston's book, *Families We Choose: Lesbians, Gays, Kinship,* utilizes field work, participant observation, and interviews with people living in the Bay Area to explore the new lesbian/gay discourse on family. She attributes this transformation in the relationship to kinship to changes in the context for coming out, the needs of building community, and the lesbian baby boom. In her empirical chapters, Weston uses coming-out stories to reveal relationships with biological families, then documents the material and symbolic aspects of lesbian/gay families and the impact of AIDS for chosen families. Weston observes provocatively, and leaves open for further discussion, that the baby boom simultaneously challenges the idea of family based on heterosexual intercourse and opposite-gender parenting while reincorporating biology.

In her book on lesbian mothers, Ellen Lewin compares results from interviews with 135 mothers: 73 lesbians and 62 heterosexual single mothers. Lewin criticizes the presumptions of psychological research regarding how the mother's sexuality or the father's absence affects children, and adopts a more sociological approach to examine the ways in which families with lesbian mothers meet the basic needs of their children.

Lewin examines how lesbians come to be mothers, the ties they form and maintain both with their biological families and their chosen families, the place of friends and lovers, relationships with the childrens' fathers, and how these mothers deal with legal threats to their rights to custody. Most intriguing is her finding that both lesbians and nonlesbians alike are heavily influenced by relatively conventional gender expectations centered on women's special vocation for nurturing and altruism. Both types of women had embarked upon a search for identity through motherhood, and motherhood indirectly enabled both lesbian and nonlesbian women to claim a specific location in the gender system. Lesbians are able to negotiate a more satisfactory relationship to traditional gender expectations than they had previously managed, and they come to share in the system of meaning that envelops motherhood in the culture. Paradoxically, then, this very process of accommodation presents them with further problems, as it frequently demands restructuring their identities to place motherhood at the core.

Identity, Difference, and Politics

In political writings about lesbian and gay communities, there is considerable debate about the ability to construct a lesbian community when its potential members are so obviously and publicly diverse. The works in this section, despite differences in the political postures of the authors, tend to work with each other in tackling various issues concerning lesbian identity and community.

In her book *The Social Construction of Lesbianism,* Kitzinger (1987) examines the social and clinical psychological, psychoanalytic, anthropological, sociological, biological, psychiatric, and sexological literature on lesbianism and male homosexuality in order to argue that the new "so-called 'gay-affirmative' research, far from being a liberating force, represents a new development in the oppression of lesbians." She argues that "the shift from 'pathological' to 'gay affirmative' models merely substitutes one depoliticized construction of the lesbian with another." Kitzinger critiques the new model as basically liberal in that it focuses on individual responsibility, internal causation, and individual solutions to problems, thus freeing the larger society from responsibility for the problems gays and lesbians face. Kitzinger maintains a radical-feminist posture; she argues that "the radical feminist argument of lesbianism is based on the belief that the institution of compulsory heterosexuality is fundamental to the patriarchal oppression of women," and takes exception to many (liberal) feminist lesbians who talk about lesbianism as no more than a choice of lifestyle, a sexual preference, the outcome of "true love," or a route to "true happiness."

Using analyses of data gathered from 120 interviews with women in and around the London area, Kitzinger suggests moving away from psychologically-driven models of the identity of individual lesbians to an examination of the origins of accounts of identity located in lesbians' sociocultural and political contexts.

Addressing some of the same concerns raised in Kitzinger's work, Arlene Stein (1993), editor of a collection of material from well-known and little-known writers, theorists, and activists, addresses the new diversity in the lesbian community, taking note of the 1990s as a historical moment in which lesbian culture is itself decentered and up for grabs. As she does in greater depth in a lengthy essay (1992), Stein explains the historical development of lesbian identity and community. She identifies several phases in community development, the first of which is marked by lesbians' struggle to rediscover roots, followed by a preoccupation with identity and with building cohesive communities in opposition to the mainstream. More recently, these seemingly unified lesbian communities have appeared to fragment as a large number of lesbians abandon a united lesbian identity to express and celebrate their individuality and differences. Stein argues that in the 1990s, it is much clearer how much of lesbian life is actually embedded in the mainstream culture, and how important it is to learn to live with the contradictions, while pushing against them. Stein suggests that it may be time to abandon the idea of "the Lesbian Community" as a singular, monolithic entity; instead, she proposes the idea of building a community through inclusion rather than exclusion.

Sociologist Vera Whisman (1993), in her contribution to Stein's volume, examines changes in lesbian alliances over the last twenty years and attempts to spell out their meanings. Lesbian feminists of the 1970s emphasized their solidarity with straight feminists by offering the notion of "woman-identified-woman" to signify the bond formed through their common stand against patriarchy. Today's younger lesbians, in contrast, often make their alliances with gay men, and are as likely to call themselves "gay girls" or "queers" as "lesbians." These younger lesbians tend to write about sex more then political theory and often define themselves as "not lesbian feminists." Today's lesbian queers see gender as a game, played with signs and symbols, whose meanings are constantly shifting and negotiable. The foundation of identity politics, the belief that lesbians share an identity and therefore a politics, is crumbling. About the movement Whisman concludes "[w]e have to minimize and maximize, create unities and simultaneously see them as false, build boundaries around ourselves, and, at the same time, smash them" (60).

Suggestions for Future Work

Sociological thinking about lesbians has vastly improved in the last decade through the thorough work of these few authors. The articles and books we have mentioned are amenable for use in upper-division and graduate courses in women's studies, sociology, and lesbian/gay/bisexual studies, and are texts upon which researchers interested in these questions must invariably build.

There is, obviously, much work still to be done. Among the most obvious immediate efforts are empirically-driven research on lesbian-sponsored activities and organizations in lesbian and gay communities at both the local and national levels, and documentation and analysis of the growth and changes in lesbian communities. Missing and very much needed are in-depth studies—through oral histories and participant observation—of the political and social lives of working-class lesbians and lesbians of color, continued examination of the crises, problems, and struggles of lesbians in health care, employment, and child care, and analyses of generational relationships among lesbians. These efforts would go a long way to making visible in a far deeper and multifaceted way the lives of lesbians in the contemporary United States.

WORKS CITED

Esterberg, Kristin. 1994. From accommodation to liberation: A movement analysis of lesbians in the homophile movement. *Gender & Society* 8, no. 3 (September):424–43.

Gould, Meredith. 1984. Lesbians and the law: Where sexism and heterosexism meet. In *Women-identified women,* edited by Trudy Darty and Sandee Potter. Palo Alto, CA: Mayfield Publishing.

Jenness, Valerie. 1995. Social movement growth, domain expansion, and framing processes: The gay/lesbian movement and violence against gay and lesbians as a social problem. *Social Problems* 42, no. 1 (February):701–26.

Jenness, Valerie and Kendal Broad. 1994. Antiviolence activism and the (in)visibility of gender. *Gender & Society* 8, no. 3 (September): 402–23.

Kitzinger, Celia. 1987. *The social construction of lesbianism.* Beverly Hills, CA: SAGE Publications.

Lewin, Ellen. 1993. *Lesbian mothers: Accounts of gender in American culture.* Ithaca and London: Cornell University Press.

Rust, Paula. 1995. *The marginal woman in the lesbian community.* New York: New York University Press.

Schneider, Beth E. 1993. Peril and promise: Lesbian workplace participation. In *Feminist Frontiers,* 3rd. ed., edited by Laurel Richardson and Verta Taylor. New York: Random House.

———. 1992. Lesbian politics and AIDS work. In *Modern homosexualities: Fragments of Lesbian and gay experience,* edited by Ken Plummer. New York and London: Routledge.

———. 1986. Coming out at work: Bridging the private/public gap. *Work and Occupations* 13, no. 4 (November):463–87.

———. 1984. The office affair: Myth and reality for heterosexual and lesbian women workers. *Sociological Perspectives* 27, no. 4 (October):443–64.

Stein, Arlene. 1993. *Sisters, sexperts, queers: Beyond the lesbian nation.* New York: Plume.

———. 1992. Sisters and queers: The decentering of lesbian feminism. *Socialist Review* 22, no. 1 (Jan–March):33–55.

Stoller, Nancy. 1995. Lesbian involvement in the AIDS epidemic: Changing roles and generational differences. In *Women resisting AIDS: Feminist strategies of empowerment*, edited by Beth E. Schneider and Nancy Stoller. Philadelphia: Temple University Press.

Taylor, Verta and Nancy Whitter. 1992. Collective identity in social movement communities: Lesbian feminist mobilization. In *Frontiers in social movement theory*, edited by Aldon D.Morris and Carol McClurg Mueller. New Haven, CT: Yale University Press.

Weitz, Rose. 1984. From accommodation to rebellion:The politicization of lesbianism. In *Women-identified women*.

Weston, Kath. 1991. *Families we choose: Lesbians, gays, kinship*. New York: Columbia University Press.

Whisman, Vera. 1993. Identity crises: Who is a lesbian anyway? In *Sisters, sexperts, queers*.

CROSS-CULTURAL LESBIAN STUDIES: PROBLEMS AND POSSIBILITIES

Evelyn Blackwood

Lesbian studies in the United States predominantly focuses on white U.S. or European lesbians, and to a lesser, though increasing extent, lesbians of color in the United States and Europe. The discussion of lesbian lives within this boundary is fairly well engaged, from the shifting contexts, meanings, bodies, identities, and politics of lesbians, to the disagreements about meanings and community, and the questioning of the category of lesbian and the hegemony and visibility of the white lesbian. But women in countries and cultures in other parts of the world are not well represented, nor can their intimate experiences and relations with other women be encapsulated easily by the same term or viewed with the same expectations. In this brief overview of "lesbian" studies cross-culturally, I will try to point out some of the pitfalls in cross-cultural studies as well as the importance it holds for lesbian studies.

The gay rights movement sparked interest in cross-cultural studies of homosexuality. The work of historian Jonathan Ned Katz (1976) provided an important early resource on gay and lesbian U.S. and Native American history. In the flush of the early gay liberation movement, gay scholars eagerly sought evidence of lesbian and gay ancestors in all corners of the world, often assuming a universal connection and commonality among all individuals who engage in same-sex sexuality. They argued against the prevailing anthropological depiction of indigenous same-sex sexual practices as deviant or outside the norm, showing that in many cultures these practices were an accepted, and in some cases highly valued, aspect of sexuality. Some efforts were made to develop preliminary transcultural typologies of homosexuality defined according to the age and relationship of the partners engaged in same-sex sexual practices.

Despite the developing interest in same-sex sexuality cross-culturally, cross-cultural lesbian studies drew the least attention in anthropological and gay studies.

As a white lesbian anthropologist I was originally drawn to the study of lesbians cross-culturally because of the lack of information available and the frequent assertion by predominantly male scholars that "lesbianism" was much less apparent cross-culturally and probably much less frequent than male homosexuality. I found that statement irritating and irresponsible: further evidence in my mind of the fact that most men anthropologists (and some women) were particularly blind to what women were doing in other cultures, as early feminist anthropologists stated often and loudly. I was convinced that more information was available and wanted to investigate the range of and constraints on women's intimate relations with women in other cultures. In a survey of anthropological texts I carried out on cross-cultural lesbian relations (Blackwood 1984a), I found more material than one would expect, given the statements of previous researchers, but none of it had ever been systematically studied nor adequately theorized. Progress in lesbian cross-cultural studies has been limited by its subsumption in the broader category of homosexuality (see Blackwood 1986). Writers continue to mistakenly conflate male and female homosexuality because they assume that a shared sexual practice, i.e., sex with a member of one's own sex, somehow means the same for both men and women. A simple glance at gay culture in the United States should have signaled the inadequacy of such a perspective (let alone attention to feminist theory). Both sociological data and folk beliefs portray gay men as quite skilled at cruising and one-time liaisons while lesbians are thought to "move in together" after the first date, suggesting that lesbians and gay men construct their sexualities quite differently. Female and male homosexual practices may be culturally defined in rather divergent ways as well. Same-sex sexuality is embedded within dominant sex and gender systems. Divergent ideological and material constraints placed on women and men cross-culturally means that sexual or intimate relations may often assume different meanings and shapes for women and men in the same culture.

The scholarship in cross-cultural lesbian studies, though limited, has begun to redress this problem. Some of the early work on lesbians, same-sex sexuality, and transgendered practices concerning peoples in Asia, Africa, the Pacific, Latin America, and Native North America includes Lorde's mention of African woman-woman marriage (1978) and Allen's discussion of Native American lesbians (1981). Since that time, other readily accessible cross-cultural studies (the majority by white European and U.S. scholars) include work on Chinese sisterhoods—women who refused marriage and formed small groups or sisterhoods, some of which were based on same-sex love relationships (Sankar 1986); "mummy-baby" relations in South Africa, probably based on a "traditional" practice of affective relations between older and younger women (Gay 1986); cross-dressing women performers of the Japanese Takarazuku Review (Robertson 1989, 1992); lesbians in Mombasa, Kenya, who may or may not also be heterosexually married (Shepherd 1987); sexual relations among black working-class women in Suriname (Wekker 1993); and articles on Cuban and Indonesian lesbians (Arguelles and Rich 1985, Weiringa 1989) and passing men (sworn virgins) in the Balkans (Gremaux 1994). A fairly substantial number of works focus on the Native American "female berdache" *[sic]*, female-bodied persons (to use Cromwell's term [1996]) who are social men (Blackwood 1984b, Midnight Sun 1988, Grahn 1986, Lang forthcoming, Medicine 1983). This Native American literature and the term *berdache* are currently undergoing serious rethinking.

Cross-cultural research on lesbians is useful in classroom studies in a number of ways. Studies of alternate genders and same-sex sexualities in other cultures illuminate the social construction of these categories. Cross-cultural studies can be used to explore diversity in forms of sexuality and sexual relations; they call into question the assumptions of "naturalness" in family and sexual forms. They problematize the Euroamerican model of sexuality and gender, a model that links sexual orientation with gender and normalizes only one form of sexuality by showing the range of practices and institutional forms of sexuality and gender cross-culturally. The presence of long-term nonheterosexual relations in other cultures problematizes the privileging of heterosexuality as the model and basic grid for family, kinship, and sexuality. Cross-cultural studies also raise questions concerning the notion of "compulsory heterosexuality" by showing that, though in all societies heterosexual marriage is expected (not always forced, however), a variety of hetero- and homosexual relations is possible in most groups during the course of an individual's lifetime.

Because sexual relations between women in other cultures arise from particular social and historical contexts of gender and sexuality, practices that may look "butch-femme" or "lesbian" to European and American lesbians may in fact mean something very different. Rubin makes the important point that "national, racial and ethnic groups differ widely in what constitutes masculinity" (1992, 470) and therefore women's expressions of that masculinity will hold different meanings. We cannot naively assume the existence of an essential sexuality, erotics, or identity for "lesbian" women worldwide. How then do we talk about, for instance, male-identified women in other cultures? How do we talk about temporary adolescent same-sex relations, or relations between women who are involved in ongoing marital heterosexual relations? Are women who engage in lesbian relations in the context of sex-segregated spaces in some Islamic cultures engaging in resistance to dominant ideology or finding release in unbearable conditions? There are no simple answers, particularly when identities of indigenous women who engage in same-sex sexuality or transgendered practices begin to reflect a growing awareness and acceptance of the Euroamerican notion of "lesbian" as a woman who loves women.

Recent work by international lesbian and gay writers is beginning to deal with the complexity of sexualities and identities in a postcolonial world. Although still few in number, these works highlight the impact of Western sexual ideology on colonized groups, showing how indigenous beliefs regarding gender and sexuality were repressed or proscribed. They also explore the complexities of accommodations and resistances to these imposed conceptions of sexuality (Chang Hall and Kauanui 1994). By rejecting anthropological and/or Western attempts to label, critique, identify, or pigeonhole indigenous sexualities and transgendered practices, indigenous writers attempt to reclaim their own subjectivities and sexualities, finding ties between contemporary and "traditional" practices (see Jacobs et al. 1996, Te

Awekotuku 1991). Yet in some cases, an emerging revisionist discourse by postcolonial lesbian and gay activists seems to reject older forms of transgender practices (here used to refer to the assumption of the opposite gender by one member of a homosexual couple). Some gay activists in the Philippines insist that gender-switching (or cross-dressing) is no longer necessary in a "modern" world in which men loving men is possible, as the Western gay model suggests (Manalansan 1994). Gayatri (1993) uses a lesbian-feminist rejection of butch-femme roles to argue that Indonesian women should be free from the confines of rigid gender roles. Ironically, at the same time in the United States, lesbian feminists are rediscovering the radical critique of heterosexuality embodied in butch-femme relationships (Kennedy and Davis 1993, Nestle 1992).

The colonization of Native American transgender/lesbian/gay studies by predominantly white anthropologists has come under increasing fire by Native American gay activists and writers (see Jacobs et al. 1996). In an effort to reclaim the terms of their identity, they have rejected the anthropologists' use of the term *berdache* as well as the rigid definitions that go along with the term. Many contemporary gay, lesbian and transgendered Native Americans call themselves *two-spirit,* a pan-Indian term referring to the presence of both male and female in a single individual. Use of this term is part of an ongoing attempt by Native Americans to deal with the complexities of their lives and their ties to their Native American cultures. For some two-spirit people it is a way to signify their difference from Western gay, lesbian and transgender identities.

As can be seen from the foregoing discussion, cross-cultural lesbian studies raise questions concerning the usefulness of a Euroamerican-dominated concept of lesbian identity. The prevalence of transgendered identities and bisexuality makes it difficult to slot other practices neatly into Western concepts of sexuality. Elliston (1995) argues that sexuality itself is not an unproblematic domain because it carries with it many of the Western assumptions about sex, sexual acts, and sexual identities. Western sexual ideology signifies an identity-based, individualistic experience that does not adequately define other forms of intimate relations between women. As Chang Hall and Kauanui (1994) argue, "The discrete analytical categories of 'homosexuality,' and more fundamentally 'sexuality' itself, are a colonial imposition which only address[es] the realities of a small part of the spectrum of Pacific people who have sexual and love relationships with members of their own sex"(76). It does not adequately represent the women I met in West Sumatra, whose gender and sexuality encompass a range of categories, including alternative genders, bisexuality, and homosexuality (Blackwood 1995). Elliston (1995) cogently expresses the problems of subsuming alternative gender and sexual categories under Western categories in her excellent critique of the concept "ritualized homosexuality." She points out that the focus on the "homosexual" element of semen practices in the anthropological literature on New Guinea imputes a Western model of sexuality and personhood that obscures the meaning of these practices in producing masculinity. Her cautionary note equally applies to lesbian studies cross-culturally. Cross-cultural studies provides the opportunity to understand local meanings of intimate relations and to question assumptions about sexuality and identity.

Given these difficulties, the continued use of the term "lesbian" for cross-cultural studies is problematic. Although Indonesians do use the term "lesbi" for female same-sex sexuality, some Indonesian women are uncomfortable with the label because of its association in the Indonesian media with Western sexuality and promiscuity (Gayatri 1993). Weiringa (1993) proposes the use of the term "homosocial" to refer to same-sex relations, which, though avoiding the problematic term "lesbian," incorporates a much broader range of relations than those based on sexual intimacy. Even within the United States, the ongoing debate over the use of the term "lesbian" to apply to cases in which genital sexual activity is absent, as in nineteenth-century female friendships (see article by Leila Rupp in this book) suggests an uncertainty about the meaning of the term. I use the term in this article realizing the irony of calling cross-cultural studies "lesbian" but wanting to hold onto a gendered signifier that terms like "same-sex sexuality" do not provide.

The trend in lesbian and gay studies cross-culturally is to a shift from the identification of patterns, traits, and roles toward a more dynamic perspective emphasizing the construction of particular gendered or sexual identities, the continual negotiation and transformation of identities in the context of dominant cultural categories, the interplay between dominant and subordinant categories and ideologies, and the conflicts among multiple identities or diverse sexual meanings. Weston (1993), for instance, argues for a move away from normative claims, fixed genders, and sexual categories, to a focus on the constructed and performative qualities of sex and gender.

The integration of cross-cultural studies into lesbian studies forces greater reflection on the meaning and coherence of "lesbian studies." How do we define "lesbian studies"? If we argue that, at a minimum, it should include only those "women" who engage in sex practices with other women (which I am not saying it should), how do we define "women," given the variability in gender representations. Does "same-sex sexuality" cover the range of practices and identities that we need to include? In delimiting lesbian/gay studies in anthropology, Weston (1993) cast her net widely. At various points in her article she used the following terms to define the subject matter: homosexual behavior and identity, 'gender bending,' multiple genders, lesbian and gay male communities, transgressive sexual practices, homosociality, same-sex sexuality, and transgendering. Although ultimately identifying her topic with queer studies, Weston chose to rely for convenience on the two terms "same-sex sexuality" and "transgendered practices" (1993, 341) as descriptive of lesbian/gay studies.

Lesbian and gay cross-cultural studies have always, at times unwittingly, now more consciously, incorporated both same-sex sexuality and transgendered practices, for example, in studies of Native American two-spirit people and Rio drag queens. The same is also true of lesbian studies. It has incorporated works on both same-sex sexuality and transgendered practices, including, for instance, studies of (mislabeled) passing "women," butch-femme relations, and masculine women, but without adequately theorizing or problematizing lesbian gender. In her discussion of butches, Rubin (1992) speaks to the lack of attention to lesbian gender. She calls for an expansive category of "lesbian" that includes the whole range of butches, from butches who are "only faintly masculine" to those who identify as men. Although I agree that we should not set up "immaculate classifications and impenetrable boundaries" (Rubin 1992, 478) in our discussion of butch or lesbian gender, there is a point beyond which the term "lesbian" is no longer useful. For instance, a female-to-male (FTM) transgender person who identifies as a man and has a woman lover cannot be called "lesbian" (see Cromwell 1996). By claiming as "lesbian" any person with a female body who engages in sex with another female body (despite FTM statements that they are men), we essentialize the gender of lesbians. This blindness to social gender means that the definition of "lesbian" ultimately depends on biology. While I am not saying that queer identities like FTMs should not be included in "lesbian studies," I am saying we need to give greater attention to the discourses, specificities, and complexities of what is called "lesbian."

If we are to develop successfully an international focus to lesbian studies, we need to set aside our own assumptions about the categories of sex, sexuality, intimacy, and women-women relationships. We need to recognize the complexities of sexualities and identities in a postcolonial world, a world in which emerging lesbian and gay activists are forging new identities that both accommodate and resist traditional and imposed conceptions of sexuality. Writings by international lesbian scholars along with their European and U.S. counterparts will provide a strong basis in the future for a developing international focus in lesbian studies. The potential is great for the development of a rich and powerful dialogue that will set the terms for new understandings and theories.

WORKS CITED
Allen, Paula Gunn. 1981. Beloved women: Lesbians in American Indian cultures. *Conditions* 7:67–87.
Arguelles, Lourdes, and B. R. Rich. 1985. Homosexuality, homophobia, and revolution: Notes toward an understanding of the Cuban lesbian and gay male experience. Parts 1 & 2. *Signs* 9, no. 4: 683–99; 11, no. 1:120–36.
Blackwood, Evelyn. 1984a. Cross-cultural dimensions of lesbian relations. Master's thesis, San Francisco State University.
———. 1984b. Sexuality and gender in certain Native American tribes: The case of cross-gender females. *Signs* 10: 27–42.
———. 1986. Breaking the mirror: The construction of lesbianism and the anthropological discourse on homosexuality. In *The many faces of homosexuality: Anthropological approaches to homosexual behavior,* edited by Evelyn Blackwood. New York: Harrington Park Press.
———. 1995. Falling in love with an-other lesbian: Reflections on identity in fieldwork. In *Taboo: Sex, identity and erotic subjectivity in anthropological fieldwork,* edited by D. Kulick and M. Willson. New York: Routledge.
Chang Hall, L. K., and J. Kehaulani Kauanui. 1994. Same-sex sexuality in Pacific literature. *Amerasia Journal* 20, no. 1:75–81.
Cromwell, Jason. 1996. Traditions of gender diversity and sexualities: A female-to-male transgendered perspective. In *Two-spirit people: The intersection of Native American gender identity, sexuality, and spirituality,* edited by Sue-Ellen Jacobs et al. Urbana-Champaign: University of Illinois Press.
Elliston, Deborah. 1995. Erotic anthropology: 'Ritualized homosexuality' in Melanesia and beyond. *American Ethnologist* 22, no. 4.
Evans-Pritchard, E. E. 1970. Sexual inversion among the Azande. *American Anthropologist* 72, no. 6:1428–34.

Gay, Judith. 1986. "Mummies and babies" and friends and lovers in Lesotho. In *The many faces of homosexuality: Anthropological approaches to homosexual behavior,* edited by Evelyn Blackwood. New York: Harrington Park Press.

Gayatri, B. J. D. 1993. Coming out but remaining hidden: A portrait of lesbians in Java. Paper presented at the International Congress of Anthropological and Ethnological Sciences, June, Mexico City, Mexico.

Grahn, Judy. 1986. Strange country this: Lesbianism and North American Indian tribes. *Journal of Homosexuality* 12, nos. 3 & 4:43–57.

Gremaux, Rene. 1994. Woman becomes man in the Balkans. In *Third sex, third gender: Beyond sexual dimorphism in culture and history,* edited by G. Herdt. New York: Zone Books.

Hart, Donn V. 1968. Homosexuality and transvestism in the Philippines. *Behavior Science Notes* 3:211–48.

Jacobs, Sue-Ellen, Sabine Lang, and Wesley Thomas, eds. Forthcoming. *Two-spirit people: Intersections on Native American gender identity, sexuality, and spirituality.* Urbana-Champaign: University of Illinois Press.

Katz, J. N. 1976. *Gay American history: Lesbian and gay men in the U.S.A.* New York: Thomas Y. Crowell.

Kennedy, Elizabeth, and Madeline Davis. 1993. *Boots of leather, slippers of gold: The history of a lesbian community.* New York: Routledge.

Lang, Sabine. 1996. Two-spirit people: Gender variance and gay identities among contemporary Native Americans. In *Two-spirit people: The intersection of Native American gender, identity, sexuality, and spirituality,* edited by Sue-Ellen Jacobs et al. Urbana-Champaign: University of Illinois Press.

Lorde, Audre. 1978. Scratching the surface: Some notes on barriers to women and loving. *The Black Scholar* 9, no. 7. Reprinted in Audre Lorde, *Sister outsider.* Freedom, CA: Crossing Press, 1984.

Manalansan, Martin F. IV. 1994. Under the shadows of Stonewall: Examining gay/lesbian transnational politics and the diasporic dilemma. Paper presented at the Sixth North American Lesbian, Gay and Bisexual Studies Conference, October, Iowa City, IA.

Medicine, Beatrice. 1983. 'Warrior women'—Sex role alternatives for Plains Indian women. In *The hidden half: Studies of Plains Indian women,* edited by P. Albers and B. Medicine. New York: University Press of America.

Midnight Sun. 1988. Sex/gender systems in Native North America. In *Living the spirit: A gay American Indian anthology,* edited by Gay American Indians and Will Roscoe. New York: St. Martin's Press.

Nestle, Joan, ed. 1992. *The persistent desire: A femme-butch reader.* Boston: Alyson Publications.

Povinelli, Beth. 1992. Blood, sex, and power: "Pitjawagaitj"/menstruation ceremonies and land politics in Aboriginal northern Australia. Paper presented at the 91st Annual Meeting of the American Anthropological Association, November, San Francisco.

Robertson, Jennifer. 1989. Gender-bending in paradise: Doing "female" and "male" in Japan. *Genders* 5:50–69.

———. 1992. The politics of androgyny in Japan: Sexuality and subversion in the theater and beyond. *American Ethnologist* 19, no. 3:1–24.

Rubin, Gayle. 1992. Of catamites and kings: Reflections on butch, gender, and boundaries. In *The persistent desire: A femme-butch reader,* edited by Joan Nestle. Boston: Alyson Publications.

Sankar, Andrea. 1986. Sisters and brothers, lovers and enemies: Marriage resistance in southern Kwangtung. In *The many faces of homosexuality: Anthropological approaches to homosexual behavior,* edited by Evelyn Blackwood. New York: Harrington Park Press.

Shepherd, Gill. 1987. Rank, gender, and homosexuality: Mombasa as a key to understanding sexual options. In *The cultural construction of sexuality,* edited by P. Caplan. New York: Tavistock.

Te Awekotuku, Ngahuia. 1991. Dykes and queers: Facts, fairy tales and fictions. In *Mana wahine Maori: Selected writings on Maori women's art, culture and politics.* Auckland, New Zealand: New Women's Press.

Thadani, Giti. 1993. Lesbian nominations and the politics of identities and languages (India). Paper presented at the 13th International Congress of Anthropological and Ethnological Sciences, June, Mexico City, Mexico.

Wekker, Gloria. 1993. Mati-ism and black lesbianism: Two idealtypical expressions of female homosexuality in black communities of the Diaspora. *Journal of Homosexuality* 24, nos. 3 & 4:145–58.

Weston, Kath. 1993. Lesbian/gay studies in the house of anthropology. *Annual Review of Anthropology* 22:339–67.

Wieringa, Saskia. 1989. An anthropological critique of constructionism: Berdaches and butches. In *Homosexualities, which homosexualities?,* edited by D. Altman et al. London: GMP.

———. 1993. Introduction: Negotiating lesbian/homosocial identity in cross-cultural perspective. Paper presented at the 13th International Congress of Anthropological and Ethnological Sciences, June, Mexico City, Mexico.

PART FIVE

*Working
with/in
Institutions*

CYBERDYKES,
OR LESBIAN STUDIES
IN THE INFORMATION AGE
Ellen Broidy

Once upon a time, not so very long ago, we all knew what lesbian meant. We understood, as well, in those simpler, less fluid days, where the library stood, literally and figuratively, with respect to lesbian topics. Suddenly, everything changed. We ceased to fix identity, theorized and conceptualized, and reconfigured lesbian studies, and in the process, fundamentally altered both the methodogical and bibliographic base of the field. This brief essay highlights some of the changes occurring in traditional and electronic information environments and attempts to provide scholars and students with lavender signposts in a shifting material and virtual terrain.

Ida VSW Red's contribution to the 1982 edition of *Lesbian Studies* tracked ten years' worth of coverage of lesbianism in standard sources available in academic and most large public libraries, including the *Readers' Guide to Periodical Literature* and the *New York Times Index*. Red pointed out that "one way to make a quick assessment of material available for a research topic is to 'read the subject' in periodical and literature indexes" (Red, 62). This should resonate with everyone who has ever tried to find information on lesbians in her local library. Since the publication of that article, however, the focus of the discussion about where and how to find "lesbians in the library" has undergone a sea change. From a preoccupation bordering on obsession with how the Library of Congress has categorized lesbians, we now find ourselves at an intellectual crossroads where the elevation of "lesbian" to subject(heading) status (hailed in less complicated times as a major victory), is increasingly read against cries of "essentialism" and dire warnings of the consequences of starting down the slippery slope of identity politics.

The central questions for today's librarians and researchers have ceased to revolve around the ability or desirability of isolating a single inoffensive yet definitive word or term. Critical theory and information technology (the ideal postmodern marriage) have combined (or conspired) to create the need to conceptualize first and then to describe bibliographically increasingly complex social and sexual constructs. Freed from the constraints of rigid classification systems yet still dependent on language as the key to identification and access, library-based research on lesbian topics remains a challenge. A changed and highly charged political, intellectual, and academic climate distinguishes today's challenges from those described a decade ago by Ida Red and others.

I leave it to other contributors to this anthology to detail the myriad and intricate transformations in lesbian scholarship. However, one academic trend, queer theory, is having such a profound impact on the approaches libraries take to lesbian studies that it deserves at least brief mention here. The very nature of "queer," challenging at every turn earlier theoretical and scholastic constructions of both women's studies and lesbian studies, combined with its undeniable appeal to a growing number of younger students, female and male, raises significant issues about how libraries acquire and organize information and then make that information accessible to the user. Does "queer" include (or subsume) lesbian? Are they mutually exclusive terms? How do libraries, still imbued with the fundamental principles of fixed categories and rigid classification schemes, assign responsibility for collection development in both lesbian studies and queer studies, particularly if "queer" signifies a resistance to categorization? Collections are put at risk and materials may fall through the cracks while champions of emerging (and competing) academic disciplines struggle for bibliographic legitimacy and collection development dollars.

From a researcher's perspective, arcane battles between collection development librarians over intellectual territory mean little; however, the outcome of those battles may well have a negative impact on the ability to identify resources relevant to lesbian studies, above and beyond the very real issue of materials simply not acquired. Although advances in information technology have loosened the linguistic knot, students still draw on class lectures and syllabi for their research vocabulary. Despite the fact that libraries have moved beyond "homosexual, see also perversion," the student coming from a classroom where "queer" is the word of choice, may still face an uphill battle when attempting to find a linguistic link to relevant and useful material.

The development of a wide range of information technologies has the potential to help researchers overcome barriers presented by both linguistic limitations and academic intrigue. Twelve years ago Ida Red's analysis of subject headings compelled us to examine the limitations of standard library tools for finding lesbians. Today, a plethora of new electronic resources, coupled with an explosion in publishing, have literally opened the floodgates to information on lesbians. The ability to use key words (significant and meaningful terms) to search for material in computerized library catalogs and periodical indexes has freed us from the grip of subject headings. Drawing on words from the titles of books, articles, videotapes, and data sets, the material practically indexes itself. Concepts such as "lesbian feminism" or "queer theory," thus far missing from the list of standard subject headings, reveal themselves to the user of an online system with key word search capability, provided the author of the book or article has been prescient enough to include at least one generally recognized term in the title of the work. We now have a range of clear avenues to materials once well hidden.

Lest we become too complacent, however, it is worth noting some of the hazards in this brave new technological world. For lesbian studies, these fall into two broad categories, source issues and equity issues. "Source issues" refers to the types of materials readily available in electronic format. For the most part, publishers continue to concentrate on computerizing existing data. That is, they take the path of least resistance and most marketability, often simply transferring a print product into machine-readable format. Caught up in the rush to digitize existing sources, publishers have paid far less attention to how those sources might be changed or enhanced. Although somewhat improved since Ida Red conducted her survey, standard periodical indexes still do a poor job of covering lesbian periodicals. Those weaknesses are transferred wholesale into the online versions. With a few notable exceptions, lesbian-focused periodicals tend to fall into the category of alternative material, which is acquired and indexed in a far from systematic fashion.

The migration from a print index that requires a visit to the library to one that can be scanned with a few key strokes on a home computer has instilled a false sense of intellectual security. The fact that a search of the online version of Current Contents covering 1 July 1989 through 21 November 1994 yields some 460 citations containing the word lesbian is actually a two-edged sword, particularly for students with little familiarity with the subject and even less research sophistication. On the one hand, the sheer number of articles indexed (and the range of journals in which they appear) reflects a mini-explosion of interest in and publishing on lesbians. On the other hand, an even cursory perusal of the journal titles indicates that the index itself, in spite of its 460 citations, is severely deficient in specifically lesbian and alternative press publications. Students, especially, get caught up in the trap of thinking that if they have located something online, they have identified what's truly significant on any given topic. The seductive nature of electronic resources, the "let your fingers do the walking" school of research, legitimates what is found while further marginalizing, if not completely obliterating, materials not represented in the database.

How aware a researcher is of the lack of specifically lesbian information in online systems depends almost entirely on whether that person has access to the necessary computer hardware. A growing reliance on technology threatens not only to obscure critical data but to exacerbate further the distinctions between information haves and have-nots. Computers cost money and most systems, even those billed as "user-friendly," require at least a modicum of specialized training. Libraries, caught between diminishing budgets and accelerating demands, have become increasingly uncritical consumers of whatever promises new technologies make to alleviate the financial burdens imposed by inflation and the escalating costs of actually purchasing materials. Many well-meaning librarians, eager to stretch shrinking dollars, have adopted an "access, not ownership" philosophy, making the "end-user" (the lesbian studies researcher) even more dependent upon computerized resources. If we add the problem of insuring equal access to computer hardware to the aforementioned intellectual limitations imposed by publishers' neglect of lesbian sources, and stir in a dose of "access, not ownership," we have a recipe for a technological revolution with seriously negative implications for lesbian studies.

It would be inaccurate, however, to cast the information "revolution" in entirely negative terms. In addition to liberating users from the shackles of rigid subject headings, new technologies, used wisely, have the potential to break down social and academic isolation, to provide researchers in lesbian studies with a new sense of community, albeit one in cyberspace. Within the past three to five years, "Lesbian Nation" (in an assortment of guises) has become an increasingly popular destination on the so-called information superhighway. While remaining cognizant of the critical concerns about equality of access (and, at the risk of overstating the point, the quality of the final product), it's hard to deny the impact of computers, and in particular their potential for opening up whole new worlds of information possibilities. Sources as wildly diverse as scholarly articles on and by lesbians in electronic journals, a listserv for lesbian graduate students, a "Queer Resources Directory," and an interactive online discussion forum focusing on the wit and wisdom of Camille Paglia coexist on the "net" and are but a few computer key strokes away for the intrepid navigator in cyberspace.

Now more than ever, on the eve of the twenty-first century, the degree to which we have access to information about our own lives and experiences depends increasingly on two key factors: the amount (and quality) of information we generate/produce about subjects of interest and the willingness to generate that information in new and technologically challenging formats. At this particular moment in our collective history, the legitimacy and viability of lesbian studies require close cooperation between scholars and activists producing data (taken in its broadest sense) and librarians and other information specialists committed to making that data accessible. In the old days (literally BC—before cyberspace), "think globally, act locally" served lesbian studies well. We fought our battles for scholarly legitimacy, whether in terms of the right to offer a class, add a book to the library, or earn tenure, at the local level, on an individual campus, or in an academic department. We reported on our victories and setbacks and connected to each other's struggles somewhat haphazardly, through irregularly published newsletters, association caucuses, and shifting personal networks. We had every reason to feel confident that we knew, or could easily imagine, what other people were doing, simply because the networks were small and the struggles depressingly similar. Information technology has changed all of that by, first and foremost, forcing a reconceptualization of the whole idea of a "network." Technology has created a "network" with the potential to transcend all borders, geographic, political, philosophical, and disciplinary. We now have the ability to "think locally, act globally," but only if we're prepared to take the initiative, learn the requisite skills, and most importantly, occupy as much cyberspace as we possibly can.

The occupation of cyberspace, going where no dyke has dared to go, presents a whole new set of challenges. Whether we like it or not, we now debate our differences and disagreements and celebrate our points of cohesion in a hitherto unimaginably public manner. For librarian and researcher alike, the struggle for a lesbian voice in this uniquely public space is alternately liberating and confining. The mini-explosion of online resources that touch on lesbian lives, including the increasingly contentious listservs, point us, hydra-like, in all directions at once. Chaos can be liberating. However, not all resources are equal, even (or especially) in cyberspace. We run the risk of being trapped in a maze of too much information, a substantial amount of which contributes more to clutter than to knowledge. As we plan for the possibilities of a "library without walls," we need to reflect on how best to incorporate new technologies into more traditional modes of operation, many of which continue to serve us well. Harking back to Ida Red's concerns about subject access, we should remember that even in this brave new technological world, many of our students (and many of us) continue to rely upon tried and true methods to approach a research question. Most people, even those quite comfortable with cruising the internet, have not yet translated that familiarity into increased research sophistication, especially as the deadline for the paper or project approaches. Given the anarchistic and chaotic nature of the net, we remain at some distance from the possibility (I resist labeling it a goal) of using computers to answer all our questions. Even with the prospect of increased order and organization, the internet probably will remain a form of hightech diversion and amusement for many of us. For the foreseeable future, we will exist in a parallel universe consisting of a largely uncharted (and possibly unchartable) virtual reality and an alternately confusing and comforting "real" world. We continue to conduct research in that real world (and advise our students to do the same), in spite of rigid classification schemes, inconvenient library hours, musty books, and missing journal issues. Realistically, lesbian studies, in all its numerous guises, will continue to occupy the middle ground between technologically advanced and traditional research sources and strategies. The more confident we are of our abilities to function in either realm, the better able we will be to insure the creation, identification, acquisition, and transmission of the critical building blocks of the discipline. In this information age, teachers, librarians, students, activists, working together on and off the net, are all the more responsible for the bibliographic viability of lesbian studies.

WORK CITED

Red, Ida VSW. 1982. "Note on 'Reading a Subject' in periodical indexes." In *Lesbian studies: present and future,* edited by Margaret Cruikshank. New York: The Feminist Press.

GLBT PROGRAM OFFICES: A ROOM OF OUR OWN

Beth Zemsky

When I was first asked to write a piece for this anthology, I hesitated. As someone who has spent most of her professional life outside of the academy working primarily as a psychotherapist, community educator, and community organizer with gay, lesbian, bisexual, and transgender communities, and who now coordinates the nonacademic Gay, Lesbian, Bisexual, and Transgender (GLBT) Programs Office at the University of Minnesota, I perceived myself as outside lesbian studies. But the more I thought about my task (with the assistance and prodding of others), the more it seemed significant for me to struggle with how to delineate the ways in which the relatively new enterprise of GLBT program offices connect to the project of lesbian studies, or more generally, GLBT studies.

History and Overview of GLBT Program Offices

Gay, lesbian, bisexual, transgender program offices[1] have existed since 1971 when the University of Michigan established its Lesbian-Gay Male Programs Office. Currently several U.S. colleges or universities have professionally staffed offices, almost all created as the outcome of surveys that investigated campus climate for gay, lesbian, bisexual, and transgender students, faculty, and staff. The specific history, environment, and local and campus politics of each university have influenced the methodology, outcomes, and implementation of the recommendations put forth in the various campus reports (a selection of which is included). I offer our experience at the University of Minnesota as an example of a successful process that has yielded many changes throughout the institution.

Efforts to evaluate campus climate for GLBT people at the University of Minnesota began as a result of extensive lobbying by student and faculty groups. In response, the president requested the appointment of a subcommittee, the Select Committee on Lesbian, Gay, and Bisexual Concerns, which operated for three years, collecting information through spoken and written testimonies, focus groups, curriculum surveys, student surveys, and audits of faculty and staff benefits at other institutions. Its effectiveness owes much to its official university status and specific mandate to conduct a university-wide study. It was also significant that the committee was predominantly comprised of openly GLBT students, faculty, and staff, as well as a cadre of vocal heterosexual allies, in a powerful example of coalition building.

In the fall of 1992, GLBT students were subjected to a number of incidents of homophobic harassment. These shocked the administration and others within the university community. In reaction to the vehemence of these attacks, the president requested that the Select Committee's survey be curtailed on the grounds that there was no need to "prove" the existence of homophobia in the face of the escalation of harassment and violence on campus. Instead, he asked the Select Committee to publish its report with concrete recommendations as to how to respond institutionally to the problems revealed through its study. The following five recommendations were proposed by the Select Committee:

- Establish a gay, lesbian, bisexual, transgender programs office.
- Provide a full benefits and privileges package for the families and children of gay and lesbian employees.
- Establish a gay and lesbian studies program.
- Develop educational training programming on gay, lesbian, bisexual, and transgender issues and concerns.
- Update all printed publications and materials to reflect diversity in sexual orientation.

At the time of this writing, four out of five of these recommendations have been either fully or partially implemented. The only recommendation that has not yet achieved significant progress is the development of a GLBT studies program.

On most campuses, surveys reveal a climate at best chilly and at worst openly hostile and intimidating to GLBT students, faculty, and staff and to the pursuit of scholarship in GLBT studies. GLBT program offices, created in the attempt to respond to these endemic campus-wide problems, take on various missions depending on the specific needs identified in the campus surveys and the possibilities for institutional support that exist within each campus structure and prevailing campus politics. As a result, each existing GLBT program office has a different mission, structure, activity schedule, and staffing pattern, and is lodged in a different position in the institution's administrative hierarchy. Most GLBT program offices are situated within Student Affairs, while others may report directly to a chancellor's office or jointly to Student and Academic Affairs. Our office at the University of Minnesota reports to Human Resources/Academic Affairs. Placement within an institutional hierarchy is no small matter given that it influences which constituency the office can serve—e.g. students only or a broader constituency that includes staff and faculty; the services it can provide—student support services, counseling, and associated programming versus the additional agenda of faculty and staff issues, domestic partnership, and academic/curricula concerns; and the amount of institutional support and validation the office may receive both in funding and in institutional decision and policy making. Placement issues are also important, given the systematic disempowerment of Student Affairs-related activities that is currently occurring on many campuses. It seems, therefore, that for GLBT program offices to be credible and effective institutionally, they need to be linked to the academic mission and academic activities of the university.

Again, I offer our program at the University of Minnesota as an example of the type of mission and services GLBT Program offices provide. The mission of the GLBT Program Office at the University of Minnesota is to:

- assist bisexual, transgender, gay, and lesbian faculty, staff, and students at the University of Minnesota in fostering a supportive community;
- educate and provide resources for all members of the University of Minnesota community about issues that impact the experience of transgender, gay, lesbian, and bisexual staff, students, and faculty; and
- support the development of curriculum and research in the area of gay, lesbian, bisexual, and transgender studies.

This mission is achieved through information and referral, advocacy, consultation, and coordination. Information about campus and community resources and events, university policies, local ordinances, and educational resources is available online via Gopher on the office's information and referral database, through walk-in and telephone requests, and through the office's information files and small research library. Assistance, support, and referrals are available to students, faculty, staff and others who perceive that they have been treated unfairly because of their sexual orientation or gender identification. Educational programming is provided through professional in-service workshops, campus events, and special guest speakers. The office also coordinates a volunteer speaker's bureau. Program development assistance is available to university groups and individuals planning projects appropriate to the needs of GLBT people. Technical assistance is available for other transgender, gay, lesbian, and bisexual organizations on campus.

Lesbian or GLBT?

Can a joint GLBT program office respond to our needs as lesbians? Do lesbians feel welcomed and included or marginalized and invisible in the alphabet soup of offices attempting to respond to the needs of multiple communities? These are difficult and often contentious questions. In my experience, how these questions are asked and how they are answered often depends on what one means by the word "lesbian" and how one positions oneself in relation to this construction. In addition, how these issues are addressed is also influenced by one's relationship to the categories "gay," "bisexual," and "transgender."

Shortly after beginning as Coordinator of the GLBT Program Office, I met with a group of lesbian faculty and staff to gain input into the development of the mission and services of the office. One woman, who is a well-known and respected feminist leader on campus, stated that while she didn't like the "L" and the "G" being together in the title and in the work of this office, she understood why the linkage was made. On the other hand, she didn't understand the inclusion of the "B" and the "T" at all. I think this faculty member spoke for many women on this campus and elsewhere who configure their identities first as women, then as lesbian, and hardly ever connect in their own identification to anything that could be defined as GLBT or "queer." For these women, GLBT program offices may not at first glance feel like rooms they can call their own.

Another example is an event I witnessed at a reading given by a very well-known lesbian feminist theorist and author. During the question-and-answer period, a number of women began discussing a declining interest in women's studies and in self-labeling as "feminist." The author suggested that perhaps this was occurring because women's studies was perceived as too radical for this generation of women. A young woman in the audience, who preceded her comments by defining herself as a "queer girl," quickly responded that the author had got it all wrong. Rather than being too radical, she perceived that women's studies and feminism were not radical enough. She added that she was concerned not only with her role as a woman, but she was also interested in issues concerning the construction of gender, sex, and sexuality. She went on to state that she hadn't felt welcome in her campus's women's center or in the women's studies classes she had taken.

In each of these examples, I believe these women perceived something to be at stake in terms of their sense of self-definition and group identity. How do we define ourselves? With whom do we ally ourselves? And for many of us, which of our multiple identities is primary for us in a particular situation? These are not solely academic questions. They also have something to do with what we need to feel safe, to feel we belong, and to believe that a field of study or an office that is supposed to address our needs will actually do so. These issues often can and do trigger deep emotional responses.

My own personal goal as Coordinator of the GLBT Program Office is to build a program and a community that is inclusive of all the various ways we as women, as lesbians, as bisexuals, as queer women, identify ourselves and lead our lives. For me, this means taking into account the fact that each of our multiple identifications tends to shift from foreground to background depending on the environment or the situations we are in and the amount of stress we are under at any particular time.[2] To respond to this, we need programs and fields of study that recognize the complexities and fluidities of our identifications, our needs, and our interests. So, whether we call a studies program or a program office "GLBT" or "lesbian," we will still need to attend to the fact that for some, "lesbian" is a classification secondary to "women," for others it is a primary identification and needs to be acknowledged as such, and for still others, "lesbian" is a way of being "gay" or "queer."

GLBT Program Offices and Lesbian or GLBT Studies

As noted above, the only recommendation set forth by the Select Committee that has not yet achieved much progress at the University of Minnesota is the creation of a GLBT studies program. Given the chilly campus climate revealed in the survey, I took it for granted when I began the GLBT Program Office that survival issues for faculty, staff, and students on campus—such as a system to respond to harassment and violence, an information and referral network, and domestic partner benefits—needed to take priority in planning my time and our programming. I soon realized, however, that in an institution of higher education, the availability of academic options quickly becomes a "survival" issue that directly effects recruitment, retention, creativity, self-esteem, and scholarly productivity for faculty as well as students. If any significant change is to be made in the overall campus climate towards lesbians and other gay, bisexual, and transgender people, it needs to include development of some type of lesbian or GLBT studies program, department, or interdisciplinary project.

As a result of the Select Committee process at the University of Minnesota, groups of students, staff, and faculty have begun to explore the possibility of coordinating and formalizing some type of academic field of study. Although more questions have emerged from these discussions than answers, these questions seem to point to the next steps in this project: How do we define who and what we are studying? Is it important to this project that we reach such a definition? Can one form an academic studies program out of an identity category, particularly one that has been constructed so differently in various places and times? What would be the core curriculum of such a program? What would be the best way to organize this project: as it is now with courses loosely offered and scattered across the curriculum? as an interdisciplinary program with a cohesiveness, however minimal, to its curriculum design? as a project subsumed under the rubric of women's studies? as a department with its own standing faculty? None of these questions has easy answers. They all require us to look both at what is optimal and what is practical. Moreover, these discussions are not solely about theory and curricula, but also about how we place ourselves in the world, as I discussed above.

In the meantime, there are a number of things that GLBT program offices can do to support the development of lesbian and GLBT studies. At the University of Minnesota, for example, our GLBT Programs Office has begun coordinating a quarterly course listing of GLBT studies courses. We have also begun gathering the names of faculty members from various disciplines interested in this project, their research interests, and their availability to serve as advisors to students. In addition, we have developed a small library of books and articles specifically chosen to be of use to faculty as they plan their syllabi and to students beginning research projects. In the near future, we also hope to have a centralized file of all syllabi of previously taught lesbian and GLBT studies courses. Lastly, we have developed a number of internet guides to conducting research on various topics concerning lesbian and GLBT studies.[3] Our intent is to be able to serve as a clearinghouse of information about lesbian and GLBT studies to facilitate the development of interest, research, and curricula in this area of study.

Conclusion

In addition to being educators, policy makers, and theorists, all of us who are in any way involved in the project of lesbian studies are also activists. Whether or not we set out to be activists, or desire to be such, involvement in a project that steps outside and challenges academic and institutional assumptions to the extent to which lesbian studies does makes us activists. While the political climate on many campuses has made claiming activist status very dangerous, I think it is important that we do not fool ourselves. One of the goals of our work is to change how knowledge about lesbians is constructed and how lesbians are treated on campus and in the culture at large. Social change, no matter what the venue, is always an activist project.

I understand our GLBT Programs Office at the University of Minnesota to be an activist enterprise within an academic environment. For lesbians on campus, I view this project as building a community in which we are able to feel strong in our identities, have access to academic resources and programs, and have the ability to work within and across communities. It is also important for me to remember that the university and academic community is only one community among many. The activist work we do on campus must take into account our relationship and responsibility to our wider off-campus communities and their social change agendas. We are in the position to serve as role models to support others in the process of identity development personally, professionally, and politically. We are also in the position to assist in the acquisition of the skills and self-confidence needed for leadership development. In addition, our work as educators and theorists makes us uniquely suited to translate the concepts of lesbian and GLBT studies to our communities—particularly to community organizing projects that would benefit from stronger theoretical underpinning. As the radical right grows in strength and in its ability to dominate how the discussion of our lives and issues is framed, the importance of our potential role as explicators of their rhetoric increases. My hope is that we can be proud of our work in asking questions, struggling to find the answers, and continuing to seek the linkage between academics and activism.

To receive or send information on campus GLBT centers, contact Curt Shepard, Director, NGLTF Campus Project, 6030 Wilshire Blvd., Ste. 200, Los Angeles, CA 90036; phone 213/934-9030; fax 213/937-0601; email cxsngltf@aol.com.

NOTES

1. These offices are called many different things depending on the university structure in which they are lodged, the mission of the specific office, who is perceived to be in the target constituency, and the politics of the local community. Choosing a name for the office itself can be a highly contentious discussion. (e.g. Are the words "bisexual" or "transgender" included or excluded? Is "lesbian" listed first or "gay"? Is it sufficient to just say "gay"? Or does one need to say "gay male"?) I have chosen to use the phrase "gay, lesbian, bisexual, transgender program office" for two reasons: (1) this name is inclusive of all the

constituency groups that might be the purview of such a office, and (2) this is what the office I coordinate was named, and so, more expedient for my purposes in this article.

2. I am indebted to Professor Larry Davis, George Warren Brown School of Social Work, Washington University, for this concept.

3. The Gay, Lesbian, Bisexual, Transgender Information and Referral Database can be found in the Gopher system under "University of Minnesota Campus Information, Information and Referral." It also can be accessed by using our Universal Resource Locator address: gopher://rodent.cis.umn.edu:11132/ or gopher://rodent:cis.umn.edu:11132/1, if using Mosaic.

SELECTED BIBLIOGRAPHY OF UNIVERSITY REPORTS

Arizona State University Campus Environment Team, *Campus Environment Team Referral Guidebook 1992–1993*. Tempe: Arizona State University.

Breaking the Silence: Final Report of the Select Committee on Lesbian, Gay, and Bisexual Concerns. Minneapolis, MN: University of Minnesota, 1 November 1993.

Chancellor's Campus-Wide Task Force on Sexual Orientation Final Report. Urbana, IL: University of Illinois-Urbana-Champaign, 19 April 1987.

Duke University Task Force on Gay, Lesbian, and Bisexual Matters 1991–1992 Report. Durham, NC: Duke University, 28 August 1992.

Gay and Lesbian Issues Committee, Issues of Concern to Gay, Lesbian, and Bisexual Students on Our Campus. Madison, WI.: University of Wisconsin-Madison, 23 January 1992.

Gay, Lesbian, Bisexual Community Concerns Advisory Committee, *The Education Climate for Gay, Lesbian and Bisexual Students at the University of California at Santa Cruz*. Santa Cruz, CA.: University of California-Santa Cruz, February 1990.

President's Select Committee for Lesbian and Gay Concerns, *In Every Classroom*. New Brunswick, NJ: Rutgers University, 1989.

Report of the Domestic Partner Benefits Task Force. Oxford, OH: Miami University, November 1992.

A Report of the Spousal Equivalency Task Force. Columbus, OH: Ohio State University, 1992.

The Study Committee on the Status of Lesbians and Gay Men, *From Invisibility to Inclusion: Opening the Doors for Lesbians and Gay Men at the University of Michigan*. Flint, MI: University of Michigan, June 1991.

University Committee on Faculty and Staff Benefits, *Report of the Subcommittee on Domestic Partners' Benefits*. Stanford, CA: Stanford University, June 1992.

University of Colorado at Boulder Task Force for Lesbian, Gay, and Bisexual Concerns, *Diversity or Discrimination? A Report on the 1991 University of Colorado at Boulder Sexual Orientation Survey*. Boulder, CO: University of Colorado at Boulder, 19 December 1991.

University-Wide Task Force on Lesbian & Gay Issues, *Moving Forward: Lesbians and Gay Men at Michigan State University*. East Lansing, MI: Michigan State University, 1992.

Update on the Reports by the University Committee on Nondiscrimination. Durham, NC: Duke University, 4 November 1993.

"SO FAR BACK IN THE CLOSET WE CAN'T EVEN SEE THE KEYHOLE": LESBIANISM, HOMOPHOBIA, AND SEXUAL POLITICS IN COLLEGIATE WOMEN'S ATHLETICS

Susan Cahn

In an era in which women's intercollegiate athletics has experienced both phenomenal growth and unfulfilled promises, to dare raise the subject of lesbianism can send shock waves through the women's sports community. The issue is so explosive that merely acknowledging the presence of lesbians or mentioning the problem of homophobia in collegiate sports can be perceived in itself as a slanderous attack on women's athletics. For instance, in August 1993 the *Austin American-Statesman* ran a story about the problems faced by the University of Texas (UT) "Lady Longhorn" women's basketball program due to its reputation as a "gay team." Although the journalists did not identify any individuals as lesbian or even broach the topic of the coaching staff's sexual preferences, UT coach and athletic director Jody Conradt described the occasion of the article's publication as "the most difficult time for me professionally, ever." And despite the objective, even sympathetic, tone of the piece, most women's sports advocates assumed that the impetus for the article came from male critics who wanted to discredit UT's nationally renowned women's athletic program.[1]

While Conradt and her supporters might appear to be overreacting to a newsworthy story (the article appeared as part of a pathbreaking three-part series on homosexuality and homophobia in men's and women's sports), subsequent events indicate that their assessment of danger was not exaggerated. Along with personally receiving hate mail, vicious phone calls, and cancellation requests for season tickets, Conradt learned that each of her new players had received, anonymously, a copy of the article in the mail. Such "negative recruiting" is a frequently used tactic. One former UT player who was considering other schools received a postcard from the Baylor basketball program which read, "Coach is outspoken against lesbianism and won't accept it."[2] Most homophobic recruiting ploys are not this explicit, with the word "lesbian" typically avoided by defenders and critics alike. College coaches may recruit high-school players by reassuring parents that all their players are "nice girls" who "look like girls." The message is clear. For women in the 1990s, though it is increasingly acceptable—even laudatory—to be a top-level athlete, to be a lesbian in sports jeopardizes one's good standing as both a woman and an athlete.

Sport and the Unleashing of Female Passion

The disruptive power of the lesbian presence in sports, whether rumored or real, has its roots in the historical relationship between women's sports and female sexuality as well as in present-day political battles over gender equity in high school and collegiate athletics. Athletics has long been the province of men. In the nineteenth and twentieth centuries in the United States, the connection between sports and masculinity has been represented in the heroic image of the virile male athlete. Therefore, when women began to claim the playing fields as their own, they challenged deeply held beliefs about both gender and sexuality, especially the powerful association between sports and masculine sexual virility. Critics of "the modern athletic girl," as she was dubbed, posited that manly sport would necessarily masculinize the female body, character, and spirit. They supposed, therefore, that the "mannish" female athlete would undoubtedly acquire masculine sexual characteristics and interests as well. One question remained, however. Would the "mannish" woman athlete simply gain the erotic appetite and sexual aggressiveness of men, or might she also seek out the normative objects of male desire—other women?

Somewhat surprisingly, early twentieth-century angst about the harmful effects of athletics on female sexuality focused on heterosexuality, not homosexuality, fearing that athletic activity might unbridle previously suppressed heterosexual desires or stimulate new ones. The responsibility for containing and protecting the female athlete's sexuality fell in large part to women physical educators who supervised the athletic activities of high-school girls and college women. Responding to public concerns about the sexually endangered athlete, women educators charted a conservative course. They developed an athletic philosophy characterized by regimented exercise, limited competition, and close supervision of student athletes. A ban on varsity competition helped secure a measure of respectability for women's athletics. Yet ironically, this approach would come to haunt the next generation of women physical educators who encountered a very different set of concerns about female athletes and their sexuality.

The transition began in the 1920s and 1930s, decades when changing sexual practices and beliefs laid the groundwork for future associations between women's athletics and "mannish" lesbianism. As modern notions of sexuality took the place of a crumbling Victorian code, assertive heterosexuality, once a sign of sexual deviance, now formed the standard of acceptable femininity. Under modern sexual codes, the sexy, feminine, spunky but ultimately compliant heterosexual female became the ideal, while sexual stigmas developed around both the "Victorian prude" and the "mannish lesbian." Women physical education students and athletes, long known for their appropriation of "mannish" games and styles, met with a new set of indictments for sexual deviance.

Over the course of the 1930s, female athletic mannishness began to connote *failed,* rather than *excessive,* heterosexuality. After two decades of tolerating or even celebrating the female athlete, college yearbooks of the 1930s began to ridicule physical education majors and Women's Athletic Association (WAA) members, portraying them as hefty, disheveled, and ugly. Although only hinted at, the impression of heterosexual "failure" contained a further possibility as well: the Amazonian athlete might not only be unattractive but unattracted to men—she might prefer women. One 1937 yearbook sarcastically titled its WAA section "Over in No Man's Land."[3] The policies which had once protected their heterosexual respectability now cast physical educators and their students as unattractive prudes, and perhaps even as man-hating lesbians.

The "Mannish Lesbian Athlete" at Mid-Century

Tentatively voiced in the 1930s, the lesbian stigma became harsher and more explicit under the impact of war-time gender disruptions and postwar fears of an imagined "homosexual menace." Earlier vague suggestions of lesbianism emerged as a full-blown stereotype of the "mannish lesbian athlete." Postwar women athletes—noted for their masculine bodies, interests, and attributes—became convenient marks for the culture's homophobic invective. College athletes, formerly accused of being unappealing to men, were increasingly charged with being uninterested in them as well.

Educators hastened to revise their policies and philosophies in accordance with the new heterosexual mandate. As early as the 1930s, physical education leaders began to de-emphasize same-sex intramural activities and team sports in favor of mixed-sex "co-recreation," touted as an "agency for social adjustment" which "provides normal social relationships."[4] Women leaders also invited psychologists to their professional conferences where they informed educators of "the different types of people who are unadjusted to heterosexual cooperative activity" and advised them on their role in fostering sexual adjustment.[5] This proactive approach to heterosexuality continued into the conservative postwar decades.

In conjunction with curricular reform, mid-century physical educators launched internal crackdowns on students and faculty who might feed the public image of mannishness. They implemented dress codes which forbade slacks and men's shirts or socks, adding as well a ban on "boyish hair cuts" and unshaven legs.[6] In the end this strategy did little to diminish the lesbian reputation of women's sports. Even on a practical level, dress and behavior codes sometimes backfired. Intentionally or not, attempts by physical educators to mollify a homophobic public merely added to the institutional bulwark which privileged heterosexuality and condemned lesbianism. The image of the "mannish lesbian athlete" survived as a symbol of female deviance, issuing a pointed announcement to *all* women that competitiveness, strength, independence, aggression, and physical intimacy among women fell outside the bounds of normal, "feminine" demeanor and would be not be tolerated. The damning associations between lesbianism, "mannishness," and women's sports persisted, forming an unwanted legacy that the next generation of women athletes would once more confront, though under far more hopeful conditions.

Lesbianism, Lavender Elephants, and Gender Politics in the Post-Title IX Era

Beginning in the early 1970s, women's athletics entered a watershed era in which longstanding barriers to full participation in sports seemed to fall almost as fast as women could push them over. Bolstered by feminism, the counterculture's concern with personal well-being, and radical critiques of inequality in U.S. education and social structure, advocates of women's sport strengthened their own critique of the male-dominated sports world and began demanding equal access to athletic resources and training. They won their most important and controversial victory with Title IX of the 1972 Educational Act, legislation which prohibited sex discrimination in any educational institution receiving federal funds. Although it would take years before federal officials definitively interpreted and began enforcing the law, the act dictated that schools at all levels establish a rough gender equality in access to coaching, scholarships, training facilities, and athletic opportunities.

Title IX, along with the broader influences of feminism and the fitness boom, ushered in two decades of significant athletic progress not limited to academic institutions. While professional athletes organized women's tours and campaigned for increased prize monies, amateur women's sports blossomed at all levels. Top-ranked athletes increased their participation in Olympic and international competitions while girls and women of lesser skill flocked to community-based youth soccer, aerobics, and adult softball programs. Girls' participation in interscholastic high-school competition jumped from three hundred thousand in 1971 to more than two million in 1992. Similar improvements occurred at the college level with an increase from sixteen thousand to over 160,000 female intercollegiate athletes between the early 1970s and late 1980s.[7]

Along with the increase in sheer numbers, women athletes have also found far greater acceptance and appreciation. Encouraged by the fitness boom and the enormous growth of women's competitive sport, a new cultural aesthetic has incorporated athleticism, muscle tone, and strength into ideals of feminine appearance. Revised beauty standards reflect significant changes in behavioral norms as well. Recent surveys have found that parents now rate athletic involvement as equally important for daughters and sons, and, as if to prove it, high-school girls have come to take athletic opportunities and scholarships so much for granted that they often view the "fuss" over gender equity as irrelevant or passé.

Given these advances, we might predict that the stigmatized image of the mannish lesbian athlete would gradually lose its potency and fade away. Yet this has not been the case. In fact, oddly enough, concerns about lesbianism in sports may even have increased in inverse relationship to the greater acceptance of women's sports in general. As women at the University of Texas discovered, when the UT program gained national prominence, rivals and detractors found lesbian-bating an all too convenient and effective tactic. Why has the disparaging image of the lesbian athlete remained a formidable force in the world of sports? The answer lies in sexual politics, both the tangible politics of competition over resources in high school and college athletic programs, and a more diffuse cultural politics involving changing definitions of femininity and appropriate female behavior.

Title IX ushered in a sea of change in school athletics, but this feminist victory did not occur without enormous opposition and a string of lawsuits that continues to this day. The National Collegiate Athletic Association (NCAA), the governing body for men's intercollegiate sports, opposed Title IX with all its might, spending years and great sums of money lobbying to overturn the act or to include within it an exemption for athletics. As it became clear that the law would stand up, individual campuses stalled or made incremental changes while at the national level the NCAA initiated what was essentially a "hostile takeover" of women's college athletics in the early 1980s. With promises of lucrative financial support and expanded television coverage, the NCAA succeeded in overpowering the much weaker Association for Intercollegiate Athletics for Women, the autonomous women's organization that had not only piloted women's intercollegiate athletics through a decade of phenomenal growth but had also become one of the most effective advocates for gender equity on college campuses.[8] In the 1990s, with the NCAA firmly in command, women's and men's sports programs have found themselves still pitted against each other in battles over resources and control.

In this polarized atmosphere, accusations of lesbianism function to discredit women's programs and place them on the defensive. There is no diabolical conspiracy at work here, and as far as I know there are no specific cases in which male administrators have publicly levelled the charge of lesbianism at women's teams. Yet women coaches have found that rumors of lesbianism, whatever their source, inflict continual damage on individual athletic programs, teams, and personal careers (many unmarried coaches, lesbians or not, feel under constant suspicion of lesbianism and some even report considering marriage as a career-saving measure).[9] The pressure to raise revenue through increased attendance encourages women's programs to seek public approval by presenting reassuring images of "normalcy." Thus, team policies prohibit athletes from going to gay bars; lesbian coaches and athletes remain so closeted that as one coach said, "we're so far back in the closet we can't even see the keyhole";[10] and, in the interest of public relations, media guides confirm players' femininity by decking them out in Playboy bunny outfits or Victorian gowns and parasols.[11]

Beyond the turf wars and budget battles of collegiate athletic departments, far more subtle forces operate to maintain the stigmatized reputation of lesbian athletes even as women's sports as a whole have gained greater acceptance. Participating and excelling in athletics no longer automatically connotes masculinity; an appreciative public generally concedes that a woman can actively pursue athletic excellence with no cost to her "femininity," however one defines it. Yet because older associations between masculinity and athletic skill linger on—as do cultural fears about physically strong and sexually independent women—a peculiar tension has taken hold of women's sports. The popularity of sports among girls and women means that athleticism is now consistent with "normal" female behavior, but ultimate acceptance hinges on an athlete's ability to reassure the public that, however exceptional her athletic talents, she is in all respects a "normal" woman.

The lesbian athlete, with her reputation for "masculine" style, body type, and desire, represents a refusal to issue this reassurance. Her sexual autonomy and her rejection of conventional femininity—as defined through heterosexuality—make her the locus for enduring fears that women in sports transgress gender lines and disrupt the social order. It is not coincidental that the years in which Martina Navratilova first revealed her bisexuality (later, lesbianism) were also those in which her superlative performance on the women's tennis tour led to assertions that she was some kind of bionic phenomenon, a genetic anomaly who fell into a unique gender category of not-woman, not-man.[12] Nor is it surprising that the charges of lesbianism are most always directed not at weak programs or losing teams, but at the best ones. Top-notch teams feature stellar athletes who disturb the still prevalent assumption that, when all is said and done, women may be welcome on the playing fields but they are in no way men's equal there; and as lesser athletes, they should also be willing to settle for smaller portions of the athletic pie.

Supporters of women's rights and women's athletics on campuses face a strategic dilemma. How do we acknowledge lesbianism and confront anti-lesbian bigotry in sports when by even raising the issue we run the risk of incurring the very prejudices we seek to abolish? The fear of exposure runs so deep that many supporters of women's sports calculate that even to admit the presence of lesbians and their contribution to sports would confirm destructive stereotypes and risk the hard-earned gains of the past two decades. Thus, it was UT's Jody Conradt and Donna Lopiano, former UT women's athletic director and current director of the Women's Sports Foundation, both defenders of sexual "diversity," who most vehemently opposed the *Austin American-Statesman's* decision to go public on the issue of lesbianism and homophobia at Texas. The dilemma is complicated by the fact that homophobic pressures are exerted from *within,* not only from outside women's sports. Male and female coaches of women's athletic teams engage in negative recruiting and lesbian labeling in order to attract the best recruits. Even those who scrupulously avoid this tactic might counsel their players and their peers to remain closeted in order to present the best (i.e., straightest) face to the public, or simply to protect their scholarships or jobs.

Under these circumstances, some advocates believe that the best strategy is to take the moral high road and not deign to notice homophobic innuendos or scurrilous lesbian attacks. But this has proven ineffective; the silence surrounding lesbianism in sports is a very loud one, and the issue is just as powerful, if not more, when left unaddressed. Pat Griffin, an educator at the University of Massachusetts, likens this silence to a large lavender elephant in the middle of the locker room, a creature carefully ignored by all and acknowledged by none.[13] Since the elephant is not going anywhere by itself, not speaking about the problem is, in effect, a way of speaking in favor of the status quo.

How then to address the issue in ways that do not jeopardize women's careers or athletic programs? One strategy is to chip away at the problem from the inside, through organizing homophobia workshops, holding team discussions on sexuality, and raising the issue at conferences and within feminist sports circles.[14] While such efforts will hopefully nurture greater understanding and toleration among players and coaches, this strategy alone will do nothing to counter the anti-lesbian hostility, lesbian-baiting, and stereotyping that persist in the broader sports world and the wider culture.

To work toward these ends will require long-term political struggle on all related fronts: lesbian and gay rights, gender equity in education and sports, and the more amorphous politics of emancipating women's bodies and challenging restrictive, binary notions of gender. In the shorter run, we need to go beyond the rather timid politics of acknowledging "diversity" (read: lesbianism) in sports and begin actively to explore, defend, and appreciate the lesbian presence in sports. For example, we can begin to investigate past and current connections among sports, sexuality, and lesbianism. Are lesbians indeed statistically over-represented in sports, and if so, why? What are the cultural dynamics at work that might make athletics, in contrast to other cultural arenas, a positive site for lesbian participation?[15] Such honest inquiries could be joined with action. If women's sports advocates initiate action directed at the general problem of homophobia—not lesbianism—we might avoid placing individuals in jeopardy while also reducing the sense of foreboding that currently pervades these discussions.[16] When accusations are leveled, we might aggressively respond with the rejoinder, "So what if every member of a team is a lesbian? Why does this make the team any less worthy of support or interest?"

In this spirit, beyond defending the right of every woman, whatever her sexuality, to athletic participation, I aspire to an active appreciation of the historic and present-day lesbian contribution to sports. Through decades of neglect and ridicule, women's athletics have benefitted enormously from the contributions of lesbians who participated as players, coaches, administrators, and fans, and in doing so have helped build an athletic tradition that serves as a foundation for the many opportunities that today's girls and young women enjoy.

NOTES

1. Quote from Helen Thompson, "A Whole New Ball Game," *Texas Monthly* (March 1994): 144. The *Austin American-Statesman* article "Diversity Creates Dilemma for Lady Horns," appeared on 3 August 1993.

2. "Diversity Creates Dilemma for Lady Horns," C3.

3. *Gopher Yearbook* (1937), University of Minnesota Archives.

4. Conference Reports, Box 17, Eastern Association of Physical Education of College Women (EAPECW), Sophia Smith Collection, Smith College, Northampton, MA.

5. National Amateur Athletic Federation—Women's Division, Newsletter #79 (1 June 1938), from Dept. of Women's P.E. Records, University of Wisconsin Archives. University of Wisconsin, Madison.

6. The 1949–50 Physical Training Staff Handbook (p.16) at the University of Texas stated "legs should be kept shaved." Box 3R213 of Dept. of Physical Training for Women Records, BTHC, Univ. of Texas. Restrictions on hair and dress are spelled out in the staff minutes and P.E. handbooks for majors at the universities of Wisconsin, Texas, and Minnesota.

7. See Vivian Acosta and Linda J. Carpenter, "Women in Intercollegiate Sport: A Longitudinal Study—Fifteen Year Update, 1977–1992" (Carpenter/Acosta, Brooklyn College, Brooklyn, NY 11210, 1992), and Linda Jean Carpenter, "The Impact of Title IX on Women's Intercollegiate Sports," in *Government and Sport,* edited by Arthur T. Johnson and James H. Frey. (Totowa, NJ: Rowman and Allanheld, 1985), 62–78.

8. For a detailed account of the NCAA-AIAW conflict, see Mary Jo Festle, "Politics and Apologies: Women's Sports in the United States, 1950–1985" (PhD dissertation, University of North Carolina, Chapel Hill, 1993).

9. See "Lesbian Issue Stirs Discussion," *Los Angeles Times* (6 April 1992): C1, C12; and "Out of the Closet," *Women's Sports and Fitness* 14 (September 1992): 62.

10. East Coast basketball coach quoted anonymously in Annette John-Hall, "Homophobia Is Repressing Female Athletes," *San Jose Mercury News* (16 April 1993): 8E.

11. In a bizarre twist of history, these media presentations have occasionally required African American athletes at southern colleges to dress up like "Southern belles" as part of an aristocratic plantation motif which flies in the face of historical accuracy; their female ancestors would most likely have been the slaves of the antebellum "ladies" they now portray.

12. Sports writers have described Navratilova as an invincible Amazon, a "bionic sci-fi creation" of her training team, and a "bleached blonde Czech bisexual defector" who was "simply too good" for the rest of the tour. Her treatment as some kind of aberrant creature was echoed by at least one woman on the tennis circuit who suggested to a reporter that for Navratilova to play as well as she did she "must have a chromosomic screw loose somewhere." For these characterizations, see *Sports Illustrated* 59 (19 September 1983): 29–31; "The Smartina Show, or Tennis in a Lethal Vein," *Sports Illustrated* 58 (4 April 1983): 34; "The Best of All Time?" *Time* 24 (16 July 1984): 61–62; and Frank Deford, "A Pair Beyond Compare," *Sports Illustrated* 64 (26 May 1986): 80.

13. Griffin is quoted in "The 'Huge Lavender Elephant': Homophobia's Contribution to the Decline of Women Coaches," *Equal Time* (12–26 April 1991): 8.

14. Dee Mosbacher is currently producing a film, titled "Out for a Change: Homophobia in Women's Sports," to be used in workshops on homophobia. For more information, write Dee Mosbacher, M. D., PhD, 3570 Clay Street, San Francisco, CA 94118.

15. For a historical exploration of these themes, see Susan Cahn, "From the 'Muscle Moll' to the 'Butch' Ballplayer: Mannishness, Lesbianism, and Homophobia in U.S. Women's Sport," *Feminist Studies* 19 (Summer 1993): 343–68, or *Coming on Strong: Gender and Sexuality in Twentieth-Century Women's Sport* (New York: Free Press, 1994), chaps. 7 & 8. For contemporary and autobiographical explorations, see Yvonne Zipter, *Diamonds Are a Dyke's Best Friend: Reflections, Reminiscences, and Reports from the Field on the Lesbian National Pastime* (Ithaca, NY: Firebrand Books, 1988) and Susan Fox Rogers, ed., *Sports Dykes: Stories from On and Off the Field* (New York: St. Martin's Press, 1994).

16. An example of this kind of proactive endeavor occurred in 1994 when the Women's Sports Foundation lent their support to the Gay Games in New York City on the grounds that the Games have traditionally been a great supporter of women athletes.

COMPLETING THE KENTE: ENABLING THE PRESENCE OF OUT BLACK LESBIANS IN ACADEMIA

Angela Bowen

When I met with the admissions committee for graduate school, a woman on the committee who was about my age asked, "Why do you want to be entering graduate school now at this stage of your life? They're very ageist in the academy, you know." My mental response was, "Oh, really, and not racist, sexist, and homophobic as well?" I took her point, but I do not see my age, or my color, or my sex as the biggest problems I will encounter within the academy. Nor do I expect the biggest obstacles to be the difficulty of the academic work, the patriarchal structure of the institutions, or the disdain, disregard, and erasure of my Black, middle-aged, woman, lesbian, feminist, community-connected self by an omniscient, omnipotent, Eurocentric patriarchy (although I am familiar with all of the above). What I am far more apprehensive about is the potential disdain, disregard, and erasure of my lesbian self by my Black heterosexual and hidden lesbian sisters, from whom I would rather anticipate comfort, encouragement, a safe retreat.

Survival in the academy without the hope of Black sisterhood would be a dim prospect indeed. Therefore, given our small numbers, imagine the joy with which I would discover the one other Black sister at a campus where I am newly hired—only to see her turn away with disdain when she realizes that she is talking to a lesbian. Since I cannot imagine retreating into the closet at this point in my life, we both end up isolated and lonely.

So, these are the questions that concern me: Will our Black heterosexual and hidden lesbian sisters enable out Black lesbians to survive? And, beyond survival, will they be allies; will they enable us to do our work? For if we are all to fulfill our mission—to water the thirsting spirits and intellects of our precious young Black women and men—we visible Black lesbians in the academy must not only survive, but thrive. If we thrive, we will have the strength to battle for broad issues within the academy, including the academic and psychic survival of our students; the addition of a further dimension to Black feminist analyses; the pursuit of scholarship in a wide variety of fields, among them, the newly emerging discipline of lesbian and gay studies.

If we thrive, that is. Hardships abound within the academy now, particularly for Black women and women of color, making it even more difficult than before (and it never was easy) to construct the networks of support that are critical in providing the lesbian visibility so necessary to our students and to our scholarship. Black heterosexual and hidden lesbian sisters can show solidarity in this endeavor by neither fearing nor undercutting us, but helping to watch our backs by feeding us the information we need to avoid traps, enabling us to be as out as possible, for all of us. That sounds like a bargain to me. It's the kind of bargain that sociologist Aldon Morris refers to in the *Origins of the Civil Rights Movement* (1984), where he writes about the bus boycotts and lunch counter sit-ins in the south in the 1950s. Black businessmen who had money and goods to offer but were vulnerable to white retaliation if they were open in their support, kept silent but contributed in the background, keeping the movement going while the churches served as movement centers. The ministers, who were not directly dependent on the white economy, could take the lead because they bore less risk. It is not too much for us to expect similar support from Black women in academe.

No evidence leads me to expect a critical mass of out Black lesbians within academia in my lifetime, or to presume that any and all Black lesbians will feel, as I and some others do, such a necessity to be out. Nevertheless, it is comforting to know that for those of us who do feel the necessity, there exists within academia a staunch group of heterosexual Black sisters who, both personally and in the work they are creating, offer consistent support to out Black lesbians. Gloria Hull has discovered and revealed lesbianism within the work of Alice Dunbar-Nelson and Angelina Weld Grimké. Barbara Christian wrote about lesbians in the novels of Ntozake Shange, Alice Walker, Gloria Naylor, and Audre Lorde. Beverly Guy-Sheftall and Johnnetta Cole have instituted lesbian-positive programs at Spelman College. There are others as well. But my larger point is that we need to make it possible for a Black lesbian to expect that she can arrive *anywhere within academia* and, knowing that she has to already battle racism, ageism, Eurocentrism, et cetera, can at least expect a homecoming from whatever Black woman she encounters, regardless of sexual orientation.

Building such networks of support would allow us to provide a visible presence to all our students, thus helping them understand that we are existing and flourishing everywhere, even on college campuses, as professors. Our visible, proud matter-of-fact acceptance of ourselves would show them that all our lives are valuable, precious, and meaningful. Students would see that we command respect for who we are and what we know, just as all their professors do. This in turn would help foster respect in heterosexual students for their peers who are lesbian, gay, or bisexual, or who may be struggling with sexual identity issues. And our visibility would allow them to carry positive images of Black lesbians in their lives beyond college. If we offered them this broader outlook, they, as well as we, would survive, thrive and contribute to the future of Africanas throughout the Diaspora.

South Africa has already reached beyond the United States in constructing a constitution which includes rights for lesbians and gay men, rights which Nelson Mandela proclaimed in a recent public statement. By embracing lesbians and gay men, Mandela honors our total humanity, for of course we are more than lesbians, just as we are more than Black, more than women, or mothers, or daughters, or teachers. The point is not that we want to make ourselves into one gigantic walking capital "L." No. We insist on claiming the lesbian identity because without it we are not whole; and without a sense of wholeness we lose our strength, our creativity, our sense of adventure, our vision.

Twenty years ago a vision of the formation of lesbian and gay studies was activated in the academy. In order to help shape the emerging discipline, one would most likely need to be out. However, even now, in 1996, the mere mention of lesbian and gay studies may cause many to twitch in their seats, for a variety of reasons, heterosexism and homophobia being only two. But the reality is that in a few years lesbian and gay studies will be a freestanding discipline. There are valid reasons for this expectation. City College of San Francisco established a gay studies department in 1989, which now grants an undergraduate two-year associate's degree. In 1991 the City University of New York Graduate School established the Center for Lesbian and Gay Studies for both academic and community scholars. Other major universities, including Duke and Harvard, support lesbian and gay studies as well.

However, within the gay and lesbian studies departments now laying the groundwork for the discipline, the prime leaders are white gay men. Unfortunately, we see very little of either community-connected / liberatory feminist theory or Black lesbians' work being studied in the rapidly expanding number of courses. Consequently, the burgeoning canon rarely includes the work of Black lesbians. If Black women scholars ignore the ramifications of this omission, we will yet again be playing catch-up for decades to come. Surely we have been down this rusty track before. So here is another case where we had better climb on board before the train leaves the station because in the not too distant future, as the momentum picks up and colleges and universities look around for us, we'll be outside on the platform clamoring and complaining when we could have been inside all along.

The majority of Black students may have little interest in lesbian and gay studies, although some who are inquiring and adventuresome will. But the course offerings will be far more crucial to Black students who know or may have begun to suspect that they might be lesbian, gay, or bisexual. It is essential that the latter group in particular be aware of the contributions Black lesbians, gay men, and bisexuals have made throughout the history of this country—indeed, the world.

It is of great importance as well to those students questioning their sexual identity who may not be able to overcome their fears enough to venture out and examine what the field has to offer, but whose awareness of the existence of these courses *and of the physical presence of out Black lesbian professors* will validate their lives. Just knowing we are there may enable them to stay on campus and continue their studies, whether or not they ever make contact. I know this to be true from my years of speaking engagements at different colleges and universities. In fact, one of the main reasons for my decision to enter academia stems from these experiences, where I could see the desperate need of many students.

And this is an important point for me. If we are out there visibly as Black lesbians, our young Black college students will be able to locate us. They need to look us in the eye and have us honestly say who we are. I remember once co-facilitating a workshop at the University of New Mexico on the visibility of lesbians within academe. There were about sixty women in the room, nearly all of them white, only a few of whom were out, and those few were generally teaching part-time or in community colleges. The reasons given were those we are all familiar with: being out would retard their careers, or keep them from getting tenure, or cause hostility, or keep the students from being able to relate to them. After about forty minutes of this, Vivien Ng spoke up. As I recall, she was the only woman of color in the room. She said that she went as an out lesbian to teach at the University of Oklahoma because the students were her priority, and she wanted to be visible as a lesbian for them. If she didn't rise in the academy, so what? She made enough to live on whether she ever got tenure or not, and that was the right decision for her, regardless of the outcome. And in fact, she had received tenure with no trouble and was very well liked and respected.[1] Ng's example was set before me at a crucial time when I was questioning whether I could pursue a graduate degree and a place within academia, being who I am. Clearly, the politics of liberation are often at odds with the politics of the academy, and I needed to discern and address the difference, as Ng had done and as each of us must do, shaping our own visions for ourselves.

If we accept W. E. B. Du Bois's concept of the "two-ness" of Black folks' vision, we must then accept that Black women bring a "three-ness" of vision to all societal relations. How, then, can Black women who accept this concept not acknowledge that Black lesbians carry a "four-ness" of vision that pushes scrutiny and clarification to yet another level? If we are truly seeking more analyses that will broaden our approaches to our feminist politics, scholarship, history, our very lives, then the vision of Black lesbian feminists is crucial.

Sometimes Black lesbians who are quite brave about being out in all other aspects of their lives are paralyzed with fear when it comes to being themselves within academia because the Black sisterhood makes it clear that it will not abide a lesbian who brings attention to her sexual identity on campus. It is all right to be one, just keep quiet about it. This silencing tactic is a reactionary holdover that refuses to recognize the radical oppositional stance of claiming lesbianism as a valid identity, not merely a "sexual preference," that old liberal canard which glosses over the political ramifications of choosing an out lesbian life. For some of us, living as an open lesbian is not a choice but a necessity, although the difference between deciding and doing so are two vastly different realities. Still, as Audre Lorde once said, as difficult as it is to be out, living in the closet is even more difficult.

So, why should we out Black lesbians expect support from Black women in the academy? Because every Black woman in the academy, whether she is a heterosexual, a closeted lesbian, or somewhere on the continuum between (Rich 1980), benefits from lesbian visibility. Our scholarship and pedagogy, our participation in lesbian and gay studies, our radical stance, the chances we take—all allow us to be seen as "bad girls," the "fringe folks." Black lesbians, by pushing the edges of expectations further within the academy, make more room for all of us.

Audre Lorde asks: "What are the tyrannies you swallow day by day and attempt to make your own until you will sicken and die of them, still in silence? I am . . . a Black woman warrior poet doing my work—come to ask you, are you doing yours?" (1984, 41–42). For some of us, our work is to affirm our lesbianism publicly in every area and in as many ways as possible. Indeed, as Adrienne Rich writes,

> For us, the process of naming and defining is not an intellectual game, but a grasping of our experience and a key to action. The word lesbian must be affirmed because to disregard it is to collaborate with silence and lying about our very existence; with the closet-game, the creation of the *unspeakable* (1979, 202).

Silences, gaps, erasures, lies. Who will rectify them if not out Black lesbians? Who has more of an investment in expunging the myths, distortions, and stereotypes and exposing the reality of our lives than out Black lesbians? Who will fight harder against the exhortations which entice us to conform, to abandon our voices and our communities and stay within the walls, within the confines of language? Who has more need to resist the insidious pressures of cooptation, the rewards of security and comfort dangled before us, urging us not to say too much, do too much, identify with our communities too much?

Yet the Black lesbian's investment in withstanding the pressures, in struggling against cooptation, does not guarantee that we will be able to call up the strength to keep doing it over and over, coming out repeatedly, writing articles without knowing if they will be rejected—not because of the worth of the work, but because of their content. Having the investment and commitment does not mean you don't have to walk the line, knowing that no matter how much you may talk or write about being a woman, being Black, a mother, a historian, a writer, or whatever else, as soon as you say you are a radical lesbian feminist, you are being "essentialist," "blatant," "political," "unprofessional," or in some other way unacceptable. Black women know the routine because we get the double dose of racism and sexism. Add homophobia to the mix (which, when it comes from Black women, raises the intensity exponentially) and you might just begin to fathom the level of pain.

The truth is that we're all in this together, each of us has our piece in the kenta cloth, and we need one another's presence to make it whole. So who among our Black heterosexual and hidden lesbian sisters will provide a safety zone when we stagger back from the front line of hostility, hatred, homophobia—the war zone? We need steady, unwavering support and encouragement. Our heterosexual sisters need the "fourth" dimension of our vision, and we all need each other's strength, courage and fortitude. Do we Black lesbians have allies? This is no mere academic question, for we are all beneficiaries of our struggle and the war really is the same, as sister Audre said in "Outlines":

> We choose the earth
> and the edge of each others battles
> the war is the same
> if we lose
> someday women's blood will congeal
> upon a dead planet
> but if we win
> there's no telling
> we seek beyond history
> for a new and more possible meeting.
> I look to meet you
> upon whatever barricade you erect or choose.[2]

Thanks to Vivien Ng for allowing me to relate her story. Thanks also to Jennifer Abod and Jacqui Alexander for their insightful comments.

NOTES

1. When I related this story in a speech at the first Midwest Conference of Lesbian and Gay Students at Oberlin a few years ago, a young man in the audience confirmed Ng's availability and openness, stating that he felt she had saved his sanity, literally. He had graduated and at the time of the conference was working at another college in administration, serving as liaison to lesbian and gay students.

2. The last two lines as presented here were spoken by Lorde at the 1990 "I Am Your Sister Conference" honoring her life. An earlier version without the final lines appears in *Sister Outsider.*

WORKS CITED

Christian, Barbara. 1985. *Black feminist criticism.* New York: Pergamon, 187–204.
Hull, Gloria, Patricia Bell Scott, and Barbara Smith, eds. 1982. *All the women are white, all the blacks are men, but some of us are brave.* New York: The Feminist Press.
Hull, Gloria. 1987. *Color, sex, and poetry.* Bloomington and Indianapolis: Indiana University Press.
Lorde, Audre. 1982. *Zami: A new spelling of my name.* Watertown, MA: Persephone.
———. 1984. *Sister outsider.* Trumansburg, NY: The Crossing Press.
Morris, Aldon. 1984. *The origins of the Civil Rights movement.* New York: The Free Press.
Rich, Adrienne. 1979. *On lies, secrets, and silence: Selected prose, 1966–78.* New York: W.W. Norton.
———. 1980. Compulsory heterosexuality and lesbian existence. In *Blood, bread, and poetry: Selected prose, 1978–1985.* New York: Virago Press & W. W. Norton.

FIGHTING REPRESSIVE TOLERANCE: LESBIAN STUDIES IN SWEDEN
Karin Lindeqvist

Sweden Should Provide Fertile Soil for Lesbian Studies

According to the United Nations, Sweden is the world's leading country in equality between women and men. Women's studies has become an (almost) accepted part of the universities, and at every Swedish university there is a forum for women researchers and for research on women. And, formally, it is comparatively easy to be a lesbian in Sweden. Open homophobia is rare. There is legal protection against discrimination; a lesbian relationship is regarded as sufficient reason to grant a residence permit to non-Swedes. Beginning January 1, 1995, lesbian and gay couples can enter what are called registered partnerships, which have all the legal consequences of a marriage except the right to adopt children together.

However promising these conditions, lesbian studies are only just beginning to take shape. So far there have been only two courses dealing with lesbianism, and to my knowledge only one completed dissertation with a lesbian subject and one in progress by lesbian researchers. In this essay I will, after presenting what has been done, try to offer some thoughts about why lesbians and lesbian perspectives are so invisible in Swedish society in general and in research and education in particular.[1]

The first course at the university level was held at Kvinnovetenskapligt Forum (Forum for women's studies) at the University of Gothenburg in 1993. It was called "Forms of Sexuality" and focused on the cultural construction of sexuality and gender and on power relations between heterosexuals and homosexuals.

The other course was not at a university but in adult education. It was called "Lesbian Life" and was held at Kvinnofolkhogskolan (Adult education college for women) in Gothenburg in 1992. It was a semester-long course with eight students from nineteen to forty-three years of age. Before that, the school had offered at least one short course (two to three days) every semester with a lesbian theme. The course was one of three women's studies courses that year but it was the one everyone noticed. A lot of feelings came up over that course.

The course investigated history, literature, and recent official documents and reports in order to see what attitudes society holds towards lesbianism. Students also participated in a radio program that documented their work in the course. The class went to Berlin, where they encountered contemporary lesbian and gay life in all its variety. The purpose of the course was not to help women come out, but to strengthen their lesbian identity, analyze heterosexism, and give students a chance to talk about lesbianism not only on a personal level but also as a political issue.

The course had several aftereffects. First, it made many people outside the school regard it as a lesbian school: it is so provocative and unusual for one out of three courses to have had a lesbian theme, that everything associated with the school is considered lesbian. The women working at the school did not hear any direct accusations but have been told secondhand that some employment exchanges would not refer unemployed women to the school. They have also warned them that they would encounter lesbians there. Second, it made the heterosexual women working there more aware of the issue of lesbian oppression, so that they have initiated discussions about lesbianism and homophobia.

Kvinnofolkhogskolan was founded by women from the women's movement, both lesbians and heterosexuals, and has a strong feminist ideology. The school wants to give women time and opportunities to explore their life conditions and potential. With that knowledge, they can then work for change on both a personal and a political level.

The school opened in 1985 on its own premises and is equal to other adult education colleges in Sweden when it comes to grants or giving credits for higher education. The planning and preparations, however, go back to 1976. From the very beginning, one of the most important ambitions was to reach immigrant women, unemployed women, and women with little formal education. The school provides child care to make it accessible to women with children. Every year the staff arranges short courses over weekends and the summer. These courses have a number of subjects—economics, dance, social work, video production, and religion. Some include lesbian contexts.

Women from about twenty nations attend the school each year and 40 percent of all students are from countries other than Sweden. They have a "sister school" in India and support their work.

Homophobic reactions from the students sometimes occur. For example, they have an annual photography course whose theme changes each year. When the theme was lesbian life, an unsigned letter was put up on the bulletin board asking whether heterosexuals were welcome at the school. The matter was resolved, however, and the course was quite successful with both lesbian and heterosexual participants.

One woman pointed out that the hardest opposition and suspicion comes not because they have lesbian courses or some of the teachers are lesbians, but because they are women organizing for women in a women-only space. This is dangerous and highly uncommon in Sweden. Something very important in this context is that Kvinnofolkhogskolan provides a place where lesbians within and outside the academic world can meet and discuss issues.

The one completed lesbian dissertation is about erotic and homosexual motifs in the Finnish-Swedish writer Tove Jansson's 1914 work.[2] Outside Scandinavia, Tove Jansson is perhaps best known as the author of the Moomin books, but she has also written novels and short stories for adult readers, among them the novel, *Rent spel* (Fair play, 1989) about the love and lives of an older lesbian couple.

The dissertation in progress is about Selma Lagerlof (1858–1940) and how images of "male" and "female" are constructed and recreated in her literary production and her private letters, to see how they are related to concepts of her time in the light of a contemporary lesbian feminist perspective.[3] This is groundbreaking work about an author whom previous researchers have desperately, almost comically, tried to "heterosexualize." As a woman writer who also wrote children's stories and used legends, folklore, ghost stories, and myths in many of her works, Lagerlof has sometimes been dismissed as dated and quaint. Her position and insights as a woman outside heterosexual institutions have always been overlooked.

Why Is the Silence around Lesbianism in Sweden so Forceful?

In Swedish culture, there is a marked tendency to avoid conflicts, to seek consensus, to find the point where everyone agrees. The welfare state was slowly built, reform by reform, agreement upon agreement. There is a long tradition of negotiations between labor and employers, tenants and landlords. When the common denominator is so desirable, you can't highlight difference. In such a "let's be friends" atmosphere, it is difficult to raise dissident voices, to find a platform for challenging heterosexual hegemony.

Open expressions of homophobia outside extreme Christian and right-wing groups are rare. Prejudice is considered bad manners. The homophobia is there, but mostly hidden in polite silence. If I should try for a rough generalization, the message from society at large would be: "OK, be a lesbian if you have to, but don't fuss over it, don't flaunt it, and don't put uncomfortable questions about heterosexism on the agenda. What you do in private is your own business, but don't try to raise lesbian feminist political issues."

Another consideration is that both the gay movement and the women's movement in Sweden have concentrated on issues of equality. The gay movement stresses the sameness between heterosexual and homosexual love, avoiding issues around difference, working hard for the right to marry and adopt children. The women's movement has focused on issues of work, wages, and child care, rather than on issues of violence against women or sexuality.

There is no strong lesbian movement in Sweden. If you want to, it's very easy to look at your lesbianism as something private. If you don't make yourself visible, you will remain invisible, and invisibility makes oppression possible. This is easy to forget when little open homophobia exists to remind you of its deadly aspects.

Also, there are few theoretical and political discussions within the lesbian community. One explanation is the lack of domestic material—almost no lesbian non-fiction books, no lesbian magazines, no public forum for sharing ideas and ideals. There are also difficulties around formulating a specific lesbian question in Sweden. Many lesbians are involved with more general women's issues (i.e. abortion is legal and available on demand, but there is strong pressure from Christian groups to put restrictions on that right), with general homosexual issues (i.e. the right to adopt children), and with minority issues (i.e. working with immigrants and nonwhite people in the antifascist and antiracist movement).

Universities in Sweden Are Slow to Accept Changes and New Perspectives

As a part of an established European male tradition of what is considered culture and science, there are rather set rules of what are to be regarded as worthy subjects for research. Theories on gender, race, ethnic background, and sexuality have difficulty being accepted. The universities are also closely linked to the state. One woman with a non-Swedish background said she felt that Swedish universities have two functions: to solve problems for the government and to serve the business world.

The universities are very male-dominated. Only 6 percent of all professors are women, and far from all of those are feminists. As one woman put it, the universities want mainstream/malestream students. Lesbian as well as feminist research is regarded with suspicion as lacking scientific relevance. If a lesbian does research about a lesbian subject, she is suspected of being biased, writing in self-interest, and committing the cardinal sin of not being objective enough. To write a paper at the pre-graduate level is quite possible and there are several in different subjects, but to get a lesbian subject approved for a dissertation is much harder. One woman has tried to get permission to write her dissertation in sociology about lesbians but has been turned down by several universities. She feels that, had she not been open as a lesbian herself, she might have had more luck. Then her research would have been accepted as it should have been from the "outside" as an established form of sociological research about deviations. She also sees a backlash against feminist-oriented research in sociology.

So far, there has not been much discussion about where lesbian studies belong. Are they to be part of women's studies or gay studies? Most of the women I talked to underlined the importance of lesbian feminist studies. There has also been little discussion of methodology and other theoretical concerns. One exception is an informal group of five to ten lesbian researchers that has been formed outside the university in Gothenburg. From that group, several lesbian research projects are forthcoming. They have written a lesbian issue of a newsletter for women's studies. And there are also plans for a book. Lesbians at other universities have expressed feeling lonely as lesbian researchers. They are often the only experts when they talk about their work or present their papers. No one else knows much about homosexuality, so there is little discussion and a lot of polite listening.

Things might change now that several lesbians have taken their doctoral degrees. Even if their dissertations did not have a lesbian theme, they now have more time and possibilities to do lesbian research, to use lesbian texts in their courses, and to encourage other women to undertake study and research in the area.

Some women have established a network with lesbian researchers in Finland. Hopefully this will lead to more contacts and inter-Nordic exchanges of ideas and experiences. Everyone agrees that there is a need for Nordic research. The situation for lesbians today and historically in the Nordic countries differs in many ways from that in the Anglo-Saxon countries. So far there are almost no books about lesbian history in Sweden; Swedish lesbian literature is a rich but largely unexplored source for researchers; little is known about lesbian self-images and sexuality, lesbians with non-Swedish backgrounds, or older lesbians. By now, it should be clear that this list could go on for a quite a while.

Interchanges among lesbian scholars and activists inside and outside Sweden could provide impetus for developing this knowledge which, in turn, can be brought into university curricula, to train new generations of lesbian scholars and teachers.

NOTES

1. In preparation for this essay I spoke to women at universities and in adult education. I want to thank Eva Borgstrom, Kerri Corley, Lilian Hultin, Elisabeth Jolly, Catharina Landstrom, Margareta Lindholm, Maggie Myers, Kerstin Sandell, Lisbeth Stenberg, Stina Sundstrom, Ingrid Svensson, and Eva Tiby for their help and time.

2. Barbro K. Gustafsson, *Stenaker och angsmark: Erotiska motiv och homosexuella skildringar i Rove Janssons senare litteratur* (Stonefield and meadowland: Erotic motifs and homosexual depictions in Tove Jansson's later literature) (PhD dissertation, University of Uppsala, 1992.)

3. Lisbeth Stenberg, *Kon och skapande—Selma Lagerlofs bilder och sjalvbilder* (Gender and creativity—Selma Lagerlof's images and self-images.) Working title of dissertation, Department of Literature, University of Gothenburg.

Beyond Backlash: Lesbian Studies in the United Kingdom

Sally R. Munt

I first started teaching lesbian studies in 1986. In several ways my initiation typifies the historical development of the subject over the past decade. I was involved with grass-roots women's studies education and a member of the Brighton Women's Studies Branch of the Workers' Educational Association, the first feminist group of its kind in the United Kingdom. The WEA is a national British liberal institution, providing education to adults who are nontraditional participants in, and determiners of, their own education. WEA students are encouraged to join their area or town branch, which operates collectively in deciding what kinds of courses to run. The WEA is a fairly devolved, localized organization, and it commands a lot of affection and loyalty from its affiliates. When I began teaching lesbian studies, a number of feminists had recently set up the Brighton Women's Studies Branch, and as its membership became predominantly dyke, we wished to offer specifically lesbian course material. The first course in the United Kingdom, "Lesbian Perspectives," taught by Flis Henwood and Jackie Stacey, was a big success. Brighton has one of the largest gay and lesbian populations in Britain and the educational institution was responding to indigenous community needs and the political changes of the past twenty years, which made lesbian education for lesbians a reality. The WEA is an example of an institution amenable to provincial radicalism due to its fringe independence. Metropolitan control over regional educational policies is anathema to the WEA's spirit of enablement and empowerment. This spirit doesn't really constitute a discourse of self-determination; rather, the model remains a "top-down" one of benign patronage and background management. As my experience unfolded, the role of the WEA as a parental institution became more transparent. In 1988 Parliament put lesbian and gay education on the agenda by discouraging it under Section 28 of the Local Government Act, which made it illegal to fund the promotion of "pretended family values." Such intolerance caused many service providers to the lesbian and gay community to back away. Liberal or left-wing organizations, who had quietly given us limited private support over the years—in a kind of private forbearance—suddenly found that a public statement of their support was beyond their means.

Meanwhile, back on the British south coast, the Bexhill-on-Sea Branch, in what is primarily a retirement resort, threatened to withdraw from the WEA, due to their proximity, in the Sussex area seasonal brochure, to the Brighton Women's Studies Branch. At issue was the advertisement for my own course entitled "Lesbian Literature." The Bexhill Branch wanted the offensive word "lesbian" eliminated. From this ensued a familiar battle over naming, including a visit from the district council chair, who nervously sat in a roomful of dykes while we told her why we needed to call the course "lesbian."

Although our district tutor, a man, offered us astonishing commitment by threatening to resign over the issue, the branch (and I, as a member) backed down. The choice was to advertise the course pseudonymously, or not run it at all. Those in the know would interpret it as a lesbian course. The new name was so discreet that I can't now remember it. Shortly afterwards I was asked to write an article for a WEA publication on lesbian education. I responded by titling it "Why We All Need Lesbian Education." Needless to say it was "edited" to pieces.

This was a bad experience, but there were positive elements. As a consequence, the dykes seceded and began issuing our own publicity, which was direct, honest, and out. The branch was for a time a political home. We ran a varied and popular lesbian studies curriculum: converts, friendships, and girlfriends were made, lost, and found again. My initiation came through developing lesbian studies out of two separable but related roots—women's studies and the local lesbian community. A liberal arts institution reluctantly facilitated its appearance, provided resources, and incorporated lesbian studies diffidently—some said inevitably—into its county provision.

This story could be replicated many times in cataloguing the growth of lesbian studies in the United Kingdom over the past ten years. Dogged persistence, incremental institutional shifts, astute and dedicated political organizing by grass-roots and professional advocates, cynical and conditional bargaining, strange alliances: with all of these, lesbian studies has seeped into the curriculum. This is an almost exclusively adult curriculum however, since it's virtually illegal to tell teenagers that lesbians are lovely, and living down your street. Adult education organizations are often staffed by people who hold dear the best tenets of a liberal education and who haven't yet ossified into bureaucrats. Adult education students tend to be extremely loyal and enthusiastic, volunteering input to their own education and contributing to the success of its execution. In addition, because they are often older, these students are more confident of their desire to learn. At the chalk face of these classes, both students and tutors often feel they are confronting the same task. Certainly, in both women's studies and lesbian studies classes of the 1980s, I felt a humility, a shared sense of purpose, and a sharp enthusiasm for teaching, all of which is more difficult to crank-start nowadays.

Most of the committed feminists teaching lesbian studies in the Brighton WEA have gone on to become full-time faculty in British universities. This career progression represents increased job security, and the completion of the PhD. In my case I expected my first appointment to mirror the collegial and optimistic working environment shared by my friends in the WEA. I'd taken feminist practice to be the norm. By the time the brutal misogynist and homophobic department I first worked in had wrought its damage, I had wised up considerably. The attacks on my professionalism—including that I "indoctrinated students with garbage," that I "didn't know what I was talking about," and that I assessed students' work according to "partial, political criteria"—were made by male leftists to discredit not just me, but the field of feminist studies. Homophobia was intrinsic to these attacks. One male lecturer would sit in to "monitor" my women's studies course. This man had tried many destructive schemes (including sexual advances), and eventually ensured that my contract was not renewed. These were very *sexual* politics. This experience also taught me that my personal identity and the subject I teach would constantly be collapsed, as an imposed subjectivity, by all facets of academe I would subsequently encounter.

Another university I taught in was incrementally more accommodating. I had more control over my subject matter, in which I included a significant amount of lesbian and gay material. I ordered every queer book I could think of through the generous library budget. Heterosexual colleagues in cultural studies seemed pleased to have gay and lesbian faculty teach "their stuff" in courses. The two academics who refused to speak to me were not typical of the generally inclusive ambience. But I received blank, disbelieving looks when I tried to explain the intimidation by homophobic students in my classes (generally young white males in U.S. street gear who would sit together at the back and either talk continuously, or stare at me antagonistically, never writing a word).

While I was teaching there, the structure of the British university system fundamentally changed. Early in the 1990s the old polytechnic sector became what were to be called "new universities." Historically, the polytechnics were colleges designed to provide vocational training for the working and lower middle classes. They received poor funding, particularly for the humanities, but given their historically left-wing status, they tended to maintain radical programs. The workforce was unionized, and generally was paid better rates and received better promotions. The polytechnics had been managed by people who understood that their employees needed their salaries, since they were usually first-generation professionals. The faculty at "old universities" have always had much more money, and still retain the idea that a liberal education can serve no greater purpose than to be "a preparation for life." Only those who don't have to worry about money can afford this view.

One of the tasks of John Major's government was to enhance the perception of a "classless society." Hence, some of the imbalances between the old and new universities were to be evened out, and we were all to compete on a "level playing field." There were two results: first, some new universities received fresh funding; second, a culture of "publish or perish" was established. Ironically, and no doubt unintentionally, lesbian, gay, and feminist studies have benefitted from these changes. Scholarships, sabbatical leaves, reductions in teaching loads, research expenses, and research fellowships have become available to younger scholars in particular, since administrators believe they publish more and are cheaper to fund. This generation, because of the groundwork laid by a handful of isolated pioneers in the 1970s and 1980s, now rests confident in the belief that lesbian studies is legitimate and credible.

My own career has benefitted from the present research-based economy. I'm now a research fellow at an "old university." I was told explicitly that I was appointed primarily because I had more publications than the other candidates. It doesn't seem to matter what I've published, only that I *have*. Years ago I understood that the liberal academic institution respected its myth of the self-regulating economy of publishing. Cynically, I know my career has been built on the paradox that capitalism, like liberalism, permits the production and consumption of all sorts of intellectual activities, including those dedicated to undermining that very system.

In 1993, the *Directory of Lesbian and Gay Studies* listed forty women teaching lesbian studies in British universities.[1] The course directory also listed thirty institutions offering lesbian and gay studies options. These figures have become increasingly anachronistic, as new courses are introduced regularly. Many other courses may contain material on lesbian sexuality or culture without openly identifying as such. Although only one lesbian and gay studies degree exists (an M.A. in "Sexual Dissidence" at the University of Sussex), all undergraduate and graduate degrees in women's studies contain some proportion of lesbian content. When I first began teaching in the 1980s, I thought that I knew, or knew of, every woman doing lesbian studies. Now I'm glad to say I don't. In recent years I've attended several major national lesbian and gay conferences with hundreds of participants, and various feminist studies conferences including a substantial diversity of lesbian papers.

Lesbian studies in the United Kingdom is a geographical and conceptual hybrid, incorporating what often appears to be, in academic and political terms, a colonial relationship with the United States. Many of the iconic texts used in the United States are imported for British use. The traffic is not equal. It used to be that every vaguely sympathetic straight student had read Andrea Dworkin; now it's more likely to be Judith Butler. Both are North American in their styles and both assume a North American reader, only of a different cultural moment. Ideologically there is a transglobal lesbian who exists in the changing texts and intertexts of cultural and racial hegemony.

In the United Kingdom, lesbian studies has its own hegemonies, but there are still substantial incompatibilities and resistances. For example, in the United States, the model for organizing and conceptualizing radical struggles is that of civil rights movements, which gives the impression of an uneasy amalgam of competing interest groups. In the United Kingdom, however, the model is that of the old male leftist imperative of Marxism and coalition. We often succeed in alliances where the United States fails. Confrontation is not our way; quiet, polite persuasion is. There are fewer of us, and we need to maintain working relations between different political and cultural interests. This can be seen positively as dialogistic, or negatively as a sell-out, depending on your position. British political groups are often effective at listening to each other, although this cooperation may only go skin deep.

Second, the lesbian and gay studies culture in the United States (as in the academic mainstream) seems oriented toward the creation of big stars. The position of professor has an aura, a mentoring authority, and a symbolic power I don't see in the United Kingdom. While we also have our mini-heroes, they appear to be more rooted in local communities and activisms. In the United States, the teacher often takes on the character-building role of mentor, whereas the British prefer to ignore the emotional undertows of instruction. Third, lesbian and gay studies in the United States has achieved greater institutional status, and hence more privilege. We in the United Kingdom occasionally feel like poor relations. Status is awarded in spite of, rather than because of, queer interventions. The financing of the U.S. academy exceeds anything teaching professionals in the United Kingdom can fantasize, resulting in a veiled awe, resentment, and envy. Moreover, the North American market determines the structure of our field: for example, editors in the United Kingdom have one major concern—will it sell in the United States?

These dynamics within lesbian and gay studies generate a culture of complaint, particularly in the United States. Countercultures often are infected with the dominant ideology, and thus the competitive and individualistic structure of the discipline causes resentment and division. Faculty seek redress for the stigma of homosexuality, requiring the inappropriate compensation of veneration from students. Graduate students expect faculty to represent them demographically, to embody their specific identities and desires, in a simple equation of "I don't see myself, therefore I will blame you," thus denying the complex pleasures and merits of cross-identification. Racial categories become the fetishized representation of difference, subsuming and ignoring other oppressions. Hence, we fail to see the subtleties of a divisive hegemony, and its real successes. In this "tyranny of co-dependence"[2] all sides trivialize the intentions and efforts of others in resisting oppressive practices. We neglect and defer the real relations of struggle with our well-funded enemies. All this results from our fixation with identity. Having been named, and contained, we now seek to reproduce the restrictions of our immediate experience.

Conceptually lesbian studies still straddles the divide between the social history of women's studies and the high theory of feminist studies and queer studies. What has become clear to me in writing this essay is that lesbian studies is indebted to women's studies, and that, in the race to emulate European philosophy, we need to remember our origins as a political movement, and not lose "street theory" to "straight theory."[3] Street theory is a sharp, accessible, and direct political analysis of what needs to be done; it is intelligent activism. We also must maintain respect for the struggles of our predecessors. When we arrogantly ignore the clashes with university authorities instigated by female faculty in the 1970s and 1980s, or the bitter fights within and on behalf of women's studies (which opened up empty spaces for us to occupy with our lesbian and gay studies in the 1990s), we waste priceless resources. At times I have despaired about how tough it is to be an out, butch, working-class lesbian teaching in a British university. But in those moments it has been older feminist and lesbian colleagues who have given me the most insight and support. There is an acute energy in each new generation full of the shock of its own exclusion, but outrage coupled with wisdom inflicts a deeper cut.

NOTES

1. Available from Ford Hickson, DOLAGS, Unit 64, Eurolink Centre, 49 Effra Road, London SW2 1BZ.

2. Thank you to Laurie Essig for the appropriation of this term.

3. The terms belong to Kath Weston; she made this point in the plenary session "The State of Queer Studies," 6th National Lesbian, Gay, and Bisexual Studies Conference, 18–21 November 1994, Iowa City, IA.

"OUT OF THE BLUE": LESBIAN STUDIES IN AOTEAROA / NEW ZEALAND

Susan Sayer

The first Hononga Wahine Takatapuhi/Lesbian Studies Conference was held in Aotearoa/New Zealand in October 1993, although there have been general lesbian conferences in the past. Maori lesbian space was provided for separate meetings and workshops. Due attention was paid to child care and dependent care, to lesbians with disabilities, and to creating a smoke-free, animal-free environment. The stated intention of the conference was "to promote and support knowledge and information about ourselves for ourselves." It was advertised "For Lesbians Only."

There were thirty-seven conference papers and workshops. These included such titles as "Dykes or Dinkies? Towards Lesbian Economics," "Lesbians in Science," "Butch Bashing," "Lesbians' Experiences in Church and Christianity," "Lesbian Feminism, Postmodernism, and Queer Theory," "Feminism and Lesbian Images," "Researching Lesbian Herstories," "Safe Sex and Sex Toys for Lesbians," "Lesbians and Violence," and "Lesbians and Publishing." As has happened elsewhere in the academy, there was dissension among lesbians as to the benefits of post-structural theory for lesbian-feminist scholarship. The Second Lesbian Studies Conference also took place at the University of Victoria, Wellington, in May 1995. A noticeable difference was the inclusion of workshops and forums on lesbian sadomasochism and on transsexual and transgender issues. The annual New Zealand Women's Studies Conference in 1994 included at least six presentations with visible lesbian studies content, including "Twenty-Five Years of Gay Liberation," "Lesbians Organizing," and "Theorizing HIV/AIDS Activism."

Exclusively lesbian studies courses are still rare in Aotearoa/New Zealand. In 1987 Cathie Dunsford taught "Unuhia Ki Te Ao Marama/Draw Forward into the World of the Light," a multicultural lesbian literature course, through the Centre for Continuing Education at Auckland University. In 1990, Alison Laurie began teaching "Lesbian Studies" at Victoria University in Wellington, a course developed in consultation "with lesbians with an interest in lesbian studies." Its changing content and structure were also the result of a collaborative process.[1] And a lesbian studies course, "Special Topic: Lives of Difference," has been taught for several years at Waikato University. This third-year course draws upon recent scholarly work in psychology, sociology, history, biography, philosophy, and literature. These latter two courses are taught within the departments of women's studies in their respective universities. Other faculty who teach lesbian courses and lesbian material include Hilary Lapsley, Marion de Ras, Janet Wilson, Lynne Alice, and Prue Hyman.

Not surprisingly, lesbian/gay/queer studies material is included in course content at both undergraduate and graduate levels primarily within women's studies, a feature of all six universities in Aotearoa/New Zealand. For example, the Feminist Studies Program at Canterbury University includes lesbian feminist theory in all core papers at graduate and undergraduate levels. At Auckland University, the developing women's studies program has a strong focus on Aotearoa/New Zealand and the Pacific and sees lesbian feminist theory as integral to its curriculum. At all universities, abundant lesbian content can be found in individual courses on gender theory, women and society, sexuality, literature, the history of feminism, and economics. It is clear that major lesbian theorists and writers are well integrated into feminist courses across the curriculum, including such New Zealand writers and theorists as Marilyn Waring, Prue Hyman, Ngahuia Te Awekotuku, Lynne Alice, Cathie Dunsford, Athina Tsoulis, Pat Rosier, Jenny Rankine, and Michele Dominy.

Central to a developing local lesbian studies are the writings of New Zealand lesbians. Cathie Dunsford, who established the first lesbian feminist publishing consultancy in Aotearoa/New Zealand, was the commissioning editor for a series of anthologies of new, feminist, lesbian, Maori, and multicultural women writers. Each book features two-thirds new writers alongside one-third established writers to ensure good sales.[2] These include several anthologies edited by Cathie Dunsford: *New Women's Fiction* (Auckland: New Women's Press, 1986); *The Exploding Frangipani: Lesbian Writing from Australia and New Zealand* (with Susan Hawthorne; Auckland: New Women's Press, 1990); *Subversive Acts* (Wellington: Penguin, 1991); and *Me and Marilyn Monroe* (Wellington: Daphne Brasell Associates Press, 1993). Other works mark a blossoming of lesbian writing in the late 1980s and early 1990s. *Spiral 7: A Collection of Lesbian Art and Writing from Aotearoa/New Zealand* was a special issue of the feminist journal edited by Heather McPherson, Julie King, Marian Evans, and Pamela Gerrish Nunn (Wellington: Spiral, 1992). *Out Front: Lesbian Political Activity in Aotearoa 1962 to 1983,* written and compiled by Julie Glamuzina (Hamilton: Lesbian Press, 1993), is a comprehensive chronology of lesbian involvement in national and international issues. Other significant works include Glamuzina and Alison Laurie's *Parker and Hulme: A Lesbian View* (Auckland: New Women's Press, 1991); Heather McPherson's poetry collections, *The Third Myth* (Tauranga: The Tauranga Moana Press, 1986) and *Other World Relations* (Wellington: Old Bags, 1991); Cathie Dunsford's *Cowrie* (Melbourne and Auckland:

Spinifex and Tandem, 1994), the first in a series of novels featuring a multiculturally-identified lesbian of the Pacific; and three novels by Renee, *Willy Nilly, Daisy and Lily,* and *Does This Make Sense to You?* (Auckland: Penguin, 1990, 1993, 1995).[3]

The future of lesbian studies seems secure as graduate students include lesbian/gay/queer studies content in their master's and doctoral programs. Lesbian scholarship at an advanced student level is on the increase with several doctorates focusing on lesbian studies completed or in process.[4] University of Waikato master's student in geography Lynda Johnston has a forthcoming publication on lesbian identities in domestic environments.[5] My own doctoral research, "Postcolonial Lesbians: Writing out of Aotearoa/New Zealand," is on the identity positions assumed by and for lesbian writers in the postcolonial context of Aotearoa/New Zealand. It places selected lesbian writings at a junction where the colonized confront the colonizers and where the colonial is confronted by the postcolonial. Where the lesbian/Other is variously colonized and invisible, I suggest that there is a sense in which lesbians are all "cultural amphibians."[6] This description is particularly apt for Aotearoa/New Zealand where Pakeha lesbians are one kind of alter/native and where Maori lesbians and lesbians of color occupy other alter/native subject positions. Hence, some lesbians of color may agree with Gayatri Spivak when she says: "[m]y biculturality is that I'm not at home in either of the places."[7]

In the early stages of my research I was warned that my "specialized" and "narrow" topic would mark me as a "professional homosexual." Although I decided that if I was to be so marked I would at least be in good company, this warning alerted me to the extent to which lesbian and gay scholarship in (though not confined to) Aotearoa/New Zealand is seen to stem from an exclusively homosexual orientation. This is an example of what Eve Kosofsky Sedgwick refers to as a "minoritizing view . . . [where] homo/heterosexual definition [is seen as] an issue of active importance primarily for a small, distinct, relatively fixed homosexual minority."[8] But by paying particular attention to geopolitical contexts, I understand lesbian studies as a mode of critical analysis, not a fixed and universal identity. With such a perspective, the contingent natures of homosexuality *and* heterosexuality cannot be glossed over. And neither can the growing interest in lesbian/gay/queer studies in Aotearoa/New Zealand and across the globe.[9]

Special thanks to Cathie Dunsford, Livia Whitman, Sarah Williams, Marion de Ras, Radhika Mohanram, Prue Hyman, Maureen Molloy, and Lynne Alice for their help in compiling the necessary material for this essay.

NOTES

1. Alison Laurie, "Speaking the Unspeakable: A Background to Teaching Lesbian Studies in Aotearoa/New Zealand," in *Feminist Voices: Women's Studies Texts for Aotearoa/New Zealand,* edited by Rosemary du Plessis (Auckland: Oxford University Press, 1992).

2. Dunsford and Associates Publishing Consultants, R D 6, Warkworth, New Zealand; Phone and Fax 64 9 422 7889.

3. Lesbian authors not mentioned specifically in this essay include Paula Boock, Jenny Fulton, Rangitunoa Black, Lisa Sabbage, Allie Eagle, Deborah Jones, Stella Duffy, Mahinarangi Tocker, Betty

Don, Catherine Dale, Sara Knox, Meliors Simms, Jenny Rankine, Aorewa McLeod, Leah Poulter, Ruth Busch, Rhona Vickoce, Fran Marno, June Joyce, Kirsten Gracie, Ruby Elizabeth, Tess Moeke-Maxwell, and Lorae Parry.

4. These are Annamarie Jagose's recently published *Lesbian Utopics* (New York and London: Routledge, 1994) and Christine Linda Atmore's study of recent New Zealand print media representations of lesbians.

5. Lynda Johnston and Gill Valentine, "At Home with Sally and Wendy: The Performance and Surveillance of Lesbian Identities in Domestic Environments," in *Mapping Desires: Geographies of Sexualities,* edited by David Bell and Gill Valentine (London: Routledge, forthcoming).

6. Edward Said, "Figures, Configurations, Transfigurations," in *From Commonwealth to Post-Colonial,* edited by Anna Rutherford (Sydney: Dangaroo Press, 1992).

7. Gayatri Chakravorty Spivak with Angela Ingram, "Postmarked Calcutta, India," in The *Post-Colonial Critic: Interviews, Strategies, Dialogue,* edited by Sarah Harasym (London: Routledge, 1990), 83.

8. Eve Kosofsky Sedgwick, *Epistemology of the Closet* (Berkeley: University of California Press, 1990), 1–2.

9. The following individuals, in addition to those mentioned in the body of the essay, are involved in lesbian studies as instructors, conference presenters, or graduate students: Nan McDonald, Frances Kell, Radhika Mohanram, Morrigan Severs, Raine Berry, Judith Dale, Kate Pulin, Ling-Yen Chua, Lynn Benson, Emma Roache, Janette Day, Marewa Glover, Jenny Fulton, Tilly Lloyd, Carolyn Gammon, Linda Evans, and Christine Linda Atmore.

PART SIX

Theorizing
Our Future

(WHITE) LESBIAN STUDIES
Sharon P. Holland

Perhaps if I had not been so badly scarred from having been born Black, poor, and female in the Deep South at a time when all Blacks were invisible . . . I might have been more enterprising. Perhaps if I hadn't had to cope with all those battles, fears, phobias, and anxieties continually raging within me, I might have gone to live in Greenwich Village, or Paris or Los Angeles, or any place except conservative Philadelphia, where we had settled. . . . —*Anita Cornwell*[1]

If Sappho literally could be regarded as the archetypal Lesbian, much of the concern about the Lesbians in the women's movement would disappear. Sappho was an educated woman at a time when most women could not read or write, a political exile, a mother, and one of the finest poets who ever lived. When virtually all women apparently lived to serve the male hierarchy and died anonymously without leaving a trace of their uniqueness, she said her name would live through history, and it has. Today she would be called a Feminist. —*Sidney Abbot and Barbara Love*[2]

In her introduction to the 1982 edition of *Lesbian Studies: Present and Future*, Margaret Cruikshank reminds us that "the concept of 'lesbian studies' is still fairly new. It means both the *grassroots cultural work* which tells us who we are and the more *formally organized courses* on lesbians which now exist in a few women's studies programs and in women's centers."[3] Later in the anthology, during a conversation with Barbara Smith, Cherríe Moraga notes, "I think basically the mentality of most [women's studies] programs is we will teach white middle-class, heterosexual women for all our courses *except* in the Lesbian literature course where we will teach white lesbians and in the Third World women's course we will teach straight Third World women. And that's it."[4] I begin here with a parallel between Moraga and Cruikshank's observations because it informs my own bittersweet relationship to lesbian studies. In contemplating this sweet and sour taste, I am reminded of Audre Lorde and her challenge to women in community with one another:

> Certainly there are very real differences between us of race, age, and sex. But it is
> not those differences between us that are separating us. It is rather our *refusal* to
> recognize those differences, and to examine the distortions which result from our
> misnaming them and their effects upon human behavior and expectation. . . .
> It is a *lifetime pursuit* for each of us to extract these distortions from our living at the
> same time as we recognize, reclaim, and define those differences upon which they
> are imposed.[5]

My emphasis on words like "refusal," "lifetime," and "pursuit" points toward
the extent to which much of the dialogue around "difference" within lesbian studies
tends to surface in the form of a refusal to see, rather than a (lifelong) commitment
to pursue. Our glimpses into the realms of "difference" seem all too fleeting—that
space is still unrehearsed. Lorde's work has had a profound influence on lesbian
lives and literature, but this effect is mediated by the often problematic intellectual
geographies or locations of lesbian "grassroots cultural work" and "more formally
organized courses" that Cruikshank perceives as operative in her introduction. I
argue here that Audre Lorde's impact has fallen between the cracks of lesbian
"culture" and lesbian "studies" and that the process of understanding this signifying
difference is a lifelong endeavor indeed. This essay is an attempt to examine this
phenomenon and to return to the unresolved space that Moraga and Smith refer to
as lesbian–of–color reality.

The Light Went On in the Closet

Recently I have been thinking about theory and practice, erasure and presence;
I have been thinking about canonized "lesbian" authors—high modernists like
Gertrude Stein and Djuna Barnes, and others like Virginia Woolf and Willa Cather
whose work is not universally approached from a decidedly lesbian perspective,
but is being read nonetheless in English classrooms on college campuses across
the country. I have also been thinking about the "mythic past" that many lesbian
authors attempt to deconstruct or reconstruct, depending upon the tenor of the
times. Most pointedly, I have been contemplating the especially annoying presence
of "Greece" as a site of (lesbian) imaginative pleasure and the extent to which
many of these early writers romanticize an earlier age, one where "homosexuals"
could be all that they could be.[6]

But, mostly I have been thinking of a way into this piece, which is supposed to
reflect on Audre Lorde's impact on lesbian studies. I find an interesting parallel
between Lorde and these early writers—a sense that she too was searching for
some kind of past (specifically, in her volume of poems, *The Black Unicorn*); some
kind of marker for belonging to a group outside of one's historical nightmare. For
this endeavor Lorde is often dismissed as too much of an essentialist, while these
same critics urge us not to judge early figures like Stein or Woolf for *their* essentialism
(for this reading of the past, replace the term "essentialist" with "avant-garde"). In
their critical hands, conceiving of a realized past is no longer essentialist; it marks

a kind of theoretical departure for their literature; it stands as a bold stroke against the numbing effect of the patriarchal narrative. For Greece, in its beauty and purity, is, after all, a legitimate site of origin that we can adhere to—but West Africa is a sign of contamination, a site of illegitimacy.[7] The opening epigraph to this piece focuses on the frustrations of Anita Cornwell as she signifies to her white lesbian audience that she is well aware that the site for traditional lesbian inquiry is not located in her neighborhood, but it doesn't make her narrative any less "lesbian"; it simply makes it more materially located, and therefore less yielding to the influences of (post)modernist romanticizing.

My ruminations here on "Greece" or, more universally, the anxiety of antiquity, are influenced by directions in recent classical/anthropological studies of Greece, which attempt to think about the region as a site of intense integration, cultural dissemination, and exchange with African communities. As linguist Martin Bernal's work has pointed out, Greece was anything *but* the site of "purity" we (or the modernists, for that matter) want it to be.[8] In addition, Toni Morrison's work on whiteness in the literary imagination has demonstrated to us that "race" is already part of the landscape of any narrative: we need only look for the marker, and the road to difference is clearly defined.[9] Given the plethora of scholarship since the mid-1970s, which acknowledges that culture does not become itself in a vacuum, but works in a larger environment of reaction and interaction, perhaps we might want to amend our examination of the ancient past; perhaps we might want to contemplate Sappho in her "exile" as not only a lyrical, exiled, "white" body, but a black body as well. But this inversion sounds very much like essentialist thinking; this inversion misses the mark of innovation.

My focus on "Greece," or what I would also call "an archaic past," is not overstated. Early debates in the delineation of homosexuality wavered between homosexuality as invention (socially constructed) or as innate (biological). In order to disprove the social construction theories, notes Diana Fuss, gay critics like Bob Gallagher and Alexander Wilson maintained that an "invention" theory "denies us a history that allows us to name Plato, Michelangelo, and Sappho as our ancestors."[10] This demonstrates that much of the anxiety about lesbian/gay identity and the struggle for institutional and intellectual space have focused upon not only a collective identity, but an identity mired in some literal location on the space/time continuum. To establish legitimacy, lesbian and gay people find themselves having to construct a her/history equally consistent with their realized subjectivities. But here is where theory without practice becomes dangerously dysfunctional—theorizing a location for a "group" is always about the politics of who/m the *individual* identifies with, and not necessarily about what is "representative" for that nebulous entity, "the group," "the collective."

This problem of differing liberatory projects is very clearly illustrated in Diana Fuss's cogently argued exploration of identity politics in lesbian and gay theory. Fuss notes that Barbara Smith's contention that "'we have an identity and therefore a politics'" means that "identity necessarily determines a particular kind of politics" (99). Fuss's analysis is impatient with Smith's didactic statement but fails to adequately account for an aspect of Smith's earlier elaboration which builds upon the notion, à la Carter G. Woodson, that to be black and female is to be divorced from the category of "humanness," and so, the struggle for "lesbian" identity is intricately linked to a journey which begins with dismantling racist notions of a self that is subhuman. Black women theorize about a location from which to derive their own empowerment; they do not speak from the position of assuming that the word "lesbian" therefore stands for a universal location to which we can all journey. Fuss's reading denies the complexity of Smith's paradigm by displacing its "human" emphasis while simultaneously reducing the category of "lesbian" to the confines of a white discourse on identity politics.

"It's Tight Like That"

I want to talk here about ownership, activism, and theory, and somehow to locate a problem in lesbian studies wherein the "colored girls" do all the soul work of the discipline, and the white women shell out the theories that decide how this soul work is going to be read, disseminated, and taught in juxtaposition to already canonized white lesbian authors. I can find no better illustration of this tension between high and low theory than Judith Roof's examination of (straight) white feminist anxiety over black and lesbian presences in her study, *A Lure of Knowledge: Lesbian Sexuality and Theory*. She notes that "While the materialist commitment to gender and the economic is a commitment to an 'analysis,' a racial or lesbian commitment is defined differently, as anachronistically political—as activism instead of analysis. Why for this moment are gender and class cerebral and race and sexual orientation experiential?"[11] While Roof intends for her explication to reach the ears of straight white feminists, I feel that the problem of "racial commitment" read as politics, read as less cerebral or theoretical, translates into readings of "queer theory" as well. Moreover, Roof surmises that white feminists often pull the "diversity" card in defense of themselves to a very conservative male academy. Much like "colored" folk on the front lines in the Vietnam and Gulf Wars, highly charged and politicized work by lesbians of color is put forth by lesbians in the academy as the first line of defense from the homophobia of heterosexual white men and women.[12] Note how many times in "lesbian" syllabi *This Bridge Called My Back* is ushered in as the "Don't mess with us, 'cause we're lesbians" aspect of a course on women's sexuality. Specifically, blackness is the fodder for a discontented lesbian studies. As Roof notes:

> If . . . third world and African-American is to feminist as feminist is to male tradition, then in the same way that feminist criticism challenges the total centered vision of male tradition, cultural diversity challenges the total centered vision of white academic feminist criticism. Intimacy in all of its connotations and implications: sharing, exposing weaknesses, giving, listening, compromising, changing in relation to an other, de-centering self, means potentially relinquishing the certitude, centrality, consistency, identity, and power of theory and position (230).

And the next query should be, "How does the problem of cultural diversity challenge/remake lesbian studies?" Furthermore, given that the fear of intimacy on a lesbian playing field is not only textual, but sexual, what does this anxiety about contamination say about the "politics" of race and sexuality? Our racial anxieties, and worst nightmares, play themselves out on this terrain of intimacy, where issues of authority and authorship converge. In no other arena is this cloak of diversity more guarded and maintained than in the lesbian community where many white lesbians feel that their lesbianism somehow automatically divests them of their own white supremacy. The anxiety of authenticity is deeply felt in more marginalized communities; it is no wonder that the subtle erasure of black lesbian experience becomes a necessity for the survival of lesbian studies as authentic *and* authenticating discourse.

"Hit the Road, Jackie"

In reviewing some of the most talked-about recent theories of lesbian studies, it is painfully obvious to me that a revolution of ideology has taken place in the emerging literature.[13] While lesbian studies grew out of the radical feminist movement, which, in turn, was sparked by the Civil Rights movement in this country, it seems to have no pretensions of feeling guilty of the same kind of "mistakes" owned in part by white straight feminism. As a matter of fact, authors like Roof cite early white heterosexist feminists as developing an exclusionary model for feminist studies that denigrates the texts of "diversity." But what is interesting about Roof's hypothesis is that anxieties over intimacy are not only felt in straight feminist communities, but also across the continuum in the lesbian community. This anxiety mediates itself in Roof's own text where "difference" and "diversity" fall into the cracks of her own discourse—where straight white feminist inclusion/exclusion is practiced in her own narrative, which privileges the voices of "traditional" lesbian practice, and relegates the presence of blackness to the space between the two halves of feminism. In another literary sphere, Ann Ducille provides a devastating metaphor for the positionality of black female bodies in the cracks of academic discourse. Cogently responding to Houston Baker's assessment of black female presence in literary discourse as the site for "the convergence of matters of race, class, and gender today" she cautions that "[o]f course, one of the dangers of standing at an intersection—particularly at such a suddenly busy, three-way intersection—is the likelihood of being run over by oncoming traffic."[14]

The intersection is quite bloody and crowded indeed. Much like Roof, other lesbian critics, or critics in lesbian studies, build their closing arguments (whenever possible) on the impending threat of blackness as a corrective to narrow thinking, while never conceding the ground for examination of "literatures" to the voices of women of color. Much of the business of lesbian studies is concerned with maintaining a purist place—we continually see studies of Stein and others which attempt to keep the status quo fully operating. However, I am not arguing solely for an inclusion of black lesbian writing in lesbian theories of the self, but rather, arguing for another revolutionary space: one that begins to ask a "how" question, rather than a "why" question; one that seeks to extrapolate a position on the nebulous inclusion of women of color in lesbian studies as caused by a much larger problem in the emerging field than mere in/exclusiveness implies.

The functionality and dysfunctionality of blackness and lesbian-ness have much to do with the competing discourses of politics as practice and academic thought as theory. This is an old, much rehearsed, and fully tiring debate in feminist studies. But I will return to this debate here because I think it will serve us well to re-examine it. Toward the close of her introduction to *Epistemology of the Closet,* Eve Kosofsky Sedgwick offers that:

> Women and men who find or fear they are homosexual, or are perceived by others to be so, are physically and mentally terrorized through the institutions of law, religion, psychology, mass culture, medicine, the military, commerce and bureaucracy, and brute violence. Political progress on these and similar life-and-death issues has depended precisely on the strength of a minority-model gay activism; it is the normalizing, persuasive analogy between the needs of gay/lesbian students and those of Black or Jewish students, for instance, and the development of the corresponding political techniques that enable progress in such arenas. And *that* side of the needed progress cannot be mobilized from within any closet; it requires very many people's risky and affirming acts of the most explicit self-identification as members of the minority affected.[15]

Sounds a lot like the dangerous intersection to me, as blackness is posited in the position of political activism (i.e., spark, fodder) but never achieves any of the rewards for such dangerous sacrifice. If you're wondering if I might be bordering on hyperbole here, think about the extent to which Stonewall is heralded by all of us as some kind of beginning for lesbian/gay/bi activism and renewed scholarship. But beyond creating what I would call the cultural moment that defines the trajectory of the field, how many of us remember that those drag queens were primarily black and Latino? Why are people of color the creators of cultural currency, but rarely its owners? Locked in Sedgwick's discursive arena of "minority-model" activism and "political techniques," the contributions of people of color are obscured by relegating their functionality as ultimately dysfunctional in the realm of discourse that matters. Here, political acts rarely take place inside the academy.

In other words, black (lesbian) identity is contained by a theorizing which calls upon (black) politics as a necessary moment; *and* it is in this space that black (lesbian) presence is engendered and simultaneously erased. What I am proposing here is that unlike straight white feminism, which, at least recently, must historicize a feminist past that includes black feminist figures, lesbian feminists in the terrain of lesbian writings have constructed a historical arena filled with the Steins and Woolfs of the world, a world where black lesbians don't produce "literature" and "theory," but they do produce "activism" and, therefore, "politics." By claiming ownership of "literature," white lesbian scholars who adhere to this standard therefore control the "discourse" which authenticates it. What perpetuates this system of analysis is the "essentialist" stance of (white) lesbian identity politics—which sees lesbianism in opposition to other categories of identity, specifically white male/female heterosexism, so much so that it is blinded by its own narrow view of subjectivity, narrativity, and historicity. Even in a playing field in which identity and subjectivity have been "outed" as malleable and performative, it is amazing how rigidly shaped and defined the roles for black presence *are* within these constantly shifting paradigms.

"Do It to Me One More Time": Reading Narrowly, Reading Lesbian

In search of an ending to this piece, I'd like to return to Diana Fuss's *Essentially Speaking*. Examining "Poststructuralist Afro-American Literary Theory" allows Fuss to focus upon the place of "race" in the politics of identity. However, her critique privileges the voices of male African Americanists like Henry Louis Gates, Houston Baker, and Anthony Appiah by rendering a full reading of their texts and marginally mentioning the works of black feminist scholars. What I am concerned with here is not Fuss's ignorance of black women's voices, but the extent to which this exclusion is symptomatic of a larger problem in lesbian studies. If lesbian critics envision the space of African-American critical production as defined and owned by men, then *readings* of black lesbian texts will suffer greatly in the context of lesbian critical analysis. Audre Lorde and other sisters writing from a woman-of-color lesbian perspective will always be read narrowly, if we are not only vigilant of the context in which their work is created, but also wary of the ways in which we construct the "other" categories to which their work speaks. Narrow readings of black women's texts will continue to render them invisible to both lesbian studies and African-American studies. Practitioners of lesbian studies need to be aware that their discursive power is being felt in other arenas, that what they say has impact beyond the limits of their own fields.

Ultimately, we cannot gauge an author's impact or influence, unless we see that person as shaped by all of their selves. A reading of a woman of color's work would be tremendously augmented by both a reading of the literary tradition from which it creates itself *and* an understanding of how she attempts to place herself within several often competing contexts. In closing, I return to Moraga and Smith's conversation. Moraga maintains: "What Lesbian feminists need to be responsible for is producing a body of literature that makes people have to get up and move. Why use the word "feminist" if you're talking about a body of literature that rationalizes people's complacency?" (64). Moraga's challenge to lesbian studies is still operative. We need to *move something,* and part of this movement might entail both complex restructuring and simple maneuvers. But we should understand that we cannot create a future for ourselves—and a future always implies a space for the young and the old—unless we understand where we have been. Lesbian studies would do well to examine the baggage it has inherited from its "cousin" programs of feminist and African-American studies. We need to learn from their mistakes and create a "new" lesbian studies—realizing that some of our own communication problems are inherited rather than owned, and therefore, can be ameliorated. We need to create a "new" lesbian studies that challenges the dichotomous paradigms of existing programs by *moving* to close the gap between "politics" and "theory," "literature" and "experience". Part of this process would be to identify those sites and locations that constitute an "original" lesbian subjectivity/identity and disrupt their meaning in the larger community of lesbians. For many of us the Americas represent both a contested site of dislocation and an odd representation of what "home" is. We might need to ask a more difficult question: Is Europe really the space from which to glean a theory of "self" when our lived experience is in the Americas? Such questions might open up the category of "lesbian" to more fruitful readings of "home."

I would like to thank Ann Ducille, whose article "The Occult of True Black Womanhood: Critical Demeanor and Black Feminist Studies," in Signs, greatly inspired this piece. I would also like to acknowledge my friends and colleagues, Yvonne Yarbro-Bejarano and Lora Romero, whose intellectual and emotional support has been invaluable. Special thanks goes to Lora Romero, who survived many of my anxiety-ridden phone calls during the last stages of writing the draft of this essay. I would also like to note that I am well aware that we have now reached a cultural moment wherein "lesbian/gay/bi studies" is being addressed as "queer studies." I don't mean to obfuscate the contributions of gay or bisexual individuals to the discourse on queer studies, but I am, for the purposes of this short piece, most intrigued by the way in which lesbian studies constructs itself as an entity and as a discipline—I am concerned with the ways in which lesbians read.

NOTES

1. Anita Cornwell, *Black Lesbian in White America* (Tallahassee, FL: The Naiad Press, 1983), 8–9.

2. Sidney Abbott and Barbara Love, eds., *Sappho Was a Right-On Woman: A Liberated View of Lesbianism* (New York: Stein and Day Publishers, 1973), 158. Throughout the book, the terms "Black" and "lesbian/gay" are considered distinct and separate categories; as a matter of fact, the authors argue that gay politics should begin to explore its own special needs and concerns outside of just "mimicking the tactics [of] the Black movement" (182).

3. Margaret Cruikshank, introduction to *Lesbian Studies: Present and Future* (New York: The Feminist Press, 1982) ix; emphasis mine.

4. Cherríe Moraga and Barbara Smith, "Lesbian Literature: A Third World Feminist Perspective," in *Lesbian Studies*, 63.

5. Audre Lorde, *Sister Outsider* (Trumansburg, NY: Crossing Press, 1984), 115, emphasis mine.

6. Perhaps a good place to start with a "lesbian" reading of this return to models in antiquity can be found in Karla Jay's *The Amazon and the Page* (Bloomington: Indiana University Press, 1988).

7. In an earlier piece, "Humanity Is Not a Luxury: Some Notes on a Recent Passing," I move back to an examination of Lorde's open letter to Mary Daly and I argue that the significance of her silence still has reverberations for the lesbian community. Daly's lack of response to Lorde's query about the place of West African goddesses in her paradigm of female empowerment tacitly implies that West Africa is not the conceivable site of any source of representative empowerment, or strength, for lesbians. Lorde's suggestion of West Africa as a location for imaginative female space is dismissed in favor of an already sufficiently broad paradigm.

8. In "Unspeakable Things Unspoken: The Afro-American Presence in American Literature," *Michigan Quarterly Review* (winter 1989): 1–34, Toni Morrison argues that, "it took some seventy years . . . to eliminate Egypt as the cradle of civilization and its model and replace it with Greece. The triumph of that process was that Greece lost its own origins and became itself original" (6).

9. See Toni Morrison, *Playing in the Dark: Whiteness and the Literary Imagination* (New York: Vintage, 1992).

10. Diana Fuss, *Essentially Speaking: Feminism, Nature and Difference* (New York: Routledge, 1989), 106.

11. Judith Roof, *A Lure of Knowledge: Lesbian Sexuality and Theory* (New York: Columbia University Press, 1991), 222.

12. There is parallel proof in Roof's own assessment of mainstream feminist studies: "Though the contributors to the anthology [*The New Feminist Criticism*] are in general conscious of questions of gender/ race/ class/ sexual orientations, in relation to the primacy of gender and class issues, race and sexual orientation are still relegated together to slim communal chunks of the book, proof of materialist/ feminist grip on diversity" (223).

13. See Judith Butler, *Bodies That Matter: On the Discursive Limits of Sex* (New York: Routledge, 1993); Judith Roof, *A Lure of Knowledge* (see note 12); Eve Kosofsky Sedgwick, *Epistemology of the Closet* (Berkeley: University of California Press, 1990); and Terry Castle, *The Apparitional Lesbian: Female Homosexuality and Modern Culture* (New York: Columbia University Press, 1993). Two books that attempt to reformulate the politics of naming lesbian and gay studies is *The Lesbian and Gay Studies Reader* (New York: Routledge, 1993), edited by Henry Abelove, Michèle Aina Barale, and David M. Halperin; and *Tilting the Tower,* edited by Linda Garber (New York: Routledge, 1994).

14. Ann Ducille, "The Occult of True Black Womanhood: Critical Demeanor and Black Feminist Studies," *Signs* 19, no. 3 (spring 1994): 593.

15. Eve Kosofsky Sedgwick, *Epistemology of the Closet* (Berkeley: University of California Press, 1990), 58.

QUEERING LESBIAN STUDIES
Judith Halberstam

Virtual Lesbians

Recently, I ventured out onto an electronic discussion net and logged into the lesbian channels. There were three separate channels: "lesbian," "lesbians," and "Sappho." While the first two channels were relatively easy to access and quite uninteresting, the last channel, "Sappho," turned out to be an intriguing talk space with restricted access. As it was an "invitation only" line, I had to ask someone already on the line to invite me into the conversation. I found a so-called operator and using my nickname, "Oddgirl," I requested access. After a short interchange between myself and an operator called "Pumpkin," I found myself on channel Sappho.

Once aboard I felt excited to be in lesbian space and in communication with a huge international range of anonymous lesbian users. The discussion in progress was about "men on lesbian channels." I learned quickly that the reason Sappho was "invitation only" was that male users, ever curious about lesbianism, were constantly trying to get onto the channel. I asked how any of them could tell from a nickname whether the user was male or female. Some nicknames, they explained, could easily be traced back to real computer addresses but others were logged on anonymously. For the anonymous users (like myself) who were protected by university generic addresses, they simply had to go on gut feeling. I immediately suggested that gut feeling was a difficult instinct to employ in a virtual space and I said that I thought it would be extremely easy to determine whether someone were male or female, straight or lesbian on line. How? they asked. Administer a simple cultural test, I answered. Ask the user what queer movies they had seen or books they had read or singers they liked or athletes they admired. Ask them to name one lesbian from history, one famous or landmark event from queer history. Silence greeted my suggestion, and I wondered whether people felt offended by something I had said. Finally, a user called Spike responded. "But Oddgirl," she said. "I don't think *I* can answer any of those questions, so if we used that as a standard to judge users, I would not count as a lesbian."

What is the correct interpretation of Spike's lack of lesbian cultural literacy? Is she young and new to lesbian culture? A lesbian in sexual practice without involvement in the nitty gritty of lesbian culture? Does she live where information about lesbian culture and history is terribly hard to come by? Is she part of a jock lesbian culture or bar culture or whatever culture uninterested in the cultural records of lesbian life in the West in the late twentieth century? At any rate, Spike's response to my pop quiz made me realize how tenuous are claims to identity within postmodern culture, and, furthermore, how strained are identifications within the weird dimensions of electronic communication.

Channel Sappho, its membership rituals, and its conversational and sexual practices seem important to me for several reasons. First, whether or not there was overt recognition of the fact, the users on this channel were engaged in subtle negotiations about what constituted "lesbian" interaction in passing judgement on and rating the lesbianism of other users. Second, it seemed as though many of the women using the channel were trying out lesbianism in a virtual space before going out and trying it in real time and space. Many of the women I talked with privately (it was possible to create private conversations simply by inviting anyone to a private channel) identified as bisexuals who had never been with a woman and wanted advice. The channel, therefore, seemed to be a flight simulator for lesbians. Third, virtual lesbianism may force users to scrutinize "real" lesbianism. Leaving the virtual space, you often begin to wonder how many of the straight people (male and female) that you encounter in your daily life enjoy a double life as lesbians (or gay men) in electronic contexts. At what point does being a virtual lesbian affect one's "real" sexual definition? Also, how do the definitional problems online (is a user really female, really a lesbian) extend to or become implicated in offline contestations of identity and practice. My online experience left me unsure about identity, sexual or otherwise. After all, the electronic personality with whom I had just interacted could easily have been a man who was adept at impersonating a lesbian.

I write of my foray into the area of lesbian studies through lesbian electronic playgrounds to emphasize both the fragility and the persistence of concepts of lesbian identity. I believe that this is the postmodern condition—a simultaneous disavowal and confirmation of desires, bodies, and identities, and the pleasure that comes from holding onto identity in the face of radical uncertainty and letting go of it even if this entails considerable risk. Identities, after all, ground bodies and even whole communities in imagined bonds of similarity and concordance.

Identity and risk go hand in hand at this particular historical moment. As Judith Butler has suggested in an essay on "gender insubordination," "What or who is it that is 'out,' made manifest and fully disclosed, when and if I reveal myself as a lesbian?"[1] She also queries: "What, if anything, can lesbians be said to share?" For Butler, the category "lesbian" describes very little and of course this is also true for all other categories of sexual identity. When Butler and other queer theorists single out lesbianism for analytic scrutiny, they already break with a philosophical tradition that understands lesbianism as the hidden or occluded sexuality: hence, Terry

Castle refers to the lesbian within Western representation as "apparitional," and film theorist Patti White discusses the "ghosting" of lesbian desire in classical cinema.[2] It is of great significance therefore that Butler makes lesbianism a kind of paradigm of desiring relations by which other geometries of desire can be mapped out. She resists, however, what we might call a cultural feminist impulse to elevate lesbian desire and desire between women in general to a moral and ethical pinnacle. Lesbianism, by virtue of its "apparitional" quality becomes a perfect place to examine the consequences—the advantages and the liabilities—of building identities around sets of sexual desires.

Lesbianism on the electronic net is very much an apparitional or virtual form. Lesbian identities assert themselves through the deliberate creation of separate space (Channel Sappho), but they simultaneously erase themselves by manifesting precisely as virtual—any body, male or female, straight or gay, might attempt to present as lesbian in this space—and the readability of any given user's lesbianism might have little or nothing to do with their actual lesbian body. Lesbianism, in this context, is a ghost in the machine, a shadowy presence that plays at code-switching and channel-surfing. Electronic models of lesbian identity force queer lesbian identifications and manifest as codes, conversations, and sets of virtual practices.

Lesbian Studies

My encounters in virtual space, the twists and turns of often contradictory identifications, prepared me somewhat for the vertiginous experience of teaching queer studies to a group of eighteen to twenty-five-year-old undergraduates. More and more, I feel, young people are coming out with much more flexible self-definitions of sexual identity. Few of the young men and women in my classes felt their sexual identities to be adequately described by the labels "gay," "lesbian," or "straight." In addition, some students cross-identified, patching together labels that worked for them from the terms available. For example, one man felt that "male lesbian" was the only term that really described both his sense of sexual identity and his sexual orientation. A young woman identified as a "stone femme" who primarily wanted to sexually dominate gay men. Not all of the students were comfortable with the label "queer," but many did find comfort in the refuge the label offered from a menu of unacceptable sexual options.

Interestingly enough, the fiercest opposition to the label queer came from white middle-class gay men who wanted to identify with mainstream political and cultural identities and felt that the only thing preventing them from total assimilation was continued homophobia. This small group of rather privileged individuals felt that there was simply nothing queer about them and they wanted to strive for acceptance rather than social change and a challenge to structures of heterosexism. In a queer issue of *The Nation*, black lesbian activist Barbara Smith points precisely to the privileges of white gay men and how they obstruct a true queer alliance.

"Does the gay and lesbian movement want to create a just society for everyone?"

asks Barbara Smith, "Or does it just want to eradicate the last little glitch that makes life difficult for privileged (white male) queers?" Smith compares the contemporary gay and lesbian struggle for civil rights with earlier political movements and she finds:

> In fact, it's gay white men's racial, gender, and class privileges, as well as the vast numbers of them who identify with the system rather than distrust it, that have made the politics of the current gay movement so different from those of other identity-based movements for social and political change.[3]

In each of three different queer classes that I have taught, some white gay men have objected to the notion of queer coalitions and, eventually, I have come even to question the efficacy of teaching gay studies and lesbian studies side by side. While I am by no means an advocate for a separatist lesbian culture, the opposition that I encountered from white gay men in the classroom made me acutely aware of the pedagogical imperative for a separate space for lesbian history and culture. Indeed, before the emergence of gay and lesbian studies, lesbian studies was inevitably taught as continuous with women's studies. While there are certainly limitations in making lesbian culture simply a subset of women's culture at large, nonetheless for the moment there may be no better disciplinary space available.

Rather than a separatist lesbian culture or pedagogy, however, I would argue for a "queer lesbian studies." "Queer" in this context performs the work of destabilizing the assumed identity in "identity politics." However, by continuing to use and rely upon the term "lesbian," we acknowledge that identity is a useful strategy for political and cultural organizing. "Lesbian" is a term that modifies and qualifies "queer," and "queer" is a term capable of challenging the stability of identities subsumed by the label "lesbian."

In recent years, "queer" has lived several different theoretical and practical lives and served multiple purposes. At the most basic level, "queer" serves as a shorthand for "gay and lesbian," and it even seems to include other underexposed sexual minorities like transgender people. But the collective project mobilized by the use of the word "queer" has very specific political dimensions. "Queer" offers a critique of traditional identity politics and it positions itself as resolutely anti-assimilationist. By this I mean that "queer" marks itself affirmatively as different or eccentric, odd or mutant, alien or outside, and it embraces peripheral localities and bodies by critiquing the notion of natural bodies and healthy or pure aims and desires.

While it seems important to me not to use "lesbian/gay" and "queer" as oppositional terms, there is certainly a critique of the growing respectability of the terms "gay" and "lesbian" within queer studies. For example, some churches now recognize gay/lesbian marriages as do some (not many) employers. While this is encouraging in terms of our civil rights, it is ominous in terms of what form of nonheterosexual desire receives official sanction. Gay and lesbian relationships, such official approval suggests, may receive institutional recognition, as long as they follow the kinship rules already established by heterosexuals. Very often, in fact, proposals for domestic partnership have much more stringent regulations for gay/lesbian couples than for heterosexual married couples. A heterosexual couple merely has to show proof of marriage while often a gay/ lesbian couple will have to prove that they have lived together for a certain amount of time and share financial interests.

Queerness refuses to be contained within strictly heterosexual models. Therefore, queer relationships may expand, redefine, or completely reject the notion of family, and they may reorganize dominant definitions of intimacy. For example, queer primary relationships may involve more than two people and thereby completely rewrite the social convention of "the couple." In this sense, queer never simply accepts a dominant model, it always challenges the conditions of acceptability and attempts to undermine institutional imperatives (to be married, to have children, to be monogamous, et cetera). But queer is not simply a sexual marker or a marker of different sexualities: as Barbara Smith's critique of gay white men indicates, race and class privilege often lead monied gays to reject identifications with the queer masses and to lobby simply for a piece of the pie. Queer, as a political as well as a sexual label, allows non-assimilationist gays and lesbians to make radical alliances with other subcultural groups in the United States and to see how race and class are always thoroughly inscribed within sexual self-definition.

Queer Lesbian Culture

In a seminal essay called "Deviance, Politics and the Media," Stuart Hall writes about the connection between deviant social groups and deviant politics, and he argues that "the crisp distinction between socially and politically deviant behavior is increasingly difficult to sustain."[4] In other words, social deviants—queers—form their own political forms of resistance that often do not have much to do with conventional politics and that have everything to do with organized forms of cultural resistance. Women's communities, and lesbian communities in particular, have long been involved in the production of queer cultures. We have also engaged in long and hard debates over what kinds of political and sexual cultures suit feminist agendas. Some of these debates have been protracted and even destructive.

In recent years, lesbians have attempted to make sense of these vigorous debates about sexuality, gender, race, and class that have shaken our communities. Alice Echols and B. Ruby Rich both wrote ground-breaking essays following the "sex wars" of the 1980s, attempting to record and historicize the battles fought over sexual expression and politics.[5] What is clear, however, is that those debates within lesbian feminist communities have, as much as anything, created, or helped to create, the queer lesbian culture that now exists within large urban centers. Queer lesbian studies must always retain a historical character, both in terms of emphasizing historical shifts within the social meaning of sexuality and also in terms of remaining aware of the history of lesbian studies and women's studies in this country. Finally, I hope that a queer lesbian studies can in the future build upon difference as much as upon commonality and hopefully side-step some of the more prescriptive tendencies of an earlier cultural feminism. Sexual difference is as important as sexual sameness, and the demonization of sexual difference is, after all, the root of homophobia. Pedagogically speaking, a queer lesbian studies should speak as much through the pervert as through the woman-loving woman.

NOTES

1. Judith Butler, "Imitation and Gender Insubordination," in *Inside/Out: Lesbian Theories, Gay Theories,* edited by Diana Fuss (New York: Routledge, 1991), 15.

2. See Terry Castle, *The Apparitional Lesbian* (New York: Columbia University Press, 1993) and Patricia White, "Female Spectator, Lesbian Specter: *The Haunting*" in *Inside/Out,* 142–72.

3. Barbara Smith, "Queer Politics: Where's the Revolution?" *The Nation* 257, no. 1 (5 July 1993): 14.

4. Stuart Hall, "Deviance, Politics and the Media," in *The Lesbian and Gay Studies Reader,* edited by Henry Abelove, Michèle Barale, and David Halperin (New York: Routledge, 1993): 63.

5. See Alice Echols, "The New Feminism of the Yin and Yang," in *Powers of Desire: The Politics of Sexuality,* edited by Ann Snitow, Christine Stansell, and Sharon Thompson (New York: Monthly Review Press, 1983): 439–59; B. Ruby Rich, "Review Essay: Feminism and Sexuality during the 1980s," *Feminist Studies* 12, no. 3 (fall 1986): 525–62.

LESBIAN STUDIES AND POSTMODERN QUEER THEORY

Harriet Malinowitz

Postmodernism took many lesbian feminists by surprise. For one thing, it threatened to disrupt much of the hard work they had done throughout the 1970s to create communities and institutions which achieved political agency through shared identification and common cause. Achieving such agency had not come easily; now there were those who would deconstruct altogether the premise of group coherence based on a shared characteristic such as gender or sexuality, insisting that identity is multiple, fragmented, and unstable—and that communities predicated on identification are hence illusory and doomed to implosion. In this view, such communities are fragile not only because the multiple threads of identities intersect in exceedingly complex and unpredictable ways (one single strand may very well be an unreliable basis upon which to forge sociopolitical alliances); but also because the meanings of even seemingly singular parts of our identities are unruly and evade consensus. With such framing principles of lesbian feminist thought as "identity" and "community" thus destabilized, postmodern theory contested at a fundamental level the very existence of knowledge as lesbian feminists had constructed it. For instance, "the authority of experience," a concept which had formed the bedrock of feminist ways of knowing since the early 1970s, appeared to yield dangerously evanescent truths when considered from a postmodern perspective. "What counts as 'experience'?" asked feminist and queer theorist Diana Fuss (113), among others, explaining, "[T]he problem with positing the category of experience as the basis of a feminist pedagogy is that the very object of our inquiry, 'female experience,' is never as unified, as knowable, as universal, and as stable as we presume it to be. . . . [E]xperience is [not] necessarily present to us—in the form of an unmediated real" (114).

The advent of postmodern theory into the realm of identity politics loomed for some lesbian feminists as an unwelcome or puzzling paradigm shift that brought with it another unanticipated transformation. "Lesbian studies," formerly in the uncontested custody of women's studies, was now simultaneously being claimed by the emerging field of lesbian and gay (or "queer") studies. As lesbians' multiple allegiances rapidly crystallized into multiple curricular, organizational, and publishing opportunities, and the contexts of their lives and work shifted, certainty about the very meaning of what it meant to be a "lesbian" was further challenged. While women's studies had posited broad definitions based on gender solidarity that aimed to be inclusive (such as Adrienne Rich's much-discussed notion of a "lesbian continuum" that included a "range . . . of woman-identified experience" [192]), queer studies relocated lesbianism within discourses of sexuality (most often lumping the girls with the boys) and then tended to dismantle the category altogether. For instance, queer theorist Judith Butler asked in an essay called "Imitation and Gender Insubordination" what it means to say that one "is" a lesbian. What criteria must one meet?

> Is it not possible to maintain and pursue heterosexual identifications and aims within homosexual practice, and homosexual identifications and aims within heterosexual practices? If a sexual identity is to be disclosed, what will be taken as the true determinant of its meaning: the phantasy structure, the act, the orifice, the gender, the anatomy? (17)

Butler's questions, in fact, hover like sky-writing captioning the internecine debates of 1970s and 1980s lesbian feminism: Can a male-to-female transsexual join a lesbian collective? Is a "political lesbian" a "real" one? What do we call a repressed married woman who lusts for her girlfriends but dies wondering? Rather than trying to answer these sorts of questions, Butler argues against questing for a source authorized to make such certifications. The project would be unfeasible not only because one subjective position would have to be arbitrarily selected (to the dismay of everyone holding all the others), but, more importantly, because it would entail a misreading of identity itself: "To claim that [my sexuality] is what I *am* is to suggest a provisional totalization of this 'I'" (15). To privilege sexuality as such a fundamental marker of selfhood is ultimately as arbitrary and misguided, Butler might say, as to assert that one's being is defined by the quality of being a nonsmoker or a crosscountry skier. Her intention is not to undermine anti-homophobic projects, but rather to cast them in new terms: "This is not to say that I will not appear at political occasions under the sign of lesbian, but that I would like to have it permanently unclear what precisely that sign signifies" (14).

The briefest and most informal inventory of actual people can confirm that it is indeed unclear precisely what the terms by which they define themselves signify. For instance, when I asked several undergraduate students who call themselves lesbian or gay what they meant when they described themselves that way, some explained that it meant being *attracted* to the same gender, others that it meant *identifying* with the same gender, and others that it meant a feeling of otherness or difference from those who conformed to gender roles. Some said they felt their gayness was something they had been born with, while others said it was something they had chosen; some—particularly women—chose it because they felt that heterosexuality was an oppressive institution; and some saw it as a lifelong state, while others saw it as an ephemeral or situational state. This variety of definitions seems to be fairly typical of the "lesbian and gay community" at large: people may share a word with which they define themselves, but the conditions signified by that word do not seem to be shared.

These two ways of viewing "identity"—as something that can form community and lead to liberatory social change, on the one hand, and, on the other, as a construction so particularized and idiosyncratically realized that the notion of a "group identity" becomes diminished to the level of a wistful fiction—have been weighed against one another primarily in academic, but also in activist, spheres. If, for example, we accept that the category "lesbian" doesn't really exist in any stable way, can any lesbian agenda exist? Membership in the category has at various points throughout the twentieth century meant risking police raids and imprisonment, street violence, incarceration in mental institutions, expulsion from jobs, families, and religious institutions, loss of child custody, dishonorable discharge from (or prohibition from entering) the military, McCarthy-ite inquisitions, disqualification from employment in education or government, and general social pariah-hood. What, then, happens when we attempt to dissolve it? What does it mean in the 1990s, when the lesbian and gay rights movement is experiencing unprecedented political power and the notion that the group is entitled to "rights" is being argued and even accepted to a far larger degree than ever before, to say that to call oneself a "lesbian" is a totalizing and ultimately meaningless fiction? In other words, how can we destabilize a category without also abandoning our claim to material and social entitlement and our repudiation of marginalization and prejudice?

Yet on the other hand, what does it mean to cling to old, comfortable identity categories for certain pragmatic reasons when we have deconstructed them precisely *because* in crucial ways they weren't really working, even for the communities built upon them? The lesbian and gay "community" has experienced the contestation and disruption of the very "affirmative" meanings with which it attempted to usurp old, homophobic ones. For example, while many (white) queer, liberal, mainstream leaders promote the idea of movement "unity," queers of color and members of other ethnic groups have said that white gays and lesbians have built a false, solipsistic, and racist image of "community" based on a gay-versus-straight opposition that was reductionistic of their personal and political experience. Many have felt that the acceptance of lesbians and gays into the military would be an important political step, while others—particularly those affiliated with feminist and leftist politics— have disparaged that goal for its implicit endorsement of a reactionary institution. Bisexuals have claimed that their existence inherently problematizes the false binary thinking that produces the homo/hetero opposition. They argue that insistence on polarization has left their needs and perspectives ignored. Nonetheless, gays and straights are politically and emotionally driven to reinscribe bisexuals as "real" denizens of specific identity categories.

These and countless other arguments have not only divided the "community," but have led to the production in the lesbian and gay press, at rallies, in courses, and in social situations of ongoing meta-narratives about the community's fragmentation. Ultimately, such fragmentation highlights a crisis of meaning about what the group actually represents or *is*. Thus, a variety of queer theorists have raised fundamental questions about what we mean—and what it is impossible for us to ever accurately signify—when we say "we." Just as the accrued experiences of participants in social movements inevitably break down myths of absolute affinity, uncompromising coalescence, and a common language, a chief project of postmodern theory has been to puncture the master cultural narratives that swallow up anarchic and infinitely complicated human difference. The object is not simply to give "silenced" discourses a chance to be heard; it is rather to expose the indeterminate and hybrid nature of all discourse, to prompt incendiary questions about what is wrong with pictures that present themselves as seamlessly composed. Yet the project is of particular importance to subjugated peoples, since master narratives become hegemonic precisely by distilling and then strategically universalizing dominant ideologies, rendering the presence of others unimaginable.

Ironically, while many lesbian feminists express indignation about postmodern theory's presumptive cancellation of "the authority of experience" and its threats to collective agency, many are also perplexed about why postmodern theorists have posited so schismatic a relation between themselves and proponents of identity politics. Certainly, those women argue, analyzing decentered subjectivity, critiquing the ways hegemonic structures reproduce themselves, and examining the ways that the notion of difference organizes society and epistemology have been some of the most basic concerns that have guided their own work. And in truth, contemporary queer theory, though appearing to some as an extraterrestrial landing and threatening to wreak perverse acts on an undefended populace, *does* count feminism as a substantial part of its mixed lineage.

I would like to focus here on a particular moment of feminism and its relationship to queer theory—the moment of late 1970s/early 1980s feminist writing about the intersections of race, gender, and sexuality. This moment constituted a highly significant point along a trajectory that extends as far back as the nineteenth century, when Sojourner Truth punctured white feminists' "we" with her "I," rendering their generalizations about womanhood obsolete and propelling the category "woman" beyond its limiting parameters. It was a moment when feminist writers of color frequently employed metaphors such as "margins," "centers," "borderlands," and "mestiza consciousness" to delineate the complexities of location, as gender, race, class, and sexuality began to crowd onto a common theoretical ground. I would like to illuminate some links as well as some significant differences that exist between the approaches and assumptions of that feminist moment from those of contemporary queer theory, whose lineage is also heavily suffused by psychoanalytic and French poststructuralist thought.

Audre Lorde is the theorist perhaps most often cited for galvanizing the lesbian feminist community to think about the nature and politics of difference. Lorde's philosophy of difference shifted the focus of analysis from one in which difference constituted a liability that must be responsibly dealt with in coalition-building to one in which it was seen as the very motor driving authentically revolutionary acts. In her essay "The Master's Tools Will Never Dismantle the Master's House," for example, she wrote, "Advocating the mere tolerance of difference between women is the grossest reformism. It is a total denial of the creative function of difference in our lives. Difference must not be merely tolerated, but seen as a fund of necessary polarities between which our creativity can spark like a dialectic" (111). For Lorde, communities needed to exploit their heterogeneity in order to realize their radical potential; without friction there is no fire. By foregrounding the dynamic and generative qualities of difference, Lorde propelled forward a new sort of feminist discourse that displaced the earlier 1970s model predicated on shared, universal female experience. In a Lordian view, obfuscating the differences that exist between women will ultimately derail any program or theory; and in fact, the number of women who responded to 1970s feminist discourse by protesting, "That's not *me* you're talking about!" serves as adequate testimonial. Lorde frequently introduced herself or was introduced by others as a "Black lesbian feminist socialist warrior poet" (sometimes adding additional descriptors such as "mother of two, including one boy, and a member of an interracial couple," her age, or her status as cancer patient and veteran of a mastectomy), thus using her multifaceted identity to disrupt simple schisms of unified insides and outsides, oppressed and oppressors. I would argue that in this sense—and in the sense that she helped many feminists realize the pointlessness of trying to reduce their experience to common denominators and to find meaning rather than voids in the spaces between them—she brought feminist praxis toward a far more postmodern interpretive arena than that in which it had heretofore conducted its work.

Still, there are some important differences between Lorde's work and postmodern queer theorizing. For example, her writing on silence may be compared to Foucault's insight that silence is not an absence, but a knowledge-field and a strategic discourse, or to Eve Kosofsky Sedgwick's radical portrayal of ignorance *not* as a vacuum, but rather as a knowing, dynamic force implicated in regimes of power, a "weighty and occupied and consequentially epistemological space" (77) which is often falsely sentimentalized "as an originary, passive innocence" (7). Lorde, too, insisted that the realm of silence offers no asylum from the perils incurred when reality is articulated; instead, it is a place in which danger incubates and is actively nourished, precisely because that is where ignorance is given free rein to exercise its powerful knowledge. However, by coming out in favor of "the transformation of silence into language and action," she implies, paradoxically, that silence is *not* a language, but rather, again in Foucault's words, "the other side from which it is separated by a strict boundary" (27). Furthermore, this transformation is for her "an act of self-revelation" (42). Absolutely central to post-structuralist theory is the notion that thought and action are the *products* of language, and that the only "self" is one which is discursively produced. Most of the body of queer theory, for example, rests on the belief that "the homosexual" is a species of human that didn't exist before the late nineteenth century—not because people didn't have same-sex desires and experiences, but because no language, and thus no conceptual apparatus, yet existed to codify those desires and experiences as an identity. (Similarly, the "political lesbian" didn't exist until the radical feminist rhetoric of the 1970s created her.) Lorde, on the other hand, seems to be positing here an inner self which precedes language, and which can decide independently of it whether or not to enter its domain and employ it as a transparent medium of expression. In this sense, Lorde's entire conceptualization of speech, silence, and truth—the latter of which she seems to consider knowable and articulable—are at complete odds with postmodern conceptions of the same.

Should this matter? To many queer theorists, it matters a lot. It drives them crazy when feminists and queers write about *a priori* authentic selves and inner truths that are presumed to exist whether or not they dare to speak their name. This is called "essentialism," a belief in a naturalized identity or self that exists prior to socialization, springing from an internal core *into* the social world. For them, it is the social world that constructs, through language, the categories within which we make ourselves intelligible to ourselves. These theorists are forever frustrated by proponents of identity politics' use of words like "lesbian" and "woman" and "Black" as if their meanings are ineffably self-identical and not infinitely problematized by their relations to other words. Like other postmodernists, they challenge the Western rationalist idea that there is a primordially apprehendable and representable reality "out there" that fills up the receptive space of consciousness. Instead, they argue that meaning is encapsulated in the inescapably social machinery of language, and available only via entry into the relational, frictional world of linguistic signs.

Those writing from the perspective of identity politics are equally frustrated. Their complaints often center around queer theorists' elitism, abstraction, their removal from materialist political reality, and their incomprehensible deconstructionist terminology. But I think there may be another issue at play. The very process of living requires constant suspension of disbelief in a nameable, manipulable Real—even for those postmodernists who most emphatically disbelieve in it. Even they can't ever step outside of the constraints of language, but must stake out provisionally determinate truths as launching sites for their philosophic acts. At the same time, if identity is a protean construct of discourse, then at least we can be selective or inventive about the language-systems and discursive rules within which we compose ourselves. Doing this self-consciously *has* been a major endeavor of lesbian feminist work.

Poststructuralist theory is attentive to the ways in which, in Western thought, an idea or a thing becomes meaningful only within a binary relationship to something else which it displaces; for instance, heterosexuality can buttress its own self-identity only by reinforcing its comprehension of itself as not-homosexual: I am confident that I am me because I know that I am not-you. Lorde's "difference" also recognizes this displacement while radically refusing it as a way of knowing. "[W]e have no patterns for relating across our human differences as equals," she writes in "Age, Race, Class, and Sex: Women Redefining Difference" (115). "[W]e do not develop tools for using human difference as a springboard for creative change within our lives. We speak not of human difference, but of human deviance." It is a misreading of Lorde to imagine her project as a pluralist one which simply celebrates the kaleidoscopic effect of diverse subjectivities. It is a project that envisions the resignification of difference itself, suggesting that social conflicts are not simply the products of variant material interests or ideologies, but of the discourses of difference that we inhabit. It is a project that is traditionally feminist in that it not only asks how we think about difference, but challenges us to examine how we feel and act about it. It is also postmodern in its premise that "truth" is always contingent upon context and positionality. In short, it is a project that exhorts us to conceive new ways of occupying intersubjective space.

A lesbian studies on the threshold of the twenty-first century needs to find ways of alchemizing its apparent contradictions into new funds of knowledge. Rather than being torn apart by theoretical polarities, we can put disparate interpretive systems into contact with one another to discover, if not common ground, then at least new kinds of conversations whose tensions can recharge our work and offer it fresh direction. Such conversations can help us make sense of, for example, the perplexing simultaneity of lesbians' categorical vaporization with our emergence into the academic limelight. Any pop psychologist waxing philosophical about possessiveness in relationships will tell you that, in order to have someone, you first have to let her go. Similarly, just as the word *lesbian* became emptied of stable meaning, we began to see it emblazoned on texts, syllabi, conference papers, course titles, and curriculum vitae. I don't believe that this was a coincidence; neither do I accept that it was evidence of homophobic backlash, rewarding us for effacing our existence, or simply the result of teaming up with men in queer studies. Rather, I believe that destabilizing the concept *lesbian* made it both available and interesting to many women for the first time, because it ceased to be a mantle of definition that displaced other identities, a monologue, a source of knowledge considered patently incompatible with other sources of knowledge, a guardian of stasis. Instead, *lesbian* became a concept that suggested polyglossia, kineticism, that invited multiple forms of intellectual inquiry. As I have shown, this destabilization was not a sudden wrenching act executed by hostile or capricious forces, but was the result of a long process in which some of lesbian feminism's most canonical theorists played crucial roles. During all those years, lesbians wanted to be represented more, and now that we are, we represent so much more.

WORKS CITED

Butler, Judith. 1990. *Gender trouble: Feminism and the subversion of identity.* New York: Routledge.
———. 1990. Imitation and gender insubordination. In *Inside/Out: Lesbian theories, gay theories,* edited by Diana Fuss. New York: Routledge.
Foucault, Michel. 1978. *The history of sexuality: An introduction.* Volume 1. Reprint 1990. New York: Vintage Books.
Fuss, Diana. 1989. *Essentially speaking: Feminism, nature, and difference.* New York: Routledge.
Lorde, Audre. 1984. *Sister outsider.* Freedom, CA: The Crossing Press.
Rich, Adrienne. 1983. Compulsory heterosexuality and lesbian existence. In *Powers of desire: The politics of sexuality,* edited by Ann Snitow, Christine Stansell, and Sharon Thompson. New York: Monthly Review Press.
Sedgwick, Eve Kosofsky. 1990. *Epistemology of the closet.* Berkeley: University of California Press.

PLACING LESBIANS

Bonnie Zimmerman

I have been thinking a lot about the place of lesbians in the academic profession these days. I recently coedited a collection of original essays, *Professions of Desire: Lesbian and Gay Studies in Literature,* published by the Modern Language Association (MLA) in 1995. This project has stirred ancient memories and focused current dilemmas for me.

In doing research for the introduction to the volume, I came to realize that I am a charter member of the Gay Caucus of the MLA. Gay men and lesbians met openly (the closet history of queers in academia merits a study in itself) for the first time in 1973 and laid the infrastructure for all subsequent gay and lesbian research, publication, pedagogy, and institution-building in the discipline of language and literature. In recovering that moment in history, I have been struck by two thoughts (aside from the very personal shock of realizing that I have been doing this stuff for twenty years).

The first is that, to a significant degree, we have lost a sense of continuity and tradition in our work. The phenomenon of cultural amnesia is notoriously widespread in the United States; we seem to delight in lopping off old branches from the tree before young shoots have attained mature growth. Contemplating the current state of the field, I have been overwhelmed by what I have referred to as the Rip Van Winkle effect: it feels as if I had closed my eyes one day and when I awoke the whole theoretical scene had shifted. So if current journalism and even scholarship imply that gay and lesbian studies burst forth, oh, four or five years ago—well, those of us who have been plowing away these past two decades may shake our heads in amusement (or bemusement), but we hardly can be surprised. On the other hand, we ought to be concerned about the distorted and one-sided perspective this gives on the theory and practice of our field.

The second point of interest to emerge from a review of the history of lesbians in the MLA is that our relation to gay literary studies has always been problematic. I have in my files a dittoed letter (a technology that in itself reveals my generational position) to "Sisters of the Gay Caucus for the Modern Languages" from Dolores

Noll, one of the cofounders (with Louis Crompton) of the caucus. I also have a hazy memory of sitting in a circle with a dozen or so other women after we had decided to form a (sub-)caucus separately from the men. Clearly, from its initiation, gay studies hasn't quite known what to do with lesbians, nor have lesbians always known what (or whether or how much) to do with gay studies. And as gay studies mutates into queer theory, the lesbian question becomes that much more urgent.

This second point resonates strongly for me today. I have been a lesbian activist and academic for over twenty years. My professional life has been located almost exclusively in women's studies. I have written and taught about women for most of that time. My career has been, in effect, if not by design, separatist—until now. Like many other feminist scholars, I have had to adjust to the undeniable reality of lesbian and gay studies and queer theory. In my case, that has meant that, for the first time, I have worked with a man on a gender-mixed subject area. I have nothing but affection and respect for my coeditor, George Haggerty, and only pride and excitement about the book we have compiled and edited. But I do think this marks a significant turning point in my career, and may be offered as a symbol of the shifts that have been occurring in lesbian studies. I want to raise here a few thoughts that puzzle, worry, and challenge me.

Lesbian studies as it developed in the 1970s and early 1980s was, in reality, lesbian feminist studies. Not every lesbian scholar identified with lesbian feminism, but in general the field was strongly and unmistakably flavored by it. Lesbian feminism is too complex a theory to cover here, but suffice it to say that it represents more than the sum of feminist theory and gay politics. It is a particular variation of feminism that grew from the perspective or subject position of (some) lesbians at a particular moment in history. Lesbian feminism is rooted in the specificity of lesbians. It assumes that lesbians differ from both heterosexual women and gay men. As a result, lesbian feminism shares a long common border with lesbian separatism, although the two philosophies are not necessarily identical.

Lesbian feminism proceeds from an analysis of gender interests—which situates lesbians primarily as women rather than homosexuals, thus distinguishing it from gay theory—which proceeds from an analysis of sexual identity and interests (a difference noted by Eve Kosofsky Sedgwick). It also bases itself in the primacy of identity, distinguishing it further from queer theory, which lays primary emphasis upon actions and performance. Accordingly, lesbian feminism does manifest a certain degree of essentialism—at least the nominal or strategic essentialism, as Teresa de Lauretis puts it, that continues to assign meaning and value to names, labels, and categories.

In the practice of lesbian feminism, the most significant factor I have observed is the boundary-crossing between scholar and writer, academy and community. If we look back to the early lesbian sessions at the MLA—for example, the exciting 1977 session, "The Transformation of Silence into Language and Action," attended by over six hundred people—we note that many participants, such as Adrienne Rich and Audre Lorde, are equally celebrated as educators, creative writers, and political theorists. Even those participants who were at that time professional academics—Julia Penelope, Judith McDaniel, Mary Daly—have come to speak and write to lesbian and feminist communities at large more than to the academy. Moreover, these early MLA panels were reprinted not in academic journals, but in the pioneering lesbian literary journal *Sinister Wisdom*.

In other words, lesbian criticism and theory (as well as theoretical and empirical work in disciplines other than literature) originated at the margins of the profession and drew its strength precisely from that marginality. It had strong ties to lesbian communities and to the not-yet-institutionalized women's studies programs emerging all over the country. It was as likely to be presented at sessions of the National Women's Studies Association as at the MLA (or AHA, APA, or any other professional association), and more likely to appear in lesbian and feminist journals than in the journals of the literary profession. Lesbian scholarship (not unlike the first generation of feminist scholarship) merged with lesbian journalism, polemics, and creative writing to create a unique genre of engaged critical theory.

As many people have pointed out, the current situation is very different. What one generation figured out in consciousness-raising groups and political collectives, another learns in the classroom. An identity hard fought for in the 1970s can be calmly deconstructed in the 1990s. The heroic pioneers of one era become the boring old fogies of the next. Lesbian feminism gives way to gay and lesbian studies, which in turn is challenged by queer theory. It's the way of the world, to be sure, but the question remains for me: what is the unregenerate lesbian feminist scholar to do in this brave new world?

I wish to approach this question from the institutional perspective. That is, where can the lesbian scholar work? Note that I am not asking where *should* she work. There are already too many prescriptions and prohibitions in the community/ profession for me to add any more. But I have found this to be a meaningful, sometimes urgent question for myself, especially once I recognized (perhaps later than most) that the hegemony of feminist discourse over lesbian theory and practice was dead. What happens to the lesbian scholar who still considers herself a lesbian feminist in the new terrain marked by gay and lesbian studies programs, gender and/or sexuality journals, and queer theory conferences?

There are many institutional questions one could address. Who will get hired in the new gay and lesbian or queer studies programs? What will constitute its curriculum? Who will edit and serve on the boards of new journals and book series, and what will get published? Who will write the textbooks, and what will they include? Who speaks at conferences and symposia? Who is training graduate students, the next generation of scholars and teachers? In short, who is or will be in charge? But I will approach the issue by offering a simple, practical example. You are a lesbian professor, and you wish to develop a course for your university. What do you teach? Exclusively lesbian material? There is certainly more than enough for half a dozen lesbian courses in the curriculum. Or a course covering a range of gay and lesbian (and what about bisexual or even transsexual) texts? Or a course on theories of sexuality that would even include radical perspectives on heterosexuality? Or, to get away from all this identity nonsense, a course on queer discourse? Now you may feel, as I certainly do, that any or all of these courses may be exciting, valuable, and necessary. But you can only put your time and energy into one of them. Which one do you teach?

Suppose you choose to develop a course on lesbians. The next question is, where do you locate it? I am not considering here the traditional disciplinary houses like departments of literature, history, anthropology and so forth. I am also assuming that you have some choice in this matter, which is not likely to be the case except at a very few highly advanced institutions. But considering how rapidly women's studies proliferated, it may not be entirely utopian to imagine a university that has programs or departments in women's studies, gay and lesbian studies, sexuality studies, and so on. Indeed, what these new programs will name themselves and how they will be structured raises many of the same questions that I am addressing here. Where does your course on lesbians belong? (Don't answer too quickly: allow me to develop my argument.)

Generally speaking, it seems to me that there are three venues for the openly lesbian academic's work. Until recently, I believe it fair to say that politically and professionally active lesbians have located themselves primarily in women's studies programs. Despite the homophobia of some women's studies programs, and the tendency for the discipline as a whole to downplay the strong lesbian presence within it, women's studies has been the logical and sympathetic home for dyke scholars. Increasingly, however, as institutions develop gay and lesbian studies foci, lesbians will feel the urge and perhaps pressure to shift their allegiance there. Instead of dealing with homophobia in women's studies, we will struggle against sexism in gay studies. That has led some lesbians to propose a third alternative: the development of an independent lesbian studies program (where, presumably, we can all process together over racism, classism, and different styles of being dykes).

Each choice has its advantages and drawbacks, and each engenders different theoretical and practical consequences. Should lesbians withdraw their specific lesbian energy from women's studies (which seems highly unlikely to me), we face the possibility of watching it become what we always feared it would be: a purely heterosexual enclave within feminism. We also face the certainty that it will collapse entirely from the withdrawal of its vital core. But if lesbians do not become involved in the creation of gay and lesbian, queer, and/or sexuality studies, then these emerging fields will realize their own tendencies to be predominantly or exclusively male-centered, not to mention white and middle-class. And to withdraw into the presumed comfort of lesbian studies—disregarding the real differences among lesbians that are as significant as differences of gender and sexuality—is to succumb to an atomizing impulse that is neither practical nor theoretically sound. On a global/political scale we can see the tragic effects of ever-spiraling nationalism; the analogy with U.S. identity politics may seem far-fetched, but it resonates with some degree of truth.

So what is my conclusion? Where, practically and theoretically, can the lesbian feminist scholar place herself? I am sure astute readers have the answer ready: anywhere and everywhere. But let us consider what this means. It means maintaining a multiple subject position that is neither comfortable, coherent, nor easy. It means being a gadfly everywhere, constantly questioning and deconstructing the metaphor of home (as Biddy Martin and Chandra Mohanty argue). It means working twice or even three times as hard as your colleagues. It means constantly inspecting one's options and choices for complex and conflicting consequences. It means agonizing over which principled position to take—not just occasionally but almost all the time. It means living with the possibility that you may not always be able to take a principled position. It means—to use my currently favorite phrase—living always with contradictions.

I am entirely sympathetic to the postmodern position that subjectivity is always, necessarily, desirably, multiple and fragmented, but I am also under no illusion that the various subject positions represented by "lesbian feminist," "gay and lesbian" (or, as I now hear it called, "lesbigay"), or "queer" are congruent. Indeed, I would argue, they are often inconsistent, contradictory, and downright hostile. That may be exciting and challenging at times, but what happens when these various discourses collide at the location occupied by the body of "the professor"? Can the "lesbian feminist" successfully assert her voice in a course on lesbian and gay studies, or queer theory? Poststructuralism has made it very easy to talk about multiple subject positions, fragmentation, deconstructing identity, and so on. But putting our theories into practice is another story entirely. We all tend to yearn after some kind of consistency, unity, and wholeness. We suffer when we feel alienated or divided within ourselves. We want the various parts of our lives to flow harmoniously together, to create coherent communities of meaning and understanding. But the challenges facing lesbian scholars, teachers, and activists in the 1990s may not allow for such nostalgic and idealistic visions.

Since I have addressed my personal history in this essay, I will use some of my current projects to illustrate the argument. Since 1979 I have taught a course on lesbians as part of the curriculum of the women's studies department at San Diego State University. There has been and still is no other institutional home for this interdisciplinary course. As I prepare to teach it again, I am aware of putting on my lesbian feminist, essentialist costume—performing my originary politics, if you like. Even the title of the course—"Women-Identified Women"—reflects its 1970s origins.[1] In this course I will insist upon lesbianism as a meaningful category, stress the politics of identity, lecture on the history and tradition of lesbians, argue for the importance of community, et cetera. At the same time I have developed a new graduate seminar on lesbian and gay theory, in which I question and undermine all those concepts— identity, history, tradition, community—in the best deconstructive and "queer" manner. Finally, I have co-facilitated a lecture series, entitled "The Queer Gaze: Lesbians and Gay Men in History and Culture," that, in the time-honored liberal, pluralist tradition, takes no particular point of view, but draws upon as many different and "balanced" approaches as possible (so much so that my colleague and I— dedicated feminists both—worried about the under-representation of men!).

Each of these subject positions that I assume in planning and teaching a course— lesbian feminist, queer theorist, liberal pluralist—seems justified to me by the aims of the particular course, the needs of its audience, and the role it plays in a particular program. But I am under no illusion that these positions do not conflict with each other. The trick—I hope—is to work with them, to articulate their principles, to raise judicious questions about them, to share one's own process and conflict as much as is appropriate in a classroom—all without entangling one's self hopelessly in confusion, and feeling finally like an intellectual fraud.

I would conclude with a few points I consider essential as we negotiate the new mine fields (to use Annette Kolodny's phrase) facing us. The first is that we need to maintain or, more accurately, restore the links between academic lesbian feminism and lesbian communities. We need always to listen to the voices of women who do not necessarily speak in the dialects of high theory and modish ideas. This is particularly important if lesbian studies is to reflect our very visible diversity of race, class, physical ability, age, and personal history—diversity that is not yet and may never be fully evident within the academy. Moreover, we need to ask how we can make our scholarship and criticism useful, and not only to ourselves as we climb the academic ladders of success.

The second point is that we continue to explore in our teaching and research the particularity of lesbian histories, perspectives, subjectivities, and identities. We have hardly, in our mere two or three decades of self-conscious existence, so thoroughly established the lesbian subject that we can now blithely discard her. Must we have post-lesbianism to go along with postfeminism?[2] The third point is a corollary to the second, that we avoid the premature merging or harmonizing of lesbian studies with gay, queer, or sexuality studies. To be sure, coalition-building may well be necessary, practical, and desirable. In the long run, however, I believe that lesbian and/or lesbian/gay/queer/sexuality studies will develop best if each constituency maintains some healthy and skeptical distance, engages in open and critical dialogue, and acknowledges both the similarities and the differences, the congruencies and the contradictions, among our multiple points of view.

I'll conclude by saying that, as much as I occasionally regret it, the answer to the dilemmas I am posing does not lie in a nostalgic return to the supposed lost utopia of the lesbian-feminist 1970s. On the one hand, I am theoretically and emotionally sympathetic to the position that we form our own separate lesbian studies programs and movement. As a pragmatist, however, I have concluded that I inevitably will live in an intellectual world shaped by clashing and competing discourses—not to mention limited material resources. The problem, as I see it, is that the discourse of lesbianism—specifically, lesbian feminism—has been all but silenced. This leads to the appropriation of our work and ideas (including feminism itself) *without* any recognition or citation of sources, the vilification of our values and continued existence, and the appalling misrepresentation and ahistorical construction of the past twenty years. To counter this, lesbian feminists need to reinsert ourselves into the debates in a forceful and intellectually impeccable way. That, to me, is the most important work facing lesbian-identified scholars today.

An earlier version of this essay appeared in *Concerns* 23, no. 3 (fall 1993): 10–16.

NOTES

1. As a matter of fact, in 1995 the department changed the title of the course to "Lesbian Lives and Cultures"—a title that still has a slightly 1970s twang to it.

2. I thank Marilyn Schuster for this observation.

WORKS CITED

de Lauretis, Teresa. 1989. The essence of the triangle, or taking the risk of essentialism seriously: Feminist theory in Italy, the U.S., and Britain. *differences* 1, no. 2:3–37.

Kolodny, Annette. 1985. Dancing through the minefield: Some obervations on the theory, practice, and politics of a feminist literary criticism. In *The New Feminist Criticism*, edited by Elaine Showalter. New York: Pantheon.

Martin, Biddy and Chandra Mohanty. 1986. Feminist politics: What's home got to do with it? In *Feminist Studies/Critical Studies*, edited by Teresa de Lauretis. Bloomington: Indiana University Press.

Sedgwick, Eve Kosofsky. 1990. *Epistemology of the closet.* Berkeley and Los Angeles: University of California Press.

BOOKLIST: TONI AND BONNIE'S FAB FIFTY PLUS ONE

The fields of lesbian, lesbigay, and queer studies are developing so rapidly that it is impossible to provide an exhaustive reading list. With a few exceptions, we have not duplicated the bibliography from the first edition of *Lesbian Studies*. Reluctantly, we have also excluded works of fiction, poetry, drama, memoir, or auto/biography, and separately published articles, no matter how influential. The reader will find more expansive bibliographies attached to many of the essays in this book. Instead, we have selected fifty-one books (with publication dates prior to June 1995, when we completed this manuscript) that we have found personally inspiring and provocative, as well as generally influential in the development of lesbian studies as a field of inquiry. Our choices reflect our individual preferences, to be sure, but we also have attempted to reflect the diversity of theoretical and disciplinary approaches current today. We hope you will agree that any lesbian teacher, scholar, or serious reader will find these to be essential components of her book collection.

Abelove, Henry, Michèle Aina Barale, and David Halperin, eds. *The Lesbian and Gay Studies Reader.* New York and London: Routledge, 1993.

Allen, Jeffner, ed. *Lesbian Philosophies and Cultures.* Albany: State University of New York Press, 1990.

Allen, Paula Gunn. *The Sacred Hoop: Recovering the Feminine in American Indian Traditions.* Boston: Beacon Press, 1986.

Anzaldúa, Gloria. *Borderlands/La Frontera: The New Mestiza.* San Francisco: Aunt Lute Books, 1987.

Balka, Christie and Andy Rose, eds. *Twice Blessed: On Being Lesbian, Gay, and Jewish.* Boston: Beacon Press, 1989.

Beck, Evelyn Torton, ed. *Nice Jewish Girls: A Lesbian Anthology.* Boston: Beacon Press, 1982, 1989.

Boston Lesbian Psychologies Collective. *Lesbian Psychologies: Explorations and*

Challenges. Urbana and Chicago: University of Illinois Press, 1987.

Bunch, Charlotte. *Passionate Politics: Feminist Theory in Action.* New York: St. Martin's Press, 1987.

Butler, Judith. *Gender Trouble: Feminism and the Subversion of Identity.* New York and London: Routledge, 1990.

———. *Bodies That Matter: On the Discursive Limits of "Sex."* New York and London: Routledge, 1993.

Card, Claudia. *Lesbian Choices.* New York: Columbia University Press, 1995.

Castle, Terry. *The Apparitional Lesbian.* New York: Columbia University Press, 1993.

Cruikshank, Margaret. *Lesbian Studies: Present and Future.* New York: The Feminist Press, 1982.

Curb, Rosemary and Nancy Manahan, eds. *Lesbian Nuns: Breaking Silence.* Tallahassee, FL: Naiad Press, 1985.

de Lauretis, Teresa. *The Practice of Love: Lesbian Sexuality and Perverse Desire.* Bloomington and Indianapolis: Indiana University Press, 1994.

Doan, Laura, ed. *The Lesbian Postmodern.* New York: Columbia University Press, 1994.

Duberman, Martin, Martha Vicinus, and George Chauncey Jr., eds. *Hidden from History: Reclaiming the Gay and Lesbian Past.* New York: Meridian, 1990.

Faderman, Lillian. *Odd Girls and Twilight Lovers: A History of Lesbian Life in Twentieth-Century America.* New York: Columbia University Press, 1991.

Frye, Marilyn. *The Politics of Reality: Essays in Feminist Theory.* Trumansburg, NY: The Crossing Press, 1983.

———. *Willful Virgin: Essays in Feminism.* Freedom, CA: The Crossing Press, 1992.

Fuss, Diana. *Inside/Out: Lesbian Theories, Gay Theories.* New York and London: Routledge, 1991.

Garber, Linda, ed. *Tilting the Tower: Lesbians Teaching Queer Subjects.* New York and London: Routledge, 1994.

Grahn, Judy. *Another Mother Tongue: Gay Words, Gay Worlds.* Boston: Beacon, 1984.

———. *The Highest Apple: Sappho and the Lesbian Poetic Tradition.* San Francisco: Spinsters Ink, 1985.

Hoagland, Sarah Lucia. *Lesbian Ethics: Toward New Value.* Palo Alto, CA: Institute of Lesbian Studies, 1988.

Hoagland, Sarah Lucia and Julia Penelope, eds. *For Lesbians Only: A Separatist Anthology.* London: Onlywomen Press, 1989.

Jay, Karla and Joanne Glasgow, eds. *Lesbian Texts and Contexts: Radical Revisions.* New York: New York University Press, 1990.

Johnson, Susan E. *Staying Power: Long Term Lesbian Couples.* Tallahassee, FL: Naiad Press, 1990.

Kennedy, Elizabeth and Madeline Davis. *Boots of Leather, Slippers of Gold: The History of a Lesbian Community.* New York and London: Routledge, 1993.

Kitzinger, Celia. *The Social Construction of Lesbianism.* London: SAGE Publications, 1987.

Krieger, Susan. *The Mirror Dance.* Philadelphia: Temple University Press, 1983.

Lorde, Audre. *A Burst of Light.* Ithaca, NY: Firebrand Books, 1988.

————. *Sister Outsider: Essays and Speeches.* Trumansburg, NY: The Crossing Press, 1984.

Meese, Elizabeth. *(Sem)erotics: Theorizing Lesbian Writing.* New York: New York University Press, 1992.

Moraga, Cherríe and Gloria Anzaldúa, eds. *This Bridge Called My Back: Writings by Radical Women of Color.* New York: Kitchen Table/Women of Color Press, 1984.

Nestle, Joan. *A Restricted Country.* Ithaca, NY: Firebrand Books, 1987.

Penelope, Julia. *Speaking Freely: Unlearning the Lies of the Father's Tongues.* New York: Pergamon, 1990.

Penelope, Julia and Susan J. Wolfe, eds. *Lesbian Culture: An Anthology.*

Pharr, Suzanne. *Homophobia: A Weapon of Sexism.* Inverness, CA: Chardon Press, 1988.

Ramos, Juanita, ed. *Compañeras: Latina Lesbians.* New York and London: Routledge, 1987.

Raymond, Janice G. *A Passion for Friends: Toward a Philosophy of Female Affection.* Boston: Beacon Press, 1986.

Rich, Adrienne. *Blood, Bread, and Poetry: Selected Prose 1979–1985.* New York: W. W. Norton, 1986.

Roof, Judith. *A Lure of Knowledge: Lesbian Sexuality and Theory.* New York: Columbia University Press, 1991.

Segrest, Mab. *Memoir of a Race Traitor.* Boston: South End Press, 1994.

Stein, Arlene, ed. *Sisters, Sexperts, Queers: Beyond the Lesbian Nation.* New York: Plume, 1993.

Trujillo, Carla, ed. *Chicana Lesbians: The Girls Our Mothers Warned Us About.* Berkeley, CA: Third Woman Press, 1991.

Weiss, Andrea. *Vampires and Violets: Lesbians in Film.* New York: Penguin, 1993.

Weston, Kath. *Families We Choose: Lesbians, Gays, Kinship.* New York: Columbia University Press, 1991.

Wittig, Monique. *The Straight Mind.* Boston: Beacon Press, 1992.

Wolfe, Susan J. and Julia Penelope. *Sexual Practice, Textual Theory: Lesbian Cultural Criticism.* Cambridge, MA and Oxford: Blackwell, 1993.

Zimmerman, Bonnie. *The Safe Sea of Women: Lesbian Fiction 1969–1989.* Boston: Beacon Press, 1990.

NOTES ON CONTRIBUTORS

LOURDES ARGUELLES (PhD, New York University) is Professor of Gender and Feminist Studies and Chicano/Latino Studies at Pitzer College, Claremont, California, and Adjunct Professor of Education at the Claremont Graduate School. Dr. Arguelles is also a psychotherapist who has worked primarily with queer peoples of color.

EVELYN TORTON BECK is Professor of Women's Studies and Jewish Studies at the University of Maryland-College Park, where she served as Director of Women's Studies from 1984 to 1993. Among her books are *The Prism of Sex* (1971) and *Nice Jewish Girls: A Lesbian Anthology* (1982, rev. ed. 1989). She has written and lectured widely on issues of difference, especially the complex intersections of misogyny with anti-Semitism and lesbophobia. She offers a course on lesbian communities and cultures across differences.

PAULA BENNETT is Associate Professor of English at Southern Illinois University, Carbondale. Since the first edition of *Lesbian Studies* she has become the proud author of *My Life a Loaded Gun: Female Creativity and Feminist Poetics* (1986, rev. ed.1990) and *Emily Dickinson: Woman Poet* (1991), plus numerous articles. However, she would still prefer to be in northern Canada, counting loons.

EVELYN BLACKWOOD is Assistant Professor of Women's Studies and Anthropology at Purdue University, West Lafayette, Indiana. She holds a PhD in anthropology from Stanford University. Her work includes a study of Native American two-spirit females, lesbian relations cross-culturally, and lesbian identity in Indonesia. She is editor of *The Many Faces of Homosexuality: Anthropology and Homosexual Behavior.*

ANGELA BOWEN, a black lesbian feminist, is a PhD candidate writing about Audre Lorde at Clark University. She was one of the organizers of the 1990 conference honoring Lorde, "I Am Your Sister: Forging Global Connections across Differences." A lifelong cultural worker, she founded an inner-city cultural center and directed it for nineteen years. Among her numerous awards are the E. Franklin Frazier Fellowship from Clark (1992–93), and the 1991–92 Naiad/NWSA dissertation award. Her ongoing research focuses on black lesbians.

ELLEN BROIDY, a lesbian luddite attempting to make peace with technology, is the History and Film Studies Librarian at the University of California, Irvine. She and her partner of fifteen years, Joan Ariel, also a UCI librarian, teach classes on surfing the net from a feminist perspective. In her spare time, she is writing a dissertation on progressive women elementary and secondary school teachers during the McCarthy era.

SUSAN CAHN teaches U.S. women's history at the State University of New York at Buffalo. She has published a feminist history of women's sports called *Coming on Strong: Gender and Sexuality in Twentieth-Century Women's Sport* (1994). Her current research is a historical study of adolescence and female sexuality.

CONNIE S. CHAN is Associate Professor of Human Services and Co-Director of the Institute of Asian American Studies at the University of Massachusetts at Boston. Her writing and research focus upon the fluidity of bicultural issues in the development of gender, cultural, and sexual identities for Asian Americans.

JO WHITEHORSE COCHRAN, a Lakota/Norwegian-American born in 1958, received an MFA in creative writing from the University of Washington. She currently lives in Seattle and works for the King County Executive as a policy and budget analyst. Her passions in life are meditating, drumming, writing, beaches, and the pursuit of the spirit within. Hello to all from Bob the Cat: he is sixteen and still going.

MARGARET CRUIKSHANK has been writing on lesbian and gay topics for the past twenty years. She teaches English, women's studies, and gay and lesbian studies at the City College of San Francisco. Her most recent books are *The Gay and Lesbian Liberation Movement* and *Fierce with Reality: An Anthology of Literature about Aging*.

SUSAN DALTON is a PhD candidate in sociology at the University of California, Santa Barbara. Her dissertation is an examination of social, legal, and ideological constructions of family and their effects on the legal treatment of lesbians and their partners and children. She is also completing research on the 1993 U.S. Senate hearings on gays in the military.

DORIS DIOSA DAVENPORT (PhD, University of Southern California, Los Angeles) is now a forty-six-year-old recovering alcoholic and "ex-academic." She lives at home in northeast Georgia where she does performance poetry and lectures on such topics as multicultural literature and education in the United States and the blues and black literature.

OLIVA M. ESPÍN is Professor of Women's Studies at San Diego State University and part-time Core Faculty at the California School of Professional Psychology. She has published on psychotherapy with Latinas, immigrant and refugee women, women's sexuality, and other topics. She has recently coedited *Shattered Societies, Shattered Lives: Refugee Women and Their Mental Health*. Her book *Latina Healers: Power, Culture and Tradition* is forthcoming. Dr. Espín received a Distinguished Professional Contribution Award from the American Psychological Association in 1991 and is Past President of the Society for the Psychological Study of Lesbian and Gay Issues.

LILLIAN FADERMAN is the author and editor of a number of works on lesbian history and literature, including *Surpassing the Love of Men, Scotch Verdict, Odd Girls and Twilight Lovers,* and *Chloe Plus Olivia.* She is the general coeditor of the Columbia University Press lesbian and gay series, Between Men/Between Women. "Who Hid Lesbian History?" was written in 1979, while she was engaged in uncovering lesbian history for *Surpassing the Love of Men.*

PAUL B. FRANKLIN is a doctoral candidate in the fine arts department at Harvard University. He is the coeditor, with Marjorie Garber and Rebecca L. Walkowitz, of *Field Work: Sites in Literary and Cultural Studies* (1995).

MARILYN FRYE is author of two collections of essays, *The Politics of Reality* (1983) and *Willful Virgin* (1992). She teaches women's studies and philosophy, mainly feminist theory, at Michigan State University. Her main research interest is the topic of *categories* and how they pertain to the mechanisms of "social construction."

JANE GURKO taught English literature and women's studies for twelve years, and since 1980 has been Associate Dean of Humanities at San Francisco State University. She still hovers protectively around the women's studies department, but increasingly is planning her retirement to the woods of northern California. Any forthcoming work will likely focus on lesbian community-building in a small town.

JUDITH HALBERSTAM is Assistant Professor of Literature at the University of California, San Diego, where she teaches the nineteenth-century novel, queer theory, feminist studies, and film. She is the author of *Skin Shows: Gothic Horror and the Technology of Monsters* (1995). She is currently at work on a book-length project on "female masculinity." She has published essays in *Feminist Studies, Social Text,* and *GLQ,* and she writes film reviews regularly for *On Our Backs* and *Girlfriends.*

KATHLEEN HICKOK is Associate Professor of English and Women's Studies at Iowa State University, where she chaired the Women's Studies Program for nearly ten years. She teaches various courses on women writers, especially African-American, Victorian, and/or lesbian writers. She lives in Ames, Iowa, with her partner, their two preschool children, two cats, and a dog.

BARBARA HILLYER teaches women's studies and human relations at the University of Oklahoma. She writes about feminist teaching, feminist theory, and disability. The sequel to *Feminism and Disability* (1993) will be about old women's experiences of disability.

SHARON P. HOLLAND is Assistant Professor of English at Stanford University. She is the author of two articles on Audre Lorde, "Humanity Is Not a Luxury: Some Notes on a Recent Passing" and "To Touch the Mother's C[o]untry: Siting Audre Lorde's Erotics," forthcoming in *Lesbian Erotics,* edited by Karla Jay. Her essay is part of a larger project involving curriculum development for a lesbian literary studies course. She is currently working on a book manuscript entitled *American Dream/American Nightmare: Death and Discourse in Native and African American Literature.*

H. PATRICIA HYNES is an environmental engineer who works in the enforcement of hazardous waste regulations. She has designed a two-story passive solar greenhouse. She was a founder of Bread and Roses, a women's vegetarian restaurant and feminist cultural center in Cambridge, Massachusetts.

YOLANDA CHÁVEZ LEYVA is a Chicana/Tejana, born and raised on both sides of the border. She believes that our survival requires an understanding of where we come from. She tries to keep memories alive by telling stories, teaching and writing, studying history as a doctoral student at the University of Arizona, and as founder of the Lesbiana Latina Archives. She lives in the desert with her compañera, Nena, and her son, Jose Miguel.

KARIN LINDEQVIST holds a bachelor of law, although she never practiced as her interest in literature proved the stronger. She and a friend opened a feminist bookstore, Kvinnobokhandeln Medusa, in 1985 in Stockholm, and she still works there. She lives with her lover, Anna-Karin Granberg, who is also her favorite author. Some of her other passions are animal rights, walking by the sea, fighting violence against women and children, opera, and vampires.

HARRIET MALINOWITZ is Assistant Professor of English at Long Island University in Brooklyn, where she teaches writing, literature, and gender studies. She is the author of *Textual Orientations: Lesbian and Gay Students and the Making of Discourse Communities* and is on the Board of Directors of the Center for Lesbian and Gay Studies in New York. She also writes lesbian/feminist stand-up comedy which her life partner, Sara Cytron, has performed around the country, including on many campuses.

JUDITH MAYNE is Professor of French and Women's Studies at Ohio State University. She is the author of several books on film, including *Cinema and Spectatorship* (1993) and *Directed by Dorothy Arzner* (1994).

TONI A. H. MCNARON, a transplanted Alabamian, is Professor of English and Women's Studies at the University of Minnesota, where she has taught for thirty years. Her publications include *Voices in the Night: Women Speaking about Incest* and *I Dwell in Possibility: A Memoir.* She is currently writing a book entitled *Poisoned Ivy*, about lesbian and gay faculty members who have worked in higher education for at least fifteen years, and planning for her retirement in 2003.

CHERRÍE MORAGA is a poet, playwright, and essayist, and coeditor with Gloria Anzaldúa of *This Bridge Called My Back: Writings by Radical Women of Color.* She is the author of numerous plays including *Shadow of a Man*, winner of the 1990 Fund for New American Plays Award, and *Heroes and Saints,* winner of the 1992 Pen West Award. Her most recent book is a collection of poems and essays entitled *The Last Generation.* She is also a recipient of the National Endowment for the Arts' Theater Playwrights' Fellowship and an artist-in-residence at Brava Theater Center of San Francisco, where she is developing a play entitled *Watsonville.* In 1994, Moraga was commissioned by Berkeley Repertory Theater to write a new play, *Mexican Medea.*

SALLY R. MUNT is Research Fellow in American Studies at the University of East Anglia, Norwich, England. She is the author of *Murder by the Book: Feminism and the Crime Novel* (1994) and the editor of *New Lesbian Criticism* (1992). At the time of writing, she is the Fulbright/American Council of Learned Societies Fellow in American Studies for 1994–95 at the Lesbian Herstory Archives, Brooklyn, New York. She is writing a new book entitled *Heroic Desire: Lesbian Identity and Cultural Space.*

VIVIEN NG is a Chinese-American lesbian who lived and worked in Oklahoma for more than twelve years until moving to Albany, New York. She is a professional historian by virtue of the fact that she makes her living teaching and writing Chinese history. She takes great pleasure in cracking open the homophobic shell of Chinese studies.

DOROTHY PAINTER completed her dissertation in 1978 on the use of humor in lesbian speech communities. Since then, she has continued to write and publish on lesbian topics while working as an academic counselor and an Adjunct Assistant Professor of Women's Studies. She is currently Interim Director of the Office of Gay, Lesbian, and Bisexual Student Services and a student in the College of Law focusing on GLB law, both at Ohio State University.

ANN PELLEGRINI received her PhD in cultural studies from Harvard University. She is now teaching in the Department of Women's Studies at Barnard College. She is the author of *Performance Anxieties: Staging Psychoanalysis, Staging Race* (1996).

JEAN K. QUAM is Director of the School of Social Work at the University of Minnesota, where she has been a faculty member for fifteen years. Her research includes articles on gay and lesbian aging in *The Gerontologist* and *Siecus Reports,* and a chapter in a forthcoming text on spirituality and aging. She is a founding member of the American Society on Aging's Lesbian and Gay Aging Issues Network and editor of their newsletter, *Outword.* She and her partner live in Minneapolis, Minnesota, with their two sons.

ANNE M. RIVERO (MSW, UCLA) is a licensed clinical social worker in the Department of Psychiatry, Kaiser Permanente, Southern California. She has been an HIV/AIDS prevention educator in communities of color, as well as a workshop presenter and research consultant in health/mental health issues for many years.

SUZANNA ROSE is Associate Professor of Psychology and Women's Studies at the University of Missouri, St. Louis. She has been teaching feminist psychology courses since 1974. A major teaching concern is how to effect social change in the classroom. Her research focuses on how gender, race, and sexual orientation affect friendships, romantic relationships, and sexuality. She has also edited two books, *Career Guide for Women Scholars and Women's Careers: Pathways and Pitfalls.*

LEILA J. RUPP teaches U.S. and European women's history and gay/lesbian history at Ohio State University. She is the author of "'Imagine My Surprise': Women's Relationships in Historical Perspective," originally published in *Frontiers* in 1980, and of "Women's Culture and Lesbian Feminist Activism: A Reconsideration of Cultural Feminism," co-authored with Verta Taylor and published in *Signs* in 1993. She is currently working on a book on the history of international women's organizations during the first wave of the international women's movement.

SUSAN SAYER is a fiction writer who tutors in women's studies and sociology at the University of Waikato, Hamilton, Aotearoa/New Zealand. She was a member of Scratching the Surface, a lesbian writing group, has been part of a feminist theory group for over ten years, and has been active in welfare rights groups and *pakeha* (white-settler) antiracist work. She works closely with other writers.

BETH E. SCHNEIDER is Professor of Sociology and Women's Studies at the University of California, Santa Barbara. She is the coeditor of three books: *The Social Context of AIDS* (1992), *Women Resisting AIDS: Feminist Strategies of Empowerment* (1995), and *Looking Out: Readings in a Lesbian and Gay Sociology* (in press). In 1995 she resumed editorship of the journal *Gender & Society.*

MAB SEGREST has written a collection of essays, *My Mama's Dead Squirrel* and more recently, a political memoir interrelating lesbianism and racism entitled *Memoir of a Race Traitor.* She lives in North Carolina where she engages in various anti-Klan and pro-lesbian/gay projects.

BARBARA SMITH is a black feminist writer and activist whose work has appeared in *Lesbian Poetry: An Anthology* and *This Bridge Called My Back: Writings by Radical Women of Color.* She coedited *Conditions 5 (The Black Women's Issue)* as well as *All the Women Are White, All the Blacks Are Men, But Some of Us Are Brave: Black Women's Studies,* and edited *Home Girls: A Black Feminist Anthology.*

LUZ MARIA (LUZMA) UMPIERRE, a native of San Juan, Puerto Rico, received her PhD in both Spanish and Latin American literatures from Bryn Mawr College. She has taught at Rutgers University, Western Kentucky University, and State University of New York College at Brockport. Her wrongful termination suit against the last institution is currently before the New York State Supreme Court and the Human Rights Commission. She has published seven books and over one hundred articles and book chapters and has received numerous awards and honors.

KATH WESTON is Associate Professor of Anthropology at Arizona State University and a member of the National Writers Union. She is the author of *Families We Choose: Lesbian, Gays, Kinship,* and a coeditor of *The Lesbian Issue: Essays from Signs.* She is currently working on a book titled *Reader Me, Gender Me.*

CAROLYN WOODWARD is Associate Professor of English at the University of New Mexico. Her publications include "'My Heart So Wrapt': Lesbian Disruptions in Eighteenth-Century British Fiction," in *Signs* (1993). She is coeditor of *Changing Our Power: An Introduction to Women's Studies* (1988; 3rd ed. 1995), and has edited Sarah Fielding and Jane Collier's 1754 work of fiction and theory, *The Cry: A New Dramatic Fable* (1995). Her book, *Reading Elsewheres in the Master House of British Fiction 1740–60* is forthcoming.

WILLA YOUNG is a doctoral candidate in sociology at Ohio State University, where she also works as Director of Women Student Services and the Rape Education and Prevention Program. Her scholarly interests include lesbian talk and the social construction of communities, social movements, feminist theory, methodology, and qualitative methods. She is available to be lesbian and to teach lesbian studies at your school. Call her.

BETH ZEMSKY is currently Coordinator of the Gay, Lesbian, Bisexual, Transgender Programs Office at the University of Minnesota. She has worked as a psychotherapist, community organizer, and educator. She did not set out to get paid to be a lesbian, but she is very glad it has turned out this way.

BONNIE ZIMMERMAN is Professor of Women's Studies at San Diego State University. She is author of *The Safe Sea of Women: Lesbian Fiction 1969–1989* and numerous articles on lesbian literature and theory. A lesbian activist since the early 1970s, she still believes in the value and necessity of waving the lesbian label around as much as possible.

INDEX